# PAINTING ON THE PAGE

SUNY Series in Latin American and Iberian Thought and Culture
Jorge J. E. Gracia, Editor

# PAINTING ON THE PAGE

*Interartistic Approaches
to Modern Hispanic Texts*

Rosemary Geisdorfer Feal
and
Carlos Feal

STATE UNIVERSITY
OF NEW YORK
PRESS

Published by
State University of New York Press, Albany

© 1995   State University of New York

Production by Susan Geraghty
Marketing by Theresa Abad Swierzowski

Printed in the United States of America

The *Program for Cultural Cooperation between Spain's Ministry of Culture and United States Universities* is gratefully acknowledged for their financial support of this publication.

For information, address State University of New York
Press, State University Plaza, Albany, N.Y., 12246

Library of Congress Cataloging-in-Publication Data

Feal, Rosemary Geisdorfer.                    1001616550
    Painting on the page : interartistic approaches to modern Hispanic
texts / Rosemary Geisdorfer Feal, Carlos Feal.
        p.   cm.—(SUNY series in Latin American and Iberian thought
and culture)
    Includes bibliographical references and index.
    ISBN 0-7914-2603-3. — ISBN 0-7914-2604-1 (pbk.)
        1. Art and literature—Spain—History—20th century.   2. Art and
literature—Latin America—History—20th century.   3. Ut pictura
poesis (Aesthetics)   4. Psychoanalysis and the arts.   5. Feminism
and the arts.   I. Feal Deibe, Carlos.   II. Title.   III. Series.
NX562.A1F43    1995
700'.1—dc20                                                    94-38023
                                                                   CIP

10  9  8  7  6  5  4  3  2  1

*For our son,*
*Jaime Carlos*

# CONTENTS

# LIST OF FIGURES

# PREFACE

Criticism in the poststructural and postmodern veins has been working toward a fuller integration of literature and other fields, especially the visual arts. Disciplinary boundaries are being crossed—and crossed out—as quickly as the cultural maps are redrawn. Those fields of representation grouped under "literature" and "the visual arts" are currently being studied in conjunction with major theoretical and methodological issues, and we are particularly invested in finding appropriate critical strategies that combine psychoanalysis, feminism, semiotics, and philosophy as they may be applied to late nineteenth- and twentieth-century Spanish and Spanish-American literature in relation to painting and to larger questions of art history. While some critics have made signal contributions in these directions, not very many relate interartistic theory to the specificity of Hispanic texts. (Incidentally, we say "Hispanic texts" as a kind of shorthand for "works written in Spanish from Spain and from Spanish-speaking countries in the Americas and the Caribbean." We recognize that it may not be a neutrally descriptive term.) This book examines the relations between Hispanic literature and the visual arts by engaging in a series of interartistic explorations, which mediate new approaches with the more traditional concepts of *ut pictura poesis* and ekphrasis. Our project entails some obvious literary-artistic connections (literary works based on paintings, literary-artistic historical movements) but emphatically seeks to broaden the interartistic theoretical rubric in an effort to probe common literary and artistic representational codes.

We contend that this systematic interpretation and application of theories of visual representation to the selected Spanish and Spanish-American texts will contribute generally to the fields of literary criticism and art history by demonstrating specific possibilities of how theory can uncover new ways of analyzing works of art. Further, we wish to add to the criticism of major figures in contemporary Spanish and Spanish-American literature and plastic arts while confirming the suitability of these creators' works for study in a comparative arts framework. It is well known to Hispanists that in the United States interdisciplinary studies of this kind typically focus on works from North America, France, or England, with the result that criticism of literature from Spain and Spanish America is often disseminated in relatively limited contexts. It is our hope that in placing Hispanic literature and art at the core of this theoretical project, the value and importance of these works will stand out more prominently on the North American critical scene from which we write. Since each chapter provides a fully articulated approach to an interartistic problem, the individual studies that make up the book will shed new light on the works of the artists under consideration from carefully constructed and integrated theoretical positions; demonstrate the deep affinities between writers of Hispanic texts and creators of visual works; raise crucial theoretical concerns that situate the art and texts beyond the historical, national, or aesthetic framework in which they have been traditionally placed, thus facilitating different "ways of seeing"; and, finally, chart new theoretical directions that may be utilized to study other artistic works, be they plastic or verbal.

"Reflections on the *Mirrored Room*: From Work to Word," the introductory chapter written in two parts (the first by Rosemary Geisdorfer Feal, and the second by both authors), gives an overview of the principal theories that approximate the literary and the visual arts. This exploration begins with a meditation on Lucas Samaras's *Mirrored Room* as metaphor for the interartistic approaches undertaken in the book. The mirror itself is a powerful vehicle that may assist in positioning the written text vis-à-vis the work of art, but to do so demands a treatment of metaphor and image along with a general consideration of the methodological potential and legitimacy of the interart comparisons. By putting into play the effects of mirrors in Samaras's work, we may see some possibilities for reflection—mental and optical—in the enterprise of comparative arts. This chapter presents a historiography with respect to the body of scholarly work that applies particular theories to literature and the visual arts. The conjunction of feminist and psychoanalytic theories is highlighted specifically for its import to the readings that comprise the core of our book, and the "new" art histories are reviewed with an eye toward mapping the critical trajectory that follows as we go from theory to application.

Chapters 2 through 6, written by Carlos Feal, address a range of modern Spanish texts, commencing with literary naturalism at the end of the nineteenth century and extending through the contemporary period. "The Temptation of Saint Julian in Emilia Pardo Bazán's *The House of Ulloa*: Bosch, Goya, and Spain's Fin de Siècle" begins with the premise that the story told in the third person is focalized through the protagonist, Julián. An analysis of Julián's vision in *Los Pazos de Ulloa* reveals that his distorted images are rooted in the unconscious and processed through his rigid religious upbringing. Moreover, these images take shape in the implicit evocation of paintings by Bosch, Goya, and artists from the Victorian age. To the extent that Julián functions as a subject of desire, however, he is trapped in his own acts of contemplation, which take on the quality of a mirror or a dream. Finally, the novelist's feminist viewpoint interferes with that of the protagonist, thereby creating fissures where the contradictions of "patriarchal" and "matriarchal" may be glimpsed.

"All the World's a Museum: The Marquis of Bradomín's Textual Exhibition" centers on Valle-Inclán's *Sonata de primavera* [Spring sonata], in which Bradomín more overtly displays the decadent fin de siècle perspective initiated in *Los Pazos de Ulloa*. As the megalomanic narrator, Bradomín aspires to take possession of the world of women around him through his aggressive vision, but this world onto which the protagonist projects his desires has the power to annihilate him. Bradomín thus resorts to freezing those women, whom he perceives as both desirable and threatening, into pictorial images. As the distanced spectator of his creations, Bradomín can exert his dominance much as a Renaissance painter does over his subjects.

The spirit of modernism that pervades Valle-Inclán's *Sonata* is continued in the narrations that make up *Víspera del gozo*, the subject of chapter 4, "The Infinite Progression: Love and Art in *Prelude to Pleasure* by Pedro Salinas." Salinas makes literary use of spatial forms by approximating temporal sequences to painting, thereby transporting the narrative flow outside of chronological time. Yet the opposite impulse is equally present in his work: there is a constant progression that seeks to surpass and replace current forms. A pictorial correlation to this impulse may be made with El Greco's work, which is infused with an intense dynamism and always seems on the verge of dissolving or unraveling. Another link between literature and painting in Salinas could be the entire history of Western art, understood figuratively by him as a progression from clumsiness, rigidity, and theatricality toward light and color.

The figure of the he-goat in Goya's *El Aquelarre* [The witches' sabbath] undergirds the structure of *Tiempo de silencio* [Time of silence], the subject of "Male (De)Signs: Art and Society in Luis Martín-Santos." This omnipresent symbol of the *homo hispanus* makes no social distinctions as it moves about in refined domains as well as abject settings. Martín-Santos's mordant critique of Spain finds correspondence in other satirical works by Goya, such as his celebrated *Caprichos*, which may be said to set the stage for several passages in the novel. Martín-Santos's "illustrated mind" also derives from Goya: building on the painter's legacy, the novelist-psychiatrist implacably demonstrates how the dream of reason produces monsters. Finally, along with the macho appears another typical Spanish figure, the bullfighter and the corresponding vision of Spain as a giant bull ring or spectacle in which everyone participates. Once again the presence of Goya is unmistakable: works with bullfighting themes, such as *Plaza partida* [Divided ring] and *Diversión de España* [Spain's amusement] serve as the visual models for this tragic and grotesque textual world.

"Exiled in *The Garden of Earthly Delights*: From Hieronymus Bosch to Francisco Ayala" examines *El jardín de las delicias* for its self-declared, explicit association between literature and the visual arts. Given that the author reproduces a series of paintings to accompany or illustrate several of his narrations, the text and the pictorial image inhabit parallel planes. The plasticity of Ayala's imagination stands out clearly when he employs the act of contemplating a painting as the departure point for a story. Through the appeal to pictorial images, a kind of fictional autobiography is also being composed, since the writer inserts his life experience in the mythic worlds evoked by artists such as Bosch, Rubens, Goya, Michelangelo, and Titian. Thus the figure of the writer becomes inseparable from the painted figures that he both animates and observes as a coparticipant in pleasure, pain, proximity to death, vehement desire, and nostalgia for paradise.

Chapters 7 through 9, written by Rosemary Geisdorfer Feal, center on contemporary texts by Spanish-American authors of the "boom" from the 1970s to the late 1980s. Through an approach derived from narratology, Lacanian psychoanalysis, and feminism, "Visions of a Painted Garden: José Donoso's Dialogue with Art" analyzes *El jardín de al lado* [The garden next door] and its relation to painting in an attempt to uncover the unconscious fantasies that give the texts and works of art their structure. Pictorial images of women in particular are called on to read the play of gender in Donoso's novel, in which the evocation of the garden of exile and desire connects once again to Bosch. From the cover image, based on a painting by Magritte, to references in the novel to Ingres and Klimt, Donoso invokes a female who is both archetypically phallic (for example, the spiderwoman) and castrated (the decapitated figure). Last, the description of a painting done by a character in the novel is linked to Dalí's *The Hallucinogenic Toreador* in terms of pictorial and psychological content, which relates to the complex narrative game of writing transexually.

"In Ekphrastic Ecstasy: Mario Vargas Llosa as the Painter of Desire" focuses on Vargas Llosa's erotic novel *Elogio de la madrastra* (In praise of the stepmother) with respect to the paintings that are reproduced as illustrations for chapters in the work, much like Ayala had done. The author's incorporation of paintings by artists such as Jordaens, Boucher, Titian, Bacon, Szyszlo, and Fra Angelico positions the depicted female body *vis-à-vis* the written objects of desire in the erotic text. An analysis of this overt dialogue with painting looks at the ways in which the relations among the actors in the oedipal triangle come into play when they are filtered through word and image. Given the scandalous novelistic interpretations that the author spins around the paintings, we may re-examine a work like Jordaens's *King Candaules* for the way it interrogates notions of complicity and exhibitionism, or look at a work like the one by Szyszlo to extract a metacommentary on the possibilities of reading abstract art as narrative painting and of making art (into) theory. Further, Vargas Llosa's play with painting falls squarely within a postmodern context, which can account for the simultaneous inscription and subversion of cultural codes.

"Dada at the Tropicana: Guillermo Cabrera Infante and Readymade Art" presents a model based on generic and formalist criteria. This study of readymade art translates Marcel Duchamp's gestures onto the contemporary Latin American literary scene by locating Cabrera Infante's *Exorcismos de esti(l)o* [Exorcizing a sty(le)] within the tradition of Dada and the found object. In keeping with the spirit of readymade art, this study underscores both the radical and the conservative nature of this kind of artistic practice: the analysis interrogates the production and reception of the readymade in the "high" cultural sphere and thus questions its status in the art world. This chapter takes Cabrera Infante at his word, which means at his wordplay: its tone marks a change from the previous studies in our book, and yet there is unity in the common search for the underlying structures of the text and the artwork. Here, the connections come from linguistics and the philosophy of aesthetics, and, accordingly, there are fewer links to feminism or psychoanalysis that may be pursued. Nevertheless, this study shows more dramatically than any other why the interartistic comparison may provide some of those elusive analytic keys without which a text remains partially unavailable to its readers. And we hope that after the solemnity of some of our earlier material, this imagined partnership between Duchamp and Cabrera Infante offers a pause that refreshes. Or, as Cabrera might add, we're all for fresh paws. The book concludes with an epi(dia)logue in four parts in which we engage each other in the issues informing this project and make some connections between the ideas developed in the preceding chapters.

We should say a word about how we worked. The initial impetus for this project came during the years when an extraordinary conjunction of comparative arts scholars were based at the University of Rochester, some of whom are cited throughout this book for their contributions to the field. As the art history collection in our personal libraries grew, so did our interest in collaborating on a common interartistic project that would encompass both Spain and Spanish America, one that would allow us to engage in methodologies that were already a part of our critical repertoire while developing new vocabularies and contexts. Each author worked autonomously, and we then set about weaving our texts so that the commonalities outweighed the idiosyncrasies. We noted that our methodological assumptions were compatible, though not uniform, and we were surprised to see just how much we had learned from others—and from each other. Although we drafted our chapters separately, we served as reciprocal readers and commentators. As for the English translations, we cite published versions of translated literary and critical texts whenever available (the page numbers refer to the bibliographic items listed in the works cited). At times we have modified the translation for reasons of clarity, precision, or to compensate for omissions; our modifications appear in brackets. In the one case (chapter 6) in which there is no published English version of the primary literary text, we have provided our own translations. When we cite from an untranslated critical work written in any language other than English, we give an English equivalent, enclosed in quotation marks, with a page reference to the original article or book in question.

# ACKNOWLEDGMENTS

This book owes its existence to many individuals, beginning with our wonderful series editor, Jorge J. E. Gracia, who showed enduring confidence in our work and extraordinary patience with our progress. *Un millón de gracias.* We wish to express our deep gratitude to colleagues past and present, near and far, who have offered their expertise and support at various stages of this project: Mieke Bal, Norman Bryson, Sara Castro-Klarén, Lou Charnon-Deutsch, Michael Ann Holly, Amy Katz Kaminsky, Lucille Kerr, Sharon Magnarelli, and Carlos Rojas. A special word of thanks goes to Debra Castillo, imaginative commentator and tireless reader of the manuscript in its several versions. We owe a personal and intellectual debt to Mary Maselli Fox, who has accompanied us throughout the intense years of work on this joint venture.

The process of turning manuscript into book was eased at every juncture by Christine Worden, acquisitions editor at SUNY Press, and Susan Geraghty, production editor. At the early stages of research, Maggie McCarthy gave capable assistance with bibliography. We appreciate the generous support provided by our respective universities in the form of leaves, time releases, and monetary grants. Carlos especially thanks Henry J. Richards, Chair of Modern Languages and Literatures, and Kerry Grant, Dean of Arts and Letters, at the University at Buffalo. Rosemary is grateful to Beth Jörgensen, Chair of Modern Languages and Cultures, and Richard Aslin, Dean of the College, at the University of Rochester, and also wants to acknowledge those who arranged for her Bridging Fellowship with Art History: Ruth Freeman, Patricia Herminghouse, and Michael Ann Holly. We hope that this book demonstrates the tangible impact on interdisciplinary scholarship that results from administrative initiatives such as the ones extended to us.

Preliminary and partial versions of several chapters have appeared previously in *España Contemporánea, MLN, Revista de Estudios Hispánicos, Criticism,* and *Revista Hispánica Moderna.*

We acknowledge the following for permission to reproduce copyrighted material:

From *The House of Ulloa* by Emilia Pardo Bazán, translated by Roser Caminals-Heath. Copyright © 1992 by the University of Georgia Press, Athens, Georgia. Reprinted by permission of the publisher.

From *The Pleasant Memoirs of the Marquis de Bradomin*, translated by May H. Brown and Thomas Walsh. Copyright © 1924, reprinted by permission of Harcourt Brace & Company.

From *To Live in Pronouns: Selected Love Poems*, by Pedro Salinas, translated by Edith Helman and Norma Farber, by permission of W. W. Norton & Company, Inc. Copyright © 1974 by Edith Helman and Norma Farber.

From *Prelude to Pleasure* by Pedro Salinas, translated by Noël Valis. Copyright © 1993 by Associated Universities Press, Inc.

Excerpts from *Time of Silence* by Luis Martín-Santos, translated by George Leeson, copyright © 1962 by Editorial Seix Barral, S.A., Barcelona, English translation copyright © 1964 and renewed 1992 by Harcourt Brace & Company, reprinted by permission of Harcourt Brace & Company

From *The Garden Next Door* by José Donoso, translated by Hardie St. Martin. Copyright © 1992 by Grove/Atlantic, Inc.

From T. S. Eliot, *Four Quartets*. Copyright © 1943, reprinted by permission of Harcourt Brace & Company.

Excerpts from *In Praise of the Stepmother* by Mario Vargas Llosa. Translated by Helen Lane. English translation copyright © 1990 by Farrar, Straus & Giroux, Inc. Originally published in Spanish as *Elogio de la madrastra*, copyright © 1988 by Mario Vargas Llosa. Reprinted by permission of Farrar, Straus & Giroux, Inc.

# CHAPTER 1

# *Reflections on the* Mirrored Room: *From Work to Word*

## IN THE *MIRRORED ROOM*

Some of my most memorable recollections of growing up in Buffalo are of visits to the Albright-Knox Art Gallery, and it is to this place that I now return, accompanied, to think through the theoretical issues involved in the study of literature and the visual arts. Only two people are allowed in the *Mirrored Room* at a time, so this chapter should read as if we two coauthors were walking through the structure—and the issues—in tandem. The native Buffalonian (that's Rosemary Geisdorfer Feal) voices an *I* when she speaks for herself in the first part of this chapter: there is a deliberate shift to a *we* when both of us are implicated or authoring, as in the second part, or when our readers are included (even spoken for), or, finally, when that old-fashioned but convenient editorial *we* gets dusted off, "as we will see." In the chapters that follow, the *we* proves useful, too, even though an *I* might be more precise: we fundamentally agree with each other in our expositions of the material, and so we have elected to smooth over the jarring effect that would be produced by dual referents for the first-person pronoun. In the epilogue, however, we each reclaim our individual *I* as we enter into explicit dialogue in two voices.

I have chosen one of the most popular works on exhibition in the contemporary collection of the Albright-Knox Art Gallery, Lucas Samaras's *Mirrored Room* (1966) (Fig. 1), as central metaphor for these reflections in this section, and the choice is far from arbitrary. I have gone through the *Mirrored Room* countless times, and have emerged with ever-evolving perceptions of the work, of the art world, and, in recent years, of my critical practice as a scholar of literature written in Spanish. Now that my own studies have placed me in closer proximity to the field of visual arts, I find myself indebted to early encounters with the *Mirrored*

1

Figure 1.
Lucas Samaras, *Mirrored Room* (1966). Albright-Knox Art Gallery,
Buffalo, New York. Gift of Seymour H. Knox, 1966.

*Room* for the rich host of interpretive possibilities it can provide
when the printed word is held up to the metaphoric mirror of
visual representation.

Lucas Samaras's *Mirrored Room* is built up around notions of
the reflected work and the reflected self. After all, what is a sculpture consisting of mirrors that make up the inside, the outside, the

ceiling, the floor, the furniture, the walls if not a stage for representation? The *Mirrored Room* holds the potential for setting off a chain of endless reflections, an event that hinges on the appearance of an eye, the presence of an *I*. Before a person enters the space of the *Mirrored Room*, the cubicle simply stands there, static, reflecting the materials of its own construction on its six surfaces. When you approach the *Mirrored Room*, you can see yourself fully reflected on the outside walls as you sneak a voyeuristic glance toward the inside, where the mirrors reflect each other in eerie tones of green, the patina caused by the steady stream of the shoeless individuals who have circulated through the room since 1966. But your corporeal integrity is dissolved when you come closer to the doorway that leads inside the structure. You then get your first glimpse of a partial image of yourself that peers back from the panels of that room where it is reflected: you see yourself peeking from some remote corner that transmits the sensation of spatial distance, and you note that your pair of eyes is already multiplied in hundreds of places. You see the beginnings of yourself being seen: you have created a spectacle of yourself in your attempt to see the *Mirrored Room*. For that *is* the experience of the *Mirrored Room*, or at least the primary one: recreating *yourself* as the object to be contemplated in all your transposed, interrupted fragments. *You* become inseparable from the *Mirrored Room* when you enter it. No longer static, potential, or theoretical, the sculpture has become a type of kinetic "happening."

But the *Mirrored Room* is located in a museum, that is, a sanctioned, institutional setting that proclaims its contents to be part of the art world. Further, Samaras's creation does not duplicate any ordinary room full of mirrors, and consequently it does not function in the manner of, say, a mirrored dressing room in a department store. This differentiating effect is of course in part attributable to the cultural, social, and psychological factors that condition viewers' subjectivity. But because it is stationed in the Albright-Knox Art Gallery, the *Mirrored Room* literally—that is, optically—reflects *other* works of art that hang on the walls of the partitioned area in which the sculpture room stands. These works change whenever the curators elect to utilize the wall space for different pieces of contemporary art, with the result that the *Mirrored Room* undergoes a shift as well: the outside walls invariably reflect their new surroundings, which are continually subject to mutation, to an always past and an always future. The *Mirrored*

*Room*, then, like moveable art, enlists constant change as its stabilizing force, but motion in this case does not alter the actual physical structure, but rather what is represented in it, or reflected. For the *Mirrored Room* contains no reflections of things or people past, because those reflections can never be etched or encoded on the structure itself: they can be preserved in an individual's memory or in a photograph. There is a 1978 photograph of Lucas Samaras inside his own sculpture: the camera has recorded the flash of its bulb, creating a view not unlike an aerial shot of a city at night. And that particular camera angle is itself partial, particular: the *experience* of being in the *Mirrored Room* cannot be recorded in a credible manner (including verbally, as I am only too well aware), and for those who have been through the structure, a photographic representation surely must seem highly distorted, even unrecognizable. As we look at the photograph of the work, it becomes obvious that this is not just a room of mirrors, it is a mirrored *room*. Like a "tiled" room or a "painted" room, "mirrored" functions in adjectival complementarity: this is not a compound noun, like the Green Room, or the Dining Room. In fact, I should probably delete the definite article in speaking of the sculpture, reporting instead that "I have gone through *Mirrored Room* countless times," which would emphasize its status as named, unique artwork and downplay its role as a variant of "room." The title of the work does not declare it to be a room made of mirrors, but a room covered over by mirrors. This grammatical distinction, I believe, proves crucial to the psychological structure of the *Mirrored Room*, that is, the function of the mirror in the psyche as Jacques Lacan views it in his formulation of the mirror stage, which will be discussed shortly.

We define ourselves in our reflections in the *Mirrored Room* as we walk around inside it. But we do not actually penetrate it, we do not go *through* the looking glass like Alice: we study surfaces. To fully grasp this experience, we need to look at the psychological dimensions of the mirror. My own observations lead me to believe that when little children approach the *Mirrored Room*, they are at once fascinated by their reflection, yet terrified at the mirage of depth that threatens to suck them into a horizontal downfall. Experiments show that when a false sense of depth is created, young children instinctively back away from the perceived abyss, but can be coaxed to cross the dangerous zone by a trusted individual (usually the mother). In the *Mirrored Room*, children seek the other to anchor their own sense of self. They delight in seeing the person who accompanies them into the room reflected endlessly, like themselves: they know that the other does not fall through, and therefore they conquer their own fear. They may be terrified by the experience, but, like on a roller-coaster ride or a walk through a haunted house, they derive the thrill from the scare, and they seek to repeat it and thereby master it. Children may think of the *Mirrored Room* in terms of a carnival fun house with concave and convex mirrors that distort the self into a laughable caricature. But this experience in the museum setting is tangibly different for them: rather than signs of sheer amusement, they utter expressions of wonder—and terror—at the sight of themselves infinitely reflected, reduced, reduplicated, and lost.

The notion of "terror" acquires even more relevance to Samaras's work if we consider the structure of his *Mirrored Cell* (drawn in 1969 and constructed in 1988, currently at the National Gallery of Art in Washington, D.C.). As its title indicates, the *Mirrored Cell* places the visitor in a room designed to imprison: the mirrored bed suggests not so much the idea of repose as of perpetual confinement; the toilet and desk do not offer relief or freedom to work, but rather threaten the inhabitant with constant surveillance, by one's own eye or by the eye of another. There is a small window that allows a viewer from the outside to observe the prisoner within: much like the panopticon as analyzed by Michel Foucault, the *Mirrored Cell* enchains the inhabitant in a psychological state of being-looked-at, a state carried to the extreme of having the spectator serve as his or her own spy while being observed potentially from the outside as well. The fascination with one's own image in the *Mirrored Room* can rapidly give way to the terror of inescapability that the *Mirrored Cell* sets up on its fragmented, reflecting surfaces. But when excised from the negative connotations of surveillance, the *Mirrored Cell* may offer an imaginary place for repose, meditation, communion, and self-contemplation, much in the manner of a monk's cell. The mirror as Samaras conceptualizes it therefore does not have to take away our soul or alienate us from ourselves; it may also give us back to ourselves.

Children in the *Mirrored Room* touch their bodies to reassure themselves of their corporeal integrity: they inquire, "Is that *me* in there?" What do we respond? Is that "us" in the *Mirrored Room*? When we cease the viewing process by exiting the structure, we are no longer constituted in the *Mirrored Room*, so in a sense it is not "us" on display at all: it is a subject viewing the momentary reflections of his or her own viewing action. Upon emerging from the *Mirrored Room*, we perhaps take another glance back in, remembering the sensations that were aroused but relinquishing their status as motion, action, or experience. There is no trace of our having been recorded in the structure; there is only the mental record of perception. This experience is both evocative of the experience of viewing a painting and profoundly different from it. Standing before a painting we construct ourselves as the viewing subject, the spectator, but we are not the "spectator in the picture" in a literal sense. Perhaps we identify with an internal spectator's position within a painting while we contemplate it, and/or we appropriate the look of another in the process of construing our own gaze; it could be that we project ourselves into the painting and/or that we allow ourselves to be imprinted by the work of art. But when spectators come face to face with themselves as the object viewed in the mirror, they inevitably assume the position of subject and object within the same physical space. If they turn away from the mirror, they no longer see themselves reconstituted there, but the structure still exists in the realm of the real, perhaps reflecting another viewer, or implacably reflecting itself. Like Narcissus, we are fascinated by our reflection, and like him, we are beckoned by the sight of ourselves and may wish to cross over the representational barrier to embrace ourselves.

Accustomed as we are to seeing ourselves in mirrors on a regular basis, we find that it is the multitude of reflections that draws us into the *Mirrored Room*, and therein lies our fascination. We look overhead and see ourselves reflected below; we look down and see ourselves reflected from above. The image that appears before us can never be located in what we think is the viewing space, for it, too, is always a reflection of another space within the chamber of mirrors. We look down and imagine that we are falling into an infinite tunnel, but we realize that it is the few panels of mirror directly above us, on the ceiling, that create this illusion of depth. We turn our gaze upward to grasp this principle of reflecting mirrors, and we see ourselves projected from the floor up, yet we never can look at the floor without viewing the ceiling. The same holds true for the sides of the room and for the corners, where the conjunction of walls creates a false "safe space" in which the infinite reflecting may be momentarily interrupted, since it projects a bisected view of our bodies back to us. We may reach out to touch a mirror panel (until the guard orders us to refrain from tactile exploration). We are permitted vision alone, yet we are compelled to seek other sensorial dimensions of the experience. The guard may even invite us to try some of the optical "tricks" known to devotees of the *Mirrored Room*, such as standing in one corner and quickly looking up and down to simulate the sensation of riding in an elevator.

In short, the *Mirrored Room* serves as a most suitable metaphor for the exploration of the boundaries of text and art, boundaries that necessarily implicate the position of a subject who seeks to project meanings onto the silver-backed surface. Samaras could hardly have chosen the mirror as prime material for his work without some awareness of the significance that the reflecting glass holds in specific cultural, historic, or mythic contexts. Further, the mirror is par excellence a gender-coded space through which women have traditionally formed an identity (or have had one constructed for them). In his literary iconology, appropriately named *Disenchanted Images*, Theodore Ziolkowski points to three familiar metaphors produced by "man's perennial fascination with mirrors": "the mirror of art, the mirror of God, and the mirror of man" (149–50). Those searching for a recognition of woman's relation to the mirror will be disenchanted with this iconology, which makes the male the originator, receptor, and interpreter of the reflecting glass: that is, he creates it, he is mirrored in it, and he projects the images of his (male) artworld and his (male) divinity back to himself.

Ziolkowski is not the only one to view the reflection in the mirror as prototypically male (I am tempted to call it a critical act of unreflective narcissism): in his illuminating study of the mirror from an anthropological perspective, James W. Fernandez concludes that the mirror can give us "some feeling that there is something of our fathers in ourselves and something of ourselves in them. It can give us some feeling that there is something of the king in everyman and something of everyman in the king. If the mirror can give us such feelings . . . the 'sensation of relief' may well be absolute" (37). If indeed felt, this relief, I would argue, derives from having one's male identity confirmed in the mirror through the channels of patriarchy: there is no intruding female image to complicate man's bonding with other men; there is no threatening female-other to contaminate transmission of the stuff of a father-king. In Lacanian terms, however, the "relief" at seeing oneself whole in the mirror, at seeing oneself male, would harbor the unease of the split that must be traced to the mirror stage: here, it is woman who holds up the little boy to the mirror, and here, he does in fact construct his identity in relation—and in opposition— to her reflection as well as his own. The little boy's awareness of his potential as father-king comes when he glimpses himself whole, distinct, but alienated; that is, when he intuits the threatened dissolution of his sense of bodily and psychic integrity by means of the separation of the self from the previous imaged unity of mother and child. No wonder Fernandez decorporealizes the experience of seeing oneself, and thus claims, following Lévi Strauss's lead, that the mind is what is reflecting upon itself in the mirror (36).[1] What better way to counter the mirror's potential for arousing fear, discomfort, unease, or disorientation than by subjugating it to the mind's control? Lucas Samaras's structure, as we have seen, has the power to reinstate some of the primitive effects of the mirror while simultaneously decontextualizing the ordinary mirror by installing it into the world of art, and, by extension, into the world of the intellect. I, too, want to view the *Mirrored Room* "in the mind's eye," but I do not wish to lose sight of the gendered, embodied experience of the self in reflection.

In response to the trope of the man-in-the-mirror, some critics have indeed focused on the specificity of the female subject in relation to her reflected self in both literature and art. In *Herself Beheld: The Literature of the Looking Glass*, Jenijoy La Belle discusses the notion of the radical otherness of woman as a cultural construct. She sees the mirror as a semiotic surface, the potential site in which woman's identity is not only established or fixed, but also threatened or undone. La Belle compares the mirror to the literary text in that both surfaces aid women in encoding and decoding their identities; we might add, however, that writing may be considered a superior vehicle in that it exacts activity and affirms power, even when it provokes the "anxiety of authorship" (as defined by Sandra Gilbert and Susan Gubar). If writing is an act of liberation for women, the mirror may also be uncovered for its positive force: "By taking the mirror into their own hands, women are eliminating the mirror as tyrant, as dominant male. . . . For women to liberate themselves as women is not to dismiss their bodies but to free them from male/mirror tyranny" (180). This "liberating" mirror, then, becomes the "other speculum of woman," the man-made object turned into instrument of feminist self-discovery and self-realization. This utopian interpretation of the mirror perhaps parallels—or reverses—the patriarchal view expounded by critics such as Fernandez. In theory, women would see their mothers in themselves and something of themselves in their mothers, or, in other words, the mirror would give us a feeling that there is something of the goddess in everywoman and something of everywoman in the goddess. This mythic elevation of the looking glass intercepts the frightening spectacle of woman as she perceives herself degraded by physical aging, or as she comes close to insanity, or as she is drawn back into the waters of undifferentiated narcissism. The dark side of the glass thus reflects both male and female subjectivity, but certainly with a set of distinctions attributable to constructions of sexual differences, and social and cultural practices (especially literary and artistic practices, to be sure).

Lucas Samaras draws on a long-standing tradition of the mirror in art, which can appear as a subject in a painting or as an actual object: archaeological artifact, architectural form. In a study of mirrors in art, Laurie Schneider traces the evolution of the reflecting glass and lists its key symbolic usages. She believes that "art *is* a mirror, a reflection of society with all its customs, beliefs, folklore, superstition, religion, even of the artist himself" (283). We might take exception to that initial interpretation, since art can rightfully be viewed as the medium that constructs those very elements she claims it reflects, culminating of course with the image of the artist *himself* as normatively male. Samaras brings this issue of constructedness to bear on the conceptualization of his *Mirrored Room*, which, as I have argued, provides passage to a double-visioned space where the subject undergoes fragmentation and dissolution at the same time that it is made present and brought into being in the mirrored chamber. The thematic structure outlined by Schneider encompasses some analogous functions: the mirror serves as symbol for human vanity, for self-portraiture, and for knowledge of self and other.[2] When read together, the studies by La Belle and Ziolkowski, which look primarily at literature, along with those by Schneider and Schwartz on the mirror in art, provide fertile ground for our interartistic work on text as the metaphoric mirror of art (or art as the metaphoric mirror of literature), and it will become our task to juxtapose these critical findings with relation to specific word-image analyses.

The function of the mirror has been examined by philosophers as well as art historians and literary critics, and a few words about the ontology of the looking glass are in order at this point. As I have claimed with regard to Samaras's *Mirrored Room*, the act of passing through the structure constitutes a type of "happening," and the viewing process should be likened to a kinetic experience. In "Mirrors, Pictures, Words, Perceptions," Virgil Aldrich distinguishes the "mirror" as "material thing" from the "mirror-in-intention," which describes the field of representation proper to the looking glass. In strict terms, "nothing *qua* seen *in the mirror* 'exists' in it, or behind it, or in front of it" (41). Rather, the mirror is "the *occasion* for an image that is quite like the original it intends" (42, our emphasis). Aldrich's language is highly technical and dense, but his description of a man in a room with a mirror merits our consideration here: "the man but not his mirror image is in the room, yet reference to him in the *room* is not reference to him in the mirror's field of representation. They are identical but not 'simply.' It is the original that 'appears' in the field—can be said to be seen in it" (53–54). For our purposes, then, the person who walks through the *Mirrored Room* must be reconstructed along the lines of a subject split into two: the original (who of course is also a viewer) and the represented self, who, to use Aldrich's expression, plays "the role of appearing" (54) in the entire room's reflecting surfaces. Since the whole of the *Mirrored Room* would coincide with the room containing a mirror of Aldrich's example, the field of representation is inseparable from the structure that should theoretically contain it and limit it. Aldrich's metaphors lend a highly appropriate tone to our comparative discussion, since they allow us to look at the *Mirrored Room* as an experience of role playing, theatricality, staging, and acting, notions, after all, that are fundamental to "representation" in the visual arts as well as in the dramatic arts.[3]

## BETWEEN VISION AND TEXT: THE LANGUAGE OF THE INTERARTS

It is significant, we think, that there is no appropriate theoretical rubric under which to place the kind of criticism that seeks to compare the visual arts to the verbal arts, or, more accurately, to use theoretical models in reading the verbal through the visual. The term *ekphrasis*, although now experiencing a revival of sorts, certainly cannot serve as the house of criticism for the word-image studies that have been appearing in recent years, nor can it easily withstand the challenges leveled at traditional notions of *ut pictura poesis* or the outright attacks aimed at the institution of art historical practices. While ekphrasis etymologically holds the potential for a wide latitude of comparative work (it comes from the Greek verb *ekphrazein*, which means "to speak out" or "tell in full"), the term rarely finds usage outside the line of inquiry that describes how a picture somehow gets painted with words. In fact, the comment that "the author paints with words" is so pervasive in ekphrastic studies that it has become a cliché, an expression that is meaningless in itself. To study the problem of ekphrasis, critics have turned to notions of time and space, metaphor, analogy, imagery, period, style, and so forth. When a poem refers to a painting, it seems logical for the critic to view the pictorial image in an effort to discern what the poet sought to capture of it; in this manner, the critic becomes the interpreter of the interpreter, the spectator not so much of the painting itself but of the poet's viewing and act of poetic interpretation (which may take shape as recreation, evocation, representation). Narrow ekphrastic studies might find, for example, that the fierce, dagger-like adjectives penned by the poet correspond to the fiery reds painted by the artist. Another study may uncover the stylistic affinities between romantic painters and poets from a historical or aesthetic perspective.

We should mention one study in ekphrastic theory that marks an important stage in the development of interartistic work, since it comes around the time when "new" methodologies in art history began to have an impact on a highly conservative field that traditionally had kept itself isolated from other disciplines. In "*Ut Pictura Noesis*? Criticism in Literary Studies and Art History," Svetlana and Paul Alpers question the ability of a painting to be "mute poesy" or that of a poem to be a "speaking picture"; further, they trace the philosophical, historical, and aesthetic grounds on which comparatists have performed ekphrastic analyses and show the inherent weaknesses in many of the approaches. However, the conclusion of their study prescribes the critic's role in most problematic terms: "The critic's writing should work along—literally, collaborate—with the intentions, both large and small, of art works." They ask, "In what sense and in what ways are intention, comprehension, historical reality, social situation and purpose, human use implicit or implicated—literally, enfolded—in works of art?" (457). For our purposes, we will frequently reverse that question and instead ask, In what sense do works of art create or prescribe social situations, historical realities, gender differences, interpretive stances, and so forth? When comparatists who operate interartistically seek only the common human dimensions and intentions in visual and verbal works of art, they function primarily as mediators and thus renounce a potential role as agitators. We resist the intentional fallacy in interartistic comparisons as vigorously as we resist it in textual studies, since we consider that the results of our methods of inquiry could rarely have been "encoded" or "enfolded" in the works. This is not to say that we willfully ignore the contexts of the works we analyze—quite the contrary. We attempt to recontextualize the material we study in light of theories that forge previously unanticipated links between verbal text and visual representation.

At this juncture, we may well ask on what basis ekphrastic correspondences have traditionally been established: on a model of intrinsic differences between the arts, or on one of inherent similarities? This stance determines the attitude of critics, even when they are not aware of it. Thus, one could elect to mediate the fundamental differences that make the visual a world apart from the verbal; one would in effect be approaching the sister arts as family therapist, reconciling their tensions and placing them in dialogue or communication with each other. Or, on the other end of the spectrum, a critic may view the sister arts as twins bound together in symbiotic similitude, their individual distinctions passing unnoticed under a shared essence if not a like appearance. Further, as Carol Plyley James remarks, when "the qualities of pictures and words are compared, a hierarchy develops: pictures are primary, present, clear; words are secondary, abstract, mediated" ("No, Says the Signified" 458). But is this observation thoroughly accurate? Certainly, the "new" art histories would attempt to prove that there is nothing unmediated, direct, or even concrete about the medium of painting, except of course its physical reality (which itself is subject to the dynamics of perception, at the very least). In fact, the visual arts may be profitably studied in terms of a complex linguistic system, as Nelson Goodman's title, *Languages of Art*, so readily suggests. Although texts themselves bear physical presence (if nothing else, as black symbols on white pages and as printed matter bound up in books), they do not achieve the immediacy of the visual image, but this gap can be bridged by interrogating both kinds of representational codes and by uncovering the illusory nature of art as a clear, primary, or direct mode of perception and comprehension.

At this stage in our discussion, the sister arts appear to enter into sibling rivalry, into vital combat for primacy: they juggle for position and hierarchy when subject to interarts comparisons.[4] French philosopher Maurice Merleau-Ponty has made original contributions to this problem. By rooting thought in perception, or, in other words, by ascribing to perception an intellectual energy of its own—"painting's mute 'thinking'" ("Eye and Mind" 285)—he erases the traditional borderline between two activities that are considered to be distinct and hierarchically subordinated (with thought holding primacy over sensorial perceptions in Plato and philosophical idealism). Thus Merleau-Ponty succeeds in introducing a temporal dimension into the domain of the visual arts, which Lessing had called spatial. Accordingly, each painting, like each perception, does not end with the initial effect of surprise that it is likely to produce; rather, it constitutes a departure point for future explorations into the reality that was initially observed. As Jacques Taminiaux notes in his essay on Merleau-Ponty, "The Thinker and the Painter," "The thing that I perceive . . . offers itself as belonging to the future, as a 'hoped-for thing' (*'la chose espérée'* in Merleau-Ponty's expression); that is, as arousing the power I have of exploring it, of investigating it from all sides. My perception is therefore the overlapping of two dimensions: the present and actual with the nonpresent and nonactual, or in other words, *the visible and the invisible"* (203). Painting, then, may be compared to a text whose final meaning inevitably slips away or one in which the real shows itself, opens up, and conceals itself all at once.

In his seminal article "Spatial Form in Modern Literature," Joseph Frank also questions the distinction established by Lessing between temporal and spatial arts, and he does so in more explicit fashion. In early twentieth-century literature Frank sees textual echoes, foreshadowings, and juxtapositions that undermine the sequence inherent in language: the readers of these modern texts, therefore, perceive them more like spatial forms than temporal developments. Or, in other words, "the synchronic relations *within* the text took precedence over diachronic referentiality," as Frank would go on to summarize in a later article ("Spatial Form:

Thirty Years After" 207). For Frank, the best works of literary modernism are analogous to sculptures or illustrated manuscripts that use figures from the Bible or from classical antiquity as an expression of a timeless complex. The coexistence of images from the past and the present contributes to turning history into myth.[5] And Frank encounters spatial elements in any narrative work of art, not only in modernist ones, since the temporal sequence is constantly distorted, thereby making it necessary to construe relations across gaps in the causal-chronological order of the text. A characteristic of narratives would indeed be this very tension between the temporality of language and the spatiality required by their artistic nature.

Though intent on correcting or extending Frank's ideas, W. J. T. Mitchell in fact corroborates them when he states that "spatial form is a crucial aspect of the experience and interpretation of literature *in all ages and cultures* ("Spatial Form in Literature" 273, our emphasis). Mitchell, however, is original in showing that spatial form does not presuppose an antithesis to temporal form, since one is inseparable from the other. That is, the notion of time cannot be conceptualized without the support of spatial imagery. Similarly, space cannot be apprehended apart from time and movement. Mitchell proceeds to suggest that "every sentence is a picture or spatial form" and at the same time "every picture is a sentence," that is, reading is visionary, while vision is the reading of an informed mind. Mitchell criticizes the distinction between temporal and spatial arts as well: "Instead of Lessing's strict opposition between literature and the visual arts as pure expressions of temporality and spatiality, we should regard literature and language as the meeting ground of these two modalities" (297). Therefore, a concern with space is not completely removed from history, contrary to what Frank's detractors have claimed. Mitchell also takes up recent deconstructionist theories to claim that their attempts to surpass formalism do not constitute a negation of spatiality but rather affirm new and more complex spatial forms. The overlaying of spatial forms onto the temporal narrative flow is, for Mitchell, a necessary element in any act of reading. The incoherence heralded by decontructionists could lose its energy if the creation of patterns of coherence is not initially established.

Another signal contribution to the study of the relations between painting and literature is Wendy Steiner's work. According to Steiner, the attempt to join both arts obeys a deeper impulse: to erase the limits between art and life, between sign and thing. Painting and literature thereby function as equals when they are understood as an "icon of reality rather than a mere conventional means of referring to it" (*Colors of Rhetoric* 2). Yet, as Steiner says, a fully iconic representation of reality is impossible. Works of art imitate not reality but sign systems or models of reality, which are always conventional. From iconicity, then, we move into iconography, or, one step further, into iconology, an approach epitomized by Erwin Panofsky. A new kind of connection develops here between the visual and the literary arts. In iconographic painting, meaning depends on the knowledge of texts on which the details of the painting are based; alternately, the details of a literary description may have their origin in allegorical pictures. In turn, iconology—or "iconography in a deeper sense," as Panofsky defines it (*Studies in Iconology* 8)—demands "more than a familiarity with specific *themes* or *concepts*" (14); it also compels us to view the work of art in relation to multiple factors.[6]

Steiner makes another fruitful correspondence between visual and literary arts when she develops ideas originally formulated by Boris Uspensky. The parallel between the two art forms may be buttressed by the different ways in which they focus on their subjects: in painting, the medieval "perspective" places the most important figure in the center of the work and subordinates other figures to it by diminishing their size and distancing them from the center. The Renaissance perspective, on the other hand, subordinates all figures to the painter's look, which then is taken over by the viewer of the painting. In this way, the painter/spectator assumes a dominant position. In literature the pre-Renaissance stance would find an equivalency in the first-person narration. Steiner says that "a technical comparison of the two arts can consider the correspondence of position and semantic weight. . . . Perspective, then, is an important part of the pragmatics of painting and finds its literary analogue in point of view" (60, 61). However, Steiner also notes some distinctions. In the medieval representational system, the character integrated with its surroundings in the painting, as the center, can see all (and we in turn see *with* him or her); to the contrary, the distant Renaissance vision "limits the perceiver's knowledge to what can be seen unidirectionally at one moment in time" (62). Conversely, first-person narration limits our vision or knowledge to what the narrating character can see, whereas an omniscient viewpoint, distanced from the action, constitutes a higher degree of narrative privilege.

Mieke Bal has also treated these problems extensively, as the title of her recent book forcefully indicates (*Reading "Rembrandt": Beyond the Word-Image Opposition*). She notes that the very expression "word and image" does not bring illumination to the complexity and subtlety of the issues involved, and its confrontational framework often plunges the critic into simplicity or confusion. Instead, she proclaims that there is "an interaction, not an opposition, between discourse and image" (*Reading "Rembrandt"* 24). Bal, like the authors previously cited, seeks to go beyond the arbitrary dichotomy, which she accomplishes by appealing to semiotics, narratology, and psychoanalysis, typically constructed through feminist ideologies. This combination proves particularly fruitful, and it is a model that informs to a large extent the interartistic readings in this study. But of course there is no step-by-step recipe for a workable theoretical model with which to approach the visual and verbal arts, something that Bal certainly emphasizes in her critiques of the history of word-image studies. Perhaps it would be an easier task to follow Bal's lead and point to the failures of interartistic approaches than to ascertain what routes ultimately prove viable. It is the accomplished readings of paintings and literary texts that chart the ground, but it is a cogent consideration of theory that prepares the ground in the first place. The language of theory may be regarded as the suturing device that holds the arts together in comparative work of the sort we undertake. Far from seamless, our studies in this book display their stitches rather blatantly, in defiance of a smooth surface, of an uncracked looking glass.

## FEMINIST REVISIONS AND PSYCHOANALYTIC INCURSIONS IN THE VISUAL

We have occasionally used terms such as *deep* and *significant* in our search for common ground between literature and the visual arts, and it would be contradictory with some of our goals if we claimed to eschew those notions in a critical study of this sort. Yet this aim of arriving at "deep significance" may be in tension with the feminist agenda that undergirds much of what is attempted here. To use Naomi Schor's notion of the detail, that which is insignificant or goes unnoticed becomes an imperative in a visual-verbal analysis. The metaphor of the female body, which Schor, among others, has appropriated for the study of literature, brings us to the larger issues of representation, visual analysis, and feminism. Here we should cite Lynda Nead's recent work, *The Female Nude*, which advances a thorough critique of Kenneth Clark's well-known distinction between the naked (the body outside of cultural representation) and the nude (the body "clothed" in art). The (female) nude, then, would be for Clark an epitome of art itself, inasmuch as the essence of art resides in transforming matter into form. Nead deconstructs Clark's arguments by showing the fragility of the border that separates the naked from the nude: "The female nude strains the value oppositions of western metaphysics to their limits. . . . we can now begin to place the female nude not only at the center of the definition of art but also on the edge of the category, pushing against the limit, brushing against obscenity" (25). In the chapters that follow, we will refer to work from the many disciplines that touch on visual representation, including film studies, analysis of popular culture, psychoanalytic theory, philosophy, semiotics, and, of course, the "new" art histories that have arisen from the intersections of these fields. Other recent studies seek to trace the evolution of sexual difference and the visual arts: of particular importance is Lisa Tickner's cogent synthesis, "Feminism, Art History, and Sexual Difference."[7] Tickner affirms that "feminist art history cannot stay art history"; that is, it cannot be contained within the traditional disciplinary boundaries that have kept art history a conservative and conservationist avenue of intellectual inquiry. To accomplish their revisionist tasks, feminist art historians need to "account for the traffic in signs between different sites of representation" (94), which is itself a mandate to discard the notion of a discrete, precious object, an individual great "artist," or a closed succession of periods and styles. Feminist art history thus must chart the "battlefields of representation" in order to articulate the production of ideology and subjectivity; to do otherwise would be to remain marginal in the object-centered critical discourse that we have inherited from romanticism and modernism.

Tickner fully realizes, however, that feminism cannot enjoy a privileged, monolithic relationship to the field of art history, since the alliances that are formed among "feminisms" are themselves the products of tensions among incompatible notions of sexual difference. When Tickner concludes that "we need to work with different frameworks in the full knowledge of their incompatibility, testing them against each other, reading them through the historical material that can itself throw light on their usefulness" (116), she perfectly describes the critical goals of many feminists who study visual representation, and her mandate aptly summarizes some of the theoretical bases for this study. This type of project runs the risk of forcing diverse methodologies upon each other, with the result that the parts may not coexist in some harmonic whole, but we insist on the validity of these approaches to accomplish a "reading against the grain." The emergence of the "new" art histories has paved the way for a study of the kind attempted here, yet their convergence on these pages presents many complications that we are obligated to point out and to defend, wherever possible.

As we have emphasized, the feminist critique of art history starts with a challenge to the discipline itself: it interrogates the way in which one chooses to study—and construct—the category of "art." To speak not only of art but also of representation is to push the field of art history further toward the theoretical apparatuses from neighboring disciplines that examine how subjects come into being and how they are recreated and reinvented textually or visually. Griselda Pollock, whose feminist interventions in art history have prepared the way for current directions in research, speaks of representation in several ways. In the first place, the term *representation* stresses that "images and texts are no mirrors of the world, merely reflecting their sources." For Pollock, representation entails refashioning: something is coded in rhetorical, textual, or pictorial terms. This conceptual framework can also provide the mechanism for articulating social processes "which determine the representation but then are actually affected and altered by the forms, practices and effects of representation." Finally, representation involves a third dimension in that it addresses a viewer-reader-consumer (*Vision and Difference* 6). Pollock links the three processes entailed in representation to the function of gender and sexual difference in order to make explicit the mechanisms of male power. She believes that "art history is not just indifferent to women" but that it is "a masculinist discourse, party to the social construction of sexual difference" (11). Like many British feminists, Pollock forges theories of representation that accommodate both materialist and psychoanalytic considerations with regard to sexual difference. Jacqueline Rose remarks that "our previous history is not the petrified block of a singular visual space since, looked at obliquely, it can always be seen to contain its moments of unease" (*Sexuality in the Field of Vision* 232–33). Feminist visual analysis actively seeks out these moments of tension or unease in an effort to fracture the illusion of a singular vision or a readily accessible representation. This act is more than a reviewing or revisioning, however, since it interrogates the mechanisms that permit us to view or envision in the first place.

The title of a collection of essays edited by Hal Foster, *Vision and Visuality*, neatly encodes the problem of representation as it concerns us here, for vision is always conditioned by subjectivity (through ideology, sexual difference, class consciousness, cultural difference, and so forth). The term *visuality* more radically questions the naturalness attributed to the act of seeing, for to look is always to interpret, to involve the body and the psyche, and to block something out, whether or not one is aware of these processes.[8] Further, viewers are as constructed by viewing as they themselves construct that which they see: we are always in a sense "looking on" even when we believe we are "just looking." Norman Bryson has pioneered the study of visuality in his work on the glance and the gaze, and he has uncovered multiple complications entailed in vision or in a given "scopic regime." The "logic of the gaze," as Bryson terms it, in fact constitutes a language of its own, one that yields surprising coherence when analyzed within the framework of ideology, psychology, and semiotics. Thus Bryson says that a painting may direct the flow of interpretation across its surface, and it can mobilize collective forms of discourse present in the social formation; above all, painting has the capacity to exceed the fixities of representation (*Vision and Painting* 170).[9]

Reference has been made to the work of Jacques Lacan, whose discussion of the mirror stage partially informed the "reading" of the *Mirrored Room* in the first part of this chapter. Another influential work by Lacan is the section of *The Four Fundamental Concepts of Psycho-Analysis* entitled "Of the Gaze as *Objet Petit a.*" Lacan questions the possibility of a distant gaze that attempts to establish domination over the contemplated object, and, in harmony with Merleau-Ponty, he locates the gaze within the scopic field where one is both a viewer and on view: "I see only from one point, but in my existence I am looked at from all sides" (*Four*

*Fundamental Concepts* 72). In keeping with this scheme, the superior relation of subject with respect to object is subverted to instead usher in "the dependence of the visible on that which places us under the eye of the seer" (72). The subject instituted by the Cartesian tradition, then, becomes the victim of an annihilating power. For Lacan, what disorganizes the field of vision is the dialectic of desire, that is, the conception of the human being as subject of desire rather than of reflexive consciousness. In this regard, the French psychoanalyst postulates a sort of "appetite of the eye on the part of the person looking" (115). That appetite is met in the showing (*le donner-à-voir*), which in turn emanates from the desire of the Other. Yet not only is the gaze (or the desire) of the Other related to a seer; paintings also function in analogous fashion, which accounts for their hypnotic effect: "in the picture, something of the gaze is always manifested . . . , something so specific to each of the painters that you will feel the presence of the gaze" (101). Understood in this way, the spectator who stands before the contemplated object (a painting or whatever) actually stands in the *place* of that object; or, in other words, the spectator is "*photo-graphed*" (106). It would be hard to imagine a better illustration of these concepts from the art world than Samaras's *Mirrored Room*.

Lacan's theories certainly are brought to bear on many of our interartistic readings, but other psychoanalytic models are employed as well (some of which may stand in opposition to his thinking). While it would be quite futile to attempt an overview of all the psychoanalytic theories that undergird these analyses, it nevertheless is imperative that we take a brief look at the ways in which psychoanalysis has been used in the service of visual analysis. In fact, this task has been partially accomplished by Ellen Handler Spitz in her *Art and Psyche*, in which she isolates three principal psychoanalytic approaches to art: the nature of the creative work and experience of the artist (pathography); the interpretation of works of art; and the nature of the aesthetic encounter with works of art (ix). The first model arose from the works of Freud himself, typified of course by his study of Leonardo da Vinci. In pathography, the psychoanalytic critic would analyze biographical data in order to show how the artist's unconscious manifests itself in his or her creative works. When clinicians undertake analyses of their artist-patients, they also may perform a pathography of artistic expression (or, as is often the case, of blocked creativity or neurotic/psychotic creativity). The analysis of literary or visual art differs markedly from clinical analysis, however. We need only to look at the bitter exchange between psychoanalyst John Gedo and art historian Theodore Reff concerning the works of Cézanne to comprehend that there are unbridgeable gaps between those who approach art as symptom of specific unresolved unconscious tensions and those who find little merit—and much harm—in "psychobiographies."

This polemic brings us to Spitz's second model of psychoanalytic interpretation, which takes as its context the work of art "conceived as autonomous and constituted by its own internal relations" (x–xi). That is, the artists' individual family histories are considered irrelevant to the study of their creative work: the critic instead addresses questions of the origin and function of individual style and artistic form. While Spitz relates this model to the study of an artwork in isolation, as do the proponents of New Criticism, for example, she does not point out that many psychoanalytically informed readings of artworks do indeed relate their findings to a larger network of social and psychological sign production that makes up systems of visual representation. Relinquishing an individual biography for the purposes of a psychoanalytic study does not automatically correlate to insulating the work. It may mean, however, that the work momentarily assumes the role of *insula* within a larger cartography of land masses that the critic interconnects. Spitz only addresses this expanded grid in her third model, which includes the work of art plus its audience. This expansion draws from object-relations theory, reader-response criticism, and phenomenology (xi), but nowhere in her models do we find the very influential work of Jacques Lacan nor the revisions and reappropriations of Lacan that psychoanalytic feminists have carried out, developments that will be foregrounded in our readings.

In his lengthy overview of psychoanalysis as it has been incorporated into the "new" art histories, Jack Spector sketches the problems of psychoanalytic approaches to art and ponders their application by art historians (50–51). Unlike Spitz, Spector attaches significant weight to the impact of Lacanian theory; his undertaking is helpful not only because of its lucid exposition of the many ways in which psychoanalysis has been called to the service of art—and vice versa—but also because he makes visible the vast potential that can be located at the crossroads of multiple theoretical paths. Spector's work further complicates the already complex field of psychoanalytic inquiry by forcing visual critics to define and defend their positions with respect to the uses (and abuses) of the Freudian legacy. As a result, it is no longer legitimate to speak of *a* psychoanalytic approach to art history, but instead we must be attuned to the conflicting ways in which our readings fundamentally implicate psychoanalysis as a force for the comprehension of creativity. That is, we must become metacritics by problematizing the psychoanalytic tools we employ precisely because they have a long history of their own and because their link to aesthetics and creativity has never been free and clear, even when it may have appeared to be so. Those practitioners of the comparative arts who have been most successful at applying psychoanalysis have also taken the most care to engage actively in metacritical and theoretical discourse: Mieke Bal, for example, devotes an entire chapter of her *Reading "Rembrandt"* to these polemical questions.

The richness and variety of approaches derived from psychoanalytic models may be observed in theoretical and critical works of the last few decades. Much attention has been devoted to the transferential relationship between analyst and analysand in addition to the hermeneutical possibilities afforded by Freud's method. Spitz's third approach once again applies here: the aesthetic encounter with works of art, onto which we may graph the analytic possibilities contained in the phenomenon of transference. This theoretical position radically alters the traditional perspective that assigns to the critic the role of analyst with the artwork functioning as the analysand. By stressing the dialogic nature of the relationship between work and interpreter, we come to appreciate how both function simultaneously as analyst and analysand. The work of art generates an abundance of unconscious material and free associations in the spectator or reader, much as the analytic situation does for the analysand.[10] To formulate this process in a way that links on to the ideas developed here, let us say that the work (text, visual art, or painting on the page) functions like a mirror (this, after all, is how Freud viewed the analyst in relation to the patient) in which the readers/spectators see themselves reflected. Individual affect is thus transferred onto the work of art, and we project our intrapsychic material onto the images that the artist convenes in his or her creation. The artist's and the receptor's fantasies therefore merge in a process of absolute mutuality. This is a veritable "mirrored room": the work sees me as much as I see it and make it an object of my own reflection. In this sense, there may be some fairly tight restrictions on critics' receptivity, and, consequently, on the reach of their exegeses. When critics enunciate an interpretation, according to André Green ("Unbinding Process" 338–39), they expose the errors and limitations of their self-analysis (and not just of the analysis of the work); that is, they lay bare the level of resistance they experience with respect to their own unconscious.[11]

To conclude this section: the identification between author and work on one hand, and between author and critic on the other—all of whom indistinguishably represent the roles of analyst, analysand, and analytic discourse—must be carried to another level, where the spectators or readers are positioned. They too achieve the status of artist when they configure the textual data in a new narrative order; that is, when they act as interpreters who ascribe a new coherence to those data or narratives. The crossover of multiple fantasies—fantasies in the text communicated to the reader, the reader's fantasies projected on the text—sets off a secondary narration, which weaves through the framework of the originary discourse and thereby alters it (a bend here, a twist there, a link soldered more securely, something jarred loose). Interpretation, as Barthes, Eco, and others posited years ago, is a text written jointly, in which both author and reader collaborate. The same may be said of the psychoanalytic encounter in its strict clinical application, as Donald P. Spence notes: "[Psychoanalytic] interpretation can be seen as a kind of artistic product" (37). Spence bases his thinking on the distinction that he makes between narrative truth and historical truth. Analysts construct (more than *re*construct) a new reality that starts from the "facts" that the patient communicates. Analysts therefore do not capture any historical truth, hidden under those facts; they are not archaeologists of the mind. Instead, they use the material (reports, dreams, free associations, body memories) offered to them—as story—by the analysand to build a somewhat different story, one that possesses narrative truth.[12] Similarly, critics carry out an ordering process when they interpret texts, be they visual or verbal; they inflect these materials in accordance with what they perceive as being present in the original and/or what they project from their own psyches. If the narrative that this interpretive scheme produces is expressed in rhetorical forms that are analogous to the languages of art, then it has an effect on readers comparable to what art succeeds in doing: it invites our concurrence, involvement, and even suspension of disbelief.

## BEYOND THE *MIRRORED ROOM*

Visitors are not allowed to see the *Mirrored Room* from the dark inside, with its door closed, and we might wonder, along with the author of *Through the Looking Glass*, what the flame of a candle would look like when it is extinguished. The door of the sculpture remains open for a smooth transition from inner-art-world to outer-art-world, our path illuminated by artificial light bouncing off the mirror panels. So now we may move forward from theory to application, from what potentially could be a herme(neu)tically sealed room of ideas bouncing off one another toward a gallery of texts and images, which we construct as the testing ground for our interartistic critical practice. Or the playground, if you prefer: it is relevant that visitors to the Albright-Knox often inquire as to the location of the *Mirrored Room* by asking for the "children's section" of the museum. Some of the authors and artists we study have made text and art a site for deep play; yet we are more than reluctant to accord permanent space in the so-called children's section to works that are very serious in their references to urgent social and psychological matters. Just as our theoretical models do not claim to be wholly compatible, neither are the subjects of our critical applications to be taken as some homogeneous block or glass cube. We are attempting to probe the viability of interartistic approaches, and our building blocks, owing to their diverse composition, might appear as stumbling blocks from time to time. We take heavy baggage with us as we exit this chapter that began in the *Mirrored Room*: the ideas discussed here at times threaten to weigh us down and encumber our readings. We nevertheless feel confident that we provide good enough mirroring of these pioneer theorists who have worked in visual and verbal representation, for without this basis there would be precious little illumination and plenty of illusion. Whatever else we attempt in our studies of "painting on the page," we uphold theoretical clarity as an ideal, and our insistence on it is reflected every step of the way.

CHAPTER 2

# The Temptation of Saint Julian in Emilia Pardo Bazán's The House of Ulloa: Bosch, Goya, and Spain's Fin de Siècle

Emilia Pardo Bazán, a feminist and the first woman in Spain to hold a university chair (though she herself never earned an advanced degree), stands as a towering figure in nineteenth-century Spanish literature. Both as an author of fiction and as a literary critic, she made her presence and her passions intensely felt in a domain that for centuries had traditionally been reserved for men only. The following analysis of *Los Pazos de Ulloa* [The house of Ulloa] (1886), Pardo Bazán's masterpiece, centers on key passages of the novel in which the role of vision is privileged. Vision in this novel frequently appeals to a pictorial model: a painting is interposed between the thing viewed and the viewer. In other words, the object of contemplation is presented in terms that correspond to a specific painting (sometimes referred to either directly or indirectly), and, extending beyond, to the language of painting, to an imaginary scene. Essential to *The House of Ulloa*, then, is the dialectic between "vision" and "visuality," concepts elaborated by Hal Foster and Norman Bryson, among others, which we discussed in the preceding chapter.

As a complementary strategy, a psychoanalytic perspective comes into play here insofar as psychoanalysis is built up around visual images and grants them primacy both in clinical and in theoretical models. Mary Anne Doane, who speaks of images in film, underscores this notion: "the fascination with psychoanalysis on the part of film theory is linked to the centrality and strength of its reliance on scenarios of vision: the primal scene, the 'look' at the mother's (castrated) body, the mirror stage. Psychoanalytic theory would appear to be dependent upon the activation of scenarios with

25

visual, auditory, and narrative dimensions" (44–45). At the same time, Doane comes close to the concepts of "vision" and "visuality" when she distinguishes between two types of vision: natural versus culturally conditioned or, in psychoanalytic terms, conscious versus unconscious: "Yet the visible in no way acts as a guarantee of epistemological certitude. Insofar as it is consistently described as a lure, a trap, or a snare, vision dramatizes the dangers of privileging consciousness" (45). Our reading of the novel will be directed by these theoretical presuppositions, which serve as a base to be further elaborated as the interartistic analysis progresses.

From the opening pages of *The House of Ulloa* we may already observe the protagonist acting in ways that signal his future behavior. While riding on horseback, Julián has trouble controlling the animal: "Demostraba el jinete escasa maestría hípica: inclinado sobre el arzón, con las piernas encogidas y a dos dedos de salir despedido por las orejas, leíase en su rostro tanto miedo al cuartago como si fuese algún corcel indómito rebosando fuerza y bríos" (*Pazos* 8) "The horseman displayed little riding skill: as he leaned over the saddlebow with his knees bent, ready to be ejected over the horse's ears, his face revealed as much terror as if the nag were a wild steed bursting with fierceness and vigor" (*House* 3). These lines neatly expose a central thread in the novel: the priest's fear of instinctual life and the difficulty he experiences in confronting that aspect of life and, by extension, the world at large.

Nevertheless, Julián will immediately encounter in Ulloa's house exactly what he most fears and attempts to keep at bay. There, in the kitchen, he comes across some hunters with their dogs; along with a few other men, the hunters take part in a feast that also includes Perucho (Julián at first mistakes this boy for one of the dogs), whom they get drunk, and, finally, Sabel, the maid, "cuyo aspecto desde el primer instante, le había desagradado de extraño modo" (21) "whose looks had strangely displeased him from the first moment" (14). Closely associated with Sabel is another woman, an old crone named María the Sage ("María la Sabia"), described in highly negative terms: "La última tertuliana que se quedaba, la que secreteaba más tiempo y más íntimamente con Sabel, era la vieja de las greñas de estopa. . . . Era imponente la fealdad de la bruja" (45) "The last guest to leave, the one who whispered the longest and most intimately to Sabel, was the old woman with coarse hair. . . . The witch's ugliness was imposing"

(36). As Darío Villanueva has shown, vision throughout the novel is fundamentally aligned with the viewpoint of the protagonist, Julián (*"Los Pazos de Ulloa*, el naturalismo y Henry James" 130). The kitchen scene is an example of this kind of focalization. The epithet *witch* that is applied to the old woman does not seem fully justified by her ugliness; it is above all the intimate link between her and the young, sensual Sabel, for whom Julián feels particular repulsion, that promotes the old woman to the rank of witch, that is, the rank of lascivious servants of the devil. By taking his eyes off Sabel, Julián sets himself apart from the other men (including the other priests), but he nevertheless comes close to these men in his negative judgment of the old woman. In this regard he is no different from the Marquis of Ulloa, Don Pedro, who, when bothered by the presence of the old woman in the kitchen, recriminates Sabel: "¿No te tengo dicho que no quiero aquí pendones?" (16) "Didn't I tell you I don't want old hags around here?" (10). Don Pedro is irritated by the proximity of Sabel, his lover, to María the Sage. Sabel's sensuality is projected onto her elderly companion, which makes the old woman a repulsive being, at least for the masculine mentality as encoded in the novel. Yet, conversely, the old woman's ugliness defiles the young girl, whose physical beauty turns to moral decrepitude. And when women are so closely identified with their bodies in patriarchal culture, the transition from sensual youth to repulsive old woman is only ever a blink of the mind's eye away.

The negative vision projected onto María the Sage—and, by extension, onto Sabel—culminates in the following passage: "Mientras hablaba con la frescachona Sabel, la fantasía de un artista podía evocar los cuadros de tentaciones de San Antonio, en que aparecen juntas una asquerosa hechicera y una mujer hermosa y sensual, con pezuña de cabra" (45) "As she talked with the buxom Sabel, an artist's fancy might have recalled the paintings of Saint Anthony's temptations, in which a loathsome sorcerer and a beautiful sensuous woman with cloven hooves appear together" (37). What began as a simple description of the kitchen feast, presided over by Sabel, "la reina de aquella pequeña corte" (44) "the queen of that little court" (36), with the old woman beside her, ends up prominently foregrounding a man (Julián-Saint Anthony), even though the priest does not seem to have eyes for this instinctual world. Julián, who is paying attention to Perucho, is in fact only mentioned in passing a few lines earlier: "y si el capellán no estuviese tan distraído con su rebelde alumno, vería algún trozo de tocino, pan o lacón" (45) "and if the chaplain had not been so distracted with his rebellious pupil, he would have seen an occasional slab of bacon, bread, or pork shoulder" (36). Thus the description that removes him from center stage ultimately suits him most aptly: he is likened to an ascetic tempted by lascivious women. Superimposed onto the novelistic text is a painting that distills and recirculates the meaning of this passage. And in keeping with the depictions of the temptations of Saint Anthony in a variety of paintings in which he turns his head away so as to avoid looking at seductive women, Julián also would seem to be refusing the sight that appears insistently before him.[1] The painting or paintings evoked therefore require the presence of Julián as the center of the scene (object of the temptations), and as the narrative subject who replaces what he has viewed or glimpsed with an interior vision corresponding to his own desire. Next the priest is taken into that realm where he is so strongly implicated: "Sin explicarse el porqué, empezó a desagradar a Julián la tertulia y las familiaridades de Sabel" (45) "Julián, though he did not know why, began to feel annoyed by Sabel's chat and familiarities" (37).

As the narration progresses, a different perspective becomes apparent: "Poco después sufrió una metamorfosis el vivir entumecido y soñoliento de los pazos. Entró allí cierta hechicera más poderosa que la señora María la *Sabia*: la política, si tal nombre merece el enredijo de intrigas y miserias que en las aldeas lo recibe" (217) "Shortly after these events the stagnant and sleepy life of the house of Ulloa underwent a change. A certain witch, more powerful than María, the Sage, entered the scene: it was politics, if a tangle of village intrigues and miseries merits this name" (195). The focus has shifted from the feminine (the witches) to the masculine (politics). The power struggles among men constitute the principal cause of the misfortunes that occur in the novel. And, on closer examination, the "sensuous woman with cloven hooves," that is, the diabolic creature,[2] turns out to be a victim of two cruel men. Don Pedro, the lover, beats her savagely and insults her: "¡Perra . . . , perra . . . , condenada . . . ; a ver si nos das pronto de cenar, o te deshago! ¡A levantarse . . . , o te levanto con la escopeta!" (66) "Bitch, damned bitch! Make supper right away or I'll beat the living daylights out of you! Get up, or I'll get you up with the gun!" (57). When in her injured condition she speaks of leaving the house, she must face the adverse will of her father, Primitivo, the butler of the manor: "¿No oyes lo que te dice el señorito? . . . Pues a hacer la cena en seguida" (68) "Didn't you hear the master? . . . Then move and get supper ready" (58). Although they engage in a rivalry for power, the marquis and the butler correspond to the same model. But there is another male bond here: between the Marquis of Ulloa and Julián, who coincide in their negative estimation of Sabel, only in part justifiable. The image of the eternal Eve becomes superimposed on the representation of Sabel in the priest's mind: "No, no era Dios, sino el pecado en la figura de Sabel, quien le arrojaba del paraíso . . ." (75) "No, it wasn't God, it was sin incarnated in Sabel that expelled him from paradise" (65). This Eve, however, would gladly leave the "paradise" to which she is confined: "Que me voy, que me voy . . . A mi casita pobre . . . ¿Quién me trajo aquí? . . ." (67) "I'm leaving. I'm going to my poor little home. Who brought me here?" (58). The dominant perspective of Julián, who at once differs from other male characters (in his behavior) and is identical to them (in his misogyny), does not offer a full account of the events that take place in the social microcosm of the manor. The narration subtly bifurcates: a feminine (even feminist) voice supplements and corrects the masculine voice, yet its urgency is not diminished by its frequent relegation to the background.[3]

That the mentality displayed by Julián is shared by Don Pedro as well may be gleaned from the disastrous marriage choice that he makes. The marquis is attracted to his coquettish cousin Rita but must overcome the temptation that she presents, much like Julián resisted Sabel. Under Julián's influence, Don Pedro ultimately shifts his attentions to his other cousin, Nucha; although she is not physically beautiful like Rita, she knows the value of defending her virtue: "¡Oh, sorpresa! La resistencia más tenaz y briosa, la protesta más desesperada, unas manitas de acero que [don Pedro] no podía cautivar, un cuerpo nervioso que se sacudía rehuyendo toda presión" (106–7) "What a surprise! He met with the most stubborn and vigorous resistance, the most desperate protest, two little hands of steel that he could not dominate, a nervous body trying to break free" (94). Julián's candidate thus triumphs, and his attraction toward Nucha is doubly justified: she simultaneously incarnates the ideal of the pure woman and that of the good mother for the priest. Just as the figure of Sabel gives way to that of the lascivious Eve, so does Julián's vision of Nucha defer to another iconographic order: the representation of the Virgin Mary: "Por lo que su madre le había contado y por lo que en Nucha veía, la señorita le inspiraba religioso respeto, semejante al que infunde el camarín que contiene una veneranda imagen" (99) "What his mother had told him of Nucha and what he saw in her filled him with religious awe, as if he were before a shrine that enclosed a revered image" (87). A dialectic is undoubtedly established between these two opposed images, as Matías Montes-Huidobro clearly articulates: "Julián decorporealizes Nucha as the only way that would permit him to escape the danger represented by the opposite sex. Protected by the chastity belt of celibacy, his psychological fears are hidden behind the adoration of the Virgin Mary" (40). True, in a text in which the voices of the narrator and of Julián coincide as often as they diverge, we at times see the narrator adopting the chaplain's perspective; the pregnant Nucha is described as follows: "En cuanto al natural aumento de su persona, no era mucho ni la afeaba, prestando solamente a su cuerpo la dulce pesadez que se nota en el de la Virgen en los cuadros que representan la Visitación. La colocación de sus manos, extendidas sobre el vientre, como para protegerlo, completaba la analogía con las pinturas de tan tierno asunto" (149) "The natural enlargement of her frame was not excessive or unbecoming; it simply lent her body that sweet gravity we see in Mary's figure in the paintings of the Visitation. The posture of her hands, spread on her belly as if to protect it, completed the analogy with the iconography of such a tender scene" (131). A pictorial object again underlies the description, but the link between Nucha and the Virgin is now reversed. Contrary to Julián, who sees a woman as if she were a Madonna, the narrator perceives the Madonna as a woman. It is Mary's pregnancy, rather than her purity, that receives emphasis here.

Chapter 19 marks the climax of the narration. One night, from the top of a staircase, the chaplain witnesses an extraordinary scene:

> Como se le hubiese acabado el aceite de su velón de tres mecheros y no pudiese rezar ni leer, bajó a la cocina en demanda de combustible. Halló muy concurrido el sarao de Sabel. En los bancos que rodeaban el fuego no cabía más gente: mozas que hilaban, otras que mondaban patatas, oyendo las chuscadas y chocarrerías del tío Pepe de Naya, vejete que era un puro costal de malicias y que, viniendo a moler un saco de trigo al molino

de Ulloa, donde pensaba pasar la noche, no encontraba malo refocilarse en los pazos con el cuenco de caldo de unto y tajadas de cerdo que la hospitalaria Sabel le ofrecía. (183)

As the oil in his lamp had burned out and he could not pray or read, he went to the kitchen for more fuel. Sabel's soirée was very well attended. The benches by the fire were occupied by girls who spun or peeled potatoes while they listened to the jokes of Uncle Pepe of Naya, an old fellow who was all mischief. Whenever Uncle Pepe came to the Ulloa mill to grind a sack of wheat, he spent the night there, after enjoying a bowl of greasy soup and pork slabs that the hospitable Sabel offered him. (163)

The presence of Sabel's perennial companion, María the Sage, the "horrenda sibila" (183) "horrendous sibyl" (164), floods the scene with characteristics of a genuine witches' sabbath. In fact, the following is said of the old woman: "ponía miedo su estoposa pelambrera, su catadura de bruja en aquelarre, más monstruosa por el bocio enorme" (184) "She was a frightful sight, with the expression of a witch at a black mass [*aquelarre*], a coarse mane, and a monstrous profile with a huge goiter" (164). Given the Hispanic context of the narration, the interartistic model for this scene would be none other than the famous painting by Goya, *El Aquelarre* [The witches' sabbath] (Museo Lázaro Galdiano, Madrid) (Fig. 2), in which a group of women surround the devil in the guise of a he-goat.[4] The figure of the he-goat may be assigned to Uncle Pepe of Naya ("vejete que era un puro costal de malicias" "an old fellow who was all mischief"), although the demonism or protagonism rather belongs to the women, especially to Sabel and to the witch María the Sage. The real devil, Primitivo, does not appear here. Vision—and the description of the spectacle—once again corresponds to the perspective of Julián, the voyeur and disguised narrator. He not only watches the scene but also transforms it in his imagination.[5] Further evidence may be found in Pardo Bazán's *La madre naturaleza* [Mother nature] (1887), the continuation of *Los Pazos*, where at the start of chapter 27 the same gathering is evoked. And once Julián ceases to be the focalizing agent, the description looks markedly different: the only witch-like connotations are owed to the fact that among those people "se pagaba tributo muy crecido a la superstición" (385) "a great tribute was paid to superstition." Nothing in this description would surprise a native of Galicia, a land rich

Figure 2
Francisco de Goya, *The Witches' Sabbath* [El Aquelarre].
Museo Lázaro Galdiano, Madrid.

in superstitious beliefs, nor would it disrupt the festive connotations of the scene: "un viejo chusco refería cuentos, y las mozas,
en ratos de buen humor, se tiroteaban coplas, improvisándolas

nuevas cuando se les acababan las antiguas" (385) "an amusing old man told stories, and the girls, in moments of good spirit, exchanged verses, improvising new ones when they ran out of old ones."

But to Julián's eyes "Sabel's soirée" presents itself quite differently. The sexual connotations are clear: we have only to underline the relationship between spinning and copulating and between gluttony and lust.[6] Everything here points to an orgy: "se veían, no lejos de la turbia luz de aceite, relieves de un festín más suculento" (183) "not far from the dim candlelight, the remains of a more succulent feast lay scattered" (163). A second pictorial referent may be brought to bear on this scene: the painting by Bosch, *The Temptation of Saint Anthony* (Museu Nacional de Arte Antiga, Lisbon) (Fig. 3), mentioned earlier. In Bosch's painting as well as in *The House of Ulloa*, there is a witch-like atmosphere aligned with the temptation of a male subject. If, therefore, Goya's *The Witches' Sabbath* and other of his works correspond to Julián's vision, then Bosch's *The Temptation of Saint Anthony* is the equivalent of the totality of this passage, encompassing at the same time the beholder (Julián–Saint Anthony) and the object of contemplation, as attractive as it is repulsive, as near as it is distant. Tolnay describes Bosch's painting in these terms: "In the center panel Bosch surrounds St Anthony with the adepts of this sect [the sect of sorcerers and witches]. . . . In depicting the orgy of the 'witches' sabbath' Bosch has included many references to lust and gluttony" (*Hieronymus Bosch* 27). And even though the novel makes no specific mention of Bosch, Flemish painting constitutes the visual analogue to the description of the kitchen in chapter 6:

> Si se encontrase allí algún maestro de la escuela pictórica flamenca, de los que han derramado la poesía y el arte sobre la prosa de la vida doméstica y material, ¡con cuánto placer vería el espectáculo de la gran cocina . . . ; los gruesos brazos del ama confundidos con la carne, no menos rolliza y sanguínea, del asado que aderezaba; las rojas mejillas de las muchachas, entretenidas en retozar con el idiota, como ninfas con un sátiro atado . . . ! (55)

> Had a master of Flemish painting—one of those who lavish poetry on the prose of domestic life—been present, how he would have rejoiced at the sight of the spacious kitchen . . . ; at the plump arms of the housekeeper that blended with the no less plump red meat of the stew she was seasoning; at the flushed

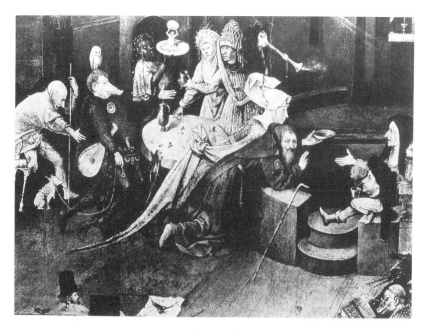

Figure 3
Hieronymus Bosch, *The Temptation of Saint Anthony* (detail of central panel). Museu Nacional de Arte Antiga, Lisbon, Portugal. Giraudon/Art Resource, New York.

girls who frolicked with the village idiot like nymphs with a captive satyr. (46)

We may observe in passing a certain resemblance between that "sátiro atado" "captive satyr," surrounded by "nymphs," and Julián–Saint Anthony as prey of female temptations.

Further, the interartistic correspondences point not only to the object viewed, but also to the place of the beholder and the peculiar manner in which the contemplation is effected. In the terrain of the visual arts, Uspensky has noted the difference between pre-Renaissance and Renaissance perspectives (134–35). In the latter, the artist contemplates the work from the outside, from a position coincidental with that of a simple viewer of the painting. But before the Renaissance, artists could situate themselves inside the painting and expose a view of the world in which they figure as the center. Carrying Uspensky's ideas one step further, Wendy Steiner formulates a parallel between pre-Renaissance vision and first-person narration: "the subjectivity of a first-person narrative can be matched in painting to such visionary scenes as Brueghel's 'Mad Mag' . . . , in which a central figure is surrounded by the dream world of her imagination" (*Colors of Rhetoric* 62). This relationship doubtless coincides with the link between Bosch's *The Temptation of Saint Anthony* and Julián's vision of the kitchen in *The House of Ulloa*, despite the fact that the novel is not written in the first person. (What matters here is not the grammatical person but rather the existence of a focalizer in the text.) The correspondence between literature and painting in this case facilitates a deeper understanding of the dominant perspective in *The House of Ulloa*, which does not emanate from some objective spectator at the margins of the narrated action, but instead comes from someone who, like Bosch's Saint Anthony, transmutes in his mind, in the theater of his mind, the world surrounding him.[7] And, in addition, the parallels with Goya would confirm the visionary nature of the scene rather than its realism.

In this dense, charged atmosphere of the kitchen, the witch tells fortunes and, as she lays down the cards, the narrative voice identifies the figures with characters in the novel:[8]

> Aquel rey de bastos, con hopalanda azul ribeteada de colorado, los pies simétricamente dispuestos, la gran maza verde al hombro, se le figurara [a Julián] bastante temible si supiese que representaba a un hombre moreno, casado (don Pedro). La sota del mismo palo se le antojaría menos fea si comprendiese que era símbolo de una señorita morena también (Nucha). A la de copas le daría un puntapié por insolente y borracha, atendido que personificaba a Sabel, una moza rubia y soltera. Lo más grave sería verse a sí mismo—un joven rubio— significado por el caballo de copas, azul por más señas, aunque ya todos estos colorines los había borrado la mugre. (184)

> That king of clubs, in his blue train trimmed with red, with his feet in a symmetrical position and the heavy green club on his shoulder, would have seemed quite formidable, had Julián realized that he represented a dark married man (Don Pedro). The [maid of the same suit] would have appeared less ugly if he had understood that it symbolized a young lady, also dark-haired (Nucha). He would have kicked the [maid of goblets] for her insolence and drunkness had he considered that it personified Sabel, a blond unmarried woman. The great shock would have been to recognize himself—a fair young man—in the [horse of

goblets], which was blue, to be precise, although all the colors were covered with filth. (164)

Figures of the same suit are related among themselves. And since clubs (*bastos*) are unequivocal phallic symbols, the king (Don Pedro) and the maid or *sota* (Nucha) of this suit are linked sexually. Here we understand the phallus in Lacanian terms as the signifier of desire. Elizabeth Grosz clarifies this meaning: "The phallus is both the signifier of the differences between the sexes and the signifier which effaces lack and thus difference. It is the term with respect to which the two sexes are defined as different, and the term which functions to bring them together, the term of their union" (117). Sabel, for her part, is the maid of goblets (*copas*), and here, too, the association with the motif of drink (and, more precisely, drunkenness) points to a world of lust. Finally, the strangest thing ("lo más grave" "the greatest shock") would be to see Julián as the "caballo de copas" "horse of goblets," thereby relating him to Sabel.

But who sees here? Who establishes these correspondences? From the distance at which he is situated, Julián would be unable to see the cards that are put down. Nevertheless, in a dream that he later has at the chapter's close, both the maid of clubs and a horse appear, although they are not of the same suit. In a deep sense, then, it is as if Julián not only saw the figures on the cards but also drew the correspondences himself. Even though he is a distant spectator, Julián seems absorbed in his own vision. What he contemplates functions as a mirror; it possesses him or traps him, disarticulating the Renaissance perspective alluded to earlier. Mary Ann Doane's words lend weight to this interpretation: "Perspective guarantees the maintenance of the subject and its place. Alternatively, in perspective's own aberration—anamorphosis— one gets a glimpse of the fascination of the gaze as the annihilating of the subject" (84). Doane here follows Lacan in his notion of "anamorphosis." For Lacan the reduction of the subject to an object, from annihilator to annihilated, obeys the instance of desire, the possession, we could say, of oneself by an uncontrollable desire: "Is it not clear that the gaze intervenes here only in as much as it is not the annihilating subject, correlative of the world of objectivity, who feels himself surprised, but the subject sustaining himself in a function of desire?" (*Four Fundamental Concepts* 84–85).[9]

In short, through his role in the scene depicted in the novel, Julián becomes a witness to the world of sexuality around him and within him. There is a common identity among the four figures, not just between Don Pedro and Sabel on one side, and Julián and Nucha on the other. The seemingly pure figures (Julián and Nucha) are contaminated by the sexuality or impurity of the other two, with whom they are related through the same suit (clubs or goblets). Moreover, both men share the color blue, which may be applied equally to the horse and to the king's train. And the two women are "sotas" "maids," a term that in one of its accepted meanings signifies "mujer insolente y desvergonzada" "insolent and shameless woman" (Real Academia, *Diccionario*) or even "prostituta" "prostitute" (Moliner, *Diccionario*).

However, the figures that appear on the cards not only bear sexual connotations that extend to all of them and join one to the other; intimately linked here to sexual significance is the code of power relations. And it is the men (king and horse) who incarnate the notion of dominance, whereas the women (the maids) are relegated to a subordinate role. Thus the *sota* is defined as follows in the *Diccionario de Autoridades*: "Dixose de la voz Italiana *Soto*, que vale debaxo, porque vá después de las figuras del Rey, y caballo, que le son superiores" "It was taken from the Italian word *Soto*, which means beneath, because it goes after the figures of the king, and horse, which are superior to it." We will return to this point shortly.

The parallel between this passage in the novel and Bosch's *The Temptation of Saint Anthony* is once again established in these lines: "Merced a la situación de la escalera, dominaba Julián la mesa, trípode y ara del temeroso rito, y sin ser visto podía ver y entreoír algo" (185) "From his location upstairs, Julián's glance took in the table, pillar, and altar of the frightful ritual, and without being seen, he was able to see and overhear some of it" (165). The transformation of "table" into "altar" and of a simple scene of local customs into a "frightful ritual" (and a few lines below into a "ejercicio de la hechicería" "practice of sorcery") equates such a spectacle with the black mass visible in the foreground of the central panel of Bosch's painting: "a tonsured demon with a pig's snout is reciting a black mass" (Lassaigne and Delevoy 24).

When Julián is discovered after accidently making a noise he returns to his room. He does not attribute the agitation that overtakes him to sexual matters but rather to a premonition of death:

"¡Tremenda situación! El capellán le daba vueltas a su cerebro excitado: a la niña la robarían para matarla de hambre; a Nucha la envenenarían tal vez" (185) "Terrible situation! The chaplain tortured his overexcited brain; they would kidnap the child and starve her to death, perhaps they would poison Nucha" (165–66). These fears are not logically derived from the scene he has witnessed. Goya's *The Witches' Sabbath*, with the dead children offered up to the he-goat by the circle of women, would again serve as an adequate pictorial representation of Julián's interior vision. If, however, Nucha and her daughter are threatened, this threat could never be attributed to the women gathered in the kitchen but instead to the absent Primitivo, the butler of the manor house, who fears loosing his power over the marquis of Ulloa.

Julián's thoughts are quickly interrupted by a scream that, for the second time, forces him out of his retreat. The new scene that he is about to observe is in close relation to the previous one: "¡Dios santo! Sí, era la escena misma, tal cual se la había figurado él . . . Nucha en pie, pero arrimada a la pared, con el rostro desencajado de espanto, los ojos, no ya vagos, sino llenos de extravío mortal; enfrente, su marido, blandiendo un arma enorme . . ." (187) "Good heavens! Yes, here was the scene, just as he had imagined it: Nucha standing against the wall, her face contorted with panic, her eyes not only vague but unbelievably astray. In front of her, her husband brandished a huge weapon" (167). What scene is this? Undoubtedly, by brandishing "a huge weapon" before his wife, Don Pedro arouses an impression of violence directed against the defenseless Nucha. Julián imagines that when Don Pedro is alone he brutally beats his wife, as he had Sabel, his lover. This explanation (or manifest content) should be probed further, for the scenes viewed and imagined conceal another one, fantasized at a deeper level: the scene of the sexual union of the parents from the child's perspective. That is, Julián would envision what Freud calls the "primal scene" (*Urszene*), usually perceived by the child as an act of violence wherein the man incarnates the role of the aggressor. Julián's fear, however, is shown to be groundless:

Julián se arrojó entre los dos . . . Nucha volvió a chillar:
—¡Ay, ay! ¡Qué hace usted! ¡Que se escapa! . . . ¡Que se escapa!
Comprendió entonces el alucinado capellán lo que ocurría, con no poca vergüenza y confusión suya . . . Por la pared tre-

paba aceleradamente, deseando huir de la luz, una araña de des-
mesurado grandor, un monstruoso vientre columpiado en ocho
velludos zancos. Su carrera era tan rápida, que inútilmente tra-
taba el señorito de alcanzarla con la bota. (187)

Julián threw himself between them. Nucha cried out again:
"What are you doing! It's running away, it's running away!"
    Then the deluded priest understood what had happened, to
his great embarrassment and confusion. A spider of incompara-
ble size and monstrous belly, swinging on eight hairy legs,
crawled rapidly up the wall, trying to escape from the light. It
raced so speedily that the marquis could not reach it with his
boot. (167)

As in the previous scene in the kitchen of the manor, Julián
ends up incorporated—physically, this time—into the world that
he observes. He translates his fantasies into actions and accordingly intervenes to separate husband and wife. And when he discovers that his imagination has erred, he feels shame. Carl
Schneider's explanation of this affect clarifies its meaning: "we
experience shame when we feel we are placed out of the context
within which we wish to be interpreted" (35). Feeling shame,
then, is associated with making oneself visible or exposing oneself in an inappropriate way: it is being out of place. That place is
exactly one of a sexual nature in the fantasy of the priest. A similar thing happened just before, when he was discovered spying:
"En un santiamén [la bruja] recogió los naipes, y el capellán bajó
algo confuso de su espionaje involuntario" (185) "She [the witch]
gathered up the cards in a jiffy. The chaplain descended, a little
embarrassed by his accidental spying" (165). Not so accidental,
in fact. Now, in the spider scene, the spying is repeated, and
along with it the unlucky exposure of the spy or of his hidden
desires.[10] We should also note that these actions occur in the hall-
way near Don Pedro's office, the same place where Julián surprised Sabel and subsequently realized that the master and his
servant had not ended their relationship: "vio salir de allí [el
despacho] a la moza, con descuidado traje y soñolienta. Las
reglas psicológicas aplicables a las conciencias culpadas exigían
que Sabel se turbase; quien se turbó fue Julián" (178) "he saw the
wench come out of it [the office], bleary eyed and with her
clothes in disarray. The psychological laws that apply to guilty
consciences required that Sabel be confused; but it was Julián

who was upset" (159). Here too the roles are twisted about so that the observer, to his embarrassment, finds himself observed in turn. The scene with Sabel implicates the one with Nucha; it and the beginning of chapter 19 provide the key to the latter passage. The realistic explanation (the motif of the spider) does not annul the fantasy, since in symbolic terms the spider is a female substitute, or, more precisely, a representation of female sexual organs.[11] This notion is quite visible when the spider is described as if it were a "monstrous belly, swinging on eight hairy legs." The boot, in turn, is a phallic symbol. Later, in Julián's dream (190), the boot gives way to the knight's lance, which he plunges into the spider.

As we noted, the child attributes violent connotations to what is called the primal scene. For Freud and his followers, violence is not really present but instead is the product of the fantasy of the child, who is unable to interpret the scene in any other terms. Freud's ideas have been questioned recently in psychoanalytic feminist readings such as the one offered by Maria Ramas: "The fantasy, quite simply, expresses erotically the essential meaning of sexual difference in patriarchal culture. . . . Even when those acting out the fantasy are of the same sex, the 'scene' depicts the submission and degradation of whoever is in the feminine position. That is to say, ultimately and always, a woman is degraded" (157). A passage in the novel justifies this feminist interpretation. After her wedding, Nucha awaits her husband in the marital bedroom: "Parecíale que aquella habitación . . . era el mismo templo en que no hacía dos horas aún se había puesto de hinojos. . . . Oyéronse en el corredor pisadas recias, crujir de botas flamantes, y la puerta se abrió" (114) "This room . . . seemed to her the same temple where barely two hours earlier she had been on her knees. . . . In the corridor she heard the creaking of brand-new boots, and the door opened" (100). In Nucha's mind, then, the bedroom where she waits for her husband is conflated with an altar where sacrifices are performed. Maryellen Bieder comments on this passage: "Nucha's perceptions at this highly charged moment dramatize from within her psyche the sacrificial nature of her marriage to Pedro. . . . Pedro, metonymically represented by his resounding boots, approaches the kneeling figure of Nucha as a conquering hero" (139).

But in addition Don Pedro is the "king," and before him Nucha is the maid (*sota*). Sexual difference, it should be emphasized, is related to the social distribution of power: in the nine-teenth-century context of the novel, there are the haves (men) and the have-nots (women). And the primal scene as fantasized by the child constitutes the typical model in which sexual relations are presented as the domination of one being by another. Don Pedro's subjugation of Nucha therefore points to the oppression of the female sex by the male sex, and in this light the master of the house appears not at all as a singular exception, but rather as the representative of his gender and of the patriarchal society described in the novel.

When Julián returns to his room he finally falls asleep. The account of the dream he then has closes the chapter:

> Empezó a soñar con los pazos, con el gran caserón . . . : era un castillote feudal hecho y derecho . . . ; indudablemente, Julián había visto alguna pintura o leído alguna medrosa descripción de esos espantajos del pasado, que nuestro siglo restaura con tanto cariño. . . . Miraba Julián fascinado hacia lo alto de la torre, cuando vio en ella alarmante figurón: un caballero con vi-sera calada, todo cubierto de hierro. . . . Julián percibía, al través de la celada, la cara de don Pedro. Furioso, amenazador, enarbolaba don Pedro un arma extraña, una bota de acero, que se disponía a dejar caer sobre la cabeza del capellán. . . . de repente sintió que se le posaba en el hombro una lechuza feísima, con greñas blancas. . . . La lechuza reía silenciosamente. . . . aso-maba un rostro de mujer, pálido, descompuesto . . . Aquella mujer sacó un pie, luego otro . . . , fue descolgándose por la ven-tana abajo . . . ¡Qué asombro! ¡Era la sota de bastos, la mis-mísima sota de bastos, muy sucia, muy pringosa! Al pie del muro la esperaba el caballo de espadas, una rara alimaña azul, con la cola rayada de negro. Mas a poco Julián reconoció su error: ¡qué caballo de espadas! No era sino San Jorge en persona, el vale-roso caballero andante de las celestiales milicias, con su dragón debajo, un dragón que parecía araña, en cuya tenazuda boca hundía la lanza con denuedo. . . . Lo sorprendente es que el lan-zazo lo sentía Julián en su propio costado . . . (188–90)

> He started to dream of the big old mansion of Ulloa. . . . it was a true feudal castle. . . . Undoubtedly, Julián had seen a painting or read a frightening description of these bogeys from the past that our century restores so lovingly. . . . Julián, fascinated, looked up at the top of the tower and saw an alarming figure in it: a knight in iron armor and a lowered visor. . . . Julián . . . rec-ognized Don Pedro's face behind the visor. Don Pedro, furious

and threatening, flourished a strange weapon, a steel boot, that he was about to drop on the priest's head. . . . Suddenly he felt a hideous owl with white hair perched on his shoulder. . . . The owl laughed quietly. . . . Behind the window he saw the pale, contorted face of a woman. This woman stepped out of the window—first one foot, then the other—and began to climb down. Astonishing! It was the [maid] of clubs, the same dirty, greasy [maid] of clubs! Under the wall the [horse] of spades, a rare blue creature with a black-striped tail. But gradually Julián realized his mistake. The [horse] of spades! It was no other than Saint George himself, the brave knight-errant of the celestial army, fighting a dragon that looked like a spider, in whose powerful mouth he thrust his spear again and again. . . . Surprisingly, Julián felt the thrusts in his own side. (168–69)

We should note how the dream's scenario (the mansion of Ulloa tranformed into a castle) becomes associated with "alguna pintura" "a painting," additional proof of the frequency with which descriptions and pictorial visions merge. Cases such as this one, which explicitly posit an interarts relation, support our assuming a plastic scene as the point of departure for other narrative sequences. On the other hand, Julián's dream obviously reiterates the themes of the last two passages we analyzed. First, Julián, replacing Nucha (or duplicating her figure), imagines himself as the victim of Don Pedro, who now threatens the priest with a "bota de acero" "steel boot." Is this an enraged response to Julián's attitude a short while back when he intervened—"se arrojó" "he threw himself"—between Don Pedro and Nucha in an attempt to fight off the supposed aggression of the husband toward his wife? Following Don Pedro's rage in the dream, a "lechuza feísima" "hideous owl" perches on the chaplain's shoulder. Once again Bosch's *The Temptation of Saint Anthony* makes an appropriate interartistic referent. In this painting, an owl sits on the head of a man with a pig's face; the link between the bird and demonic sensuality thus stands out clearly. The owl covering the heads of a pair of tangled lovers also appears as a symbol of lust in another painting by Bosch, *The Earthly Paradise* (Museo del Prado), as well as in Goya's *Capricho 75*, "No hay quién nos desate?" "Can't anyone untie us?" which displays thematic and formal devices analogous to Bosch's *The Earthly Paradise*. In addition, the "white hair" of the owl establishes a parallel with the witch María the Sage, one that becomes even more convincing if we note the definition of the word *bruxa* given by the *Dicciona-rio de Autoridades*: "Ave nocturna semejante à la Lechúza . . . tiene el instinto de chupar a los niños que maman" "Nocturnal bird similar to the Owl . . . which has the instinct of preying on breast-feeding infants." Goya's *The Witches' Sabbath* comes immediately to mind again, but with the notable peculiarity that it is Julián, the dreamer, who now appears as a child threatened by the trio of owl-witch-death.

The dream continues with the appearance of the "sota de bastos" "maid of clubs" (Nucha), who looks "muy sucia, muy pringosa" "very dirty, very greasy." The filthy condition of the cards affects the figure of the woman, who obviously is distanced from the model of the Virgin. It is precisely this transformation from Virgin (pure mother) to lascivious woman or mother that takes place in the imagination of the child who contemplates the primal scene. The "caballo de espadas" "horse of spades" waits for the "sota de bastos" "maid of clubs." It is quite evident, we believe, that the horse is Julián. To call him "caballo de copas" "horse of goblets" would have made the meaning too explicit, and, consequently, intolerable to the conscious mind. Julián is not only associated with the horse of goblets but also, since the beginning of the novel, with the horse as a beast (and with the difficulty in controlling it). The priest would thus play the role of rescuing a woman trapped in a tower like a new Saint Barbara (a figure that appears in his dream). At the top of the tower is also the "knight" (Don Pedro), who may be seen as a representative of patriarchal authority in his role as prison guard. In Freudian terms, Julián's dream exposes a repressed desire. And since the priest's fantasy of liberating Nucha from her husband's power emerges clearly further ahead in the novel, the dream implies a premonition of sorts.

Yet at this point the dreamer must turn back. The strong social and religious barriers against which his desire runs up demands a correction: "¡qué caballo de espadas! No era sino San Jorge en persona" "The horse of spades! It was no other than Saint George himself." Even in his dreams Julián has gone too far. The correction (or censorship) transforms the horse, symbol of lust, into Saint George, the "valeroso caballero andante de las celestiales milicias" "brave knight-errant of the celestial army"; that is, someone who does not represent the instinctual passions, but instead incarnates in Christian terms the victory against the instincts or the forces of evil (the dragon). The famous legend of Saint George and the dragon calls for further analysis, however. Adrienne Munich has shown how in Victorian times this legend was merged with the myth of Perseus and Andromeda, which captured the imaginations of many visual artists. In the classical myth Perseus liberates Andromeda, who is tied to a rock as a victim to be sacrificed to a horrid sea monster. Perseus marries her after having liberated her. Saint George, conflated with Perseus, marries Princess Sabra after slaying the dragon. Munich writes: "The Princess has unaccountably dressed as a bride when she goes to be eaten by the dragon, her wedding gown suggesting a rivalry between the monster and the saint" (13). In the Victorian version of the legend of Saint George, then, the woman becomes an object of dispute. And, in Julián's specific case, the woman also functions as a prohibited object, insofar as she is the legitimate spouse of another man (and insofar as Julián, a priest, has renounced women).

If we relate this dream to the Victorian version of the legend of Saint George, the three terms would be: Julián–Saint George, Don Pedro–dragon, and Nucha–victim of the dragon.[12] But from a Christian perspective—such as Julián's—the priest can hardly be equated to a saint. His illicit desire, as manifested in the dream, would associate him instead with the dragon, with the instincts that he has failed to master, as his efforts to control his horse at the beginning of the novel remind us. In fact, the identification of Julián with the dragon is ultimately produced in the dream. Through the figure of the dragon, then, two apparently opposite men are again placed in an intimate association: Julián and Don Pedro. However, Don Pedro, even if he represents a degenerate human being, acts with marital, and consequently legal, authority. In his role as "caballero con visera calada" "knight in iron armor and a lowered visor" he is in a way identified with Saint George, the "caballero andante de las celestiales milicias" "knight-errant of the celestial army," thereby displacing Julián from such a heroic role and relegating him to that of the dragon, a masochistic position. Julián's punishment in the dream—a sword pierces him as it goes through the dragon—should then be attributed to a paternal *imago*, seen either as an exterior force or as an inner one in the form of moral conscience (the introjected father).

To sum up: the dream lays bare both a forbidden unconscious wish and the moral reprobation of that wish. The presumed liberator is transformed into a victim, fused with Nucha, in the shape of a dragon-spider. Don Pedro's power is harnessed against the two of them when he brandishes the steel boot or the lance. But the dream also uncovers that at bottom Julián defers to patriarchal power. He thus prevents Nucha, whose only recourse is the priest, from shaking off her status as victim. The myth of Perseus-Andromeda, reflected in Saint George, never becomes fully realized, owing to the lack of a true liberator.[13] However, the combination of dragon-spider, into whose mouth the masculine figure plunges his phallic lance, associates Nucha as well as Julián with the legendary dragon. Munich has noted in the representations of the myth that she studies how the dragon encodes both masculine and feminine traits: "In the mythological version the monster merges male and female characteristics: its roaring jaws the female, its writhing length of body the male. The intimacy between St. George and the dragon also suggests sexual symbolism. Substituting monster for maiden, the male limb enters the monster's head" (108).[14]

The identification of Nucha with the dragon-spider carries her degradation to the maximum, a process that began when she was linked to the "sota de bastos" "maid of clubs," "very dirty, very greasy." Conceived in these terms, Nucha is truly indistinguishable from the other maid, the diabolical Sabel. Julián's dream reveals the magnitude of his repressions: the abject image of Nucha, along with his fear before this image. At this point Nucha is more closely associated with Eve or Medusa than with Andromeda, let alone the Virgin.[15] Or, in other words, she is associated with the "bad" mother, the witch, who is the constant companion of the young temptress and whom we saw represented by the owl perched on the shoulder of a petrified Julián: "Quiso gritar; en sueños el grito se queda helado en la garganta siempre. La lechuza reía silenciosamente" (189) "He tried to scream, but in dreams the scream always freezes in the throat. The owl laughed quietly" (169). In short, by making the dream expose a repressed unconscious reality, Pardo Bazán anticipates the discovery that a few years later would be accomplished by Freud. This case is not unique, however, among writers of that time. Ronald R. Thomas has devoted a book to this topic, in which he shows how nineteenth-century novelists influenced Freud: "Freud was a great admirer of the fiction of Arthur Conan Doyle, as well as that of Dickens. . . . There, dreams figure importantly . . . not only as sites where illicit desires are expressed and enacted but as places where the laws of social repression are inscribed and enforced" (191).

The fantasy of escaping from Ulloa's house is later expressed by Nucha:

—Es preciso—declaró Nucha, sin apartar de él sus ojos, más que vagos, extraviados ya—que me ayude usted a salir de aquí. De esta casa.
—A . . . , a . . . salir . . . —tartamudeó Julián, aturdido. (260)

"You must," Nucha stated, fixing her eyes—now vacant rather than vague—on him. "You must help me flee this place."
"Fl . . . flee," Julián stammered, astounded. (234)

Julián retreats in cowardice. Nucha's determination is portrayed as if it were the raving of a madwoman, but her reasons are entirely valid. Once more the narrator, apparently conforming to a masculine perspective, plays a double role: "El tono, la expresión, la actitud eran como de quien tiene perturbadas sus facultades mentales; de mujer impulsada por excitación nerviosa que raya en desvarío" (261) "Her tone, expression, and attitude were those of a woman who has lost her mind, a woman compelled by nervous excitement bordering on delirium" (234).[16]

Julián, disarmed, ends up succumbing to Nucha's insistent attitude: "A fuer de criatura candorosa, una fuga tan absurda le pareció hasta fácil. . . . Además, ¿qué cosa en el mundo dejaría él de intentar por secar aquellos ojos puros, por sosegar aquel anheloso pecho, por ver de nuevo a la señorita segura, honrada, respetada, cercada de miramientos, en la casa paterna?" (265–66) "Being so naive, he found such an absurd escape easy. . . . Besides, he would attempt anything in the world to dry the tears from those pure eyes, to soothe that anxious bosom, to see his mistress safe, honored, respected, surrounded by loving care in the paternal home" (238). Julián's reflections occlude a later fantasy, which we will analyze shortly. And his candor does not only concern the idea of a flight, but also the way in which he idealizes the "casa paterna" "paternal home." In La madre naturaleza (319) we are apprised of the existence of a desperate letter written by Nucha to her father, a letter that receives no reply in The House of Ulloa. Following her marriage to Don Pedro, Nucha is abandoned by her father to her own misfortunes.[17]

Julián's fantasy is spelled out as follows: "Se representaba la escena de la escapatoria. Sería al amanecer. Nucha iría envuelta en muchos abrigos. Él cargaría con la niña, dormidita y arropadísima también" (266) "He pictured the scene of the flight. It would take place at dawn. Nucha would be wrapped in plenty of warm clothing. He would carry the sleeping baby, who would also be wrapped" (238). This imaginary scene doubtless finds correspondence in the biblical theme of the flight to Egypt, a subject of frequent pictorial representations. The parallel is strengthened by the fact that the little girl, whose life is in danger, is called "Manolita," a feminine diminutive of Manuel. But of course when the flight is fantasized in these terms, the earlier notion of restoring the woman to the paternal home is lost. Nucha would no longer have need of a father since she has found a replacement husband: Julián, who occupies Saint Joseph's position. Julián himself establishes this association earlier on in the novel: "Una penosa idea le ocurría de cuando en cuando. Acordábase que había soñado con instituir en aquella casa el matrimonio cristiano cortado por el patrón de la Sacra Familia. Pues bien: el santo grupo estaba disuelto; allí faltaba San José o le sustituía un clérigo, que era peor" (177) "A painful thought haunted him from time to time. He remembered his dream of instituting in this home a Christian marriage modeled after the Holy Family. Alas! The holy group was incomplete: Saint Joseph either was missing or, worse yet, had been replaced by a priest" (158).

A curious transformation may be observed if we compare what takes place here with Julián's previous dream, a dream that also reveals a wish to flee from Ulloa's house. The religious images in the chapel, the place where Julián and Nucha now meet, appear to endorse the decision at which the two have arrived:

Ni la Purísima de sueltos tirabuzones y traje blanco y azul, ni el San Antonio que hacía fiestas a un Niño Jesús regordete, ni el San Pedro con la tiara y las llaves, ni siquiera el Arcángel San Miguel, el caballero de la ardiente espada, siempre dispuesto a rajar y hendir a Satanás, revelaban en sus rostros pintados de fresco el más leve enojo contra el capellán, ocupado en combinar los preliminares de un rapto en toda regla, arrebatando una hija a su padre y una mujer legítima a su dueño. (266)

Neither the Virgin Mary with loose curls and a white and blue robe on her body; nor Saint Anthony, cuddling a chubby Baby Jesus; nor Saint Peter, with his triple crown and keys; nor even the archangel Saint Michael, the knight with the flaming sword, always ready to cleave and strike Satan—none of them revealed on their freshly painted faces the slightest anger against this chaplain engrossed in the preliminaries of a regular abduction, whereby he would snatch a daughter away from her father and a wife away from her lawful husband. (238–39)

Julián's fantasy is represented, on the one hand, in the most extreme terms: "rapto en toda regla" "a regular abduction," an outrageous attack against patriarchal authority from whom a legitimate daughter and wife would be wrested. On the other hand, both the Virgin and the saints approve. The figure of the Archangel Saint Michael offers commonalities with that of Saint George in Julián's dream. Both are, so to speak, knights-errant in heavenly service who slay the primordial enemy (the dragon).[18] But the difference between them is also obvious: in the dream, Saint George attacks the dreamer (Julián), which we take to be a kind of divine reproval. The heavenly and paternal orders form an alliance, thereby conforming to a traditional view of human existence, and they infiltrate Julián's afflicted consciousness as he recriminates himself. Now, however, the heavenly order of which Saint Michael is part lends approbation to Julián's behavior, and the priest is no longer associated with a dragon, devil, or other sinful being that must be fought.

The change in Julián may be noticed not only in relation to the dream. Earlier the priest overtly expressed his patriarchal conception of duty: "Pero, ¡ay!, nadie puede usurpar el puesto del amo de la casa, del jefe de la familia; y el jefe . . ." (242) "But, alas! no one can take the place of the master of the house; and the master of the house . . ." (217). Nucha, in contrast, says to Julián: "No obedecería si usted me mandase quedarme aquí . . . Ya sé que es mi obligación: la mujer no debe apartarse del marido" (262) "I wouldn't obey if you ordered me to stay here. I know it's my duty: a wife must not leave her husband" (235). Nucha's triumph over Julián's mentality is reinforced by the feminine narrative voice, which condones the escape plan in spite of its violent resistance to social norms oppressive to women. We should note that the same reversal of roles we discussed earlier is produced anew in the chapel. Although the images of the Virgin and the saints are described in minute detail, they are looking in addition to being looked at (if indeed they are) by Nucha and Julián. But the subject transformed into object of vision no longer feels shame, even though the dimension of desire is still implied in the scene. If the episode in the chapel is interpreted as a reflection of Julián's own vision, then it may be claimed that he experiences, if only momentarily, an ideological transformation toward the realm of feminist values held by the author herself.

The escape plan nevertheless fails when Don Pedro catches the pair. The accusing look finally makes its appearance, and it sets into motion a sense of guilt and shame. Don Pedro has been tipped off by the first person to discover Julián and Nucha, his illegitimate son by Sabel, Perucho. Don Pedro's reaction is to be expected: he flies into a rage against his wife and the chaplain. Perucho will also be witness to this confrontation: "El niño recordó entonces escenas análogas, pero cuyo teatro era la cocina de los pazos, y las víctimas su madre y él; el señorito tenía entonces la misma cara, idéntico tono de voz. . . . No cabía duda de que el señorito se disponía a acogotar a su esposa y al capellán" (275) "The boy then recalled similar scenes in the kitchen of the house of Ulloa, whose victims had been his mother and himself. On those occasions the master had the same expression on his face and the same tone of voice. . . . That the master was going to knock down his wife and the chaplain was beyond question" (246–47). This scene is highly reminiscent of the early one in which Julián observes the pair and sees the husband positioned before his wife in what seemed to be a threatening stance. Now, as we see, there is yet another precedent brought to bear. The child remembers analogous scenes where the only change is the identity of the victim: instead of Nucha (and Julián), his own mother (and himself). If Julián symbolically functions as a child who in chapter 19 fantasized a "primal scene," then the transition from him to Perucho as focalizer of the story makes sense. The scene is repeated, and in it appear the same notes of brutality—only this time they are not imaginary.

Accused of having dealings with Nucha, Julián is forced to leave the region of Ulloa, to which he will not return until ten years later as the priest of its humble parish. Nucha is buried in the atrium of the church, and the priest pauses before her tomb: "allí descansaba Nucha, la señorita Marcelina, la santa, la virgencita siempre cándida y celeste" (291) "there rested Nucha, Señorita Marcelina, the saint, the victim, the little virgin, always candid and heavenly" (259). Once more Nucha is the "virgencita" "little virgin," who, being deceased, fully becomes for Julián an erotic object, representative of what Bram Dijkstra calls "the Victorian ideal of passive womanhood" (58). Julián finally dares to give carnal expression to his love since the fervent and disquieting body of Nucha has been replaced by cold stone: "besó ardientemente la pared del nicho, sollozando como un niño o mujer, frotando las mejillas contra la superficie, clavando las uñas en la cal, hasta arrancarla . . ." (291) "[he] kissed the grave ardently, crying like a child or a woman, rubbing his cheeks against the cold surface, and digging his nails into the lime until it came off" (259). The lack of ardor (of "excitación nerviosa" "nervous excitation" or "desvarío" "delirium") in the case of the woman opens up a path for the secret impulses, the delirium of the "hombre acostumbrado a dominar todo arranque pasional" (288) "man used to repress[ing] every outburst of passion" (256), who is now caught in the rapture of a veritable necrophilia, that is, in Dijkstra's words again, "a necrophiliac preoccupation with the erotic potential of a woman when in a state of virtually guaranteed passivity" (58).

Villanueva has noted the "unrestrained lyricism of some of the scenes in the last two chapters of *The House of Ulloa*" ("*Los pazos*, novela en la encrucijada" 35), and, comparing Pardo Bazán to Joris-Karl Huysmans, he sees *The House of Ulloa* as a work that shows "a very pronounced current of decadent art" (33). John W. Kronik arrives at a similar conclusion: "it was to be expected that [Pardo Bazán] would soundly and directly condemn French decadence, since she in her strong Catholic morality would feel offended. . . . But this did not happen" (171–72).[19] In this light, the Galician writer stands out not as a simple naturalist (Catholic or otherwise), as she was most commonly classified by critics, but as a forerunner of the soon-to-arrive literary modernism, and of Valle-Inclán in particular.

To conclude, then: Julián, the protagonist of *The House of Ulloa*, is revealed to be a delicate, tender individual, capable of feeling profound displeasure toward the brutality of men; notwithstanding, he exposes his own deeply rooted masculine prejudices. The male-based duality of woman (pure angel and lascivious monster), so dear to the romantic sensibility, is perpetuated in Julián, who in turn anticipates the modernist vision in which these two feminine extremes are reconfigured within a framework of decadence. Nothing has changed nor is any change imminent; Emilia Pardo Bazán's masterpiece nevertheless stands as unimpeachable testimony of the absolute necessity for social transformation.

# CHAPTER 3

# All the World's a Museum: The Marquis of Bradomín's Textual Exhibition

The fin de siècle ideology in Spain, which had an infancy of sorts in *The House of Ulloa*, fully matures into outright decadence in Valle-Inclán's *Sonata de primavera* [Spring sonata], published in 1904. Although they belong to different literary generations, Emilia Pardo Bazán and Ramón María del Valle-Inclán, two highly acclaimed Galician authors, share an undeniable affinity for certain themes that typify the cultural milieu they inhabited at the end of the nineteenth century. Pardo Bazán is precocious in that she anticipates literary currents and demonstrates early feminist attitudes, whereas by European standards Valle-Inclán straggles slightly behind. Valle-Inclán may come a bit late in a chronological scheme, but he is the author who brings the turn-of-the-century mentality to full fruition in his country: the four *Sonatas*, which center on the seasons of the year, are unanimously considered the height of modernist prose in Spain.

Specifically, the dominant perspective both in *The House of Ulloa* and in *Spring Sonata* corresponds to a young male character who acts simultaneously as a voyeur—he looks on—and as a viewer—he mentally processes what he observes. Although in one case the look emanates from a shame-filled priest (Julián), and in the other from a petulant seducer (Bradomín), the two men, attracted as they are to forbidden women, reveal at bottom a shared bond in their misogyny and lust in addition to a common perception of the female as a destructive being. In both texts, narrative viewpoint is aligned with the visual arts, either implicitly, as we have shown with respect to *The House of Ulloa*, or in more direct fashion, as *Spring Sonata* demonstrates in its references to famous paintings, which are contemplated by the young protagonist or evoked by him as an old man telling of his conquests. There is no basic difference between the description of characters and that of paintings: they possess equal referential standing. The life that is narrated has been reduced to the dimensions of a series of artworks, which in the novel serve as constant props for vision (or as the anchor to hold it down). This analysis will thus look beyond the decorative function of the visual arts in this early work by Valle-Inclán in an attempt to probe the structural function of these paintings contained in the text.

*Spring Sonata* begins its narrative course with bad omens for Bradomín, the young marquis, who by papal designation is transporting the cardinal's hat to Liguria for Monsignor Estefano Gaetani. Upon arrival, he discovers that the monsignor is dying: "¡Nuestro amantísimo padre, Excelencia . . . ! Nuestro amantísimo padre, nuestro maestro, nuestro guía, está en trance de muerte" (*Sonatas* 18) "Our beloved father, Excellency!—our beloved father, our master, our guide, is at the point of death" (*Pleasant Memoirs* 3), exclaims the attendant who receives him. The imminent death of His Grace comes on the heels of the death of his eldest brother, Prince Filipo Gaetani, about whom the attendant informs: "no hace el año que falleció en una cacería (19) "Hardly a year has passed since he was killed while hunting" (3). Moreover, in explaining why His Holiness has named him for such a lofty mission as transporting the cardinal's hat, Bradomín proudly relates his genealogy: "Yo soy Bibiena di Rienzo, por la línea de mi abuela paterna, Julia Aldegrina, hija del príncipe Máximo de Bibiena que murió en 1770, envenenado por la famosa comedianta Simoneta la Corticelli, que tiene un largo capítulo en las Memorias del Caballero de Seingalt" (17) "I am a Bibiena de Rienzo, through my paternal grandmother, Julia Aldegrina, daughter of that Prince Maximo of Bibiena who died in 1770, victim of the poison of the [actress] Simoneta la Corticelli, the story of [whom] fills a long chapter in the Memoirs of the Caballero de Seingalt" (3). Now would it not have been sufficient for him to simply state that he is the Marquis of Bradomín? There is a displacement here from the masculine lineage, passed from father to son through the title of marquis, to the lineage of the paternal grandmother, whose own father died of poisoning at the hands of an actress named in the memoirs of Casanova, the infamous Don Juan. There is a notable excess in deaths of paternal figures: the demise of the bishop is even more lamentable in that it frustrates his ambition, manifested later, to become pope one day; the passing of Prince Filipo is even sadder in that he leaves no male heirs; and the death of Bradomín's great-grandfather is even more ill-fated in that it was carried out by a cunning actress. Prince Má-ximo de Bibiena seems suspiciously like a womanizer, a victim of his own intrigues—a bad sign for his great-grandson, who preco-ciously plots out a similar path for himself.

Beneath Bradomín's boastful pride, then, lies a basic uncer-tainty, or the constant presumption of a threat. His arrogant image teeters wherever it attempts to stand firm. What was his father like, the man who is never mentioned either here or in the other *Sonatas*?[1] We may gather that he died young, since Bra-domín is already a marquis at twenty (his age in *Spring Sonata*). Perhaps he was poisoned, like his maternal grandfather, or maybe he died while hunting, like Filipo Gaetani, who could be seen as a mythic brother of the son-lover Adonis, or of the Actaeon pursued by Diana. In any event, the papal envoy carries a hat that doesn't have a head to sit on. The pope's decision is thwarted and the sol-emn mission charged to the young messenger is stripped of mean-ing, thus becoming much ado about nothing.

Before entering the Clementine residence where the monsignor is agonizing, Bradomín catches a glimpse of an image: "El tardo paso de las mulas me dejó vislumbrar una Madona: Sostenía al Niño en el regazo, y el Niño, riente y desnudo, tendía los brazos para alcanzar un pez que los dedos virginales de la madre le mos-traban en alto, como en un juego cándido y celeste" (16) "As the coach passed slowly I was able to distinguish the picture of a Madonna; she [held the Child in her lap], and he, smiling and naked, stretched out his arms toward a little fish which the [vir-ginal fingers of the mother showed to him in innocent and] celes-tial play" (2). Alonso Zamora Vicente (99) compares this Virgin to the famous *Madonna of the Fish* by Raphael in the Prado Museum (Fig. 4). Despite the similarities, however, there are some noteworthy differences. In Raphael's painting, Tobias, supported from above by the Archangel Raphael, displays the fish to the Christ-child; the Virgin, the Christ-child and Saint Geronimo all look toward Tobias. In Valle-Inclán's version, however, there is only room for the Virgin and the Child, and it is the Virgin who holds up the fish. If the fish takes on therapeutic significance when associated with Tobias (Wehle 172), then a variation in context will alter that meaning: in the *Sonata*, the fish-phallus would solidify the intimate bond between mother and son.[2] Clearly this

Figure 4
Raphael, *Madonna of the Fish*. Prado, Madrid.

function stands in opposition to another one that Lacan also discerned: the phallus as the third term, representative of the father, which accomplishes the separation between mother and child. Paternal absence in the textual world of the *Sonatas* places (or expresses a desire to place) Bradomín within the register of the imaginary, that is, outside the realm of the Lacanian symbolic order.[3] The image of the Virgin and Child, glimpsed in shadows, perfectly encodes the representation of desire. Marilyn A. Lavin points out the frequency with which "the Madonna and the Child, as opposed to the adult Christ, are depicted as the *Sponsus-Sponsa*" (194). Lavin attributes the presence of a smiling angel in numerous works with this theme to the bliss experienced by the angel who witnesses the betrothal of this saintly couple. The angel thus serves as the groom's friend. In Valle-Inclán's text the angel is done away with, but his laughter or smile is manifested through the Christ-child himself, the Groom: "riente y desnudo" "smiling and naked."[4]

To be sure, Valle-Inclán could have cited any number of versions of the Madonna and Child in which the pair appears unaccompanied. If he chose the *Madonna of the Fish*, erasing from that painting all references to third parties, perhaps it is because the fish—passed from Tobias's hand to the Virgin's—sexualizes the scene or, in other words, renders the sexual content of the scene patent.[5] The image perceived by the young marquis thus serves as an exemplary preamble to his erotic story, which adapts itself well to the mythic model of the Madonna and Child while in keeping with a modernist or decadent vision. The sacred and the profane become fused as they mutually transform each other.

In the same room where the monsignor is about to expire, Bradomín finds the Princess Gaetani and her five daughters praying. This is his description of the mother: "La Princesa Gaetani era una dama todavía hermosa, blanca y rubia. . . . me recordaba el retrato de María de Médicis, pintado cuando sus bodas con el Rey de Francia, por Pedro Pablo Rubens" (20–21) "The Princess Gaetani was still a beautiful woman. . . . [She] recalled the portrait of Marie de Médicis, painted at the time of her marriage to the King of France by Peter Paul Rubens" (5). These lines present a problem: there is in fact a portrait of the betrothal of Maria de' Medici by Rubens (part of a series of twenty-four paintings based on her life). The majority of these paintings, including the wedding portrait, are housed in the Louvre.[6] Nevertheless, it is difficult not to think immediately of another portrait of Maria de' Medici by Rubens: one that hangs in the Prado, the location of so many of the works to which Valle-Inclán alludes in *Spring Sonata*. Harry B. Wehle makes the following comment about the portrait of that splendid matron: "At the time when she sat to Rubens for this likeness, she was approaching the age of fifty and had been a widow for more than twelve years, since the death of Henry IV in 1610" (156). The two visions of Maria de' Medici seem to be superimposed in the mind of the writer. Besides the possible physical resemblance (unsubstantiatable, in any case), the similarity between Princess Gaetani and the Maria de' Medici painted by Rubens would be based on their mature age and their widowhood, common to both the princess and Maria de' Medici in the Prado's version—but not the Louvre's. Yet by transporting Maria de' Medici back to the moment of her marriage, the narrator strips her of her status of widow and mother. Or rather, he turns her (and, indirectly, Princess Gaetani) into a virgin mother.

The princess addresses Bradomín as follows: "¿Qué sabes de tu madre? De niño te parecías mucho a ella, ahora no . . . ¡Cuántas veces te tuve en mi regazo! ¿No te acuerdas de mí?" (23) "[What do you know about your mother?] As a child you were very like her, but now you are changed. How often I have held you in my arms! Don't you remember anything about me?" (5–6). Bradomín thinks back: "La hija del Marqués de Agar . . ." (23) "The daughter of the Marquis de Agar" (6). This is interesting, because Agar is also the paternal surname of Bradomín's mother, as the *Sonata de otoño* [Autumn sonata] (1902) makes clear: "María Soledad Carlota Elena Agar y Bendaña" (*Sonatas* 383). Even if the narrator does not emphasize the point, this new finding of his mother's last name underlines the maternal nature of the one who carries it, the princess. She introduces her daughters in this fashion: "María del Rosario, María del Carmen, María del Pilar, María de la Soledad, María de las Nieves . . ." (24). The mother's name is never stated, but she, too, is endowed with a virginal grace through her association with so many Marías (and earlier, with Maria de' Medici). Her negative side nevertheless breaks through, as seen in the following description: "en el fondo dorado de sus ojos yo creí ver la llama de un fanatismo trágico y sombrío" (25) "in the depths of her golden eyes I fancied I beheld the light of a dark and tragic fanaticism" (7). The resemblance between this woman and Bradomín's mother becomes apparent if we compare these lines with a passage from *Autumn Sonata* that describes María Soledad, the marquise of Bradomín: "De reclamar varonía las premáticas nobiliarias . . . hubiera entrado en un convento, y hubiera sido santa a la española, guerrera y fanática" (383) "[Had the nobiliary rules limited aristocratic titles to men] she would have [entered a convent and] been a saint in the Spanish manner, [a warrior and a fanatic]" (204).

Bradomín accepts the invitation to move into the Gaetani palace. The butler, Polonio, shows him into the room he will occupy. There are some paintings hanging on the wall: "Eran antiguos lienzos de la escuela florentina, que representaban escenas bíblicas:—Moisés salvado de las aguas, Susana y los ancianos, Judith con la cabeza de Holofernes—" (34) "They were ancient [paintings] of the Florentine School and represented scenes from the Bible—Moses [saved from the waters], Susanna and the Elders, Judith with the head of Holofernes" (12). Zamora Vicente identifies these works of art: "he saw these paintings in the Prado. They are not Florentine, but Venitian. . . . And the three cited paintings—the one of Judith by Tintoretto, and the other two by Veronese—are very near to each other spatially. The Prado and the illustrated magazines of the time are the two great fountains from which Valle-Inclán drank his artistic culture" (99–100). These paintings may be integrated structurally in the *Spring Sonata*. *Judith and Holofernes*, by Tintoretto, hints at a threat against the marquis, which in fact presents itself immediately in the text: it is the threat unleashed by female or maternal power. Here, Valle-Inclán is taking up a theme that appeals to the artistic sensibilities at the end of the nineteenth century:

> Symbolic castration, woman's lust for man's severed head, the seat of the brain, that "great clot of seminal fluid" Ezra Pound would still be talking about in the 1920s, was obviously the supreme act of the male's physical submission to woman's predatory desire. Turn-of-the-century artists searched far and wide to come up with instructive examples of such emasculating feminine perfidy. (Dijkstra 375)

Together with Salome, Judith becomes an exemplary representation of the ominous woman.[7] This threat, however, is not carried out in *Spring Sonata*. Bradomín, with difficulty, manages to escape unscathed: *Moses Saved from the Waters*, by Veronese (Fig. 5), points to the terrible risk that the marquis succeeds in avoiding. The affinities between the *Sonata* and this painting are heightened by the presence of six women in Veronese's work: an old woman and five young ones surrounding Moses. Moreover, a musical quality has been ascribed to this most exquisite picture: "The charm of Paolo Veronese's rare small compositions . . .

Figure 5
Paolo Veronese, *Moses Saved from the Waters*. Prado, Madrid.

could be compared to a musician, accustomed to the symphonic power of the organ, improvising delicate variations on a spinet. To continue the musical metaphor, the composition flows along in continuously legato rhythms" (Pallucchini 49). Finally, Veronese's *Susanna and the Elders* is also inscribed in the *Sonata*, if we take into account that the narrative viewpoint corresponds to an old man who revives his loves of the past as he remembers them. That narrator, who has lived through it all, inhabits the soul of his past self—the young lover or even the papal envoy—and contaminates him with a cynicism inappropriate for such a tender age. That is, peeking out at a tempting young woman through the eyes of the young Bradomín is in fact a cynical old man, the narrator in the discourse time (*temps de l'énonciation*). And, of course, the male spectator of this scene may also look on, in identification with Bradomín or with the elders in their role as voyeurs. Margaret R. Miles describes the impulse in the numerous pictorial versions of this biblical theme in the following terms: "These paintings attempt to reproduce, in the eyes of an assumed male viewer, the Elders' intense erotic attraction, projected and displayed on Susanna's flesh" (123). Susanna, then, is a most appropriate model for María Rosario, subjected as she will be to the constant visual inspection of her admirer, the marquis.

The following dialogue between Bradomín and Polonio is a model of Valle-Inclán's irony:

> —¿Qué os parece? Son todos de la misma mano. ¡Y qué mano . . . !
> Yo le interrumpí:
> —¿Sin duda, Andrea del Sarto?
> El Señor Polonio adquirió un continente grave, casi solemne:
> —Atribuidos a Rafael. (35)

> "What do you think of them? They are all by the same hand, and such a hand!"
> I interrupted to say: "Andrea del Sarto, no doubt [?]"
> Messer Polonius assumed an almost solemn air: "Attributed to Raphael." (12)

Of course, both the marquis and the butler are mistaken in their identifications. The implied author hovers above the two of them and delights in the artistic ignorance of those who think themselves connoisseurs. This interchange constitutes a verbal duel between two characters destined to hate each other. Painting is nothing more than a pretext for the men to continue to launch their word-weapons:

> —Reparad que tan sólo digo atribuidos. En mi humilde parecer valen más que si fuesen de Rafael . . . ¡Yo los creo del Divino!
> —¿Quién es el Divino?

El mayordomo abrió los brazos definitivamente conster-
nado:

—¿Y vos me lo preguntáis, Excelencia? ¡Quién puede ser
sino Leonardo de Vinci . . . !

Y guardó silencio, contemplándome con verdadera lástima.
Yo apenas disimulé una sonrisa burlona. (35)

"Notice that I merely say, attributed. In my humble opinion
they are more precious than works by Raphael—I believe them
to be painted by the Divine One!"

"Who is the Divine One?"

The major-domo threw back his hands in consternation:
"Can your Excellency ask me that? Who else but Leonardo da
Vinci?"

And he [kept silent, looking at me with real pity]. I could
hardly hide a mocking smile. (12)

At the same time that the butler denies that Raphael is the author
of the works in question and attributes them instead to Leonardo,
he also robs Raphael of the title "the Divine One." But is the butler ignorant, or does he really endeavor to mock Bradomín, since
he looks on him "con verdadera lástima" "with real pity"? And
does Bradomín truly not know the answer? And what provokes
the "sonrisa burlona" "mocking smile," the butler's error that
Bradomín caught, or the need to keep up a front? The text offers
hints that the first conjecture is correct, since some pages later the
narrator mentions "aquel retrato que del divino César Borgia
pintó el divino Rafael de Sancio" (87) "that portrait of [the divine]
Cesare Borgia painted by the divine Raphael Sanzio" (40). The old
narrator is correcting Polonio. Like the two characters, the readers
must keep alert lest they themselves become objects of derision.

At this point the butler retreats, perhaps to initiate another
round: "Excelencia, acaso tengáis razón. Andrea del Sarto pintó
mucho en el taller de Leonardo, y sus cuadros de esa época se parecen
tanto, que más de una vez han sido confundidos . . . En el mismo
Vaticano hay un ejemplo: La Madona de la Rosa. Unos la juzgan
del Vinci y otros del Sarto. Yo la creo del marido de Doña Lucrecia
del Fede, pero tocada por el Divino" (36) "Perhaps your Excellency
is right. Andrea del Sarto painted for a time in the studio of Leonardo
and their pictures from that period are so much alike that they are
easily confused. In the Vatican there is an example of this, the
Madonna of the Rose. Some declare it is Leonardo's; others say it
is by del Sarto. My opinion is that it is by the husband of Donna

Lucretia de Fede, touched over by the Divine One" (13). Polonio's data are once again easy to refute: the *Madonna of the Rose* was painted neither by Sarto nor by da Vinci, who differ so notably anyway, but by Raphael, and—no surprise here—the work hangs in the Prado. The harangue delivered by the butler, who like Shakespeare's Polonius is a flatterer and a fake, produces only one true statement: Lucrezia del Fede was in fact Andrea del Sarto's wife, a widow at the time they married (Wehle 188). She is the supposed model for his *Portrait of a Woman*, also located in the Prado; the same model also appears in several of del Sarto's *Madonna* paintings. Is this another virginal widow, like the Princess Gaetani or the Maria de' Medici whom the narrator of the *Sonatas* imagines?

From his vantage point on a palace balcony, the marquis contemplates the princess's daughters as they stroll about the garden: "En el fondo, caminando por los tortuosos senderos de un laberinto, las cinco hermanas se aparecían con las faldas llenas de rosas, como en una fábula antigua" (37) "Passing through the twisted paths of the labyrinth below, the five sisters were to be seen with their aprons filled with roses as in some ancient myth" (13). This vision of the five young women may be approximated to certain paintings from the Pre-Raphaelite school, such as Dante Gabriel Rossetti's *The Bower Meadow*, in which two women in the foreground play musical instruments, while two women dance behind them and a fifth wanders off into the background. Groups of four or five women also appear in works by Edward Burne-Jones; they are either dancing (*The Mill*), sleeping (*Panel from Briar Rose Series: The Sleeping Beauty*), or paying homage to Venus (*Laus Veneris*). In *The Mirror of Venus* and *The Golden Stairs* (Fig. 6), also by Burne-Jones, the female figures are even more numerous, their presence multiplied by their reflections in the water or as they descend the steps of a curved staircase one behind the other in an unending line. In short, both the *Sonata* and these paintings contain an overwhelming feminine realm, which blends complacently and unjarringly into the surrounding atmosphere.[8] Bradomín describes the five sisters as follows: "Cuando hablaban, el rumor de sus voces se perdía en los rumores de la tarde, y sólo la onda primaveral de sus risas se levantaba armónica bajo la sombra de los clásicos laureles" (39) "When they spoke their voices died away among the little sounds of evening and only the springtime wave of their laughter rose harmoniously in the shadows of the classic laurels" (14). A common language applies

Figure 6
Sir Edward Burne-Jones, *The Golden Stairs* (1880). Tate Gallery,
London, Great Britain. Art Resource, New York.

both to the women and to the setting in which they move about,
thereby making them indistinguishable from their surroundings.
The motif of the roses that the young women weave into wreaths
contributes to this identification. Eva Lloréns, referring to another

text by Valle-Inclán—his short story "Eulalia," from *Corte de amor* [Court of love] (1903)—mentions "the presence of flowers, the integration of the female figure into a landscape, within which she functions rhythmically" (52). The same could be said of *Spring Sonata*.

The narrator's gaze shifts from the paintings and then the garden to the princess's living room: "Amorcillos con guirnaldas, ninfas vestidas de encajes, galantes cazadores y venados de enramada cornamenta poblaban la tapicería del muro, y sobre las consolas, en graciosos grupos de porcelana, duques pastores ceñían el florido talle de marquesas aldeanas" (39) "Cupids in garlands, nymphs in laces, gallant huntsmen and antlered stags filled the tapestries on the walls, and on the consoles in graceful groups of porcelain [dukes dressed as shepherds held tight to flowered waists] of rural marquises" (15). The description of these women ("ninfas" "nymphs" and "marquesas aldeanas" "rural marquises") in the tapestries and ceramics found in the living room does not differ fundamentally from the way the sisters in the garden were described. Life and art are conflated here: to be enjoyed, life must take on the proportions of a work of art, an object of distant and fervent contemplation. Through his gaze as a connoisseur of beauty, Bradomín establishes his authority.

This realm of the five Marías, which at first glance does not pose a threat in that it has been reduced to a pleasant work of art, is nevertheless depicted as a self-sufficient enclosure. Like the women in the paintings by Rossetti and Burne-Jones, the sisters in the spring garden seem to emerge as autonomous beings; they do not call to anyone outside the scene that they create, and, moreover, they offer a mute protest against the intrusion of any male presence. In a latter passage, the sisters evoke a famous painting in the narrator's mind: "salieron de la estancia con alegre murmullo, en un grupo casto y primaveral como aquel que pintó Sandro Boticelli [sic]" (75) "[they] hurried out of the [room], lightly chattering like a chaste springtime group painted by Sandro Botticelli" (33). This is, of course, a reference to the famous *Primavera* [Spring] (Fig. 7).[9] The affinity between *Spring* and the *Spring Sonata* is undeniable. Camille Paglia's (occasionally acute) observations are relevant here: "Botticelli's personalities have a fixity and dreamy apartness. They offer themselves to the eye and yet rebuff our intimacy" (153). Botticelli and Valle-Inclán therefore coincide in their ability to create an atmosphere that is both seductive and remote.

Figure 7

Sandro Botticelli, *Spring* [La Primavera]. Uffizi, Florence, Italy. Alinari/Art Resource, New York.

Bradomín would like to frolic about in this overwhelmingly feminine universe, but without relinquishing his control. He would want to join the women in this modernist pastoral, thereby taking the place of the false "hunters" (exempt as such from the perils of the hunt) and the "dukes" who encircle the "flowered waists" of the ladies as if they were so many trees (and about as dangerous, too). Or Bradomín would wish to take Mercurio's place in *Spring*, a pictorial figure of whom Paglia says: "Like the Graces' impenetrable female circle, androgynous Mercury is narcissistic and self-complete" (152). But unlike Mercurio, Bradomín, though narcissistic, is not a self-sufficient person. He needs to conquer the love of women, or to reconquer the primordial mother-son union, to feed his narcissism.

The allusion to Botticelli raises certain questions. In a passage from the beginning of the *Sonata* that we have previously cited, Bradomín speaks of the woman who poisoned his great-grandfather: "Simoneta la Corticelli, que tiene un largo capítulo en las Memorias del Caballero de Seingalt" "Simoneta la Corticelli, the story of [whom] fills a long chapter in the Memoirs of the Caballero de Seingalt." There is a slight error here: the Corticelli woman (whom Casanova never calls by her given name) was in reality Marianna, not Simoneta.[10] But there is a Simonetta Vespucci, the supposed model for Venus in Botticelli's *Spring*, and also the model for Judith in his *The Return of Judith* (Uffizi, Florence).[11] Isn't there a confusion in the narrator's mind—intentional or otherwise—between Simonetta Vespucci and Marianna la Corticelli? And insofar as Venus (Spring) is linked with María Rosario, would it not be possible to ascribe to her the traits of the *femme fatale*, by way of Simonetta, the model for both Venus and Judith? These traits are equally present in Marianna la Corticelli, the lovesick dancer, whom Bradomín transforms into a murderous actress. Incidentally, María Rosario's negative side does not escape the marquis's notice: "Aquella niña era cruel, como todas las santas que tremolan en la tersa diestra la palma virginal" (52) "This maiden was as cruel as all the saints in whose white hands tremble the virginal palms" (22).

This threatening side of María Rosario is nevertheless counterbalanced by the insistent vision of her as a Madonna; Bradomín accordingly presents the eldest and the youngest sisters as follows: "Yo veía cómo la infantil y rubia guedeja de María Nieves desbordaba sobre el brazo de María Rosario, y hallaba en aquel grupo la gracia cándida de esos cuadros antiguos que pintaron los monjes de la Virgen" (43) "I saw the blonde, baby tresses of Maria Nieves fall across the arms of Maria Rosario and recalled the simple beauty of the old paintings where the monks depicted the Virgin" (17). But this vision also encodes a problematic reversal, since the Son's place is taken up by a female figure. The Virgin evoked in these lines does not identically resemble any painted version. The daughter, María Rosario, becomes a mother (a virginal mother) when she holds her little sister in her arms. This pair consisting of the eldest and youngest sisters, remains inaccessible to men, as did the group of the five. The attraction that the marquis feels toward María Rosario manifests itself in short order:

> Mi aliento casi rozaba su nuca, que era blanca como la de una estatua y exhalaba no sé qué aroma de flor y de doncella.
> —¡Os adoro! ¡Os adoro!
> Ella suspiró con angustia:
> —¡Dejadme! ¡Por favor, dejadme! (49)

> My breath almost brushed against her neck which was white as marble and exhaled some strange perfume, as of a virginal flower.
> "I adore you! I adore you!"
> In dread she whispered: "Leave me! Please leave me!" (20)

At the same time that Bradomín is attracted to María Rosario, he also immobilizes her, turning her into a kind of sculptured figure ("nuca . . . blanca como la de una estatua" "neck . . . white as marble"), or he compares her with a flower. Besides, the passion that this woman arouses in the marquis is undeniably connected to her imminent destiny: she is about to enter a convent, which reinforces her aura of virginal innocence. Although Bradomín and María Rosario are both twenty, she must turn away from worldly experience and knowledge as a future nun. Here is another scene in which the young woman becomes subjected to the attention of her admirer: "desde el fondo de un sillón, oculto en la sombra, contemplaba a María Rosario: Parecía sumida en un ensueño: Su boca, pálida de ideales nostalgias, permanecía anhelante, como si hablase con las almas invisibles, y sus ojos inmóviles, abiertos sobre el infinito, miraban sin ver" (50) "From the depths of a chair hidden in the shadows . . . I could watch Maria Rosario. She seemed lost in a dream; her lips, pallid with ideal yearnings, remained parted as though she were speaking with invisible spir-

Figure 8
Dante Gabriel Rossetti, *Beata Beatrix* (1864). Tate Gallery, London,
Great Britain. Art Resource, New York.

its, her motionless eyes looking into some infinity which they
could not see" (20). Rossetti's well-known painting *Beata Beatrix*
(Fig. 8) offers a magnificent pictorial equivalent to this textual
description. Timothy Hilton has this to say about the woman
whom Rossetti portrays in his masterpiece: "She looks as if she is

in ecstasy; and, as for instance in Bernini's *St Teresa*, it looks as much a sexual as a religious ecstasy" (181).[12]

The marquis derives pleasure from disturbing the calm of this woman who is bound to her forthcoming vows of chastity: "María Rosario se detuvo bajo la lámpara y me miró con ojos asustados, enrojeciendo de pronto" (49) "Maria Rosario paused under a lamp and gazed upon me with frightened eyes and a sudden blush" (20). The colors that emanate repeatedly from the young woman's face—or, put another way, her proximity to flowers—permit connections not only with Botticelli's *Spring* but also with the *Madonna of the Rose*, to which we made reference earlier.[13] The comparison with the Virgin is explicitly established: "María Rosario lloraba en silencio, y resplandecía hermosa y cándida como una Madona. . . . Yo recordé entonces los antiguos cuadros, vistos tantas veces en un antiguo monasterio de la Umbría, tablas prerrafaélicas que pintó en el retiro de su celda un monje desconocido" (61) "Maria Rosario wept softly in her serene beauty like [a] Madonna. . . . I recalled some ancient paintings I had seen years before in a poor Umbrian monastery, primitive scenes painted in the privacy of his cell by some unknown monk" (26–27). By distancing this woman as a virgin or as a pictorial object, Bradomín can freely give rein to a relation with her. He observes her on the sly, so that she cannot see him in return, or he fixes his eyes on her with seductive impertinence: "Y miré a María Rosario, que bajó la cabeza y se puso encendida como una rosa" (64), "I looked over at Maria Rosario [who lowered her head and turned red like a rose]" (28). Despite his fondness for paintings predating Raphael, Bradomín's visual practice follows the later perspective of the Renaissance. No matter what the narrator insinuates, it is not the humble attitude of a medieval monk before the innocence of the Madonna that we see manifested here. Instead, the perspective is one of dominance, which is established through possession of the contemplated object.[14]

It may also be said that turning a woman into a madonna is one of Bradomín's favorite devices, and it even occurs in cases where there is no easy justification. One such example was his desire to remake Princess Gaetani as a virgin. And in *Autumn Sonata*, Concha undergoes the same modification: "Concha tenía la palidez delicada y enferma de una Dolorosa" (318) "Concha was pale with the frail delicate pallor of a Dolorosa" (166). Doña Margarita in *Winter Sonata* is depicted in like terms: "me pareció que sus ojos de Madona, bellos y castos, estaban arrasados de lágrimas" (*Sonatas* 456) "it seemed to me that those madonna-like eyes, so pure and beautiful, were brimming with tears" (*Pleasant Memoirs* 245). In each instance, Bradomín establishes his superiority before these modest, pale, or tearful madonnas. The woman does not modify her virginal appearance even as she ages, nor does Bradomín curb his aggressive Don Juan style as the four seasons progress. In addition, the old narrator is always on standby to help out the young protagonist. As the spectator looking back on his life, the narrator can protect the individual that he was in the past and save him from amorous attacks but without dulling the effect of those potent forces on his juvenile self.[15]

In this regard, the following description of the palace garden is of interest: "Los tritones y las sirenas de las fuentes borboteaban su risa quimérica, y las aguas de plata corrían con juvenil murmullo por las barbas limosas de los viejos monstruos marinos que se inclinaban para besar a las sirenas, presas en sus brazos" (38–39) "The Tritons and Sirens of the fountains sputtered in fantastic laughter and the silvery waters murmured youthfully through the mossy beards of the [old] sea-monsters bending to kiss the . . . Sirens [imprisoned in their arms]" (14). The dominion of the "sirenas" "sirens" yields to that of the "viejos monstruos marinos" "old sea-monsters," which signals a vestige of triumphant masculinity in that redoubt of overwhelming feminine presence. Bradomín would really need to join this legion of old sea-monsters in order to confront the powerful siren who holds up his very own coat of arms: "una sirena abraza y sostiene tu escudo en la iglesia de Lantañón" (358) "a siren clasps your [coat of arms] in the Church of Lantañon" (189), he is told by his uncle, Don Juan Manuel Montenegro, in *Autumn Sonata*.

Bradomín's superiority in *Spring Sonata* is based on sexual experience, which stands in contrast to the modesty and fear that María Rosario feels: "Viéndola a tal extremo temerosa, yo sentía halagado mi orgullo donjuanesco, y algunas veces, sólo por turbarla, cruzaba de un lado al otro" (82–83) "[Seeing her so afraid] flattered my pride as a Don Juan, and sometimes merely to torment her I would pass from one side to another" (38). Alone in the garden, he remembers, with some confusion, "otros tiempos y otros amores" (84) "[other times and other loves]." The viewpoint of the protagonist and that of the old narrator seem to overlap here. Although he is young, Bradomín has already grown

weary of life, which causes him to feel alienated from earthly pleasures, including love; he considers himself a "místico galante" (86)
"mystical gallant" (40). The obvious irony in these words should
not occlude their ultimate truth: the desire to enjoy love without
becoming its prisoner. Or, in other words, Bradomín wishes to
know the temptation of love while resisting it: "La pobre [María
Rosario] no sabía que lo mejor de la santidad son las tentaciones"
(52) "[Poor Maria Rosario] did not know that the best part of
sanctity lies in the temptation" (22). María Rosario's mutism irri-
tates the marquis. "¿Qué siente ella . . . ? ¿Qué siente ella por
mí . . . ?" (84, 85) "What does she [feel]? What does she [feel for]
me?" (39), he asks himself insistently. He sets his sights on becoming "Confesor de Princesas" (86) "Confessor of Princesses" (40),
which would allow him access to—and power over—the female
soul while keeping his own inner self well concealed.

One night, when the marquis glimpses María Rosario in her
living room, he feels the urge to enter into that space: "pasó por
mí . . . un impulso ardiente, y después una sacudida fría y cruel:
La audacia que se admira en los labios y en los ojos de aquel
retrato que del divino César Borgia pintó el divino Rafael de Sancio" (87) "I felt . . . an ardent impulse and then [a cold and cruel
shiver], the boldness admired in the lips and eyes of that portrait
of [the divine] Cesare Borgia painted by the divine Raphael de
Sanzio" (40). This must be a reference to the portrait of Cesare
Borgia formerly attributed to Raphael.[16] By identifying with Borgia, Bradomín may place himself among those characters whom
he (and his creator, Valle-Inclán) admires, like Juan de Guzmán in
Summer Sonata: "Era hermoso como un bastardo de César Borgia" (221) "he was as handsome as some bastard son of Cesare
Borgia" (113) or like Don Juan Manuel in Autumn Sonata, of
whom Concha remarks: "Ese no tiene escrúpulos. Es otro descendiente de los Borgias" (347) "He has no scruples—another
descendant of the Borgias" (183). Here we detect a note of praise
for illegitimacy, also present in Cesare Borgia himself, son of Pope
Alexander VI.[17] Bradomín thus defies the law by opposing legitimate descent. The rejection of the law goes hand in hand with the
rebuke of the father, who is never mentioned in the Sonatas. But
in the father's absence, Bradomín must identify with strong masculine figures if he is to be successful at holding the feminine or
maternal realm at bay.

There is a delicious irony here: given that the portrait evoked in the text lacks a fixed referent to the identity of both the subject and the painter—the supposed "divine Cesare Borgia" and the "divine Raphael"—perhaps Bradomín, despite himself, winds up confused with an unknown character in a painting by an anonymous artist. After all, that anonymity, though unsolicited, would be a consequence directly related to the obliteration of an individual or historic personality, which then becomes replaced by a mythic one.[18] And Bradomín is engaged in exactly this process. If on the one hand myth—exemplified by Cesare Borgia or by the nostalgia of a heroic Renaissance man—insulates the marquis from a threatening universe, on the other hand it annihilates him, thereby substituting a mask for his face.[19]

María Rosario faints when she sees Bradomín enter her room; he then deposits her inert body on the bed. If his penetration into that space and the woman's falling faint symbolically equal a sexual union, it should also be noted that fainting (comparable to a kind of death) places a definitive separation between the two, parallel to the one that exists between the mother as object of desire and the son. María Rosario remains an inaccessible figure for Bradomín at all times. But his crime does not go unpunished: a pair of invisible hands draw back the curtain, which lets in the light of the moon (a maternal deity). The luminous atmosphere of the garden where the sisters move about has given way to the realm of shadows. This contrast is similar to the one that exists in paintings by Veronese and, especially, Tintoretto, the master of chiaroscuro and author of *Judith with the Head of Holofernes*. An analogous transition from light to dark may be found in Pre-Raphaelite paintings if we compare the earlier works with some later ones, as for example, Rossetti's *Astarte Syriaca*, which Hilton describes in these terms: "she is dusky, sombre, mysterious, and to give oneself to her worship is to abandon the world of light" (187).

At the princess's instigation, Polonio stabs Bradomín. The eclipsed paternal figure may be perceived in Polonio, and the onomastic resemblance between the butler and Shakespeare's Polonius intensifies this comparison.[20] Nevertheless, Valle-Inclán's Polonio could never constitute a real threat to the marquis, since he derives from a degraded and ridiculous character.[21] Bradomín, then, does not need to kill the old servant. He thus differs as well from the traditional Don Juan, who kills the Commander, another paternal figure. It would be superfluous to do away with someone who, like Polonio, carries his own annihilation in his name. The most the butler can accomplish is injuring Bradomín's shoulder. His power is entirely borrowed, whereas the princess—the mother—stands as the true rival, and Bradomín must free himself from her *imago*. The maternal figure is split into both the princess and María Rosario, the eldest sister. The princess rejects him while María Rosario seems to give secret consent, yet ultimately remains inaccessible.

Bradomín oscillates between the desire to stay and the wish to flee the palace at Liguria: "Ahora mi voluntad flaqueaba, sentíame vencido y sólo quería abandonar el Palacio" (97) "My will seemed weakened, I felt myself conquered and I [only] wished to steal . . . from the palace" (45). Here escaping would be equivalent to a failure of will, a defeat before the princess. But, from another perspective, the defeat would consist in staying behind, that is, remaining subject to the maternal empire that reigns in the palace. Although Bradomín apparently defies the mother, at bottom he is subjected to her rule, displaying as he does an attraction to an impossible woman. He cannot abandon Liguria no matter how hard he tries; he is unsuccessful at breaking the bond, or the spell, that holds him in the maternal sphere, both pleasurable and suffocating.

The motif of the ring that has been robbed from Bradomín and that the old sorceress has in her power fits well the context of the *Sonata*.[22] The old woman is obviously a maternal *imago*. The ring, a legacy from the grandfather, the Marquis of Bradomín, is associated with virility: "Excelencia, nunca os hubiera hecho morir, pero os hubiera quitado la lozanía . . ." (111) "Excellency, I should never have procured your death; I would only have destroyed your virility" (52), the old woman says to the marquis.[23] Later she insists on the ring's crucial role in an act of sorcery: "Me mandaban privaros de toda vuestra fuerza viril . . . Hubierais quedado como un niño acabado de nacer" (112–13) "They wanted [me] to deprive you of your manly strength. You would have been like a new-born infant" (53). The decadent imagination reigns supreme.[24] By means of the ring, Bradomín is able to establish his paternal filiation. He must resort to the ring in order to escape those maternal powers that threaten to destroy his manhood.

It is not Bradomín who will be annihilated, however, but rather a woman, as if only her destruction could save him from the threat he feels. In the final combat between the marquis and María Rosario, she calls on her youngest sister to repel Bradomín's assault: "La llamaba con un afán angustioso y poderoso que encendía el candor de su carne con divinas rosas" (127) "She called her with [an anguished and profound zeal that illumined the innocence of her flesh with divine roses]" (61). A chain of sorts between mothers and daughters is set in motion here. María Rosario, owing to her age, is like a mother to María Nieves, who "adormecía a su muñeca con las viejas tonadillas del tiempo de las abuelas" (130) "[was] singing her doll to sleep with an old lullaby [from the time of the grandmothers]" (63). The chain is prolonged to include imaginarily past generations (the "time of the grandmothers") and future ones (the doll as child of the little girl). Bradomín attempts to penetrate and thereby ravage this closed matriarchal world, where all the voices—María Rosario has joined in with her mother—implore him to leave.

The chain ultimately breaks at its weakest link. The window suddenly flies open, and the little girl, seated on the sill, falls to her death in the garden below.[25] "¡Fue Satanás!" (136, 137, 138) "It was Satan!" (66, 67), María Rosario repeatedly claims. Bradomín, the indirect cause of the tragedy, thus finds himself endowed with the devil's prestige—or stigma. Far from being destroyed, he asserts his satanic power to destroy, since he cannot convincingly develop any capacity to love. And he is the one who first picks up the bloodied child and carries her up the stairway like a priest offering a sacrificial victim. There is a parallel here between the marquis and King Lear, who holds Cordelia's cadaver in his arms. Janet Adelman (126) sees a reversed pietà in the ending to Shakespeare's tragedy, and the same could be said of the ending to the *Sonata*. Throughout the work, Bradomín never succeeds in occupying the place of the Son; his mystical betrothals with the Mother fail endlessly. Entrance into an exclusively female world, which at first seemed to exempt Bradomín from rivalries with other men (save a clumsy maternal emissary like Polonio), reveals its disastrous potential for the young marquis. That world of women shuts him out, no matter how often he succeeds in bringing an erotic blush of roses to an innocent virgin's face. Bradomín travels down a path strewn with male cadavers: Monsignor Gaetani, Prince Filipo Gaetani, his own father the Marquis of Bradomín (never named), and his great-grandfather who was poisoned by an actress. If Bradomín does not encounter a true obstacle in any man, neither does any man come to the aid of this orphan. He therefore must imagine himself as the Machiavellian Cesare Borgia, or, as we have just suggested, King Lear: he becomes the father of an innocent victim rather than the victim of an implacable maternal *imago*. But this radical inversion of roles does not ultimately allow Bradomín privileged access to that female universe, the "coro angustiado de las hermanas" (137) "the chorus of anguished sisters" (66), to whom he delivers the dead body of their youngest sister. Immediately thereafter, he flees from the Gaetani palace.[26]

Bradomín's forced escape nevertheless is compensated, in his masculine fantasy, by his later telling of the destruction he wreaked, as if somehow María Nieves's death were not enough. As a consequence of this tragedy, María Rosario loses her mind. The old narrator evokes María Rosario, now elderly and alienated, her maternal aspects reinforced by old age: "¡Pobre sombra envejecida, arrugada, miedosa, que vaga todavía por aquellas estancias y todavía cree verme acechándola en la oscuridad!" (137–38) "Poor creature, aged, wrinkled, timorous, still wandering through those rooms and still imagining that I am lurking in the shadows!" (67). Another famous Shakespearean character, Ophelia, comes to mind here. Her tragic figure is split in two: the dead María Nieves and the insane María Rosario. Valle-Inclán once again finds himself on common ground with the aesthetic currents of his time, in which there was a marked fascination for the Ophelia whom Bram Dijkstra describes as "the later nineteenth-century's all-time favorite example of the love-crazed self-sacrificial woman who most perfectly demonstrated her devotion to her man by descending into madness, who surrounded herself with flowers to show her equivalence to them" (42). Dijkstra supports the popularity of this character by reproducing paintings by artists such as Arthur Hughes, John Everett Millais, Ernest Hébert, Adolphe Dagnan-Bouveret, Madeleine Lemaire, and Georg Richard Falkenberg; in all these works the Shakespearean heroine appears with a copious floral surround.[27]

The Gaetani palace, then, may be seen as a reflection of the Shakespearean castle of Elsinore, complete with its Polonius and, implicitly, its Ophelia and Hamlet, duplicated in the figures of Cordelia and Lear.[28] The substance of the Marquis of Bradomín and María Rosario is therefore injected into these already mythic representations, or vice versa. The readers of the *Sonatas* thus become an audience who watches them, and the text turns into a theatre. Or it becomes a museum where a series of pictorial subjects are gathered—Judith and Holofernes, Moses saved from the waters, Susanna and the elders. These figures join parallel literary characters: Bradomín about to lose his virility, or saved *in extremis*, or the eternal pursuer of a Susanna ravaged by insanity and the unforgiving passage of time, not to mention the multiple virgins and decadent Ophelias adorned with flowers. The sparse action of this narrative, where death and springtime are fused, is repeatedly mollified in spatial figurations, a most appropriate enclave for myth.[29] This is modernism at its highest.

But does Bradomín truly disappear behind the characters that he represents? It should be said that from this amalgam of different models—the gallant mystic, Hamlet the mother's boy, the audacious Cesare Borgia, the cruel and sorrowful Lear—there emerges a unique literary representation or, rather, a new version of the Don Juan type, that demonic seducer who lies in the heart of all the previously mentioned models: "Un Don Juan admirable. ¡El más admirable tal vez!" (*Sonatas* 11) "He was an [admirable] Don Juan—perhaps the most admirable of all time" (*Pleasant Memoirs*, Prefatory Note), as the very author designates him. And, although the character thus conceived is largely a product of modernist or decadent sensibilities (especially concerning the particular vision of women), it would be wrong to think that Bradomín does not transcend the limits of his time or that he fails to achieve an original place in that historical scheme. After all, a literary character is constructed not unlike an ordinary person who must forge an identity by appealing to the available cultural discourses (while at the same time resisting them). This in fact describes how Ramón del Valle-Inclán lived his own life, flamboyantly acting out the role that he carefully elaborated for himself. Miguel de Unamuno highlights this aspect of the Galician writer better than anyone else when, in his necrological tribute, he states: "En su vida se ponía a menudo en jarras . . . ; alguna que otra vez se encampanaba. Y so capa, se reía. Como buen actor se comportaba en su casa como en escena. El hizo de todo, muy seriamente, una gran farsa" (42) "In his lifetime he often stood defiantly with his hands on his hips . . . ; sometimes he was a braggart. And he would laugh to himself. Like a good actor, he behaved at home like he did on the stage. He turned everything, most seriously, into a grand farce." This is where Valle-Inclán's work (and life) should be situated: in that slippery zone between seriousness and farce. It would not make sense to discard the comic or ironic elements (an irony both modernist and Galician) that infiltrate all of his writing, nor to view them as simple posturing, the destructive (or deconstructive) move of a nihilist.[30] Perceptible behind the distanced and deformed vision of Bradomín's erotic adventures is the affective nearness of that bygone spring, which the old narrator remembers: "¡Han pasado muchos años y todavía el recuerdo me hace suspirar!" (50) "Many years have passed, and still this memory makes me sigh" (21). And, in *Winter Sonata*, Bradomín shudders when he learns that the aged Princess Gaetani has always vilified him by calling him the "peor de los hombres" (499) "wickedest of men" (270), as one of her granddaughters testifies. Although there is undoubtedly an element of vanity in knowing himself the object of a curse that would make him the "wickedest of men" (a title that Miguel de Mañara, the infamous Don Juan, takes on for himself), Bradomín never ceases to feel authentic anguish. A threatening figure still enshrouds the decrepit seducer even in the winter of his life: "Todo el pasado, tumultuoso y estéril, echaba sobre mí ahogándome, sus aguas amargas" (499) "All of that tumultuous, fruitless past came pouring over me to drown me in its bitter waters" (271). The image of drowning is especially persuasive: Bradomín now drowns once again in the realm of the maternal, which is incarnated in the "abuela" "grandmother," who has placed a weighty curse on him. At the end of his life, this Moses/marquis, the eternal child, slips back into the bitter waters from which he was saved, in an endless series of deaths and rebirths, like the cyclical time of the seasons.

# CHAPTER 4

# The Infinite Progression: Love and Art in Prelude to Pleasure by Pedro Salinas

*Víspera del gozo* [Prelude to pleasure] (1926), Pedro Salinas's first work in prose, followed the publication of a collection of poetry in 1923 entitled *Presagios* [Presages], which initiated his literary renown. While Salinas has been heralded as one of Spain's most original modern poets, it is his contributions to fiction in *Prelude to Pleasure* that particularly interest us here for their relationship to the visual arts. Of this book's seven short narrative pieces, the three central ones, "Cita de los tres" [Rendezvous for three], "Delirios del chopo y el ciprés" [Delirium of poplar and cypress], and "Aurora de verdad" [True Aurora], connect most directly to painting and sculpture and will therefore be the primary focus of this interartistic analysis, but we will also make references to Salinas's poetry where relevant. In fact, these prose texts stand up well when compared with Salinas's poetry in his best-known books such as *La voz a ti debida* [The voice owed to you] and *Razón de amor* [Love's reason] from 1933 and 1936 respectively, works that established him as the most salient "love poet" among the distinguished members of Spain's Generation of 1927, which among others includes Jorge Guillén, Federico García Lorca, Vicente Aleixandre, Luis Cernuda, and Rafael Alberti.

Even though the narrations in *Prelude to Pleasure* are temporally distant from what in Hispanic letters is called "modernismo" (the movement that Nicaraguan Rubén Darío initiated at the end of the nineteenth century), Salinas remains faithful to the spirit of European modernism.[1] Marianna Torgovnick considers this literary modality, which she places approximately between the years of 1880 and 1940 (11), to be "the richest period . . . in the novel's relationship to the visual arts" (13). Torgovnick stresses the notion of spatial form, one of the legacies of formalist criticism associated most closely to Joseph Frank. Formalist criticism lends itself well to the analysis of modernist literature precisely because it has been influenced by modernism itself, according to Torgovnick (35). Murray Krieger establishes the same connection: "the spatialization of temporal sequence in literature became [with the New Criticism] the object of aesthetic worship" (204). In the works of T. S. Eliot or Joseph Frank, Krieger sees "the crowning idolatry of fixed poetic structure in the modernist movement in both poetry and criticism" (204).

This framework in part accommodates *Prelude to Pleasure*, but our analysis will not be restricted to spatial form, since we are also confronted with a powerful dynamism, central to Salinas's oeuvre. Running throughout his prose and poetic texts, then, are two opposite impulses: a desire for repose, and, simultaneously, a dissatisfaction with the achieved state of calm, which triggers new, interminable searches.[2]

The very title of "Rendezvous for Three" alludes to the oedipal triangulation, which, according to Lacan, characterizes the symbolic order. Initially, however, the text presents a world of pleasure, exemplified by the imaginary city of Sarracín, or, more concretely, by the clock that strikes six even though it is only a quarter to six. (Mis)guided by that clock, Angel arrives fifteen minutes early at the cathedral, where he is to meet a beloved woman. He thus enjoys the imminence of the encounter, the prelude to pleasure, which becomes more valuable inasmuch as the rendezvous may never actually happen. But Angel is not yet overcome with doubts, and for the moment he immerses himself in the voluptuous sensation of altered time; that is, a state that resembles a kind of paradise, severed from rigid constrictions and laws: "el tiempo estaba desnudo y se comportaba liberal y graciosamente, como en una fiesta báquica el cuerpo que soltó corsé y tirantes, ligas y corchetes, todo lo que le ceñía oprimido y estricto y se muestra ahora desenvuelto y rosado sin dejar ya dudas respecto a su entrega total" (*Víspera* 38) "time was naked and behaved in a liberal and [charming] fashion, as in a Bacchic festival when the body loosens corset and suspenders, garters and clasps, everything that fits it oppressively, rigidly, and reveals itself free and easy, rosy, leaving no doubt of its complete surrender" (*Prelude* 34).

His fantasy, as we see, begins by evoking "naked time," a world exempt from temporality, and then opens into a "Bacchic festival," at the center of which is the image of a woman in the

Figure 9
Titian, *Bacchanal.* Prado, Madrid.

process of undressing. The action described in the above passage, however, transports the reader indirectly into the art world where there are abundant representations of ancient Bacchic festivals. A pictorial vision is thus inscribed on "naked time." One of the most famous artistic *Bacchanals,* by Titian, is found in the Prado Museum (Fig. 9): Salinas could well have had that painting in mind as he wrote his narration.[3] A nude woman, fully illuminated, dominates this picture: "the dancing movements and the swaying bodies convey the spirit of Bacchanalian abandon, and the extraordinary beauty of the sleeping nude Ariadne brought the picture great renown," writes Harold E. Wethey (37). Abandoned by Theseus, Ariadne, semireclining, seems to offer herself fully to the spectator of such a beautiful scene. No third party emerges in the painting to contend with the observer for that "easy, rosy" body. Berenson remarks: "look at the 'Bacchanals' [by Titian] in Madrid, or at the 'Bacchus and Ariadne' in the National Gallery.

How brim-full they are of exuberant joy! you see no sign of a struggle of inner and outer conditions, but life so free, so strong, so glowing, that it almost intoxicates" (19). There is, however, a difference between these two paintings by Titian. In *Bacchus and Ariadne*, the god embraces his wife, whom he carries off with him. The most the spectator can do with respect to Ariadne, then, is to form part of a triangle: an exclusive, imaginary relation with her is thus thwarted.

But one could also dispute that the Ariadne in the *Baccanal* in the Prado may be associated with a woman's body that leaves "no doubt of its complete surrender." Immersed in her dreamlike state, Ariadne rebuffs all contact with exterior reality. Besides, when she enters into the realm of artistic representation, the woman takes part in a system of patriarchal forces: she is first subjected to the desire of the painter before she becomes the subject of the spectator's gaze.[4] Salinas's story oscillates from the start between two opposing visions: that of the woman who surrenders, like in a Bacchic festival, outside of customary rules, and that of the same woman as an inaccessible creature, under the desire (or the empire) of the Other. Both the nude body of the woman and the imaginary Bacchic festival exist within social constructions, which regulate all apparent excesses.[5]

Returning to the character Angel, it may be observed that his fantasies of a "naked time" run up against the inexorable dimension of real time, silently marked by the courthouse clock: "reloj mudo y sin campana, dechado perfecto de una justicia, casi divina, que no yerra nunca y se cumple en secreto" (42) "mute and bell-less, the perfect model of a nearly divine justice that never errs and is carried out in secret" (36). The Lacanian law of the father thus asserts itself before the other clocks of the city, deliciously in error and daringly in violation of the rules. An interesting stylistic variation (omitted in the English translation) reflects this duality of the world inhabited by the protagonist. Though he is called "Angel" for the most part, on two occasions (37, 49) the narrator calls him "Jorge"; in so doing, he removes the character from an angelic paradise and instead associates him with the legendary Saint George, destined to battle the dragon and the forces of evil. In this regard, it is worth noting that in the last narration in *Prelude to Pleasure*, "Livia Schubert, incompleta" [Livia Schubert, incomplete], the train in which Livia departs, leaving behind her lover, is compared to a dragon.[6]

A threatening atmosphere develops in "Rendezvous for Three" when the much-awaited hour of six arrives, but Matilde, the beloved woman, does not. Angel/Jorge shows signs of desperation:

"Apenas si son las seis, decía, aún puede venir." Aunque él sabía que las seis estaban allí hacía diez minutos, como está la muerte, sorda y segura, a nuestro lado los quince últimos días de la vida, y nosotros inocentes, disimulando, haciéndonos los distraídos, animados y hervidores de proyectos como si así pudiéramos escaparla. (43)

"It's barely six," he'd say, "she could still come." Even though he knew that six o'clock had been there for ten minutes, the way death, stealthy and certain, is at our side the last fifteen days of our life. Yet we play the innocent, dissimulating, pretending not to notice, bustling and bubbling with projects as if somehow we could escape it. (37)

The prelude to pleasure, from this viewpoint, may turn into the brink of catastrophe. The double resonance of six, which can give as well as take away, may be perceived in the two contradictory adjectives that Salinas assigns to it: "aquella hora irisada, mate, de las seis" (45) "that iridescent . . . [matte] hour of six o'clock" (38). And the matte, dull hour is connected with Matilde, the woman capable of inflicting death (by killing with love), but also capable of giving life: "recordaba Angel que esta cifra [las seis] le sirvió a él, de pronto, para explicarse el mundo, que un momento antes, cuando no sabía si podría verla o no se le aparecía como un problema confuso o insoluble" (45–46) "It was, Angel remembered, as though that number [six] suddenly served to explain the world to him, that world which a moment before, when he did not know if he would be able to see her or not, seemed like an insoluble and confusing problem" (38). Everything becomes clear, or the real emerges, as a result of an intimate encounter with a woman, representative of that originary state before the institution of the law and of language.[7] The world thus is reborn from its own ruins, as it is in these haunting lines from a poem in *La voz a ti debida*: "Amor, amor, catástrofe. / ¡Qué hundimiento del mundo!" (*Poesías* 150) "Love, love, catastrophe. / What a collapse of the world!" (*To Live* 45). True reality is encoded in the hour of six, not insofar as "six" is objectively measured by the courthouse clock, but as a promise or prelude to pleasure—the amorous rendezvous. That is, true reality agrees with the Freudian pleasure principle, rather than with the reality principle. Six o'clock is not six o'clock: it is not yet six, or it will always be six, a time before time, a world before the world: "Y ya siento entre tactos, / entre abrazos, tu piel, / que me entrega el retorno / al palpitar primero, / sin luz, antes del mundo, / total, sin forma, caos" (*Poesías* 151) "And now as I touch, as I embrace, / I feel your skin / giving me the way back / to the first pulsation / before light was, before the world was: / total, formless, chaos" (*To Live* 47).

Yet as the story advances, following Angel's disappointment when he sees that Matilde is not coming, a new situation occurs: "Pero, al fin y al cabo, ¿qué más le daba? Porque lo curioso estaba en que esa cita, esperada por él desde el día antes, no era con él. Si Matilde había quedado en venir a la catedral a las seis era por ver a Alfonso de Padilla" (46) "But in the end, what did it matter? Because the funny thing was that this meeting, which he had looked forward to since yesterday, wasn't with him. If Matilde had agreed to come to the cathedral at six o'clock it was to see Alfonso de Padilla" (38). The rival, the discordant third party, makes his appearance here. To be sure, Matilde looks straight at Angel when she announces that she will go to see Alfonso de Padilla: "Mañana, a las seis, iré a la catedral" (47) "Tomorrow, at six, I'll go to the cathedral" (38). Angel's hope in going to the cathedral is thus justified. Nevertheless, it is obvious that the dual (or imaginary) relationship, patterned after the link between mother and child, yields to the symbolic order, where the father figure causes the rupture of that early union. Alfonso de Padilla lies transfixed and immobile within the maternal surround of the church. Or, more precisely, the reference is to the tomb with the statue of the character of that name, as the text clarifies later. That Alfonso de Padilla has no real existence does not diminish his importance, which is conferred by his symbolic status as carrier of the law (*porteur de la loi*).

This statue-character has certain traits that surprise Angel (and, consequently, the readers):

> Tenía en la mano derecha un libro abierto, pero sin leer. . . . Y el libro manaba una tristeza de alcándara sin pájaro, porque la mirada que un momento antes descansaba en él, doble, negra y buida como unas garras, se le había escapado ahora, en desconocido vuelo, a cazas de altanería, sin duda muy recóndi-

tas, porque no estaba el mirar fuera de los ojos, sino tornado hacia los adentros del mancebo, tras una presa que nadie podía ver. (47–48)

In his right hand he held an open book, but unread. . . . From the book flowed the sadness of a perch without its bird, for the gaze that a moment before rested on it, double, black and pointed like claws, escaped now, on an unknown flight. The hawk was off hunting, no doubt, something well-concealed, because the searching look was not aimed outside himself but turned toward the inner recesses of the youth, after an invisible prey. (38–39)

This description corresponds exactly to one of the most famous sepulchral statues in the history of Spanish sculpture: the *Doncel de Sigüenza*, found in the cathedral of that city (Fig. 10). But it is crucial to note how the Doncel or nobleman, initially set up as an amorous rival (and, as such, a paternal figure) to the protagonist, eventually occupies the same place as Angel: an exponent of human desire, ever unsatisfiable. Alfonso de Padilla remains cloistered in a definitive solitude, while at the same time he displays an attitude of searching or longing for something beyond himself.

Matilde finally arrives when a disappointed Angel/Jorge is preparing to leave: "Pero de pronto el cortinón de la puerta del fondo de la iglesia se alzó: por allí entraban desatados, alegres, como una jauría, un tropel de rayos de sol, dorados, rojos, leonados, aullantes, saltando todos alrededor de una figura encendida y gallarda de mujer, rubia y esbelta, que traía bajo el brazo un carcaj parecido a una sombrilla corta" (49) "But suddenly the curtain belonging to the door in the back of the church was lifted: like a loosed pack of happy hounds, a rushing throng of the sun's rays, golden, red, and tawny, came in, all of them howling and leaping around the brightly lit and handsome figure of a woman, blond and slim, carrying underneath her arm a quiver that looked like a small parasol" (39). If on the one hand Angel's desire seems to find completion with Matilde's arrival, there is on the other hand something disquieting in her sudden appearance on the scene: she is introduced as a new "Diana cazadora" (49) "huntress Diana" (39). When the curtain in the church opens up, Angel's vision is reminiscent of the sight of Diana surprised in the nude by Actaeon, who pays for his audacity with his life. At the same time, it should be noted that the lifting of the curtain (*cortinón*) in the

Figure 10
Anonymous, *Tomb of Martin Vázquez de Arce*
*(The Young Nobleman of Sigüenza)*. Cathedral of Sigüenza, Spain.

church echoes the lifting of a theatre curtain; a fictitious world is thus presented for the spectators—Angel and the readers of the story. The vision of Matilde as Diana transports her to the realm of the visual arts, where that ancient goddess appears insistently: "Los árboles que se entrevieron un instante, . . . antes de que la puerta se cerrara, no eran ya . . . sino una espesa selva de Argólida, que recorría ardorosa y virgen, esta Diana cazadora" (49) "The trees glimpsed for an instant . . . before the door closed . . . had been transformed . . . into a dense woodland of Argolis through which the huntress Diana, ardent and virginal, ran" (39). Diana resembles the nude Ariadne here, subject of the previously evoked Bacchic festival. And these two figures constitute the object of an insistent desire that reaches toward both body and spirit. In addition to their splendid beauty, both Diana and Ariadne belong among the heavenly bodies, as moon, in the first case, and as a constellation of stars, in the second.[8]

The threat that Matilde incarnates is nevertheless extinguished when the curtain falls back into place and the sunrays are obscured: "Ya la cortina estaba otra vez caída, y con ello los canes de la diosa, dorada escolta del crepúsculo, desaparecidos" (49–50) "Now the curtain had once more fallen, and with it the hounds of the goddess, her golden scolt of twilight, disappeared" (39). The fearsome Diana is thereby transformed into a "respetuosa y tímida . . . señorita . . . , la figura misma, los rasgos exactos de Matilde" (50), "respectful and timid . . . young lady . . . , the very figure, the exact features of Matilde" (40). It is as if Diana shifted from her role as Actaeon's antagonist to her relation with Endymion: "Endymion was a beautiful youth. . . . One calm, clear night, Diana, the Moon, looked down and saw him sleeping. The cold heart of the virgin goddess was warmed by his surpassing beauty, and she came down to him, kissed him, and watched over him while he slept" (Bulfinch 235). When she is inside the church enveloped in shadows, Matilde turns into a beneficent Diana/moon, whereas outside of that enclosure, furtively glimpsed, she takes on the factions of the destructive Diana who drives Actaeon to his death. The narration concludes when the cathedral is about to close and Matilde and Angel, having been deprived of enough time to look at the young nobleman's statue, leave the building together:

> Angel sentía un placer satánico y secreto, porque él se marchaba con Matilde, andando a su lado, de carne y hueso, por una tarde palpitante y verdadera, mientras que su bello rival aborrecible, Alfonso de Padilla, señor de Olmos Albos, paje de la reina Católica, muerto en un romance fronterizo, frente a la vega de Granada, se quedaría encerrado en la iglesia, a la sombra de un florido dosel de piedra, en su sepulcro gótico, deshecha ya la cita de los tres. (50)

> Angel felt a secret, satanic pleasure, because he was leaving with Matilde, walking by her side, in flesh and blood, on this pulsating, [true] afternoon, while his gorgeous hated rival, Alfonso de Padilla, lord of Olmos Albos and page of Queen Isabella, having met death in a frontier ballad, before the Plain of Granada, would lie shut up in the church, in the shadow of a flowery canopy of stone, in his Gothic grave, the rendezvous for three now ended. (40)

A happy ending? In a way, yes. Once the triangulation of the symbolic order has been put to an end, the originary union of two,

toward which desire is aimed, may be reconstituted. Ellie Ragland-Sullivan summarizes Lacan's thinking on this point: "The
Imaginary order, based on primal fusion, will constantly try to
overthrow the Symbolic order of difference in its quest for unity
(*jouissance*)" (304). Angel seems to establish intimate contact
with the real world (a woman of "flesh and blood," "this pulsat-
ing, true afternoon"), whereas Alfonso de Padilla, the detested
rival, is reduced to the status of a fictive being: "muerto en un
romance fronterizo" "having met death in a frontier ballad."[9]
Nothing but a signifier, we might say: trapped in a sign system.
Yet the course of the narration has plotted a path that allows us
to subvert this affirmative ending. When Matilde and Angel walk
out into the light of day, the woman once again becomes surrounded by sunrays, that is, the metaphoric hounds of the huntress Diana. What, then, is the final metamorphosis: Diana into
Matilde (the moon-lover) as she enters the church, or Matilde into
the inaccessible Diana as she abandons the protective maternal
enclave? Note that the couple's exit is described in the following
terms: "Salieron juntos, perseguidos, echados como de un frus-
trado paraíso, por las llaves y el paso del sacristán" (50) "They left
together, pursued, ejected, as from a frustrated paradise, by the
keys and footsteps of the sexton" (40). Sinful sensuality is introduced twice in this imaginary paradise: by means of the "easy,
rosy" body of a woman at a "Bacchic festival" and through the
image of a woman whom the sexton immediately recognizes as a
"pagan goddess" (49; 39). Both splendid visions burst forth into
an atmosphere not quite prepared to receive them: a city presided
over by a "Gothic cathedral" (49; 39). That the city is named
"Sarracín" also implies an anomaly: Saracenic sensuality (equally
pagan) infiltrates the domains of Christianity, which claims to
have subjugated it.[10] Yet Christianity clamors for its rights.
Angel's "satanic pleasure" when he walks off with Matilde places
him in relation to God, and therefore to a power that cannot be
vanquished. This is a world ruled by the "name" (*nom*) or "no"
(*non*) of the father. The symbolic order, whether in the church, in
the form of a funerary sculpture (like the Commander's image in
the Don Juan myth), or outside of the church (paradise lost),
resists all efforts to displace it. And, to add to Angel's woes, there
is a threat from an exclusively feminine origin: the untouchable
huntress Diana.

Finally, projected onto Alfonso de Padilla is the figure of a young man who, "shut up in the church"—the mother church—incarnates the human ideal of plenitude. Paradoxically, in this light (or darkness, as it were), the defeated rival ends up in a triumphant position. Yet, as we have pointed out, the young man from his solitary and introspective depths incarnates the desire that afflicts Angel as well. The pleasure (*jouissance*) that Angel ultimately experiences does not come about only as a result of the dissolution of the "rendezvous for three" with its suppression of the discordant third person. It also results from Angel's own desire being projected onto the young man (the double), and thus from his apparent triumph over lack (*manque-à-être*), where desire originates. But the projection is always reascribed to its source, Angel, or, at a level beyond, the narrator, both of whom, like Alfonso de Padilla, are signifiers of a subject (subject of desire) that they represent for another signifier: Matilde, the woman as embodiment of the real, the height of that prelude to pleasure.[11]

"Delirium of Poplar and Cypress" [Delirios del chopo y el ciprés], the shortest of all the narrations in *Prelude to Pleasure*, is a kind of lyrical parenthesis placed at the center of the work. The narrator contemplates two trees in the distance as he rides on a train. From the train they both seem the same, "tan el uno del otro, como los dos palos de una inmensa hache frustrada" (53) "one as like the other as the two [posts] of an immense frustrated H" (41). He feels compelled, however, to view them more closely, and his imagination wanders away from the train to become convinced "por minuciosos testimonios de visión y palpo de que aquellos dos árboles tan iguales eran un chopo y un ciprés" (53–54) "by the [detailed testimony] of sight and touch that the two identical trees were a poplar and a cypress" (41). The traveler thus wishes to interrupt if only for a moment the temporal flow of his trip or his life in order to cling to something that urgently calls out to him from its apparent state of calm. In rejecting the role of fleeting and distant spectator, the traveler behaves much like a painter, in exact accordance with the terms of Merleau-Ponty: "The painter, [whoever] he is, *while he is painting* practices a magical theory of vision. He is obliged to admit that objects before him pass into him or else that . . . the mind goes out through the eyes to wander among objects; for the painter never ceases adjusting his clairvoyance to them" ("Eye and Mind" 260). Returning to the train, the traveler writes in a notebook: "A lo lejos, iguales; a lo cerca, tan paralelos, que nunca se encontrarán" (54) "From a distance, the same; close up, so parallel that they will never meet" (41). Like two lovers who long irresistibly for each other, the two trees—separate and parallel—can only meet in infinity. Their fusion takes place when the viewer observes them at a distance; when he approaches in answer to their call, however, the spectator establishes differences between them. The poplar and the cypress, now differentiated, exhibit a condition that may be compared to what the poet-painter experiences in his desire to fuse with them. The thwarted union functions as a departure point for their desire to find each other. Such an encounter nevertheless demands the previous existence of two different and autonomous beings. As the beginning of this narration demonstrates, the "H" (union) cannot be formed (or consummated) if the two posts come so close together that there is no room for the horizontal bar between them. That which separates—that bar or barrier—is also what permits union.[12]

When the narrator differentiates the trees, he endows them with specific personalities. He describes the poplar: "lleno, rebosado, ahogado en tu forma del minuto por la afluencia de tantas formas en tu entraña que ya quieren ensayarse. . . . tu forma no se acertará sino en la torturada sucesión de las infinitas deformaciones" (54–55), "full, overflowing, the form you assumed one minute ago overwhelmed by the rush of so many forms into your heart that now want to try themselves out. . . . your form will only take shape in the agonizing succession of infinite deformations" (41–42). Here is another infinite progression: one that, like love, leads to an achieved form. But it is the cypress, not the poplar, that seems to incarnate the ideal of perfection: "Raíz certera, hincada en tierra apenas y que da ya con el jugo de la soterrada disciplina. Con hidalgo señorío de la forma lograda, tu empeño vital se concentra en la fiera y confiada existencia de un recto perfil sobre blandos paisajes azules o escabrosos cielos atormentados" (53) "A well-aimed root, barely thrust into the earth, already exuding the sap of subterranean discipline. With the [noble-like dignity] of the achieved form, all your efforts in life are concentrated in insisting, fiercely confident, on a straight profile projected against soft blue landscapes or tormented, jagged skies" (42). What the poplar strives to be, the cypress already is, without any apparent effort. Yet it is true that the cypress, though confident and sure, also reaches for a goal: a heavenly goal, toward which it directs its "empeño vital" "efforts in life." The cypress does not retreat into narcissistic contentment; the "jugo de la soterrada disciplina" "sap of subterranean discipline" pushes it toward something outside the self. The cypress, a kind of ascetic firmly rooted on the Castilian plain, subjects itself to a constant spiritual exercise. If to the human eye the cypress looks perfect, there nevertheless is an infinite distance with respect to the heavens toward which it reaches. The poplar and the cypress clamor equally for the poet-narrator's attention as examples of two impulses of analogous nature: a desire for plenitude in both cases.

The "incidental anecdote"—as the poet calls it (42)—that comes after the vision of the two trees transports the reader to an urban interior: a museum. This is where the narrating subject takes his companion, who is feeling nostalgic for the "suelo y los chopos de Castilla" (56) "earth and poplars of Castile" (42). Nostalgia for reality: "Te llevé a la sala de retratos, y allí, en los ojillos de un personaje desconocido (traje negro, barba lacia, color terrosa), estaba tu árbol de Castilla. . . . Tú, por broma, escribiste en el catálogo: 'Identificado este retrato de desconocido, por el Greco. Retrato de chopo con vagos accesorios fisonómicos e indumentarios . . .'" (56–57) "I took you to the portrait gallery, and there, in the dark eyes of an unknown personage (black suit, limp beard, earth tones) was your tree of Castile. . . . You wrote as a joke, in the catalogue: '[The unknown man in El Greco's portrait has been identified. It is the] portrait of a poplar, vaguely attired, anatomy uncertain . . .'" (42). Not only the portrait but also the museum is identified: the Prado, where *Portrait of an Unknown Man* by El Greco (Fig. 11) hangs. The metamorphosis of tree into portrait is not arbitrary, given the previous description of the poplar in human terms as one who beckons to the spectator and questions him. The spectator's attitude, extended to his companion, corroborates the philosophical position that Merleau-Ponty outlines:

> Inevitably the roles between him [the painter] and the visible are reversed. That is why so many painters have said that things look at them. As André Marchand says, after Klee: "In a forest, I have felt many times over that it was not I who looked at the forest. Some days I felt that the trees were looking at me, were speaking to me." ("Eye and Mind" 261)

Figure 11
El Greco, *Portrait of an Unknown Man*. Prado, Madrid.

But isn't the nostalgia for poplars what makes that very tree, and no other, comparable to the character whose portrait El Greco painted? Why not the cypress, with its "noble-like dignity" and elongated form, against "tormented, jagged skies"? Through El Greco, the correspondence could be made with either of these trees. Antonina Vallentin describes the *Retrato de un desconocido* [Portrait of an unknown man] as follows: "By means of the mobility of the expression, a temperament—one could even say a characteristic mentality—is revealed. It is the face of a disillusioned man, of a sensitive man hurt too often. . . . But the man has not drawn inward to himself, recoiled in his dreams; there is something in him that is very attentive, an air of concentration" (278).

Ultimately, the desired object (the tree) is in turn transformed into a subject, that is, into the counterpart of he who searches for it.

The transformation of the poplar into a painting by El Greco, which takes place in the museum, decidedly colors the last paragraphs of the story. Even though El Greco is not mentioned again, his memory—inscribed with traces of all Spanish religious painting—is present in the evocation of both the poplar and the cypress: "por los viales de Castilla los chopos desnudos se contorsionan con secos chasquidos de esqueletos mondos, para flagelarse los blancos huesos, miserias finales" (57) "by the roads of Castile naked poplars twist and turn with the dry clicking of stripped skeletons, flagellating their white bones, [final agonies]" (43). Pagan sensuality, which burst forth so vibrantly in "Rendezvous for Three," beats a retreat here. The soul prepares for death, and the cypress manifests a desire for salvation: "ya se le ve al ciprés, ahuesado y ahusado, ese blancor largo e incorpóreo de las figuraciones, con que se representan en los cuadros las almas que, rozadas por las manos de dos ángeles, ascienden a los cielos merecidos" (58) "we see the cypress, bones splintered and spindled, that long, incorporeal whiteness like the configurations in paintings meant to represent souls, lightly held by the hands of two angels as they ascend to a well-deserved heaven" (43). Among the paintings that are generically named, one stands out in the imagination: the *Entierro del Conde de Orgaz* [Burial of the count of Orgaz] (Church of Santo Tomé, Toledo), El Greco's masterpiece. In that painting the soul of the deceased count in fact appears in the center of the work as a "blancor largo" "long . . . whiteness" carried up to heaven by an angel.

But the poplar also incarnates the same impulse toward salvation. Its aspiration to become "achieved form" does not differ from the cypress's desire. Salinas recognizes this common destiny when he calls the poplar *"madera de cruz"* (58) *"wood for a cross"* (43). The *Crucifixion* by El Greco may be said to function as the principal interartistic referent within the context of this poetic prose. The expression *long whiteness*, associated originally with the souls, applies equally well to the crucified Christ of El Greco. And, while not particularly "incorporeal," the extraordinary elongation of this Christ—together with the fact that he departs from this world—lends a spiritual dimension to his image, surrounded as it is by two angels who receive his blood (if not his soul) in their hands. It is entirely possible that these two paintings

by El Greco—the *Burial* and the *Crucifixion*—have become inter-
mingled in the writer's imagination as he projects their vision onto
the trees in his "Delirium." In the case of the poplar, however,
reaching out toward something beyond itself carries as much significance as the actual encounter. For the desired union never
takes place: "tú, centinela de todos, defiendes en la aparente calma
total el desesperado deber de las ansias delicadas" (58) "you, [sen-
tinel of us all, defend in complete apparent calm the desperate
duty of delicate yearnings]" (43). Despair, anxiety—the poplar
(like the cypress) exemplarily illustrates the measure of human
aspirations. Salvation, for the poplar, could only happen in the
sense that a poem from *Razón de amor* elucidates: "nos llenará la
vida / este puro volar sin hora quieta, / este vivir buscándola: / y
es ya la salvación querer salvarnos" "Our life will be filled / by this
pure flight with no calm hour, / this living in search of it: / and our
wanting to be saved / is already salvation" (*Poesías* 213).

To conclude, "Delirium of Poplar and Cypress" encompasses
a double striving, central to Salinas, which, in Murray Krieger's
words, could be expressed as the conflict between a feeling of
exhilaration and one of authentic exasperation. The first affect
derives from the conversion of the poet into a painter, who, by
evading the confines of a supposedly temporal art form, accedes
to the realm of immutable spatial forms, thought of as more suitable to create the impression of naturalness in its bare immediacy.
The poet touches the world, seizing it by means of "minuciosos
testimonios de visión y palpo" "the detailed testimony of sight
and touch"—as the beginning of the narration posits—and by
means of the connections that he establishes between the objects
described and specific paintings. Yet it may also be said that this
calm proves exasperating insofar as it detains the progression of
life: consequently, there arises a desire to break away from the
limits of purely spatial forms. Krieger remarks: "every tendency in
the verbal sequence to freeze itself into a shape . . . is inevitably
accompanied by a counter-tendency for that sequence to free itself
from the limited enclosure of the frozen, sensible image into an
unbounded temporal flow" (10).

Salinas is successful in resolving this tension by appealing to a
highly original visual artist: El Greco, the painter of what Eugenio
d'Ors calls "forms that fly" (69). That is, Salinas, without renouncing the materiality of painting, focuses his attention on a painter-
poet in the artistic canon whose figures—like the poplar—are

"twisted" or in the throws of "the desperate duty of delicate yearnings." D'Ors has characterized this phenomenon better than anyone: "If Poussin, Mantegna, Raphael himself, are situated closely with sculpture and architecture, and they represent the domain of spatial values, then we now [with El Greco and Goya] reach those ardent regions in which painting, motivated by a feverish ambition of expression, is at the point of volatilizing its materiality in order to turn it into music or poetry—into *lyricism* and *character*" (58). Salinas's desire, therefore, speaks of calm—the kind attained by means of the visual arts—but it is a quietude throughout which an internal dynamism flows, an impulse toward increasingly higher reaches. In the next narration, "Aurora de verdad" (True Aurora), a new version of this dual stance will be elaborated.

From the very beginning of this narration, as the title announces, woman is intimately connected to the real: "Las citas con Aurora eran siempre por la mañana" (61) "He always met Aurora in the morning" (44). The name "Aurora" ("Dawn") applies both to the woman and to the start of the day. Upon waking, Jorge reads in his agenda: "Mañana a las diez, cita con Aurora" (62) "10:00 tomorrow, meet Aurora" (44). Although Jorge cannot get Aurora off his mind all night, the woman who appears in his dreams seems "irreal y discursiva" (62) "unreal and [discursive]"— like the product of the imagination that she is, we could say— whereas the person whom he is soon to meet in the museum comes across as "verdadera y silenciosa" (62–63) "real [and] silent" (44).

On his way to the museum Jorge detects traces or memories of his beloved in other women whom he sees. Since she is fused with the world, it is natural that her image would appear, fragmented, in the multiple forms that cross Jorge's path. In order to reconstruct Aurora with the pieces of this puzzle, Jorge turns to "la imagen ejemplar que llevaba grabada en el corazón" (65) "the exemplary image he wore engraved in his heart" (46). But his efforts prove futile: "no podía encontrarse realmente con Aurora entera y cabal hasta que la tuviera delante, porque siempre le faltaban unas cuantas cosas esenciales" (66) "Jorge couldn't really have Aurora complete and of a piece until she was standing there before him. He would always be missing certain essential things" (46). That is, he would be missing the essence of her very presence, "Aurora in the Flesh," as the title of the published English translation would have it.

Aurora and Jorge have agreed to meet at the museum, in the gallery devoted to the English landscape artist, Turner. The narrative voice (which may or may not correspond to Jorge) offers the reader the following thoughts: "Así que Aurora será el único ser vivo poblador de aquel paraíso ultraterrenal, la Eva creada al revés, antes que el hombre y esperándole en un mundo recién inventado" (67) "Aurora would be the only being inhabiting that [otherwordly] paradise, Eve created in reverse, before man and waiting for him in a world recently invented" (47). The start of the day here evokes the beginning of the world. But in this auroral vision, it is the woman who is born first. Aurora and the world precede everyone and everything else, instead of functioning, androcentrically, as pure mental constructs.

When Jorge arrives at the Turner gallery, he does not find Aurora there: "Eva, Aurora, no estaba, la creación se había retrasado" (68) "Eve, Aurora, wasn't there, creation had been postponed" (47). Alone, Jorge gives free rein to his imagination and conjures up an image of Aurora "casi completa, tocada, vestida, calzada con aquellas impalpables prendas espigadas en el camino y el recuerdo" (68) "almost complete, adorned from top to toe in those intangible garments [gathered] on the way and in his memory" (47). As he leans out from a balcony that looks over some nearby docks—the outside world—Jorge thinks he sees a female figure approaching whom he identifies with his beloved: "su corpiño azul, su rosado descote respondía a la imagen interior de Aurora trazada por Jorge sobre su imagen real de la víspera" (68–69) "the blue bodice, and rosy décolletage corresponded to the inner image of Aurora traced by Jorge over her real image of the evening before" (47). At that very moment, without Jorge's knowing it, Aurora enters the room: her prodigious apparition breaks the stretch of landscapes on the walls. When he turns around and sees her, he is taken by surprise:

> Porque Aurora llevaba un sombrerito obscuro de gamuza, traje gris y sin descote. . . . La creación fidelísima de la mañana y el pensamiento, la figura inventada y esperada se venía abajo de un golpe, porque Jorge la había labrado con lo conocido, con los datos de ayer, con el pasado. Y lo que tenía delante, intacta y novísima, en la virginal pureza del paraíso, tendiéndole la mano, contra costumbre sin guante, era la vida de hoy, era Aurora de verdad. (69)

Aurora was wearing a dark little chamois hat, a gray suit with no décolletage at all. . . . This morning's highly faithful creation and the thought itself, the figure invented and expected came crashing down all at once, because Jorge had fashioned it with what he knew, with yesterday's facts, with the past. And what he had before him, intact and brand-new, in the virginal purity of paradise, holding out her hand to him, strangely without gloves, was life itself today. [It was the true Aurora]. (47–48)

The sensation of a new, auroral world enters into verbal collision with the traditional images of that world ("blue," "rosy") as depicted in Jorge's imagination. The true Aurora refutes the usual signs of her identity, that is, imaginary signs. In Salinas's logic, the world must incessantly renew itself, day after day, in order that it may stand firm as what it is: different from what we think it to be. The final Aurora—woman, world—has been liberated from the self that thinks her, that turns her into an extension of his mind.[13]

This literary statement would seem to constitute the fullest possible declaration of anti-Platonism or anti-idealism, two philosophical attitudes with which Salinas has often been linked by critics.[14] This point deserves further elaboration here. When Jorge is heading toward the museum, as we noted, he comes across multiple signs that refer him to his beloved or remind him of her. The reflections of the narrator at this moment should in reality be attributed to the character, given the correction that Jorge's ideas ultimately undergo: "Porque no hallaba a Aurora de pronto, de una vez, por súbita aparición ante la vista, sino poco a poco, por lentos avances, como da el filósofo con la verdad, a fuerza de elaboraciones interiores prendidas en severos datos reales" (63) "Not that he found Aurora suddenly, all at once, or that she unexpectedly materialized before his very eyes. No, it came little by little, advancing slowly, the way the philosopher happens upon truth, by [the force of inner elaborations] based on [harsh], real data" (45). Jorge takes these real data as his departure point from which he then retreats to an inner world where truth resides. Subsequently the outline of a woman passerby resembles Aurora for him. Are the beings of this world mere shadows or reflections of pure ideas that exist somewhere beyond, as they are in Plato's conception? Or do they only exist in the mind of the one who thinks them? Neither, in fact. The final, triumphal apparition of Aurora demonstrates beyond a doubt the risks of straying too far from the data of perception. Aurora's presence—the true Aurora—corrects all philosophic idealism and, further, the dreams of all passionate lovers.[15]

The real data must therefore be renewed in a continual process so that we do not lose our bearings or substitute vain abstractions in their place. These abstractions come between the subject and the real, thereby preventing us from seeing the world before us, let alone the world that lies distant from our vision. It then becomes a matter of recovering an unknown perspective, as if the world were being viewed for the first time.[16] In a poem from *Fábula y signo* [Fable and sign] (1931), "Lo nunca igual" [Never the same], Salinas has expounded this theme:

> Si esto que ahora vuelvo a ver
> yo no lo vi nunca, no.
> Dicen que es lo mismo, que es
> lo de ayer, lo de entonces. . . .
> ¡Mentira! Si yo ya sé
> que se murió todo eso
> en otoño, al irme yo.
> Que esto ahora . . .
> es otra cosa, otra tierra
> que brotaron anteayer,
> nuevas, tiernas, recentísimas,
> tan parecidas a aquellas
> que todos me dicen: "Mira,
> aquí vivías tú, aquí." (*Poesías* 100)

> This that I now see again
> I never saw before, no.
> They say that it is the same, it is
> the same as yesterday, as then. . . .
> A lie! I already know
> that everything died
> in autumn, when I left.
> That this, now . . .
> is another thing, another land
> that sprung up before yesterday,
> new, tender, just recent,
> so much like those other ones
> that everyone tells me: "Look,
> here is where you used to live, here."

Distant from the philosophical models mentioned earlier, Salinas concurs instead with thinkers from the end of the nineteenth century, who stressed the dividing line between abstraction and sensation.[17] But Salinas, pointing to the future, also coincides with the tenets of existential phenomenology as represented by Merleau-Ponty. In opposition to the *cogito* of the idealist tradition, Merleau-Ponty situates *percipio*, which is necessarily held up by a corporeal support. Vision is always incarnated. For Merleau-Ponty, when the reflective effort intervenes, we miss the relationship with the world, that is, the opening to it. Reflection, therefore, must yield to a sort of *hyper-reflection* (*surréflexion*) that would not lose sight of the raw thing and the raw perception, that would speak not according to the law of the word meanings inherent in a given language, but would use them to express our mute contact with the things when they are not yet things said (*The Visible and the Invisible* 35–36, 38). Mark C. Taylor has extracted the consequence of this philosophic (or perhaps nonphilosophic) posture: "This ever-present, though always inaccessible, origin effectively deconstitutes (or deconstructs) the subject's constitutive or constructive acts" (68). In analogous fashion, the apparition of Aurora in Salinas's narration knocks down the reflections and imaginary constructions that Jorge had built up.

We might wonder why Jorge and Aurora arrange to meet in a museum of art. Wouldn't it be more understandable for them to choose a natural landscape, in principle a more appropriate setting for the appearance of the true Aurora? Once again Merleau-Ponty's ideas are pertinent to this discussion. He claims that art, and especially painting, reveals a layer of raw meaning, prior to all intellectual appreciation: "Essence and existence, imaginary and real, visible and invisible—a painting mixes up all our categories in laying out its oneiric universe of carnal essences, of effective likenesses, of mute meanings" ("Eye and Mind" 263). The paintings that surround the two lovers when Aurora appears would then be the artistic equivalent of a revelation of being. Aurora emerges as a new creature before Jorge's eyes, just as the world does before the surprised look of the painter (and the spectator of the picture). Merleau-Ponty sees an example of this phenomenon in Cézanne: "it is Cézanne's genius that when the over-all composition of the picture is seen globally, perspective distortions . . . contribute . . . to the impression of an emerging order, of an object in the act of appearing, organizing itself before our eyes"

("Cézanne's Doubt" 238). Understood in this fashion, the author of "True Aurora" indirectly calls out for his narration to be assimilated to painting. Literary form aspires to speak with the immediacy of pictorial form, that silent language of pure presence.

Krieger makes an interesting critical move when he refers to the biblical motif of original sin to contrast the two languages (literary and pictorial): "The movement from natural-sign to conventional-sign-representation—from pictures to writing—has been conceived as a fall, analogous to and accompanying the Fall of man in theology" (156). The truth in these words may be appreciated if we remember that Jorge imagines the union with Aurora as a kind of encounter in a paradisiac world, a "mundo recién inventado" "world recently invented." To meet this woman, a new Eve before the fall, is therefore to become integrated—or reintegrated—in a universe from which both language and thought alienate us.

Of course, the phenomenon of presence, through which the being-in-itself (object) and the being-for-itself (subject) are no longer perceived in opposition, can only take place in a precarious or incomplete manner. Yet this fact does not diminish the value of perception, according to Merleau-Ponty:

> Each perception envelops the possibility of its own replacement by another, and thus a sort of disavowal from the things. But this also means that each perception is the term of an approach, of a series of "illusions" that were not merely simple "thoughts" in the restrictive sense of Being-for-itself and the "merely thought of," but possibilities that could have been, radiations of this unique world that "there is." (*The Visible and the Invisible* 41).

There is a circumstance in Salinas's narrative that deserves attention in this respect:

> Aurora y Jorge habían convenido en citarse cada día en una sala distinta, por orden estrictamente cronológico, lo cual . . . ofrecía a Aurora un fondo cambiante y siempre bellísimo, de acentuada progresión hacia la luz y el color, haciéndola pasar por delicadas transiciones, del ambiente de rocas, torpe y seco de Giotto, a las flores de Renoir, de una concepción del mundo teatral y enfática al modo veneciano, a esta liberalidad alegre, jugosa y semidesnuda, de los paisajes con ninfas, pintados hace diez años. (67)

> Aurora and Jorge had agreed to meet every day in a different gallery, following a strictly chronological order. This . . . gave

Aurora a mutable and exquisite backdrop for advancing more and more toward light and color. Thus she would pass through delicate transitions, from the rocky settings, [clumsy] and dry, of Giotto to the flowers of Renoir, from a theatrical, solemn conception of the world in the Venetian manner to that gay, tempting and half-naked liberality of landscapes filled with nymphs, painted ten years ago. (46–47)

The meetings with Aurora, related to paintings that belong to different periods, display the quality of a progression. The history of painting is thus contemplated in Hegelian fashion as an advancement toward increasingly achieved forms, toward light and color, away from that which is clumsy, dry, or theatrical. Consequently, the lovers' reunion—one point in a series within a temporal flow—always reveals something that falls short or is left unfinished and that furthermore could never constitute a mere repetition. Rather, their encounters would be like a (more or less victorious) siege on the real, which in turn shows itself as present and absent, as visible and invisible.

It should be remarked that Aurora's appearance takes place in the gallery devoted to Turner, a romantic landscape artist. It is well known that in romanticism the landscape acquires an aesthetic importance that it had never before enjoyed. A new vision of the world is thus ushered in, which allows Jorge's vision of Aurora—also new, in its own way—to be highlighted. The woman emerges out of nowhere, with a painting as her backdrop: "Amanecer entre rocas" (69) "Dawn amongst Rocks."[18] This vision, however, should not be considered definitive, since romanticism in general and Turner in particular stand out for their heavy dramatism, quite distant from any serene or calming effect.[19] And, in addition, the narrator himself clearly establishes that this artistic period must be substituted by others that follow it, such as impressionism, with its prodigious display of light and color, and paintings of more recent times that hang in the museum.

The tension that characterizes Salinas's poetry may be felt in his prose as well: the unflagging impulse that propels the lovers toward increasingly distant heights, or, rather, toward levels that are more fully real, more revealing of authentic being. The chronological progression of paintings in the museum, then, is equivalent to the internal force that moves El Greco's figures—evoked in the previous narration—and places them, in the words of D'Ors, under the domain of "the forms that fly." Painting, in a certain sense, cancels itself out, just as in the museum each picture, representative of an epoch, annuls an earlier picture or epoch in order to express a new discovery, to instantiate a new world before the spectator's eyes. This is an infinite progression, whereas in El Greco we see a progression toward infinity. Salinas encompasses both impulses, as may be seen in these lines from *La voz a ti debida*:

> Y al otro lado ya
> de cómputos, de sinos,
> entregarnos a ciegas
> —¡exceso, qué penúltimo!—
> a un gran fondo azaroso
> que irresistiblemente
> está
> cantándonos a gritos
> fúlgidos de futuro:
> "Eso no es nada, aún.
> Buscaos bien, hay más." (*Poesías* 153)

> And now beyond
> computations, beyond destinies,
> let us surrender blindly—
> next-to-the-last excess!—
> to a great perilous depth
> irresistibly
> singing to us
> in a loud voice
> and bright with the future:
> "That's nothing, so far.
> Search well within yourselves, there's more." (*To Live* 51)

The following lines from the same collection also illustrate this point: "Y no te acabaré / por mucho que te pida / a ti, infinita, no" (*Poesías* 172–73) "And I will not exhaust you / no matter how much I ask of you, / you, infinite one, no." Infinitude, however, does not remove the woman from this world but instead beckons toward the lover and incites his perpetual striving.

The similarities between Salinas and Merleau-Ponty stand out once more in the following words of the French philosopher:

> What I can conclude from these disillusions or deceptions, therefore, is that perhaps "reality" does not belong definitively to any particular perception, that in this sense it lies *always further on*;

but this does not authorize me to break or to ignore the bond that joins them one after the other to the real, . . . so that . . . the "probable" evokes a definitive experience of the "real" whose accomplishment is only deferred. (*The Visible and the Invisible* 40–41)[20]

In parallel fashion, the poet awaits the day on which the probable lover becomes real, that is, realizes herself by bringing her possibilities to life, by making the invisible visible: "Y que a mi amor entonces, le conteste / la nueva criatura que tú eras" (*La voz a ti debida, Poesías* 176) "And let my love be answered / by the new-born person you were" (*To Live* 109). That which is new is what one already *was* (in potentiality).

Woven throughout all of these narrations, then, is an essential theme: desire as a constitutive dimension of the subject, whether that subject is the protagonist or the narrator, or is instead represented through a tree that is likened to El Greco's portrait of an unknown man. That desire, which is rooted in the individual's solitude, aspires toward the encounter with another being, with the world. The search for love corresponds exactly to the poetic search for a form that would make language—an instrument of separation—into its exact opposite, a means of salvation. Unlike written language, pictorial language seduces the spectator through its mute, immediate signification, the sudden outburst of reality that the senses capture before the intellect comes fully into play. In short, this process is one of seeing through new eyes, and there is no one more endowed than a painter with the ability to reach that previously unattained vision.[21] Salinas rejects an idealistic stance in which the beloved would be viewed as a mere projection of the *I*; he therefore affirms the subjectivity of the other, even if that recognition stands in the way of the desire for fusion. In Salinas's version of paradise, Eve precedes Adam: she does not derive from him or depend on him. Ultimately, the ideal is not simply to fuse with the Other or that which is other (something only possible in the imaginary), no matter how attractive that may be, but rather to be witness to a continual recreation, an incessant unfolding of the invisible (or potential) made visible. This infinite progression lends a pervasive sense of dynamism to all of Salinas's works, but it also exasperates whatever pleasure is achieved, since it is always a prelude to pleasure of even greater magnitude.

# CHAPTER 5

# Male (De)Signs:
# Art and Society in Luis Martín-Santos

Martín-Santos's *Tiempo de silencio* [Time of silence], reprinted continuously and translated into many languages since its publication in 1962, holds an undisputable place of prestige in the history of twentieth-century Spanish literature. This novel, with its astonishing stylistic renovations, definitively changed the course of Spanish fiction writing, which was heavily dominated by the social realism that had set in after the Spanish civil war (1936–1939). This analysis seeks to add to the extensive bibliography on *Time of Silence* by foregrounding the relations between visual and verbal arts, an approach that casts new light on this novel—incidentally, the only one ever completed by the psychiatrist-author, who perished in a car accident at thirty-nine.

*Time of Silence* contains as its visual center a most powerful image: Goya's *El Aquelarre* [The witches' sabbath] (Fig. 2), which we also adduced to explicate Julián's vision in *The House of Ulloa*. In Pardo Bazán's novel this pictorial model was merely implied, whereas in Martín-Santos the visual referent and its author are named explicitly. In addition, Martín-Santos—like Francisco Ayala in a story that we will analyze in the next chapter—performs a double reading of Goya's painting, a process that may serve as a structural base for the exposition of the plot lines in *Time of Silence*. As Goya's visual contest is transferred onto the literary creation, then, the facts of the novel may also be read in a double light depending on which of two forces is foregrounded—patriarchal or matriarchal. Although they are not overtly identified in the novel, several other works by Goya (most notably some of his *Caprichos*) undergird Martín-Santos's descriptions, and these pictorial images contribute to the satirical, grotesque tone of the author's lucid and merciless vision of Spain. In this fashion, a continuity or dialogue between painter and writer emerges: both function as supreme analysts of their nation, subjected as they were to similar obsessions and atrocious experiences.

The protagonist of *Time of Silence*, Pedro, a young laboratory researcher, views a reproduction of *El Aquelarre* at his friend Matías's house: "*Scène de sorcellerie: Le Grand Bouc—1798— (H.—0,43; L.—0,30. Madrid. Musée Lázaro. Le grand bouc, el gran macho, el gran buco, el buco émissaire, el capro hispánico bien desarrollado. El cabrón expiatorio. ¡No! El gran buco en el esplendor de su gloria, en la prepotencia del dominio, en el usufructo de la adoración centrípeta*" (*Tiempo* 155) "*Scène de sorcellerie: Le Grand Bouc—1798—(H. 43 cm.; L. 30 cm.). Madrid. Musée Lazaro.* The great goat, the great male, the great buck, the scapegoat, the [well developed] Hispanic billy-goat. The . . . expiatory goat? No! The great buck in the splendor of his glory, in the supreme power of his dominion, the center of [centripetal] adoration" (*Time* 127). The narrator's comments apply most remarkably to Goya's famous painting, in which a scene of the witches' sabbath—women encircling the he-goat-devil—turns into a scene of seduction.[1]

Further ahead in the novel, the figure of the he-goat is superimposed onto that of a lecturer who seduces a group of distinguished women with his words. In turn, the lecturer, who is called "el gran matón de la metafísica" (157) "the great bully of metaphysics" (128), may be readily associated with the Spanish philosopher José Ortega y Gasset (though he is never named). Pedro and Matías attend this lecture and the reception following it in the speaker's honor given by Matías's mother.[2] The equivalence between the philosopher and Goya's he-goat would seem to testify to the Marxist notion that all ideology is really iconology. Like a camera obscura (the model that Marx utilized), the mind creates images: that is, concepts rooted in images. Or, in W. J. T. Mitchell's words referring to Marx's ideas: "the camera obscura of ideology produces the 'idols of the mind'" (*Iconology* 162–63). The women who surround the savage *macho*, as well as the female audience who hears the aristocratic thinker, feel compelled to bow down before these idols. The power exerted by the philosopher and his ideas is based on a primitive model: ideas seduce not only because they are expressed with charming eloquence, but also because they have become fetishes, and, as such, objects of idolatry. If the he-goat does not merit the cult that is paid to him, neither does his successor, the stiff, modern philosopher, who stands on the "escenario del cine" (160–61) "movie stage," from which he delivers his lecture while in the basement of the same building a "baile de criadas" (160) "[maids'] dance" (131) is taking place.

But Ortega is not the only figure onto whom the image of the "great male" is projected. Rather, it would seem that this "capro hispánico" "Hispanic billy-goat" represents a collectivity in which Pedro is prominently included. A succinct review of the events in Pedro's life is in order here. The previous night—a Saturday, evocative of a witches' sabbath—Pedro was involved in two decisive acts: the defloration of Dorita and the abortion performed on Florita. Called too late to the scene, when Florita's abortion has already been induced, Pedro immediately grasps the futility of his intervention: "tal hurgar cuidadoso con la cucharilla . . . carecía de toda utilidad" (134) "all this . . . careful scraping with the spoon . . . was completely useless" (110). He persists, however, as if the body of this woman aroused in him instincts more sadistic than benevolent: "La muerta no sufría y se dejaba con docilidad imponer unas maniobras que ya no tenían que ver con ella. . . . Pedro . . . continuaba automáticamente el raspado y una vez concluido, taponaba con la gasa limpia destinada a los ratones" (135) "The dead girl no longer suffered, and lay there tamely submitting to manipulations that [did not concern her. Pedro] continued automatically with the scraping [and, when it was completed,] he applied some clean gauze intended for the mice" (111). As for Dorita, Pedro is drunk when he has sexual relations with her, and one may assume that he acts with violence, as his subsequent fantasies reveal: "Como el asesino con su cuchillo del que caen gotas de sangre. Como el matador con el estoque que ha clavado una vez pero que ha de seguir clavando en una pesadilla una vez y otra vez, toda la vida, . . . en el toro que no muere" (119–20) "Like a murderer [with his knife that drips blood]. Like the bullfighter who has [thrust his sword once], but has to keep on [thrusting it] again and again in a nightmare, . . . all his life, . . . into the bull, which doesn't die" (98). Dorita, then, is equated with a bull (a victim), whereas Florita is compared to one of Pedro's laboratory rats.

It should also be noted that the he-goat receives aborted fetuses from women—"cuerpos abortados yacen resucitacalcitrantes" (157) "aborted bodies lie [resuscitacalcitrant]" (129)—and that Pedro takes part in an abortion. For the narrator, the "aborted bodies" or "niños muertos" (159) "dead children"

(131), visible in *El Aquelarre*, would be a result of the harsh conditions of Spanish life, of the misery that affects the people and that the elite Spanish philosopher chooses to ignore or to hide beneath the captivating beauty of his esteemed prose: "aficionas a la gente bien tiernamente a la filosofía, . . . con tan sublime estilo, . . . que te perdonarán los niños muertos que no dijeras de qué estaban muriendo" (159) "you [tenderly] win people over to philosophy, . . . in such sublime style . . . that the dead children will forgive you for not saying why they were dying" (131). Yet how can we ignore that other abortion, so central to the novel, in which the intellectual master has no part to play?

There is no doubt that Pedro's conduct with regard to Dorita and Florita, who are frequently confused in his mind, floods him with remorseful feelings; yet he simultaneously displays boastful arrogance over these same acts. We could note his "alegría de varón triunfante" "joy of the triumphant male," and the "kikirikí" "cock-a-doodle-doo" (*Tiempo* 119), which he lets out when alone in his room after having had sex with Dorita. Similarly, at the reception given following the lecture, Pedro tries to make himself look important by evoking his participation (a dismal failure, of course) with respect to Florita: "Ayer noche he estado operando" (172) "I had to operate last night" (142). The "operation" would allow him access to that distinguished world that both repels him and attracts him, a world where the lecturer, the "great male" or "bully," is the apple bearer in place of a female-Eve: "levantará su otra pezuña, la derecha, y en ella depositará una manzana" (156) "He will lift up his other hoof, the right, and he will take an apple in it" (128). Despite appearances to the contrary, lust is not embodied here in "una mujer desnuda con una manzana en la mano" (170) "a naked woman with an apple in her hand" (140), as another passage in the novel states, but, significantly, in a man.

Pedro's lustful attitude emerges with regard to the hostess, Matías's mother: "Pedro la vigila con mirada posesiva; le parece que tiene ya derechos sobre esta mujer" (172) "Pedro looked at her possessively. He felt that he had some rights over this woman" (142). But at that moment he is overcome once more with guilt feelings: "el cadáver de Florita se presenta en medio del salón" (173) "Florita's [dead] body appeared in the room" (142). Pedro experiences a vision of Florita (meshed in part with Dorita) in which her blood, shed during the horrifying "operation" that he had boasted about, invades the room: "Obstinadamente desnuda deja que su sangre corretee caprichosamente entre los muebles y entre las piernas de los desmesurados contertulios. Sin duda es uno de los objetos que éstos no deben ver, pues aunque pasen a su lado o bien lo pisen distraídamente, no lo advierten" (173) "Obstinately naked, its blood flowed capriciously between the furniture and the legs of the [inordinate] guests. It was doubtless one of the things they were taught to ignore, for [even if] they walked right by it or absentmindedly stepped on it . . . they did not notice it" (142). What society does not see—or refuses to see—is the sacrifice of the woman, represented here by Florita. And "society" here does not simply refer to the high society, "la très haute" (162) to which Pedro aspires. After the abortion, Muecas and Amador try to "desembarazarse del cadáver de Florita (al mismo tiempo que cadáver cuerpo de delito)" (163) "[get rid of] Florita's body (corpse and corpus delicti)" (134). Specifically, Muecas, Florita's father, is the person who caused the abortion to take place, according to his other daughter (139; 114). And Muecas is also responsible for Florita's pregnancy—"incestuoso padre" (186) "incestuous father" (152), he is labeled—in addition to having assaulted his wife: "el mismo hombre que la violó con dolor" (247) "the man who had violated her in pain" (205), as she would later recall.

Along with Goya's he-goat, then, appears the shadow of another *macho*, one who not only receives dead or aborted children as offerings, but who actually procures them. Projected onto the most humble Muecas is the ancient figure of Agamemnon sacrificing his daughter and, even beyond, the life that she carries in her womb. Pedro's reflections at the end of the novel, after the death of Dorita (clearly now the second victim), allude to woman's significance as sacrificial offering on the altar of a victorious patriarchy: "Cuidadosamente estudió el llamado Goethe las motivaciones del sacrificio de Ifigenia y habiéndolas perfectamente comprendido, diose con afán a ponerlas en tragedia" (285) "Goethe studied carefully the motives for Iphigenia's sacrifice, and having understood them he set to work to turn them into a tragedy" (238). Martín-Santos, the psychiatrist by profession, could also be said to have understood the motives behind this myth, which he displays in the form of a tragic novel.

By means of the domination that Muecas asserts over his wife and daughters, then, a parallel is established between him and the lecturer or he-goat: "Porque el Muecas se sentía, sin saber bien lo que significaba esta palabra, patriarca bíblico al que todas aquellas mujeres pertenecían" (66) "Because Muecas, without knowing what the word meant, felt that he was a Biblical patriarch to whom all these women belonged" (53). Patriarchal society manifests itself as much in refined environments as it does in the slums of Madrid, where Muecas acts like lord and master. Another *macho* in the novel is Dorita's deceased grandfather, whose widow remembers the physical violence he showed toward her (22–23; 17). Finally, the *machista* attitude appears in the extreme in Cartucho who, like Muecas, considers Florita to be his exclusive possession: he blames Pedro for her pregnancy and lethal abortion, and avenges her death by killing Dorita, Pedro's girlfriend. It should also be noted that during the autopsy performed on Florita, the victimization of her body is perpetuated, as her mother's outraged cry reveals: "Que me la están rajando toda, la pobre, que me la están abriendo" (239) "They're opening her up and cutting her all to pieces" (197–98). Dorita will not escape the fate of an autopsy either, as Pedro's final meditation indicates; he also censures the practice, though with less anger: "también a esta su autopsia. ¿Qué querrán saber? . . . No saben para qué las abren: un mito, una superstición, una recolección de cadáveres" (287). "[This one also got her autopsy.] What did they want to know? . . . [They] don't know why they open them up. A myth, a superstition, a [harvesting] of corpses" (240).[3]

As we have seen, the figure of the he-goat encompasses a series of men, even though the only explicit association is with the lecturer.[4] Further, these men belong to very different social strata: high society (the lecturer), the bourgeoisie (Pedro), the marginal classes (Muecas and Cartucho). There are vast divergences among these individuals according to their education and economic power, something that the novel highlights, but these divergences do not preclude a shared mind-set in regard to sexuality.[5] The figure of the he-goat thus presides over widely diverse worlds: from Matías's house, where Pedro views *El Aquelarre*, to the slum residences where acts of incest and a botched abortion take place, to the lower-middle-class pension, where a drunk man deflowers a woman and causes her to bleed copiously.

How can we account for these events? Muecas's domination over his wife and daughters would seem to lend support to Freud's contention that the father holds power over the primitive hoard, of which the shacks would be an appropriate representation. There is a continuous line, traversed without difficulty by the social classes, extending from this lowly world of the slums to the selective environment that serves as the setting for the lecturer's eloquent performance. All social classes coincide in their enactment of the same phenomenon: male supremacy. But do the so-called advanced stages of human social organization reproduce the more primitive, supposedly natural, modalities? Or should we say instead that the members of oppressed groups adopt or replicate the mentality of the ruling class on their own level? In the microcosm of the slums, therefore, patriarchal domination as embodied by Muecas functions as the reflection of the social oppression suffered by him and his peers.[6]

True, in Pedro's case, the woman apparently is not taken against her will, but has instead consented to relations with him, yet she has also been offered to him by her mother and grandmother. In this light, one could say that Pedro has fallen into a trap that these women have set for him. The grandmother, an old *celestina* or go-between who has prostituted her own daughter, now attempts to take advantage of the granddaughter, not precisely by prostituting her, but by marrying her off to Pedro, one of the boarders. Goya's pictorial model—implicit this time—once again comes to mind here as fundamental to the novel's content and tone. The theme of prostitution and procuring is one that Goya treated on many occasions. For example, in *Capricho 68*, *¡Linda maestra!* [Pretty teacher], two women, an old lady and a young girl, are shown flying on a broomstick. The meaning of this image is made clear by the old woman's pose as a procuress, similar to the figure in another work by Goya, *Maja y celestina en un balcón* [Maja and celestina on a balcony], Col. Bartolomé March Servera (Pérez Sánchez and Sayre 159), as well as by the sexual connotations ascribed to the act of flying and to the broomstick. This is the explanation found in the manuscript in the Biblioteca Nacional, Madrid: "Las Viejas quitan la escoba de las manos á las que tienen buenos vigotes; las dan lecciones de volar por el mundo; metiendolas por primera vez, aunque sea un palo de escoba entre las piernas" "Old women snatch the broom from the hands of those who have abundant pubic hair [literally, good mustaches]; they give them lessons on flying around [having orgasms]; penetrating them for the first time, even if it be a broomstick between the legs" (Pérez Sánchez and Sayre 126). Even in the detail of the mustache, the relationship between these two women corresponds to the one that exists in *Time of Silence* between the grandmother and the daughter she has prostituted. The old woman muses: "Ella [Dorita] ha salido más finolis que mi propia hija, tan a lo mi marido hecha, con su bigote oscuro y esos brazos fuertes" (23) "She [Dorita] has turned out more delicate than my own daughter, who is like my husband, with her dark mustache, [and] her strong arms" (17).

Another relevant example may be found in *Capricho 31, Ruega por ella* [She prays for her] (Fig. 12). Goya's engraving displays close affinities with the boarding house in *Time of Silence*, where the classic pair (old and young women) is substituted with a trio. A passage from the novel confirms the links: "[Dorita] se balanceaba sin tregua permitiendo que, quien atentamente la observara, pudiera comprobar la eficacia motriz de muy limitadas contracciones de los músculos largos de su suave pantorrilla" (45) "[Dorita] rocked backwards and forward endlessly, revealing to those who cared to watch the small muscular contractions of her broad, smooth calves" (35). In *Capricho 31*, we should also note the long, loose hair of the young woman: "the hair let down, and the comb are . . . symbols of Lust" (Lorenzo de Márquez lxxxv). This motif is similarly present in the novel: "su cabellera [de Dorita]—más abundante que lo fuera nunca la de sus dos madres—colgaba en cascadas ondulantes" (45) "her hair, more abundant than the hair of [her two mothers] had ever been, fell in cascades of golden waves" (35).

Such a charged atmosphere does not seem to bode well for the innocent researcher, Pedro. A contemporaneous explanation of *Capricho 15, Bellos consejos* [Pretty teachings] is most applicable here: "Los consejos son dignos de quien los da. Lo peor es que la señorita va a seguirlos al pie de la letra. ¡Desdichado del que se acerque!" "The advice is worthy of [the one] who gives it. The worst of it is that the girl will follow it absolutely to the letter. Unhappy the man who gets anywhere near her" (Goya, *Caprichos*). A warning like this emanates from a collective way of thinking, which Edith Helman articulates: "In other *Caprichos* of a similar setting, the victims are not the prostitutes, but rather the clients; this is the traditional point of view from Ovid in his *Ars amatoria* onward" (83). The narrator of *Time of Silence* prolongs Goya's sarcasm, applying it to the underworld of Spanish postwar society.[7] He makes this harsh commentary on the female triad in

Figure 12
Goya, *Los Caprichos, plate 32: She prays for her.*

the boarding house: "tres vulgares y derrotadas mujeres" (46) "three vulgar and [defeated] women" (36). Yet prostitution or the sale of female bodies forms part of the abuses of a male dominated society. Further ahead in the novel this other perspective is communicated with equal attention to the two parties involved: "sólo sobre el telón de fondo de la vileza de un hombre, la impudicia femenina despide sus más detonantes destellos" (276) "only against the background of man's vileness does feminine shamelessness detonate its most glittering sparkles" (230).

In the final instance, the "great male" once again rears his head. His virtual presence in the universe of the boarding house is demanded by the patriarchal imperative, and the man destined to incarnate this presence is none other than Pedro. Thus, on one occasion, the young researcher exclaims before the three women: "No me interesan más luchas que las de los virus con los anticuerpos" (46) "The only battles I'm interested in are those between the virus and the antibodies" (37). Such a proclamation of knowledge is met with the answer that, at least unconsciously, it seeks: "Palabras cabalísticas. . . . Pues, aunque ninguna de las tres mujeres pudieran entenderlas, las recibían sonrientes y alegres como demostración viva de la superior esencia de que su joven caballero estaba conferido" (47) "Cabalistic words . . . , and even though not one of the three women understood what he was talking about, they smiled happily and took it as clear evidence of their young man's superior knowledge" (37). On this point Pedro is not essentially different from the philosopher, who with his dazzling rhetoric seduces the dumbstruck women raptly listening to him. Once again, it is abundantly clear that the philosopher is not the only one identified with the he-goat. Rather, the figure of Ortega functions more like a "buco émissaire" or "scapegoat" of the crimes committed by others. It is significant in this respect that the title of Goya's painting (*El Aquelarre*) is given in French and in a form (*Le Grand Bouc*) that links to another term, *bouc émissaire*, which is absent in the title and meaning of Goya's work.[8]

It would therefore be inappropriate to consider Pedro a simple "victim," as he is called at one point in the novel (*Tiempo* 46). More exactly, this role belongs to Dorita. The following lines, though filled with rancor against women, allude to this victimization: "Dispuestas estaban las tres [abuela, madre e hija] a ofrecer el holocausto con distintos grados de premeditación y de cinismo" (44) "The three of them [grandmother, mother, and daughter] were willing to offer the sacrifice with differing degrees of premeditation and cynicism." If we keep in mind Dorita's final destiny—her horrible death and the appalling acts performed on her cadaver—, a destiny she fully shares with Florita, then the term "holocausto" "sacrifice" as applied to women is neither ironic nor excessive.

Following Florita's abortion, Pedro, with the assistance of his friend Matías, finds refuge in a brothel. Night has closed in: "Cuando la grata y envolvedora tiniebla hubo con el nuevo crepúsculo restablecido el predominio de la verdad . . . , cuando Doña Luisa tomó de nuevo el aspecto providente y confidencial de gran madre fálica . . . , Matías conoció que era llegada la hora de la confesión de boca" (185) "When the pleasant veil of twilight had dropped . . . so that truth . . . once more predominated . . . ; when Doña Luisa had once more taken on the providential and confidential aspect of great phallic mother . . . , Matías knew that the time for confession had come" (151–52). The narrator adopts his usual ironic stance; he expresses himself in a way that is closely aligned with Pedro's intimate thoughts and feelings. Pedro would be the one who considers the night to be hospitable to truth, and thus he clings to night rather than plunge himself into that diurnal vertigo full of deceptions and dangers from which he seeks escape. Unable to face up to life, Pedro regresses to this other dark, maternal world—womb, rather—, represented by Doña Luisa, the owner of the brothel, the "great phallic mother." This would be the primitive or archaic mother of early childhood, the one who exists before the consciousness of sexual division and gender differences sets in. Pedro's conduct must thereby be understood as an enactment of unconscious forces, because in terms of pure logic it makes little sense.

Yet it is significant that the maternal *imago* is incarnated in a madam, a prostitute. In this guise she represents the bad mother, the castrating woman (another acceptable meaning of the term phallic mother).[9] In keeping with this negative image, the word "avernos" (186) "infernal abyss" is employed in reference to the brothel. The hoped-for paradise (the place safe from evil) is thus transformed into its opposite, hell. And the bad mother here naturally becomes a seductive mother: Doña Luisa feels an attraction to Pedro as she strokes his hand. This touch repels Pedro: "La mano de Pedro fina, pero no tanto como hubiera sido si él fuera un hábil quirurgo dispuesto a seguir los derroteros triunfales que la otra vieja (la de la pensión) soñaba, transmitió por sus nervios sensitivos hasta el alma encogida del muchacho una clara repulsión" (186) "[Pedro's delicate hand, but not as delicate] as it would have been if he were a skillful surgeon [willing to follow the triumphant path that the other old lady (from the boarding house) dreamed of, transmitted a clear] shudder of revulsion through [its] sensitive nerves to [the young man's timid soul]" (153). It is obvious that Pedro is infantilized: he regresses to a primitive world that distances him from the lofty destinies ("hábil quirurgo," "skillful surgeon") that Dorita's grandmother had fantasized for him. For Doña Luisa, Pedro would be at most an able abortionist in defiance of Spanish law at that time. Doña Luisa also imagines Pedro as a part or extension of herself that she could call upon at will to provide the abortion services she requires: "Pero no se atrevió todavía a hacer valer el poder que pudiera haber alcanzado sobre tan empecatadas manos, sino que se contentó con gozar de ellas por un instante en su estado de pura posibilidad no manifestada, con la sensualidad huraña del asesino a sueldo que acaricia un revólver reluciente que todavía no ha empezado a disparar" (187) "But she did not yet dare to [make use of the power that she could have attained over such damned hands, and instead] was satisfied . . . to savor them [for a moment] in their unrevealed potentiality with the same sensual aloofness of the paid killer who fondles a [gleaming] revolver [that he has not yet begun to fire]" (153). We do not see any evidence here of the preoedipal or prenatal fusion that Pedro seeks; this fusion is instead a most threatening one, since it concerns a "paid killer" who turns Pedro into a "revolver." In Doña Luisa's mind, Pedro, in addition to being an object of desire, is also a possible criminal in the future (not only in the past). Pedro has ended up in a snare, a place where he cannot find escape from the worldly risks he flees. Doña Luisa attempts to confirm him in his role of illegal abortionist, that is, the very role he so desperately wishes to cast off.

A pictorial image that suggests the horrifying atmosphere in which the unfortunate man is trapped may be brought to bear: Goya's well-known *Capricho 43, El sueño de la razón produce monstruos* [The sleep of reason produces monsters] (Fig. 13). Pedro, by taking refuge in a brothel, acts like a person devoid of the light of reason. The darkness that enshrouds both Pedro and the sleeping figure in Goya's *Capricho* joins the two individuals. The motif of the black cat also turns up both in the engraving and in the novel: "A cat has joined those night-thriving creatures. . . . Traditionally allied through its color to the Prince of Darkness, it stares from the print. . . . [T]he cat was also associated with Sloth and Lust" (Pérez Sánchez and Sayre 115, 117). "Doña Luisa se levantó con trabajo, haciendo saltar al suelo el gato negro" (184) "She [Doña Luisa] got up slowly and the black cat had to jump

Figure 13
Goya, *Los Caprichos, plate 43: The sleep of reason produces monsters.*

down" (151). But in the old lady's mind it is Pedro, rather than the black cat, who is associated with the Prince of Darkness, owing to his "demoníaca belleza" (186) "demoniac beauty" (153). From the enlightened perspective of Goya and Martín-Santos, then, truth would not reside in shadows or in dreams.[10]

*Capricho 71, Si amanece, nos vamos* [When day breaks we will be off], is also of interest to our discussion. Here is the explanation given in the Ayala manuscript: "Conferencian de noche las alcahuetas sobre el modo de echarse criaturas al cinto" "The old hags confer at night about how to gorge themselves on creatures" (Helman 239). Alfonso E. Pérez Sánchez comments: "Dawn . . . banishes the sprites, witches, and hobgoblins, whose domains are darkness and night. The dawn was the luminous splendor of science, of knowledge, of revealed and triumphant truth, following the kind of permanent night that seemed to be Spain's recent history" (xxiii). As we may note, the historical context that Goya invokes resembles Martín-Santos's view of Spain as obscurantist, which sets off an identical reaction in both creators: bitter censure and the need to implant urgent reforms. Yet Goya also feels what Nigel Glendinning calls "an enlightened fascination with the irrational: the dark side of the human spirit" (lxxi); Martín-Santos, psychiatrist-novelist, experiences the same fascination.[11] Through the figure of Pedro, representative of the Spanish male, the novelist convenes the phantoms of his character and his people (including himself as implied author) in order to subject them to an analysis, or psychoanalysis, of the most implacable kind.[12]

At the brothel, Pedro imagines himself as a fetus: "le parecía que había dejado de respirar y que quedaba inmóvil en aquel espacio sumergido en que todo (el alimento, el aire, el amor, la respiración) se lo introducían por un tubo de goma mientras que él permanecía inerte" (187) "[it seemed to him that] he had stopped breathing and was standing motionless in [that submerged space in which] everything—food, air, love, and breath—was being poured into him through a rubber tube [while he remained inert]" (153). Another work by Goya seems most pertinent here: one of his *Sueños* [Dreams] from the Prado Museum, entitled *La enfermedad de la razón* [The Illness of reason]. Eleanor A. Sayre describes it in these terms: "A man in shirt sleeves and three wenches, two of them unmistakably whores, tend a pair of immobile nobles. . . . They seem to see nothing, and certainly hear nothing. . . . Their helplessness is emphasized in that one noble is propped up by a cushion, and the other has to be held upright so that the pair may be fed with spoons" (Pérez Sánchez and Sayre 119). Insofar as it is a critique of nobility, the situation depicted in the *Sueño* does not correspond exactly to the scene in which Pedro finds himself, but there is a like quality in his captivity within the atmosphere of the brothel. Matías (if not Pedro) may nevertheless be identified with the noblemen of Goya's painting, as a specimen of the leisure classes; and it is Matías, we should remember, who, thanks to his connections to Doña Luisa, procures refuge for Pedro in that underworld of the brothel and accompanies him during this scene.

At this point the narrative takes a turn. The perverse Doña Luisa momentarily resembles a good mother—the ultimate constant object of human desire, according to Freud:

> Doña Luisa hizo entonces el gesto tanto tiempo esperado, el gran gesto hacia el que había estado caminando durante toda la noche y desde hacía tantos años; rodeó con su robusto brazo el cuello del muchacho e hizo caer la cabeza en su regazo sobre los blandos almohadones de los pechos, apretando la nariz contra la piel arrugada de su cuello, haciéndole respirar la mezcla residual de los perfumes que ella había echado sobre su carne cuando a los quince años la vendía ya profesionalmente, cuando se exhibía—torpe tonadillera—en los barracones libres de la república, cuando—querida de un concejal—ocultaba su papo bajo suntuosos renards argentés. (187–88)

> Doña Luisa then made the long-awaited gesture, the great gesture toward [which he had been walking] throughout the night and for so many years. She placed her robust [arm] around the young man's neck and pulled his head down over the soft cushions of her breast, pressing his nose against the wrinkled skin of her neck so that he could smell the residual mixture of the perfumes with which she had smothered her flesh from the time she had begun to sell that flesh professionally at the age of fifteen, when she [appeared] as a third-rate singer in the [free burlesque theatres] of the Republic—when, as the mistress of a [councilman], she had hidden her double chin beneath sumptuous [renards argentés]. (153–54)

Irony once again corrodes this passage. The solemn tone ("great gesture toward which he had been walking throughout the night and for so many years") falls apart when the person who incarnates that great gesture is none other than a wrinkled old prostitute. The Great Mother turns into a character from an *esperpento*, that farce-like literary modality named by Valle-Inclán.[13] Nevertheless, when the narrator evokes the young age (fifteen) at which this woman had to make a life for herself, a reader might experience a compassionate response. Doña Luisa may thus be seen as a victim, more precisely, a victim exploited by male society, whether this be Republican or dictatorial (governments change, but prostitution and the social order that sustains it continue). And we might also note that the authorities, the representatives of the people symbolized by that anonymous councilman, are directly implicated in the trafficking in human flesh.

Prison, another symbolic maternal womb where he later winds up, also serves to shelter Pedro from the risks of an active life: "Aquí se está bien. Vuelto a la cuna. A un vientre. Aquí protegido" (219) "It's all right here. Back to the cradle. To [a] womb. Protected [here]" (181). Sexuality and marriage are key elements of that dreaded life: "Fuera de tantas preocupaciones, fuera del dinero que tenía que ganar, fuera de la mujer con la que me tenía que casar" (220) "Away from all worries. Away from the need to earn money. Away from the woman I would have had to marry" (181). This is not the first time that this particular fear manifests itself, a fear related to the fantasy of woman as a devouring or destructive being. The atmosphere at the boarding house as viewed in light of Goya's *Caprichos* hinted at that constant menace. Pedro's thoughts after having had sexual relations with Dorita are quite revealing in this respect: "allá el torero ha de seguir clavando su estoque en el toro que no muere, que crece, crece y que revienta y lo envuelve en toda su materia negra como un pulpo amoroso ya sin cuernos, amor mío, amor mío" (120) "the bullfighter has to stand there thrusting his sword into the bull, which doesn't die, but grows and grows till it bursts and covers everything with its black [matter, like an amorous octopus], without horns now, my love, my love" (98). The fantasy of the loving, enveloping woman-bull-octopus is met with another fantasy, which functions as a counterattack: the bullfighter is obliged to thrust his sword into the bull over and over again. Male violence would thus be a reaction to the imaginary aggression displayed by the woman. There is considerable overlap between this fantasy and one formulated by Matías, Pedro's intimate friend (and in a sense his double). Matías is reflecting on the scene he witnessed at his house when Dorita came to tell Pedro of the danger he was in: "Vagina dentata, castración afectiva, emasculación posesiva, mío, mío, tú eres mío, ¿quién quiere quitármelo?" (198), "The toothed vagina, affective castration, possessive emasculation. Mine, mine, you're mine. Who wants to take him away from me?" (163).[14]

Dorita is presented in the novel as a link in a chain that includes the two previous generations. In this way, Dorita is inseparable from her mother and grandmother, who both also experience attraction to Pedro and vicariously live out the youngest woman's love relationship.[15] True, he could separate Dorita from the two older women (by running away with her, for example), or he could simply abandon her. If he does not, and instead feels forced to marry Dorita, it is because of the pressure—apparently impossible for him to resist—exerted by the mother and grandmother. Pedro is thus configured as the prey of a matriarchal world: possessed and not possessing, we could say, with words spoken by his friend Matías: "¿Cuándo dejarás de buscar lo que buscas y te entregarás a las jóvenes apenas núbiles y . . . al fin sólo veas en Eva, la limpia libre de todo parto, poseída y no ya poseedora?" (199) "When will you abandon what you are seeking and [give yourself] to adolescent girls . . . and . . . finally see in Eve only the pure female, free from all childbirth, possessed and no longer possessing?" (163). Matías is referring to his own problems, but his words, by extension, are entirely applicable to Pedro.

The reaction against matriarchal domination is embodied precisely in the he-goat, the "great male" of Goya's painting. He truly possesses and is not possessed by the women (maternal figures) who kneel down in a circle around his upright figure. The fascination that this creature holds over Pedro (and Matías) is quite understandable: "El gran macho cabrío en el aquelarre, rodeado de sus mujeres embobadas, las recibía con un gesto altivo, con la enhiesta cabeza dominando no sólo a cada una de las mujeres tiradas por el suelo, sino también a cuantos inermes espectadores se atrevieran a fijar en el cuadro su mirada" (155) "The great billy-goat . . . in a witches' Sabbath, surrounded by his bewitched women, [received them with a haughty gesture], the raised head dominating not only the women [lying] on the ground but also any unwary spectator who dared to look at the picture" (127). Nevertheless, Pedro is identified not only with the he-goat. In his fantasies of "retroceso intrafetal" (199) "intrafetal regression" (163) he also is compared with the dead children who are offered up in sacrifice. Pedro, then, becomes annihilated as an individual in this imaginary return to the womb. He oscillates between two poles: in order to avoid being destroyed he must arm himself with the power to destroy. He defeats the woman-bull in his imaginary guise as bullfighter, or he cruelly wields a surgical instrument intended for laboratory animals: "los materiales necesarios que, aptos para perros y otros animales superiores fámulos de la ciencia, habían de servir también . . . para la indigna estirpe del siempre-humillado Muecas" (126) "the necessary materials which, since they were fit to be used on dogs and other superior animal servants of science, could also . . . be used for the unworthy off-spring of the [ever-humiliated] Muecas" (103). Pedro faces up to the witches (bad mothers) by turning himself into an abortionist— a he-goat to whom aborted fetuses are offered—so that he can prevent being aborted, or being the victim of sacrifice himself. Here are the reflections of a narrator indistinguishable from Pedro concerning *El Aquelarre*: "¿Y por qué ahorcados los que de tal guisa penden? ¿Y con qué ahorcados? ¿Acaso con el cordón vivificante por donde sangre venosa aerificada y sangre arterial carbonificada burbujeantemente se deslizan?" (156) "And why are these hung by the neck? And with what are they hung? Perhaps with the umbilical cord in which bubbled the oxygenized blood of the veins and the oxidized blood of the arteries" (128).[16] And when he is not associated with a fetus, Pedro is identified with the rats, the very objects of his research: "Yo también, puesto en celo, calentado pródigamente como las ratonas del Muecas, acariciado de putas, mimado de viejas, . . . pendiente de una bolsita en el cuello recalentador de la ciudad" (121), "I also . . . in heat, [bountifully warmed] like Muecas' mice, caressed by whores, pampered by old women, . . . hanging in a bag around the warm [neck of the city]" (99). On one hand, he is a researcher-he–goat-seducer-surgeon, and on the other, a miserable fetus-rat, possessed by those whom he attempted to possess.

The struggle takes shape between those formidable rivals, exemplified in Goya's *El Aquelarre*: the he-goat and the witches. The fearsome image of the witch is projected on all female characters, whether Dorita, Florita, or the women who attended the philosopher's lecture and the party in his honor, at which Matías's mother holds a prominent position: "pajarita preciosa pero también hábil pajarera, la señora de la casa volaba de rama en rama entonando canciones más complejas que . . . tenían también fines más útiles de apareamiento y tercería de grupos" (165–66) "[a precious little bird but also a skilled] bird-catcher, [the lady of the house] fluttered from bough to bough singing more complicated songs which . . . also served the more [useful] purposes of [pairing off people and pandering for them]" (136). The mother is cast in the mould of a matchmaker or go-between (*tercera*). Goya's *Capricho 19, Todos caerán* [All will fall], provides a pictorial equivalent to this passage. Helman describes it as follows: "A bird with the head and bust of a woman sits in a treetop as a lure to seduce the bird-men that fly around it" (84).

Thus the power of the male over the witches, as manifested in *El Aquelarre*, takes a new form in the novel. The outrageous displays of *machismo* never succeed in establishing an uncontested supremacy, and they therefore must be repeated constantly, much like the bullfighter's sword thrusts.[17] It is interesting that Dorita, seemingly naive or defenseless, faces the effigy of the "buco dominador" (173) "dominating buck" (143) without fear when Matías leads her to his room to meet with Pedro. These are Matías's thoughts after that meeting takes place: "Y ella, ignorante del lujo asiático de la mansión señorial, . . . como si todo aquello no fueran sino bambalinas y decorados abstractos, actuando en la cúspide de su maestría" (199) "There she is, oblivious to the Asiatic luxury of the family mansion, . . . [acting with the highest expertise], as if all this [were] nothing but painted stage sets, and fake" (164). Finally, it should be remembered that this negative image of women is projected onto Spain, the bad mother, or onto the city of Madrid. Psychology and sociology are inextricably fused here. The enlightened though rabid critique of the country (or, rather, the motherland) is based on the dream of reason, a reason that gives way to horrendous fantasies (of infantile origin) about women, who are perceived as the ultimate source of all threat.

The convoluted style of the novel may be understood from this perspective as an attempt to gain distance from the narrated events by analyzing them scientifically or trivializing them through irony (which acts as a valid critique of a perverse political system). But that language also assumes the proportions of a rite of incantation.[18] Wouldn't it be plausible to say that the narrator, and not just the characters, identifies in his own way with the he-goat, the sorcerer who casts a spell over bewitched women—like the lecturer with his jargon—, and thereby keeps them in check?

And, along the same lines, the narrator seduces his readers, as does the he-goat with regard to his "inermes espectadores" "unwary spectators." Yet the very threat that is kept off at a distance ends up revealing its powers of entrapment, like that "pulpo amoroso" "amorous octopus" that Dorita becomes in Pedro's fantasy. If the dream of reason produces monsters, then reason, when it seeks to exercise total dominion, in turn falls completely under the sway of the phantasmal realm over which it attempted to reign.[19]

Paradoxically, then, the narrator winds up embracing Spain's myths, as if they were repositories of true reality: "Si el visitante ilustre se obstina en que le sean mostrados majas y toreros, si el pintor genial pinta con los milagrosos pinceles majas y toreros, . . . esto debe significar algo" (223) "If the illustrious foreign visitor insists on being shown *majas* and bullfighters, and if the great artist paints *majas* and bullfighters with his wonderful brushes, . . . then there must be a reason for this" (184). The canonization of this Spain promoted in the "prospectos de más éxito turístico" (223) "most successful tourist brochures" implies the triumph of conventionality over the forces that oppose those invading clichés. It is the "España de pandereta" (223) "Spain of tambourines" (184), denounced by Antonio Machado in a famous poem, that imposes its values just as it claimed a military victory. The nightmarish images, stirred up by Goya's genius, consequently overwhelm the narrator, whose only recourse is to unravel them—or scrape them brutally from the feminized body of Spain—to expose their bitter truth. The figure of the bullfighter provokes the following commentary: "No debe bastar ser pobre, ni comer poco, ni presentar un cráneo de apariencia dolicocefálica, ni tener la piel delicadamente morena para quedar definido como ejemplar de cierto tipo de hombre al que inexorablemente pertenecemos y que tanto nos desagrada" (224) "It is not enough to be poor, to eat little, to have dolichocephallic skulls and slightly dark skins for us to be defined as [exemplary] of a certain type to which we belong inexorably [and that displeases us so much]" (184–85). Despite his displeasure, the narrator must recognize himself as part of the very historical circumstances that are the object of his critique. He speaks simultaneously as analyst and analysand, thus through his example inviting the readers to carry out the same process within themselves. In the above sentence, the term "dolicocefálica" "dolichocephallic" stands out (the normal form in Spanish would be *dolicocéfala*): it seems to indicate, by means of the cranium, the phallocentrism of the bullfighter or the Spaniard, as Pedro's case illustrates when he is compared to a bullfighter who boasts of his dominance ("cock-a-doodle-doo") in the act of coitus.

Yet, according to the narrator, this phallocentrism is not sufficient to explain the custom of the bullfight nor its powers of fascination. The bullfighter also acts as the "hostia emisaria del odio popular" (225) "chosen victim of popular hatred" (185); the excited Spanish spectators therefore identify with both the bullfighter and the bull in their thirst for blood: "¿Pero qué toro llevamos dentro que presta su poder y su fuerza al animal de cuello robustísimo que recorre los bordes de la circunferencia?" (225) "But what [bull do we carry] inside us that lends power and strength to the animal with the mighty muscular neck which charges around the arena?" (185). In his four lithographs entitled the *Toros de Burdeos* [Bulls of Bordeaux] (Real Academia de Bellas Artes de San Fernando, Madrid), Goya—from a place of exile similar to the interior exile known to Martín-Santos—presents a horrifying vision of tauromachia, which bears notable correspondences to the scenes depicted in *Time of Silence*. In these pictures, the audience has invaded the ring in order to participate in the bullfight; in two of them, *Diversión de España* [Spain's amusement] (Fig. 14) and *Plaza partida* [Divided ring], the bulls are also multiplied. This differs notably from the usual spectacle and reminds one instead of a pitched battle between bulls and bullfighters. Enrique Lafuente Ferrari describes these two lithographs as follows: "The bullfight acquires an epic tone; the audience, present and hypnotized in the ring, is associated with the stages of a battle. . . . A boy falls down and the bull gores him blindly; the witnesses that come to the rescue do not seem to show fear or pity, they are simply grotesque, like in a tragic carnival of drunkenness and barbarism" (25).

Pedro goes back to Dorita once he is released from prison after Muecas's wife testifies that he was not responsible for Florita's abortion.[20] With Dorita and her mother (the inseparable pair) he attends a musical revue, which gives him a new basis for reflecting on the "buen pueblo" (272) "good people" (227). These people, the spectators, see the woman—woman of the people, "como ellos, casi igual que ellos" (272) "like them, almost like them"—as the

Figure 14
Goya, *Spain's Amusement* [Diversión de España].
Real Academia de Bellas Artes de San Fernando, Madrid.

possible avenger of the oppressions they have suffered at the hands of the powerful. Woman, represented by the starlet in the musical revue, elicits the admiration of the "señores prosternados (que ocupan los palcos proscenios, las plateas)" (273) "adoring gentlemen who occupy the boxes, the front stalls" (227). She brings these high personages down to size as they adore her, the popular goddess, a truly common (Pandemian) Aphrodite. Hence the enthusiasm of the people who, in identifying with one of their own, gain access to the bastion of the dominant class. Female victory is exemplified by the mention of native Spaniard Eugenia de Montijo, who married Napoleon III. Once again the narrator indulges in irony by presenting marriage, in opposition to concubinage, as proof of a licit agreement, "instituido sobre antiquísimas instituciones, bendecido por el necesario número de varones tonsurados" (273) "based on ancient institutions, blessed by the necessary number of tonsured males" (227). The narrative, however, suggests other less flattering perspectives. Marriage is not always de rigueur: "El amor del pueblo, para quienes lo quieren y comprenden, es amor no com-

prado, no mercantilizado, sino simplemente arrebatado, como co-
rresponde, amor de buena ley" (273) "What the . . . people mean
by love is love that is not bought or sold, but [simply ravished, like
it should be,] fully legalized" (227). What law is this? Is it marriage
or abduction? A similar vision appeared a few lines earlier: the
adored woman (of the people) is "la misma hembra tan taurina-
mente perseguida, tan amanoladamente raptada desde un baile de
candil y palmatoria hasta las caballerizas de palacio para regodeo
de reyes" (273) "the same female so [bullishly] pursued and [in a
Madrilenian fashion] abducted from a [candlelight ball] to the palace stables for the amusement of kings" (227). Here we perceive
an allusion to Jupiter, who, assuming the form of a bull, abducted
Europa. The father of the gods, along with kings, now becomes the
one to incarnate a *machista* attitude. Is this to mean that the power
of a woman (a bull, in Pedro's imagination) can only be combatted
with an analogous force? And as for the "oprimiente-oprimido"
(272) "oppressing and oppressed" (227) people (that is, men), with
whom do they identify in all these abductions and ravishings? The
common woman "like them," or a person of the same sex?

In any event, the people enjoy these exchanges, whether they
identify with the ravished (but also ravishing) woman, or with
those common kings who, like themselves, "con menestrales jue-
gan a la brisca" (273) "play cards with workmen" (227). This is
why the people do not complain: "olvida [el pueblo] sus enajena-
ciones y conmovido en las fibras más íntimas de un orgullo con-
descendiente, admite en voz baja—pero sincerísima—que vivan-
las-caenas" (273) "[they] will forget [their alienations] and be
moved to the most intimate fibers of their condescending pride to
admit in low but very sincere voices—'[Long live the] chains!'"
(227). No matter who their tyrants are—Ferdinand VII or Francisco Franco—the people accept them, those very people who rose
up heroically against the French invaders before welcoming El
Deseado ("the Desired One," as Ferdinand VII was called). But
through the marriage of the most Spanish Eugenia, who seduces
with the "arts" of "any woman of the people" (274; 228), they
ingratiate themselves with the descendant of Napoleón, the
"destructor de cuantas bibliotecas habían osado distribuir por la
piel de toro los venales ministros de Carlos III" (274) "destroyer
of [all the] libraries which the venal ministers of Carlos III had
dared to distribute over . . . Spain—the bull's hide" (228). The
narrator's perspective clearly corresponds to that of the Enlight-

enment, and it is thus no coincidence that Goya's shadow once again is cast over the novel—Goya, who reviled the Spanish people as much as he exalted them in their mixture of villainy and grandeur: the "vencido pueblo que retrató el sordo a la luz de un farol entre mameluco y mameluco" (274) "conquered people whom the deaf man portrayed by the light of a street lamp surging among the mamelukes" (228).[21] Yet Goya as painter of the Enlightenment may also be viewed in another way, exemplified by the "duquesas desnudas ante las paletas de los pintores plebeyos" (273) "nude duchesses posing before the palettes of plebeian painters" (227). These duchesses turned into common women for the "regodeo" "amusement" of the plebeians, then, are the equivalents of the *amanolados* or common kings. The people manage to conquer the grandees of Spain through their preferred painter, as they did before through the popular starlet.[22] The he-goat emerges from the painting where Goya captured him in order to hide under the painter's skin, bringing with him his powers of seduction: "¿Pues, para qué tiene tan listo el ojo? ¡Para mirarnos mejor! ¿Para qué tiene tan alto el cuerno? ¡Para encornarnos mejor!" (157) "Then, why is his eye so clear? To see us better! Why is his horn lifted so high? To gore us the better!" (129). The "great bully of metaphysics," to whom these words apply, is now in the company of the great bully of painting. Both men are enlightened *machos*, all degrees of difference in education and social origin between them having been eradicated.

After the musical revue has ended, the Dora-Dorita-Pedro trio proceeds to an open-air dance, where disaster strikes when Cartucho, who has been following Pedro about implacably, kills Dorita with a knife. Labanyi sees the equivalent of a Jungian *shadow* in Cartucho, who would thus represent the unconscious, repressed side of Pedro (*Ironía e historia* 111–12, *Myth and History* 76–77). But Labanyi does not take this interpretation further: the (innocent) victim of Pedro's destructive impulses is a woman, not a man. More than Pedro's rival, Cartucho becomes his double. As such he satisfies the protagonist's deep desire to gain release from the maternal *imago*, which is projected constantly onto Dorita.[23]

Pedro's sadistic tendencies may also be glimpsed in his final meditation in the train that takes him away from Madrid toward the small town where he will practice medicine: "Miraré las mozas castellanas, gruesas en las piernas como perdices cebadas y que, como ellas, pueden ser saboreadas con los dientes y con la boca o bien ser derribadas al suelo de un bastonazo" (290), "I shall look at the Castilian girls, fat in the legs as corn-fed partridges, whom you can savor with tongue and teeth, just like partridges, and whom you can bring to the ground [with one blow of a stick]" (243). This contemplative-digestive-annihilating activity is one that Pedro shares with other individuals: "mirando sus piernas, sentado en el casino con dos, cinco, siete, catorce señores" (288) "[looking] at their legs . . . as I sit in the café . . . with two, five, seven, fourteen men" (241). The character's degradation culminates when he invokes "la puta que [lo] parió" (294) "the whore who bore [him]" (247). The bad mother visibly rears her ferocious head and, once more, her negative image coincides with that of the nation, represented here by the Castilian landscape: "Somos mojamas tendidas al aire purísimo de la meseta que están colgadas de un alambre oxidado" (292) "We are dried mummies stretched out in the pure air of the [Castilian plain], hanging by a rusty wire" (245). Once again the vision of the hanging fetuses from Goya's *El Aquelarre* is present in this frightening phantasmagoria, in which Pedro's castration applies to an entire people.[24]

Castration, however, seems to offer some solace for the protagonist (just as prison did): "Es cómodo ser eunuco, es tranquilo, estar desprovisto de testículos, es agradable" (293) "It is comfortable to be a eunuch, it is peaceful, it is pleasant to be deprived of testicles" (245). In his fantasy, Pedro defends against his own violence, present in the sexual relation through the image of the bullfighter who must thrust his sword over and over. Cartucho's well-aimed stab of the knife relieves Pedro of his burden as imaginary "assassin," and frees him at last from the threat posed by the female body. Self-castration should place him safely beyond future repetitions of his amorous story.[25]

At the same time, the protagonist levies a type of masculine protest when he assigns an exaggerated phallicism to the man who announces the departure of the train (the very train Pedro is riding in):

El hombre fálico de la gorra roja terminada en punta de cilindro rojo . . . orgulloso de su gran prepucio rojo-cefálico, con su pito en la mano, con un palo enrollado, dotado de múltiples atributos que desencadenarán la marcha erecta del órgano gigante que se clavará en el vientre de las montañas mientras yo me estoy dejando capar. (291)

> There is the phallic man in the red cap [ending in a red cylinder top . . . proud of his big red cephallic prepuce, with his whistle in his hand], a flag rolled around a stick, possessing the power to unleash the gigantic organ which [will thrust] itself into the belly of the mountain, while I am allowing myself to be castrated. (244)

Immense phallic power, bordering on the grotesque, coexists here with the opposite notion of castration. Resorting to phallic prowess is clearly a defense against castration fears. The text indirectly points to the weakness or impotence of those who display immoderate power: the *macho* or his political correlative, the dictator.

The novel, however, posits another kind of man in contrast to Pedro: Miguel de Cervantes, who seems capable of resisting collective pressures and of showing a possible human liberation. During Pedro's walk around the old quarter of Madrid where Cervantes lived, his thoughts (confused with the narrator's voice) are addressed to the author of the *Quixote*:

> Cervantes, Cervantes. ¿Puede realmente haber existido en semejante pueblo, en tal ciudad como ésta, en tales calles insignificantes y vulgares un hombre que tuviera esa visión de lo humano, esa creencia en la libertad, esa melancolía desengañada tan lejana de todo heroísmo como de toda exageración, de todo fanatismo como de toda certeza? (74)

> Cervantes, Cervantes. Was it possible that a man with such a vision of mankind, such a belief in liberty, with that disillusioned melancholy as remote from all heroism as from all exaggeration, . . . from [all] fanaticism as from all certainty, could have lived [in such a city as this, in such insignificant and ordinary streets?]. (60)

Distant from all heroism, Cervantes paradoxically becomes the true hero of the novel, a model to emulate.[26] This would be the myth or utopia that the author of *Time of Silence* proclaims, in opposition to fanaticisms and dogmas; yet, for it to be sustained, one would have to face rival myths—male (de)signs—which foment injustice and destruction. Only by achieving awareness of these myths, by plunging into the depths of a collective as well as an individual unconscious, could their power be reduced—if not eradicated.

# CHAPTER 6

# *Exiled in* The Garden
# of Earthly Delights:
# *From Hieronymus Bosch
# to Francisco Ayala*

Francisco Ayala belongs to the generation of writers whose incipient literary careers were truncated by the Spanish civil war (1936–39), and he is also one of the vast group of exiles, which includes prominent intellectuals and artists, who were forced to abandon Spain as a result of the "disasters of the war," to invoke Goya once again. Ayala made his exiled home in places such as Argentina, Puerto Rico, and the United States until his definitive return to Spain in 1976, following Franco's death. His distinguished literary oeuvre, officially recognized with many honors over the years, was awarded the 1991 Premio Cervantes de Literatura, considered the equivalent of a Nobel Prize in Hispanic letters.

The work to be analyzed in this chapter, *El jardín de las delicias* [The garden of earthly delights] (1971), not only marks a high point in Ayala's prose writing; it also presents an exemplary case study for the relations between literature and the visual arts. The book is composed of a series of stories, divided into two parts: *Diablo mundo* [Devil's world] and *Días felices* [Happy days]. Many of the stories in the second part are accompanied by reproductions of well-known paintings or sculptures. Ayala has made use of this technique previously, although he never developed it as extensively as we find here. For example, in *Los usurpadores* [The usurpers] (1949), stories such as "San Juan de Dios" [Saint John of God] and "El Hechizado" [The Bewitched One] draw their inspiration from the act of viewing certain paintings.[1] The following words by Ayala are significant in this regard: "More than one critic has suggested—and I hold it to be true—that my literary imagination is of a plastic nature, and, specifically, that my imagination shows a strong pictorial inflexion" (*El tiempo y yo* 21). In light of these declarations it would be appropriate to think, along with Estelle Irizarry, that "the stories [in *El jardín de las delicias*] may be considered true illustrations of the paintings depicted, since the visual experience seems anterior to the literary creation" (258).

For our purposes we will limit our analysis to the stories connected to pictorial representations: this approach does not destroy the unity of *The Garden of Earthly Delights*, a unity produced effortlessly through the juxtaposition of (quite dissimilar) stories that allow for independent readings. Ayala confirms this perspective: "I am surprised to see that it is a highly unified work; . . . it consists of very heterogeneous pieces, written during phases very distant from one another, and each one conceived and executed with absolute autonomy" (Amorós 4). To facilitate our analysis, we have organized the stories by predominant themes into the following three sections: "Paradise and Death," "Earthly Delights," and "The Two Loves or the Two Venuses."

## PARADISE AND DEATH

In this section we include the following stories: "Nuestro jardín" [Our garden], "Postrimerías" [Final stages], "*Au cochon de lait*," and "En la Sixtina" [In the Sistine Chapel]. The pictorial illustration that corresponds to "Nuestro jardín" is a painting done by Ayala's own mother, which confers onto this text a supposed autobiographical character, typical of many stories in the book. Nevertheless, there is no mention in the first lines that the object described is a painting, nor is its authorship revealed: "En el centro, bajo la balaustrada de macetas floridas, la fuente redonda . . . y junto a ella . . . el aro de juguete, azul y rojo, que una niña ha dejado caer" "In the center, beneath the balustrade of blooming flowerpots, the round fountain . . . and beside it . . . the toy hoop, blue and red, that a little girl had let fall" (95).[2] The initial paragraph narrows in on the description of the "[d]os círculos, el aro y la fuente" "two circles, the hoop and the fountain" (95), thereby omitting the girl interposed between them. Doubtless, any circular form exerts a powerful attraction,[3] but in this specific instance there are further reasons for displacing the girl and denying her the right to constitute the center (which she in fact occupies in the painting). It is subsequently revealed that the painter is the narrator's mother, and the theme is a garden that evokes his childhood; the relationship between garden and narrator has already been announced in the title, "Our Garden." But in the mother's painting—or in the garden of childhood—the son has no place; worse yet, an unknown girl substitutes for him. The girl thus breaks the harmonious circle for the narrator-viewer.[4] Furthermore, he notices that the fountain and hoop actually have an oblong shape: "la mano que los trazó en el lienzo supo—cuestión de perspectiva—invitar así a la ilusión del círculo," "the hand that traced them on the canvas knew—a question of perspective—how to invite the illusion of a circle" (95). That is the point: creating an illusion. The son prolongs the gesture of his mother's hand, and, by means of his perception and subsequent description of the painting, he marginalizes the obstructing little female figure that was improperly placed there.

The presence of the girl in the painting thus disturbs the narrator, who transmits these childhood memories: "¿Quién es esa niña? Dímelo, mamá" "Who is that girl? Tell me, Mama" (95). She replies: "Tu prima Laura" "your cousin Laura" (95). When the mother sees her son's surprised reaction—"Laura es una mujer" "Laura is a woman" (95)—she clarifies the obvious: "Laurita tenía la edad que tú tienes ahora; y tú, mono, ni siquiera habías nacido" "Laura was the same age that you are now; and you, doll, weren't even born yet" (96). The infantile paradise represented in the painting therefore corresponds to a moment that actually precedes birth. By the time the narrator is born, the garden has been disposed of: it belongs to others. It exists only as painting or representation: "Nuestro jardín, yo nunca lo había visto sino pintado en el cuadro" "I had never seen our garden except as it was painted in the picture" (96).[5]

The child asks another question: "Y ¿no podrías llevarme una vez a que vea el jardín?" "And couldn't you take me to see that garden one time?" (97). This wish goes unfulfilled. The most the child can do is glimpse the garden from the outside when his mother takes him there one day: "Ven, mira; ése es 'nuestro' jardín—señalando a lo alto de una tapia, en verdad un fuerte muro coronado por una hilera de balaustres" "Come here, look; that is 'our' garden—she said, pointing to the top of a wall, a strong one indeed, crowned with a row of balusters" (97). This, then, is truly an inaccessible garden or paradise.

In the story, memories of childhood alternate with descriptions of the present. The narrator is a mature man who, "al cabo de los años mil" "after a thousand years" (95), sees the painting again, at his brother's house, "al otro lado del océano" "on the other side of the ocean" (95). He later adds: "Lo he mirado sin prisa (ya nunca tengo prisa yo; yo estoy ya del otro lado)" "I have contemplated it unhurriedly (I'm never in a hurry anymore; I am already on the other side)" (95). That other side brings him closer to death, since he perceives himself on the last leg of life's journey. It is as if he were now struggling with the forces that lead him to his final destination, in an attempt to recuperate the past through the object that recalls it. But the painting, inscribed in the symbolic order, cannot replace the real, the pristine garden. In Lacanian terms, the real has become inaccessible, irrecoverable. In this manner the narrator carries the condition of exile, long borne by Ayala, to its extreme. If the writer's political exile will fortunately come to an end one day, it is not so for the other kind of exile, which derives from the simple fact of birth. The narrator's nephew, who joins him in contemplating the painting, asks the final questions, to which the story (*imago hominis*) has already responded: "Esa niña que recoge el aro, ¿no era una prima de papá y tuya? . . . Papá nunca vio el jardín del bisabuelo; y tú, ¿lo viste alguna vez, tío?" "That girl who is picking up the hoop, wasn't she a cousin of Papa's and yours? . . . Papa never saw great-grandfather's garden; and you, did you ever see it, Uncle?" (98).

The evocation of death becomes explicit in the story entitled "Postrimerías" [Final stages]. The narrator and his companion view a painting with that title by Valdés Leal at the Hospital de la Caridad (Seville). In a typically Spanish baroque way, the painting (reproduced in Ayala's book) displays the dead body of an illustrious person, and, consequently, it indicates where worldly glory ends. In fact, Jonathan Brown mentions this same painting under the title of *Finis Gloriae Mundi* ("Hieroglyphs" 128). It is of even greater interest to note that the design of the Hospital de la Caridad owes to the directives of Miguel Mañara, the famous seventeenth-century Sevillian character who was confused with Don Juan and as such inspired many literary works. After his religious conversion Mañara was appointed leader (*hermano mayor*) of the hospital, a charitable institution. Brown writes: "It has long been known that the paintings were inspired by Mañara and, to some extent, they reflect his personal obsession with death" ("Hiero-glyphs" 136).

But in "Final Stages" another painting from the hospital is also mentioned: "pasando de Valdés, el tétrico, al dulce Murillo, nos pusimos a contemplar la *Santa Isabel de Hungría* que, con sus manos de reina, cura a los leprosos" "going from the gloomy Valdés to the sweet Murillo, we then stopped to contemplate *Saint Isabel of Hungary* who, with her queenly hands, cures lepers" (113). The transit accomplished here is one programmed for the visitor, as Brown explains: "visitors to the church must experience the agony of Valdés's Hell [located just inside the entrance] before entering the promised land of Murillo's acts of mercy" (*Golden Age* 266). It is clear, then, that Mañara arranged the paintings in the Hospital de la Caridad like elements in a story to point the way toward the means of salvation in the face of death. And this narrative in the form of successive pictures determines the course (or discourse) of Ayala's story, in which the implied author identifies with Mañara, the former Don Juan obsessed with death and salvation.

The two visitors emerge from the interior of the hospital and step onto a patio, "una delicia" "a delight," and then "enfrente, al otro lado de la calle, un vivero de plantas y pájaros. . . " "across the street, a vivarium of plants and birds" (113). Isn't this a para-dise, after having faced Valdés's macabre vision, with the "sweet Murillo" as intermediary? A biographical motif that Ayala men-tions in his *Recuerdos y olvidos* comes to mind again here: the portrait of Saint John of God hung in his family home. It is inter-esting that the same saint appears in another painting by Murillo in the Sevillian hospital: *Caridad de San Juan de Dios* [Saint John of God's charity], although this fact is not noted in "Final Stages." If we superimpose *Recuerdos* onto this story, the meaning becomes apparent. The Hospital de la Caridad, with its *San Juan de Dios*, is transformed into an image of childhood paradise, par-adise lost and, somehow, now recovered. Before walking out on the patio and the street, then, the narrator must have experienced a paradisiacal vision, or, in other words, a sensation of a return to a happy world. Consequently, it is not only the abundance of plants and birds but also the correspondence between the narra-tor's "today" and the author's distant "yesterday" that may account for the bliss expressed in the following sentence: "Otro día más; un día largo, lento, caluroso, feliz" "Another day; a long day, slow, warm, happy" (113).

Further on, when the pair goes to a park, the woman stops to stroke a mangy dog, much to the narrator's displeasure. The story concludes:

> Conseguí alejar al perro. Y después, ya no tardamos mucho en regresarnos al hotel.
> Señor, ¡qué días tan felices! Pero luego . . .

> I got the dog away from us. And afterward, it did not take us long to return to the hotel. Lord, what happy days! But then . . . (114–15).

The image of Saint Isabel of Hungary healing lepers, viewed earlier, is undoubtedly projected onto the narrator's companion. But if we continue to associate the art collection of the hospital with the paintings in the author's childhood home, then the figure of a good mother is also projected onto this anonymous woman. This link between the two women is all the more plausible because Ayala's memory of *San Juan de Dios* includes reference to his mother's charitable spirit: "My mother felt particular veneration toward that saint [Saint John of God], who founded a hospitable community in Granada" (*Recuerdos* 57). In "Final Stages," then, charity is not only the road to salvation, but it is also the motif to which Ayala's memory turns as he seeks to recover the lost infantile paradise. This would be another means of (earthly) salvation—against the ravishes of time.

The story ends as it began, with an evocation of death. As we have noted, the trajectory of the text resembles the one taken by the visitor to the Hospital de la Caridad: there, at the entrance, the visitor encounters the two morbid paintings by Valdés Leal—the one mentioned by Ayala and the one entitled *In Ictu Oculi*, both quite unforgettable. Yet there is also a pleasurable interlude with two actants: the "sweet Murillo," the painter of works of charity, and the sweet, charitable woman, who (reminiscent of the mother) displays her magnanimous spirit in a sumptuous Sevillian park.

"*Au cochon de lait*" takes place in the mundane atmosphere of a restaurant, the same setting for another story in the book, "Magia, I." In Ayala's work one finds, in effect, abundant references to food and drink. But that pleasurable world—the garden of earthly delights, including love, of course—like Bosch's painting of the same name, is flanked by the proximity of the beyond, either in its infernal or in its heavenly dimension. Ayala's story utilizes Botticelli's *Spring* (Fig. 7) as its pictorial background. The figure of Venus occupies the central position in this painting: "Vasari described it simply as 'Venus whom the Graces bedeck with flowers, denoting Spring'" (Hall 264). Above Venus's head, Cupid flies about in the form of an angel, and to the left, Mercury appears. These figures, transformed into modern literary characters, enter the restaurant where the narrator is seated:

> vimos irrumpir en el comedor a la famosa Primavera, no precedida ahora por la fragancia de Flora ni flanqueada de las Gracias, sino escoltada por un angelote hermoso de tres o cuatro años, fruto de su vientre, y un caballero, su gallardo esposo, que en el cuadro original figura bajo el atuendo de Mercurio, y que en la actualidad debe de ocuparse efectivamente en actividades comerciales.

> we saw the famous Spring enter into the dining room, not preceded this time by the fragrance of Flora nor surrounded by the Graces, but instead escorted by a beautiful little angel of three or four years of age, fruit of her womb, and a gentleman, her gallant husband, who in the original painting appears in the guise of Mercury, and who in these modern times probably is in fact involved in commercial activities. (131)

This literary transposition is entirely justifiable. Cupid (or Eros) is the son of Hermes (Mercury) and Aphrodite (Venus), according to the most widely accepted genealogy (Grimal 147). It is equally understandable that the modern descendant of Mercury, god of commerce, would seem to have dealings in the business world. The prose of life substitutes for the poetry of myth, but the kinships remain intact. The story does take some unexpected turns, however. The description of Spring (never explicitly associated with Venus) adheres to Botticelli's pictorial version: "esos ojos vivaces de tierna y alegre inocencia y la dulce inflexión del cuello sobre un hombro muy suave" "those lively eyes with their tender and joyful innocence and the sweet curve of her neck on a very soft shoulder" (131). Her image changes, though, after she orders the specialty of the restaurant, "el famoso *cochon de lait* al horno" "the famous roasted *cochon de lait*" (131).

The presentation of this dish is made both in solemn and in comic terms: "su triunfal entrada repetirá en parodia bufa la aparición reciente de la Primavera; quien, desde su trono, se dispone ahora a recibirlo con la mejor gracia" "its triumphal entrance is going to be a burlesque parody of the recent appearance of Spring, who, from her throne, gets ready to receive it with the highest grace" (132). Somewhere inside the bourgeois Spring still dwells that ancient goddess, who receives the suckling pig as if it were a sacrificial victim.[6] But Ayala's narration would seem to contradict more than support Botticelli's image of Venus as incarnation of Spring. The text presents recurring visions of death and sacrifice. The suckling pig (*cochon de lait*), served on a platter, takes the place of the tender infant (Adonis) with whom Venus falls in love when she sees him.

Instead of Spring or goddess of life, Ayala's character ends up reigning as goddess of death. Or, in other words, she reveals the other side of the Mother Goddess who, in mythology, corresponds to Persephone, companion of Hades, the infernal god of the dead.[7] The first paragraph of the story is relevant in this context: "Así [*Au cochon de lait*] se llama el restaurant donde, años atrás, un camarero demasiado entusiasta se aplicó a recitar en honor nuestro, hasta decir 'basta,' las estancias de la Divina Comedia, mientras afuera, en la calle, bullía multitudinosa la *comédie humaine*" "That is the name [*Au cochon de lait*] of the restaurant where, years ago, an overly enthusiastic waiter began to recite stanzas from the *Divine Comedy* in our honor until we said 'enough,' while outside, in the street, the multitudinous *comédie humaine* bustled about" (131). Dante's poem transports us to the beyond, with which the restaurant is then associated, while outside the worldly traffic flows on in its usual fashion.[8] The narrator also remarks at the beginning: "hasta recupero el rincón mismo en que un día paladeara las delicias culinarias del menú con el aderezo añadido por el imprevisto despliegue de la imaginería dantesca" "I'm even able to recover the very same spot where, one day, I tasted the culinary delights of the menu, with the seasoning added by the unexpected display of Dantean imagery" (131). The "Dantean imagery," when not present in the waiter's recital, may be glimpsed in the description of Spring that appears in the story. We have compared Spring to Persephone. In the *Divina Commedia* the figure of this goddess (under her Roman name *Proserpina*) is evoked when the poet contemplates Matelda:

> Tu me fai rimembrar dove e qual era
> Proserpina nel tempo che perdette
> la madre lei, ed ella primavera. (*Purgatorio* 28, 49–51)

Thou makest me to remember, where and what Proserpine
was in the time her mother lost her, and she lost the spring.
(*Divine Comedy* 362)

A double, contradictory process may be observed here. Spring
(Venus), the goddess of love, turns into the infernal Persephone;
yet by means of the passage from Dante, it is possible to ascend to
Spring once again, that is, to a state before the fall, similar to the
biblical Eden.[9]

The title of Ayala's collection, *El jardín de las delicias*, comes
to mind again here. The cover of the book reproduces the two side
panels (paradise and hell) from Bosch's famous triptych, *The Garden of Earthly Delights* (Fig. 15). Heaven and hell are even closer
to each other in Ayala than they are in Bosch.[10] In addition, there
is a strict correspondence between Dante's *Commedia* and
Bosch's *The Garden of Earthly Delights* with its reversed position
of the two lateral panels: in both cases paradise follows hell. Consequently, in Ayala's work, the basic model represented by Bosch
is both affirmed and subverted: paradise is found at the beginning
(remote and lost), but it is just as much a possible ending toward
which humans reach from their horrid and delightful world, comparable to the central panel of *The Garden of Earthly Delights*.[11]

The vision of death as the antechamber to the beyond constitutes the theme of "En la Sixtina" [In the Sistine Chapel]. The
story centers on the act of viewing Michelangelo's the *Last Judgment* (Fig. 16), the lower right corner of which is reproduced in
the book. Upon arriving at the Vatican the narrator and his companion find themselves mixed in among the multitudes who wish
to enter the famous site: "Nos miramos el uno al otro con una sonrisa—¿qué hacerle sino seguir adelante?—y adelante fuimos" "We
looked at each other with a smile—what else could we do but go
on?—and so on we went" (151). Inside the chapel the narrator's
attitude stands in contrast to the one displayed by the colorful
crowd that surrounds him: "Pero ¿sabía de veras esta multitud lo
que miraba, lo que anhelaba, lo que quizá temía?" "But did this
crowd really know what it was looking at, what it desired, what
it perhaps feared?" (152). The sacred and thrilling nature of the
mural paintings does not greatly move these people, who come
from all parts of the world, exemplified by the "walkirias de min-
ifalda, pies roñosos y espléndidas trenzas rubias que devoraban

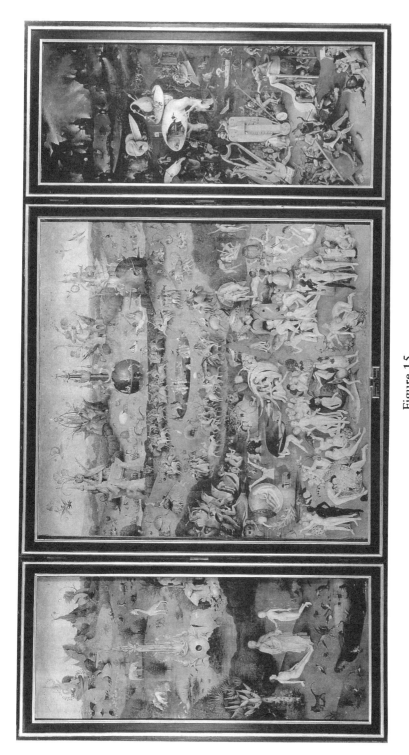

Figure 15

Bosch, *The Garden of Earthly Delights*. Prado, Madrid.

Figure 16

Michelangelo, *Last Judgment.* Sistine Chapel, Vatican Palace, Vatican State. Alinari/Art Resource, New York.

sandwiches y se llamaban a gritos" "Valkyries in miniskirts, with their filthy feet and splendid blond braids, who devoured sandwiches and shouted to one another" (152). This lack of reverence or of religious and artistic sensitivity stands out in even greater contrast when compared not only to the narrator's stance, but also to the attitude displayed by Michelangelo's contemporaries, the original viewers of the *Last Judgment*: "When, in 1541, the fresco was unveiled, the public was genuinely shocked by this apocalyptic scene, the seething mass of naked bodies racked by the agonies of the damned, by torments mental and physical," as Rosabianca Skira-Venturi writes (64). In fact, Michelangelo takes up a theme that, although present in the paintings found in many medieval Italian churches, crops up less frequently in the Renaissance; it is the advances of the Reformation, and the subsequent crisis in the church, that moves Pope Paul III to commission Michelangelo's famous painting for the altar of the Sistine Chapel. According to Robert S. Liebert, "the new pope deemed it necessary to remind his flock dramatically that Heaven is reserved only for those who live by the Faith" (333).

In addition, Michelangelo deviates from previous tradition, which placed the condemned souls and those who are saved on different planes, thereby exposing the outcome of the Last Judgment more than the process itself. Charles de Tolnay comments on this change: "In evoking the moment of the arrival of Christ just before the decision, in depicting an imminent event rather than a past fact, Michelangelo succeeded in creating in the spectator a tension of fear" (*Michelangelo* 32). But it bears repeating that the incredulous humanity of modern times remains impassive before such a dramatic representation of that inevitable future actualized by Michelangelo. In contrast, the narrator does not place himself on the margins of those who receive divine sentence in the mural. There is no essential difference for him between the position of spectator and that of object of contemplation: "Sobre todos nosotros, como sobre los muertos a quienes despiertan de su tumba, para convocarlos al juicio, se precipitaban desde la altura, soplando sus mudas trompetas, los terribles querubines del lado izquierdo" "The terrible cherubs on the left side, blowing on their mute trumpets, pounced down on us from their heights, like they do on the dead whom they awaken from their graves to call them to judgment" (152). The narrator perceives the universal dimension of this judgment, in which he includes himself as one of the accused. He is thus likened to Michelangelo himself, whose self-portrait may be observed in the skin shown to the Redeemer by Saint Bartholomew at a central point in the painting.[12] Leo Steinberg situates the effigy of the artist in a long diagonal that, crossing through the imposing figure of Christ, traverses the *Last Judgment* from the upper left to the lower right corner. Steinberg draws out the consequences of this observation: "the Last Judgment conceived as more than a fable, and more than a warning to others, is real only to the extent that the man who tells of it knows himself to be the first on trial. . . . It had to be Michelangelo who was the first in line, because the narration was his" ("Line of Fate" 109). As the narration of the Judgment is displaced through Michelangelo onto Ayala, the new narrator of this eternal story must somehow appear at the forefront.

The diagonal suggested by Steinberg culminates in an infernal scene, the one shown in the corner reproduced in Ayala's book, to which this passage refers: "a la derecha, con sus orejas de burro, reclutaba eternamente Carón a los condenados al infierno" "To the right, with his donkey ears, Charon was eternally rounding up those who were condemned to hell" (152). Michelangelo's vision recalls Dante's, as Ascanio Condivi noted: "we see Charon with his bark, exactly as Dante describes him in his *Inferno*, in the muddy waters of Acheron, raising his oar to strike any laggard soul" (in Liebert 339). The narrator thus identifies not only with Michelangelo, but also with Dante, whose *Divina Commedia* is mentioned in "*Au cochon de lait*," as we have remarked. One might even say that the narrator of "In the Sistine Chapel" hears the appeal that Charon makes to the Florentine poet: "E tu che se' costì, anima viva, / pàrtiti da cotesti che son morti" (*Inferno* 3, 88–89) "And thou who art there, alive, depart thee from these who are dead" (*Divine Comedy* 31). The narrator is so overwhelmed that he experiences the need to escape to the outdoors:

> Entre tantos pecadores impenitentes, distraídos con la idea de que, tras el Juicio Final, saldríamos otra vez de la Sixtina y, ya en la calle, satisfechos de haber cumplido nuestro deber, buscaríamos alguna *trattoria* ahí mismo en el Travestere para comer *spaghetti* y paladear un vasito de *chianti*, podían distinguirse los tenaces judíos que, desde los cuatro puntos cardinales, traen su arrogancia y su cámara fotográfica al seno mismo de la Gran Meretriz y disparan a traición sus *flashes* contra la imagen del

Redentor, sin que la imponente majestad que Miguel Angel supo darle alcance a intimidarlos.

Among so many unrepentant sinners—reassured with the idea that, following the Final Judgment, we would all leave the Sistine Chapel again and, once back on the street, satisfied that we had fulfilled our obligation, we would seek out a *trattoria* right there in the Travestere to eat *spaghetti* and taste a little glass of *chianti*—the tenacious Jews stood out, who, from the four cardinal points, bring their arrogance and their cameras to the very womb of the Great Whore and treacherously shoot their flashes at the image of the Redeemer, while the impotent majesty with which Michelangelo endowed him fails to intimidate them. (152–53)

Although in principle they remain apart from the common tourists, the narrator and his companion also seek solace in the highly touristic trappings of *trattorias* and *spaghetti*. After all, they didn't take the precaution of bringing along a sandwich in order to help shut out the visions of the great beyond.

The last lines of this story reveal how difficult it is to abandon that world in which everyone dances about in a metaphoric kettle that resembles Charon's boat: "Y todos, como masa espesa en colosal olla que desborda lentamente por un lado mientras por el otro sigue colmándose, girábamos juntos dentro de la Sixtina; girábamos y girábamos sin término" "And all the people, like a thick concoction in a colossal kettle that slowly overflows on one side while it continues to heap up on the other, were whirling around inside the Sistine Chapel; we whirled and whirled endlessly" (153). These lines subtly point to the extraordinary dynamism of the *Final Judgment*. In contrast to medieval representations of this theme, with their hierarchical, static division of planes, Michelangelo offers a vision of souls that strive to reach the heights or who resist the descent to hell.[13] Ultimately, both in the mural and in Ayala's story, we witness a representation of an anguished desire for salvation that does not slacken until the last moment.

This interartistic analysis is not based only on the fact that here, as well as in other cases, the details of a description correspond to the traits of a painting. The work of art is reproduced in the text and thus closely, inextricably even, linked to it. The narration's spatial form (Joseph Frank's term)—that is, the textual presence of echoes, juxtapositions, foreshadowings and returns—

is thereby enhanced by painting's authentic spatial form. In this fashion, the writer stresses the concept of circular time, which, in Murray Krieger's words, amounts to "a claim for a redemption of time, a notion that, because it cannot escape its theological source, firmly ties down the formal to a universal thematic" (222). Krieger is referring to modernist literature while also wondering whether the formal processes designated by Frank might not be connected to a theological doctrine (as is obviously the case with an author such as T. S. Eliot, for example). These observations apply to Ayala's writing as well, where the spirit of modernism seems to revive. This is corroborated by the narrator of "Our Garden," who in harmony with his painter-mother invites the reader into the "illusion of the circle." But the term *illusion* is key here, since it injects a note of skepticism into the expression of human desire, a desire incessantly heard as well as frustrated.

## EARTHLY DELIGHTS

Eschatology disappears in the next two stories that we analyze, "San Silvestre" [Saint Silvester] and "Mientras tú duermes" [While you are sleeping], which focus on carnal delights rather than a spiritual afterlife. In "Saint Silvester," the narrator evokes a youthful past; a foreign atmosphere is ushered in by the German term *Sylversterabend* (105), which replaces the Spanish *Noche Vieja* or *Año Viejo* (New Year's Eve). The term alludes to a custom that does not exist in the narrator's country: a license to absolute freedom on the last night of the year.

This note of foreignness expands in the second paragraph. The narrator belongs to a group of students who come from other lands that are "cálidas, secas, quemadas, ásperas" "warm, dry, scorched, rugged" (105). There is undoubtedly an autobiographical basis for this story, since Ayala went to Berlin on a fellowship when he was twenty-three years old. And, in keeping with the conventions of the autobiographical mode, there is a distinct temporal distance between the subject or *I* of the discourse and the subject of the story. This tale is told long after the action occurred, or, more precisely, long after the foreign study experience on which it is affectively based.

There is a marked contrast between the "tierras cálidas" "warm lands," where the narrator and his group come from, and the "país húmedo, verde y misterioso, selva de maravilla" "green, mysterious and humid country, jungle of wonder" (105), to which they have arrived. The characteristics of the foreign country make sense at a deeper level, since the atmosphere primarily evoked here corresponds to a feminine world as contemplated by these young men, full of ardor like their native lands: "si tan intensamente, tan dolientemente nos sentíamos llamados por las secretas voces de aquella selva . . . es porque tales señales provenían sobre todo de mujeres" "If we felt so intensely, so painfully beckoned by the secret voices of that jungle . . . it is because those signals emanated above all from women" (105). The association between "jungle" and "women" turns the female foreigners into nymphs of sorts, inhabitants of the (Germanic) forest. It is appropriate that the first painting that illustrates this story is Rubens's *Nymphs and Satyrs* (Fig. 17). The satyrs of course emerge in the guise of the young men: "nosotros los oscuros, los barbudos, los peludos" "We are the dark, bearded, hairy ones" (106). The contrast between white and dark planes finds exact correspondence in Rubens's painting, in which the "white" and "opulent" blonde women (106) appear bathed in light, whereas the men, the satyrs, hide in the shadows among the branches of the trees. It is also of interest to note that this painting hangs in the Prado. From the perspective of the exiled author, the museum in Madrid is evocative of his youth, of the "días felices" "happy days," the title of the section that includes "Saint Silvester." In this sense the narrator would be feeling nostalgia for both Germany, where he studied, and the Prado, in his native country, distant and lost at the time the story was written. In addition, Rubens's painting, with its frank pagan sensuality, strikes a vivid contrast to the Spanish artistic tradition that normally eschews mythological themes, owing to the influence of the church.[14] The Dutch painter therefore furnishes a mark of difference with respect to things Spanish that is similar to the one introduced in equal proportion by the German setting of the story. That is, the note of liberty resounding in the disciplined and ardent world of the author is signaled as much by Rubens's painting as by Germany on New Year's Eve.

Saint Silvester's night thereby functions as a kind of initiation ceremony, a true cross between two worlds: New Year's Eve and New Year's Day. In this framework, the initiator is the "viejo marqués de Saint-Denis, gordo y jocundo" "old marquis of Saint-Denis, plump and jocund" (106), who leads his acolytes to "la Franziskaner Keller, local bien espacioso . . . , fiel a su popular cerveza, aquella famosa Bockbier cuya excelencia proclama, trepado sobre un tonel en medio de la sala, un enorme cabrío de *papier mâché*" "the Franziskaner Keller, a roomy locale . . . , faithful to its popular beer, that famous Bockbier whose excellent quality is proclaimed by an enormous *papier mâché* goat sitting upright on a barrel in the middle of the room" (106). Another painting illustrates the story at this point: Goya's *El Aquelarre* [The witches' sabbath] (Fig. 2), with its group of women surrounding the he-goat-devil. In the Franziskaner Keller, the he-goat corresponds to the marquis— "diablo viejo" "old devil" (106)—who heads up the group of students. His followers are "estudiantes nuevos y bisoños" "new and inexperienced students" (107), that is, the initiates. The more seasoned fellows already manage things on their own: "quienes ya llevaban tiempo y estaban algo familiarizados con el país se atenían cada cual a sus compromisos propios" "those who had already

Figure 17
Peter Paul Rubens, *Nymphs and Satyrs*. Prado, Madrid.

been there awhile and were somewhat familiar with the country kept busy with their own engagements" (107).

At the pub, the satyrs go off one by one from the group in pursuit of the nymphs. The narrator stresses the animal-like characteristics of the first one to break loose, the "simio del cigarro, Lucio González, . . . un mono escapado de los experimentos del Dr. Köhler en Tenerife" "ape with the cigarette, Lucio González, . . . a monkey that escaped from Dr. Köhler's experiments in Tenerife" (108). The monkey takes his revenge here against German science. And at the same time, he honors his Greco-Roman forebears, since satyrs in fact assumed animal form, be it that of a horse from the waist down, or a he-goat (Grimal 416). Naturally, the behavior displayed by Lucio (Lucifer?) receives the marquis's approbation: "¡Así, así me gusta a mí! ¡Esa es la juventud! Muchachos, tomad ejemplo" "That's it, that's what I like! That's youth! Boys, take a lesson" (108). Similar exclamations appear in short order: "¡Arriba, muchachos, arriba!" "Go to it, guys, go!" (108). Or "¡Bien por el peruano!" "Good for the Peruvian!" following the spectacle of Zaldívar, "abrazado con seriedad intensa, en el vértigo del vals vienés, a una walkiria casi albina" "embracing a nearly albino Valkyrie with intense seriousness, in the vertigo of a Viennese waltz" (108). Yet it is no longer the marquis but the narrator himself who bursts forth with jubilant shouts mixed into the story. "¡Arriba, muchachos, arriba!" "Go to it, guys, go!" is spoken by the subject of the discourse in identification with the marquis. The former inexperienced student has become an old satyr (which brings to mind that other sensual marquis and master narrator: the aged Bradomín in Valle-Inclán's *Sonatas*). From the vantage point of old age, the narrator looks back nostalgically over his youthful days, and, egging on the young men, addresses himself (the youth he was) as would a father proud of his lineage: "¡Bien por el peruano!" "Good for the Peruvian!" It is left to the Spanish church, whose dictates do not govern over this pleasurably pagan world, to raise the accusation of demonism.

We might wonder at this point why Ayala did not choose another painting by Rubens to illustrate his narration: *Diana y sus ninfas perseguidas por faunos* [Diana and her nymphs surprised by satyrs], also in the Prado Museum. In this painting, the fauns display an aggressive and violent stance that differs notably from their attitude in *Nymphs and Satyrs*. The nymphs in the painting that Ayala reproduces have nothing to fear in the men; rather, the women seem to reach out their hands to them or ignore them with Olympic disdain, as does the figure in the foreground to the left, modeled after Hélène Fourment, the painter's second wife (Lorente 2, 16). She turns her back on the satyrs in order to look in the direction of the viewer of the painting. Of course, we could interpret that the nymph seems to offer herself up to the possessive gaze of the painter or masculine spectator, thereby making him one more satyr—or satirizing him, so to speak—and exposing his naked desires at the same time that she exposes herself to him. Yet, needless to say, the viewer is not inherently or exclusively fixed in this role of male voyeur, since identificatory positions are mobile within the complex pictorial-spectatorial sign system.

The narrative perspective shifts when the protagonist stops observing his companions or the marquis, who has also joined in the dancing, to instead notice someone watching him: "desde una mesa próxima, era observado yo a mi vez por dos mujeres" "from a nearby table, I in turn was being observed by two women" (109). These two women who look alike are later defined as possibly being "madre e hija" "mother and daughter" (109). At that moment the narrator perceives that he has been left alone, and he starts moving toward the other table where the two unknown women smile to him. And when he proposes a dance, it is the mother who takes up the offer. On the dance floor, his eyes "escapan buscando a lo lejos . . . la figura solitaria de la muchacha" "escape in search of the far-off . . . solitary figure of the girl" (110). But despite his insistence, the girl only concedes one dance to him: "Se negaba y se negaba y se negaba; y como yo, excitado, quisiera forzarle la mano y sacarla por fuerza, su madre . . . , quizá envidiosa y ávida ella misma, me tomó del brazo y me condujo con severa dulzura hacia el centro del salón" "She kept on saying no and saying no and saying no; and since I in my excited state wanted to grab her hand and force her to dance, her mother . . . perhaps envious and avid herself, led me off by the arm with harsh sweetness toward the center of the room" (111). It is clear that the satyr has encountered a rival who surpasses him in strength, someone who places herself between him and the nymph. There is nothing here that deviates from mythology, since nymphs do not always give in to the fury of the satyrs. They serve men's enemies, such as the goddess Diana and Circe the sorceress (Grimal 320), or they seduce beautiful young men like Hilas (Grimal 216). Erich Neumann establishes the link between the nymphs and the Great Mother, the Greek Aphrodite: "[Aphrodite] is split up and personalized in the form of nymphs, sirens, water spirits, and dryads. . . . Structurally [the nymphs] remain partial aspects of the [Great Mother] archetype and are psychic fragmentations of it" (*Origins* 89, 90). In this light, the elder of the two women in Ayala's story would resort to the younger version of herself to attract the young man, thus thwarting his initiation (that is, his emancipation from the maternal figure).

In the painting by Rubens that accompanies the narration, there is a kind of power balance between the nymphs and the satyrs. This equilibrium collapses in favor of the fauns in Rubens's *Diana and Her Nymphs Surprised by Satyrs*, which for a moment could be viewed as a pictorial exemplification of "Saint Silvester." But at the end of the story the balance shifts to the other side, where feminine power reigns, and it is Goya's *El Aquelarre* in one of its possible readings that serves to illustrate this point. In Goya's painting, the women offer up children—innocent victims—to the he-goat. Further, the children being offered are supplemented by the bodies of some others, already dead. Rubens's nymphs have thus turned into witches (bad mothers) who suck children's blood. Yet the passage from Rubens's nymphs to Goya's witches is not so abrupt. Pedro de Valencia, a sixteenth-century humanist, saw "traces of the ancient mysteries of Bacchus and nothing else in the sexual orgies [of the witches]" (Helman 192). And, in addition, "Satyrs and nymphs or maenads are [Dionysos's] regular companions" (Carpenter 37–38). In *El Aquelarre* the devil-he-goat adorns his head and horns with grape leaves, thereby merging with Dionysus-Bacchus.

To return to a main thematic thread, we note that two groups are counterposed here. On one side the marquis of Saint-Denis, a new Dyonisus (or devil), presides over the satyr-students, and on the other side the nymphs or Germanic Valkyries either engage with the satyrs or resist them through a mother figure. She incarnates the archetype that Neumann described, which may be extended to all the nymphs when we perceive them as partial aspects or psychic fragments of the Great Mother. And surely this same archetype applies well to Rubens's opulent women, those splendid matrons to whom the young women in the pub are compared. It is worth noting here that Dionysus was raised by nymphs (Carpenter 73); his servants therefore also function as his caretakers, and in that regard he is subordinated to them.

The story approaches its end as midnight draws near. The narrator's attempts to win over the girl have failed repeatedly: "Siempre, para exasperación mía, acudía la otra al rescate, ofreciéndoseme en cambio. ¡Qué! No era el cuerpo maduro de la matrona lo que quería yo, sino a la jovencita arisca y temerosa" "to my exasperation, the other one always rushed to the rescue, offering herself to me instead. Bah! It wasn't the mature body of this matron that I wanted, but rather the shy and fearful young woman" (111–12). We could say, then, that the foreign student never exits from New Year's Eve to enter the New Year; new life does not crystallize for him: "Los ojos se me cerraron, y tengo la memoria imprecisa de que unos dedos cariñosos me acariciaban los párpados; de que mi cabeza reposaba, feliz, sobre un regazo cálido. Más, no puedo recordar; más, no recuerdo" "My eyes closed, and I have the imprecise recollection that my eyelids were being caressed by affectionate fingers, that my head was resting, happily, in a warm lap. More, I cannot remember; more, I do not remember" (112). As we note the oppressive nature of this contact, we should also point to the complacency that it arouses in the narrator, "resting, happily, in a warm lap."

The first rays of morning sun surprise the young man who is laid out on the floor of the pub, that wondrous, mythic cave: "En todo lo alto, encaramado siempre, triunfaba el cabrío de la Bockbier" "From the heights, perched like always, the Bockbier goat reigned triumphant" (112). Is it the "goat" that triumphs here, or is it the maternal *imago*, which, as we pointed out, keeps a tight grip on the narrator? In fact, when the narrator's eyes open, they are greeted with the spectacle of a brigade of cleaning women: "Y enfrente de mí, muertas de risa, me contemplaban unas viejas armadas de escobas. . . . *Glückliches Neu Jahr!* ¡Feliz año nuevo, jovencito!—me saludaron" "And in front of me, dying of laughter, some old women armed with brooms were looking at me. . . . *Glückliches Neu Jahr*! Happy New Year, young man!—they wished me" (112). These old women with their brooms undoubtedly strike a resemblance to witches, and it is they who get the last (triumphant) laugh.

The one-page story "Mientras tú duermes" [While you are sleeping] (157) should be read in relation to the aquatint by Picasso that accompanies it: *Minotauro y durmiente* [Faun unveiling a sleeping woman] (Fig. 18). Picasso developed an early interest in the theme of the sleeping woman; his innovation consists in not only depicting the woman but also introducing a male figure (himself) in a contemplative mode. This duality is already manifest in an a watercolor from 1904.[15] The Minotaur, a most significant image in Picasso's art, first appears in works that date to 1933 (Penrose 171). As critics have shown, the Minotaur should be considered an alter ego of the painter himself.[16] It seems appropriate that Ayala, who often reifies male libido through satyrs and beasts, would superimpose Picasso's mythic monster onto the narrator of "While You Are Sleeping." The Minotaur highlights the animal or instinctual side of man, a precise meaning that Picasso's artistic production frequently exemplifies. Along these lines, the Picassian Minotaur has been interpreted as an exponent of the subversive eruption of sexuality into the artist's studio (M. Gedo 221). Yet the Minotaur does not always assume such a representational stance; in Picasso's artistic imagination, this mythical being takes on a variety of behaviors and poses. He thus may appear violent—a violator or rapist even—as well as weak, deserving of compassion, blinded, or in the throes of death. It should be remembered in this respect that the figure of the Minotaur in Picasso is linked to the tauromachian bull, another central focus of the Spanish painter's work. And the bull, of course, is principally a sacrificial victim. In the etching that Ayala selected to illustrate his text (or that inspires it), the Minotaur hardly displays a violent attitude. He lifts up the veil that shields the sleeping woman, contemplates her, and reaches out a hand. What follows that scene is left open; that is, the viewer cannot know if the Minotaur will in fact disturb the woman's peaceful sleep.

In Ayala's story, written like the others in first person, the *I* never abandons the initial contemplative state. The image conveyed is also one of meditation, something that distinguishes this *I* from Picasso's Minotaurs. For they may exhibit expressions of calm, desperation, or defeat, but never engage in the kind of reflections that Ayala's protagonist incarnates. Besides, painting, in theory, lacks the capacity to transmit reflections of this nature.

The first paragraph of the story communicates an affirmative tone, initiated with an *I* (normally emphatic in Spanish): "Yo te estoy mirando" "I am looking at you." But the woman is not merely an object of contemplation: the onlooker immediately reveals himself to be her lover when he calls forth an image of the awakened woman and the "llamaradas" "sudden blazes" of love between

Figure 18
Pablo Picasso, *Faun Unveiling a Sleeping Woman* [Minotauro y
durmiente] (1936). The Museum of Modern Art, New York.
Abby Aldrich Rockefeller Fund.

them. The overwhelming sensation of amorous desire before the
sleeping nude woman associates the narrator-contemplator with
the Minotaur. The assertive tone continues until the end of the paragraph. Even though she is asleep, the woman still surrenders—"se
me entrega de otro modo" "she surrenders herself to me in another
way"—to the man whose eyes caress her mouth, throat, and chest.
He possesses her with his look, so to speak.

The second paragraph alters this pleasurable state. It begins
with a question: "¿Se entrega?" "Does she surrender?" which
casts the previous affirmations in doubt. Moreover, the reply to
that question is negative: "No, no se entrega" "No, she does not
surrender." It is precisely because the contemplated woman is not
a distant being that she retains the possibility of distancing herself
from the one with whom she has an intimate relationship. And
this process takes place (or at least the narrator thinks it does) as
she sleeps. Sleep, curiously, is compared to a "selva" "jungle," in
which there is a "gruta" "cave" where the woman hides, like a

nymph. The Minotaur thus encounters a being with strengths comparable to his own. She is not a simple prey, but a fiercely aloof or evasive figure. Yet the description of this woman also includes delicate aspects, like the "blando ritmo de la respiración" "bland rhythm of breathing." All these aspects, delicate or fierce, may nevertheless be understood as a projection of the speaking subject's traits onto the woman. His own delicateness, which colors his desire, manifests itself in the following thought: "si me atrevo a besar tu pie, tu pie me responde, no tú" "If I dare to kiss your foot, your foot responds to me, not you."[17] This sleeping woman might offer herself corporally to the man, who can look at her or even touch her at will, but she nevertheless is absent in spirit. When she closes her eyes, she closes off the other's access to her soul, her privacy, in order to retreat into her own inner world. The narrator makes a final, desperate attempt to be included in her sleep; but his questions, indicative of his anxieties, never receive an affirmative answer: "¿Qué estarás soñando lejos de mí?" "What could you be dreaming of far from me?" Maybe he is excluded from her dreamworld ("¿Aparezco quizá yo dentro de tu sueño?" "Perhaps I appear in your dream?"), or the woman isn't dreaming, or she refuses to tell him what she has dreamed ("o quizá me digas que no, que no has soñado nada, que no lo recuerdas . . ." "or maybe you will tell me no, that you haven't dreamed anything, that you don't remember . . ."). Here, then, the act of awakening does not guarantee a resumption of a lost intimacy. Asleep or awake, the woman signals an area of reclusion, a metaphoric "room of one's own" that resists visitation, even by the loved one. The sleeping woman thus offers an exemplary illustration of a distinctive human trait: the impossibility of total contact or connection between two people, or, put another way, the need to protect a private zone from the other's reach. Curiously, this human drama is incarnated in the figures of a Minotaur and a nymph-like woman in repose, hidden in the jungle of her sleep.[18]

Moreover, the title "Mientras tú duermes," "While You Are Sleeping," precedes the first sentence, which we viewed as an initial affirmation of the self: "Yo te estoy mirando" "I am looking at you." But does this interpretation hold? The title, followed by the unusual placement of a comma, must be processed as the beginning of the text; or, in other words, the title forms part of the first sentence.[19] The *you* consequently comes before the *I*: thus the self-emphasis disappears. While she sleeps, the woman is not so much effaced as the man who contemplates her. He cannot be present to himself without the active and watchful presence of the woman; looking *on* is not enough, since he must also be looked *at*—and seen—if he is to feel himself fully alive.

Of course, the theme of the Minotaur also refers to the labyrinth in which Minos imprisoned the monster, according to the Greek legend. In this fashion, the narrator-Minotaur may be viewed as lost in a labyrinth. Jorge Luis Borges develops this tragic aspect of the Minotaur in "La casa de Asterión" [The house of Asterion], one of the stories from *El Aleph* (1949). This relation between Borges and Ayala is more than casual. In "Magia, II" there is an explicit reference to another story from *El Aleph*: "¿Recuerdas—me habías preguntado—aquel cuento de Borges sobre *Los dos reyes y los dos laberintos?*" "Do you remember—you had asked me—that story by Borges about *The Two Kings and the Two Labyrinths?*" (145). Both Hispanic authors superimpose the tragic character of the Minotaur onto his bestial nature.

But to the monster's tragedy we must add the woman's. In this respect, it is noteworthy that in multiple versions of the theme of the sleeping woman in Picasso—*Faun Unveiling a Sleeping Woman* among them—she assumes a position similar to the Vatican's *Sleeping Ariadne* (Ries 143). And Ariadne, even though she helps her beloved Theseus escape unharmed from the labyrinth, is subsequently abandoned by him: "After a stay on the Isle of Naxos, Theseus abandoned her as she lay sleeping by the riverbank" (Grimal 50). Man sees the woman's sleep as an occasion to flee from her.[20]

To some extent, the destinies of the Minotaur and Ariadne coincide (it is relevant that they are children of the same mother, Pasiphae.)[21] His labyrinth corresponds to her sleep, the state in which she is abandoned. The concept of the two labyrinths (of Borgesian origin) resurfaces clearly in "Magia, II": "Tú, la reina de Saba . . . , me acusaste de haberte encerrado, para castigo de tu soberbio laberinto, en un laberinto de arena: mi propio desierto" "You, the queen of Sheba . . . , accused me of having locked you up, as punishment for your arrogant labyrinth, in a labyrinth of sand: my own desert" (145). But here the woman seems to be secluded in the man's sleep rather than in her own. In any event, the tragic note ultimately prevails, something that the ellipsis following the last sentence of "While You Are Sleeping" would appear to confirm. It is as if the speaking *I* must renounce the process of reflection, which leads him further astray. Her sleep gives rise to his nightmare: the horrible vision of a man awake and alone.

## THE TWO LOVES OR THE TWO VENUSES

The visions of earthly love that were the focus of the previous section stand in contrast to spiritual love as manifested in "Magia, I" [Magic, I], "El leoncillo de barro negro" [The little black clay lion], and "Amor sagrado y amor profano" [Sacred and profane love]. A Christian-Platonic perspective informs these stories, which thread together the idea of liberation from carnal passions and the wish to make earth into the paradise the author searches for incessantly with an exasperation that increases with age.

"Magia, I" shares the setting of a restaurant with a story discussed earlier in this chapter, "*Au cochon de lait.*" The couple in "Magia, I" have tea at the narrator's home before going to the restaurant: "yo mismo preparé las dos tazas, echando, en el fondo de cada una, una cucharadita de hojillas, oscuras como hormigas, para verter luego encima de ellas el agua caliente. No tenía yo ni tetera, ni colador, ni nada; en mi casa no hay nada de nada" "I prepared the two cups myself, placing a spoonful of little leaves, dark like ants, at the bottom of each cup, and then pouring the hot water over them. I didn't have a teapot, or a strainer, or anything; in my house there is nothing at all" (141). This narration is best understood by connecting it to "El leoncillo de barro negro," which functions as its counterpoint. In this story the house becomes a metaphoric hermitage: "Ella y yo le llamamos mi ermita al apartamento sucinto donde, como un San Jerónimo en la jungla de asfalto, paso las horas de mi vejez con algún libro que apenas leo y muchos pensamientos que a veces me fatigan" "She and I call the succinct apartment my hermitage, where, like a Saint Geronimo in the asphalt jungle, I spend the hours of my old age with some book that I hardly read and many thoughts that at times fatigue me" (149). Even if he is not explicitly presented as such, the man who receives the woman in "Magia, I" is also a kind of hermit, since he has "nothing at all" and can only offer "little leaves, dark like ants." Old age takes away his material goods and loads him up instead with "many thoughts."

Something as basic as aspirin cannot be found in his stark surroundings either, and thus the narrator resorts to alleviating the woman's headache with "suaves roces" "soft rubbing" (141) on her forehead and temples. The magic is so powerful that it works. The couple then goes to a restaurant, since the cupboard is literally bare at the narrator's apartment. But even in this public setting they remain isolated and indifferent to those around them: "En medio de la gente, seguíamos estando los dos solos, como si flotáramos en el vacío" "In the midst of the people, the two of us remained alone, as if we were floating in a vacuum" (141). They manage to exit from this vacuum shortly thereafter, not to enter into a lovers' paradise but, to the contrary, into the supposedly abolished "devil's world": "cuajó de pronto en torno de mí todo aquello en que antes apenas si había reparado: la sala del restaurante anodino, con sus muebles y sus horribles lámparas, y aquellas caras, aquellos bultos, aquellos cuerpos" "all of a sudden everything that I had hardly noticed before crystallized around me: the dining room of the ordinary restaurant, with its furniture and its horrible lamps, and those faces, those shapes, those bodies" (142). The pictorial model for this narration is understandably one of Goya's black paintings, *Dos viejos comiendo sopas* [Two old men eating soup] (Fig. 19). Specifically, the parallel is established through the following passage: "y yo temblaba de que, al fin, terminaras también por descubrir a las dos brujas que, en un rincón, engullían infatigablemente, con sus fláccidos, pintarrajeados, pringosos e insaciables hocicos, atroces alimentos" "And I trembled with the fear that after all, you, too, would end up discovering the two witches in the corner who tirelessly were gobbling down atrocious food with their flaccid, smeared, greasy and insatiable snouts" (142). The sex change of these horrid creatures stands out immediately: Goya's old men become old women, or, more precisely, "brujas" "witches," perhaps in an attempt to associate the painted figures more clearly with the Parcae. Lorente in effect describes *Two Old Men Eating Soup* as follows: "the two leering cadaverous figures, enacting the drama of human existence, appear to have risen from their coffins to find nourishment" (2, 157).

Ayala animates the background of Goya's painting, thereby transforming it from the blackness surrounding the old men into the social setting of a restaurant, where the frightful apparition is relegated to a corner. The contrast is even more violent here than in the related story "*Au cochon de lait*," where the devouring side of Spring is in part occluded beneath notes of irony. In "Magia, I" there is no room for irony, since the narrator seems to lack control

Figure 19
Goya, *Two Old Men Eating Soup*. Prado, Madrid.

over the situation and thus cannot allow himself so much as a smile. In this regard Ayala resembles Goya, whose *Two Old Men Eating Soup* is interpreted as follows by Fred Licht: "The fantastic personages that the artist projects are not summoned up by the artist. . . . Instead, they impose themselves *on him*, and though he is frightened, he is nevertheless compelled by his most intimate nature to do their bidding" (192). Of course, the capacity to organize these visions through art constitutes a victory for both painter and writer, which Licht notes (in markedly elitist terms): "Whatever happens, whatever terrors the hollow, indifferent world may hold, the artist, unlike the common man, recognizes in himself the power of perception and of creation based on his perceptions" (192).

Not only should Ayala's story be related to Goya's artistic vision, but also to the painting that gives the book its title, *El jardín de las delicias*, or, more exactly, to the right panel (hell) (Fig. 20). In the open hindquarters of the monster who occupies the center of this panel, some people engage in drinking: "a witch is serving the sinners seated at table" (Tolnay, *Hieronymus Bosch* 32). In "Magia, I" witch-like or demoniac traits are also attributed to the cashier ("aquel diablo epiceno" "that ambiguous devil"), to the waiters ("aquellos tres canguros que melancólicamente pasaban en fila por entre las mesas" "those three kangaroos who moved mel-

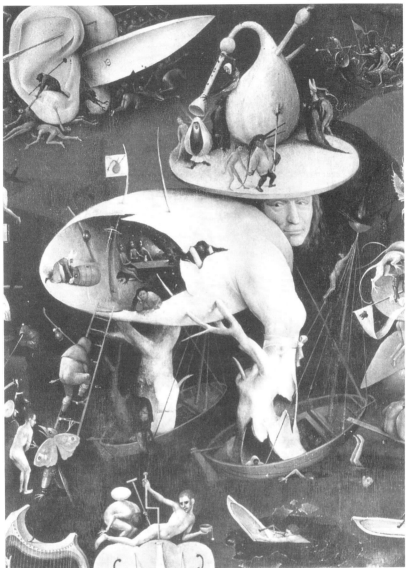

Figure 20
Bosch, *The Garden of Earthly Delights* (detail of right wing: Hell).
Prado, Madrid.

ancholically in a row among the tables"), and to other customers
(142–43). Tolnay's remarks on Bosch apply equally well to Ayala:
"The earth itself has become a hell" (32). There is another parallel
worthy of mention. Just as the narrator who introduces the story
contemplates the spectacle that surrounds him, so does Bosch in

his painting by means of a self-representation in the hostelry scene: "Apart from them [the sinners seated at table], a corpulent man in the attitude of melancholy sits with closed eyes above the abyss; when we recognize in his features the face of Hieronymus Bosch, the whole picture appears in a new light: the artist himself is dreaming this dream, his soul is the place of the thousand agonies and the thousand torments" (Tolnay, *Hieronymus Bosch* 32). Tolnay compares this vision to the one presented in the *Divina Commedia*, an interartistic link that allows us to join "Magia, I" to "*Au cochon de lait*" with its "imprevisto despliegue de imaginería dantesca" "unexpected display of Dantean imagery."

In this infernal atmosphere the narrator thinks he spots an innocent figure: "Acudió la camarera con la cuenta, y al pronto me pareció una especie de ángel adolescente que tuvieran secuestrado y cautivo en esa gruta; pero hubo un instante en que también creí detectar algún destello malvado en su aparente inocencia" "The waitress came over with the check, and suddenly she seemed to me like a kind of adolescent angel whom they had kidnapped and detained in that cavern; but there was also an instant when I thought I detected a flash of wickedness in her innocent appearance" (143). The term "gruta" "cavern" brings us back to "El leoncillo de barro negro," in which the protagonist plays the role of a penitent Saint Geronimo. As for the "adolescent angel whom they had kidnapped" (and in whom innocence and malevolence coexist), the metaphor anticipates a similar one applied to the narrator's companion. He believes that she, too, has been bewitched: "Y me acordé del cuento . . . de la princesa por malas artes convertida en paloma. Le habían clavado en la cabeza un alfiler, y el encantamiento no se desharía hasta que alguien lograra extraer ese alfiler de la cabecita al ave espantadiza y desconfiada" "And I remembered the story . . . of the princess turned into a dove by evil magic. They had stuck a pin into her head, and the spell could not be broken until someone managed to pull out the pin from the little head of the frightened and distrustful bird" (143).

In order to understand this enigmatic ending we must offer a brief analysis of "The Little Black Clay Lion," illustrated by Alonso Cano's *San Jerónimo* from the Prado Museum. The narrator places the statue of the lion next to a portrait of his innocent "niñita" "little girl" (149) and what he mysteriously calls "la imagen plural de este ángel mío, ella, la mensajera divina cuyas manos alimentan mi existencia, alma y cuerpo" "the plural image of this angel of mine, she, the divine messenger whose hands nourish my existence, body and soul" (149). Although the lion supposedly can do no harm to the girl, the presence of the animal next to the other angel worries this modern-day Saint Geronimo: "Bien puede un ángel ser princesa transformada en melancólica paloma por arte de hechicería, aquella mujer única, ella, a quien yo siempre quise, he querido y quiero desencantar" "An angel could well be a princess turned into a melancholy dove by a spell, that unique woman, she, whom I always wanted, have wanted, and want to disenchant" (149–50). The painting provides the key to these mysteries. Saint Geronimo, in his cavern with a lion nearby, receives a visit from the angel who announces the Last Judgment with his trumpet.[22] There is no greater liberation than death, which here is the death of passion as symbolized by the lion as well as the dove. This second symbolism is more complex, however. The dove often represents the spirit, as do birds in general: "Birds which can fly high into the sky symbolize . . . freedom . . . of the soul to soar, to rise seemingly free from what binds us to earthly existence" (Bettelheim 101). In this light the dove functions as the equivalent of the angel; but in another context it is an emblem of the Great Mother, the earthly Venus: "The dove specially was her attribute, both as Aphrodite and as Mary (dove of the Holy Ghost)" (Neumann, *Origins* 76).

The paradox is thus resolved: as a dove representing Venus, the woman is bewitched and subjected to earthly passions, which she shares with man—the lion perpetually tempted.[23] Yet once the pin is removed from her head, the dove turns into a princess-angel, the pure being that she was before abandoning paradise. Hell would be the indomitable passions. The desired transformation of the woman runs parallel to that of the man, that elderly figure haunted in his desert by fatiguing thoughts and frightening visions.

"El teléfono suena; suena su voz dulcísima anunciándome que viene a verme en mi ermita" (150) "The telephone rings; her most sweet voice rings as she announces that she will come to visit me in my hermitage" (150). The angel's trumpet is replaced by the phone, and the woman's voice turns angelic, whereas it had earlier been associated with "el vuelo vertiginoso del Apocalipsis" "the vertiginous flight of the Apocalypse" (149). In his excitement, the narrator makes a clumsy move that topples the lion, which breaks into pieces: "sus fauces están abiertas con no sé qué promesa de mieles en la muerte, como las del león que mató Hércules hebreo" "its jaws are opened with I don't know what promise of honey in death, like the honey in the lion that the Hebrew Hercules killed" (150). The destructive element here is symbolized by devouring passions. "The Hebrew Hercules" is Samson: an etching by Dürer, *Samson Killing the Lion*, illustrates this passage. Sweetness now emerges from the dead lion, that is, the very narrator who leaves behind his violent instincts. The biblical model is quite apparent: "And after a time he [Samson] . . . turned aside to see the carcass of the lion: and, behold, *there was* a swarm of bees and honey in the carcass of the lion" (*Holy Bible*, Judges 14.8). As we have already noted, both man and woman are transformed. She looks radiant right away: "Hoy se encuentra a sí misma, libre entre mis brazos. . . . Me dice: '¿Sabes? Esto es hermoso'; me dice: 'Cuánta paz'. Y yo la beso en la frente" "Today she finds herself, free in my arms. . . . She says to me: 'You know? This is beautiful'; she says to me: 'So peaceful.' And I kiss her on the forehead" (150). Masters of their own passions rather than subject to them, the lovers freely surrender to each other. In contrast to the inferno of "Magia, I," a utopian paradise on earth takes over here.[24]

The narration entitled "Amor sagrado y amor profano" [Sacred and profane love] offers some fruitful avenues to pursue as we conclude this chapter on Francisco Ayala. Initially, the narrator of the story boasts of having found "el equilibrio tenso, la milagrosa suspensión de una lucha larguísima y atroz con el ángel, súbitamente resuelta en abrazo de amor infinito" "the tense equilibrium, the miraculous suspension of a very long and atrocious battle with the angel, suddenly resolved in an embrace of infinite love" (163). The battle between Jacob and the angel (Genesis 32. 24–32) constitutes an obvious intertext here. Jacob ends up both victorious and vanquished when the angel injures him in the thigh but then blesses him and reveals his divine face. "I have seen God face to face, and my life is preserved," Jacob exclaims. The victory of Ayala's modern Jacob would of course consist in having triumphed over profane love, lowly carnal impulses (a triumph also seen in "El leoncillo de barro negro"). These verses cited later in the story reinforce this parallel: "*El amor, un león / que come corazón*" "*Love, a lion / that eats the heart*" (163). Along with lionly love there exists another kind, "el amor único del ángel que, desde su esquina, plegadas las alas, me atraía siempre, y siempre se me quería hurtar" "the unique love of the angel who, from the corner, with her wings folded, always attracted me, and always tried to escape from me" (163).

The dividing line between both worlds or both loves is not so clear, however. The figure of the angel later takes material form in the sculpture that stands at the entrance to the Cathedral of Reims; *El jardín* includes a reproduction of its smiling face. For the narrator, the ambiguous smile of this famous angel reminds him of the woman who currently serves as object of his adoration. He says in reference to her: "Leve desdén burlesco riza su boca alzando un poquito la comisura izquierda; y ¿qué falta hace entonces pedir corroboración a su mirada para sentirse expulsado del paraíso?" "Slight mocking disdain curls her mouth, raising the left side a little; and what then would be the use of seeking corroboration in her look to feel oneself expelled from paradise?" (163). The angel or the angelic woman thus carries too much of a terrestrial charge to function only as an image of pure love beyond the storm of passions. The second illustration for this text is Titian's painting of the same title, *Sacred and Profane Love* (Fig. 21), which contains representations of the two Venuses differentiated by Plato: the heavenly Venus and the earthly Venus (Hall 262).[25] It is of interest that the celestial Venus appears nude, with a flock of sheep dotting the landscape behind her. The terrestrial Venus, on the other hand, is clothed; the animals in the background (rabbits) possess an undeniable sexual connotation.[26] In Ayala's narration, the two opposing loves are also represented by different animals: "Hay el manso amor de los corderos, que lastimeros balan; el ronco, venustino amor de la paloma, que rodea y arrulla" "There is the tame love of the sheep, which bleat pitifully; the throaty, Venus-like love of the dove, which encircles and coos" (164). The dove, as in "Magia, I," is associated with the sensual world (Pandemian Aphrodite). In its double signification, spiritual and terrestrial, the dove exemplarily represents Venus; it mediates the transit from profane love to divine love, while at the same time it encodes the always possible fall from celestial heights. That is, the dove incarnates the notion of a battle between opposites, which at most may be resolved in "equilibrio tenso" "tense equilibrium," or "milagrosa suspensión" "miraculous suspension," as we saw at the beginning of the story.

Yet the nude admits a similar conflictive meaning. Kenneth Clark formulated the distinction that associates the naked with the (feminine) body unclothed, "huddled and defenseless" (3); the nude, in contrast, is a "balanced, prosperous and confident body: the body re-formed" (3). Titian's painting appears to offer a perfect illustration of Clark's ideas, which in our times may be seen to reinscribe the very Renaissance doctrines that he studies in his critical work: "It seemed then [during the Renaissance] that there was no concept, however sublime, that could not be expressed by the naked body" (26). Here, form or spirit triumphs over materiality: "The nude remains the most complete example of the transmutation of matter into form" (27). But a victory or transmutation such as this is always suspect. Matter and the senses constantly threaten to overturn the constructions built up on them. Lynda Nead accordingly locates the female nude on the border between art and that which most seems to oppose it, obscenity: "The female nude marks both the internal limit of art and the external limit of obscenity. This is the symbolic importance of the female nude. . . . And whilst the female nude can behave well, it involves a risk and threatens to destabilize the very foundations of our sense of order" (25).

In *Sacred and Profane Love* by Titian the joint appearance of the clothed and the nude women disrupts the intention of the work. The twin Venuses supposedly establish a radical difference in accordance with the Neoplatonic line of thinking. Yet these two women who bear an undeniable physical resemblance may be seen as one, clothed *and* nude. That is, a narrative intrudes between them: one that tells of the act of unclothing. In this fashion the nude cannot be so easily separated from the naked. Even works of art such as Titian's force somewhat the equation of the two categories differentiated by Clark (or by Plato).[27]

In truth, the nude can only be sustained when it is situated in abstract space and time, on the margin of any narrative.[28] However, at the moment when the nude forms part of an event (or, in W. J. T. Mitchell's words, when we see or read the picture as if it were a sentence), the naked reappears. And what could be easier than to endow Titian's *Sacred and Profane Love* with a narrative if, as it happens in Ayala, the painting is evoked in a text with the same title. The narrator's attempts to freeze time by recurring to the static forms of painting may hardly be called a guaranteed success. The language of art tells us otherwise.

Another painting by Titian, the *Bacchanal* (discussed in chapter 4 with relation to Salinas) deserves mention again here. A female nude (Ariadne) also figures prominently in this work, but what surprises the spectator is that this nude, like the representation of Vic-

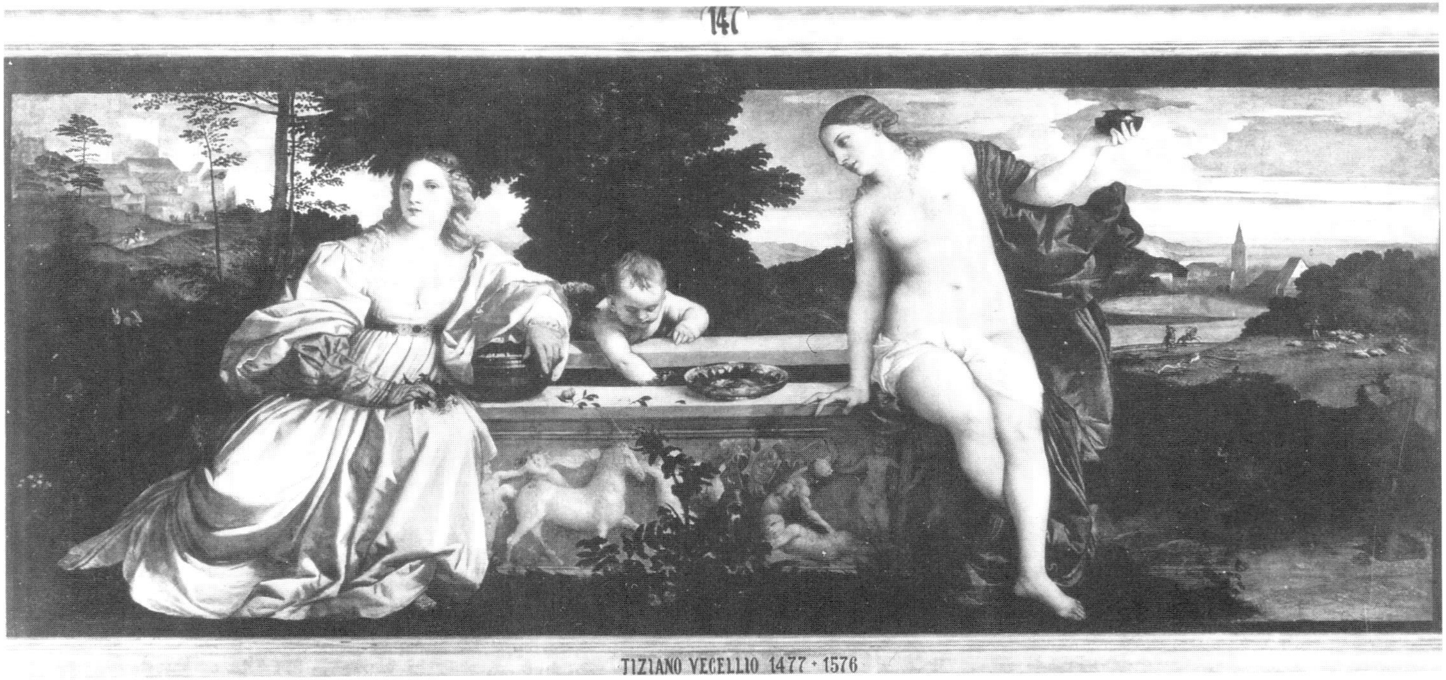

TIZIANO VECELLIO 1477 - 1576

Figure 21

Titian, *Sacred and Profane Love*. Galleria Borghese, Rome, Italy. Alinari/Art Resource, New York.

torine Meurent in *Le Déjeuner sur l'herbe*, is surrounded by people who are dressed, for the most part. In addition, if we recall that the depicted scene is precisely a Bacchic festival, then the argumental sequence may be established in this instance as well.[29] The act of unclothing in that particular licentious context affects Ariadne, whose body now appears to be naked rather than nude. We should recall that the sleeping Ariadne in Roman and Hellenistic sculptures is shown clothed except for one exposed breast (see chapter 4, note 8). Perhaps Salinas perceives this motif in a description that we have linked to Titian's *Bacchanal*: "el tiempo estaba desnudo y se comportaba liberal y graciosamente, como en una fiesta báquica el cuerpo que soltó corsé y tirantes, liga y corchetes, todo lo que le ceñía oprimido y estricto y se muestra ahora desenvuelto y rosado sin dejar ya dudas respecto a su entrega total" (*Víspera* 38) "time was naked and behaved in a liberal and [charming] fashion, as in a Bacchic festival when the body loosens corset and suspenders, garters and clasps, everything that fits it oppressively, rigidly, and reveals itself free and easy, rosy, leaving no doubt of its complete surrender" (*Prelude* 34).

Another pertinent example from art history is Goya's two *Majas*. Emilia Pardo Bazán, as previously indicated, considers the clothed *Maja* "even more disquieting beneath her clothes."[30] But the disquieting or obscene aspects of the clothed *Maja* come about as a result of the inevitable comparison with the naked figure, since the same woman is depicted in both paintings, which are displayed in the Prado Museum one beside the other. Here, too, the beholder effortlessly supplies a narrative: the clothed *Maja* is about to undress, hence her obscenity. And, further, the model is supposedly the Duchess of Alba, whom the *vox populi* made out to be Goya's lover. Nead's words once again are relevant: "If . . . the purity of the female body depends upon stasis, both of the body that is displayed and the body that is viewing, then movement begins to toy with the possibility of obscenity" (85). The naked *Maja*, understood as the result of a process, at the very least exhibits a kind of stasis that cannot be attributed to the clothed one, who in this sense is more carnal, not (yet) tamed by the powers of artistic sublimation. Or we might say that the clothed *Maja* possesses a more active nature, and is thereby more "disquieting" than her naked sister-self (although signs of activity of course pass from one to the other). In the retrospective light of Goya, *Sacred and Profane Love* by Titian defies the Platonic reading that has been performed on it. The two Venuses are too close—like the side-by-side *Majas*—to be appointed representatives of two opposite worlds, one celestial and the other earthly.[31]

We also have analyzed, in Ayala's writing, the theme of the Minotaur or the satyrs in the presence of the female nude body; their animal forms incessantly suggest the possible rupture of equilibrium, or the alteration of any stasis to which that nude figure may lay claim. The balance would always hinge on unstable forces. The narrative previously adduced with respect to Titian and Goya has as its equivalent in Picasso the multiple versions of the theme of the Minotaur and the woman from the Vollard Suite.[32] In some of these works, grouped by Bolliger under the title "Battle of Love" (numbers 28–32), the imprecise limits of the figures, in their jumbled mix, produce the impression of a kind of return to chaos, which would appear to contradict Clark's idea of the "transformation of matter into form" operated by the nude.[33]

In Ayala's "Amor sagrado y amor profano," the last paragraph sets forth the scope of this difficult and precarious victory over the senses. The narrator, a glass of whiskey at his side, leafs through a magazine in which there is an advertisement for rum with this image: "una mujer espléndida alza su copa y brinda" "a splendid woman lifting up her glass and toasting" (164). The first paragraph of the story contained the same elements (drink, a magazine); they resurface at the end following the meditations contained in the interposing text. Through the vision of the "splendid woman," the narration returns to the level above which it had sought to rise. Commercial art transforms the woman into one more commodity, roughly equivalent to the rum that she is peddling. There is no possibility of a victorious conversion of matter into form or of sublimation of the body, characteristic of "high culture." Charles Bernheimer makes the following remarks concerning Manet's *Olympia* (the model for which supposedly was a prostitute): "*Olympia* traps the male viewer by making him unconsciously aware of an anxiety about sexual difference that he thought he had mastered but that now returns. This return is all the more unsettling in that its vehicle is an image of woman as publicly available commodity displayed for male consumption" ("Uncanny Lure" 21). In effect, the vision of the woman in the advertisement perturbs the narrator by reminding him of loves past, loves that he nevertheless casts aside as definitively ended: "De pronto (sólo por un instante, es cierto: ya pasó) un sutil esti-

lete se me ha hundido en las carnes. (Ya pasó: ¡Adiós, amores! . . .
También yo, como la mujer del anuncio, levanto mi vaso y bebo
un trago)" "All of a sudden (only for an instant, it is true: it's over
now) a subtle stiletto has been plunged into my flesh. (It's over
now: Farewell, loves! . . . Like the woman in the advertisement, I,
too, lift up my glass and take a drink)" (164). The narration thus
concludes on an ambiguous note. The farewell to an amorous past
is solemnized through the Bacchic gesture, which brings the narrator close to that "splendid woman," as if the two of them were
toasting together at the same time that he takes leave of her (or of
what she signifies). Several etchings by Picasso come to mind here,
such as numbers 83, 85, and 92 of the Vollard Suite (*Drinking
Minotaur and Reclining Woman*; *Drinking Minotaur and Sculptor with Two Models*; *Minotaur, Drinking Sculptor, and Three
Models*), in which the artist in his studio, or his double, the Minotaur, raises a glass beside equally "splendid" women. The renun-
ciation of love therefore coexists with images that express a vital
excess or overflow. "Amor sagrado y amor profano" may thus be
perfectly integrated into *El jardín de las delicias*, a work that Carolyn Richmond claims is "above all, a celebration of life" (222).

Richmond points to the profound lived experience as reflected
in the pages of Ayala's book, which she characterizes with the
term "imaginary autobiography" (213). Similarly, Irizarry views
*Días felices* [Happy days], the second part of *El jardín*, as "a kind
of fictitious autobiography" (257). The imaginary or fictitious elements of the the text derive from the insertion of invented material, which the reader cannot sort out from lived circumstances
without the author's help (or without extratextual evidence).
Ayala comments on this aspect in relation to "Nuestro jardín":
"The only element there that was taken from reality is . . . the oil
painting that gave rise to the story. But everything that is narrated
in it is a complete invention on the writer's part; nothing, absolutely nothing, that is told had taken place before outside of the
scope of the written work" (*El tiempo y yo* 64).

Paradoxically, literary invention, by projecting subjective
experience onto a generic human level, underscores veracity or
truth because readers are taken into the narrator's world and identify with him. Certain thematic constants (the universal fantasy of
a lost paradise, youthful emancipation, the proximity of death,
incommunication between lovers, violence and control of the passions) serve to implicate readers in the text. Instead of feeling like

distanced spectators, we may experience ourselves as co-authors of the text; or, in other words, we see ourselves reflected in the figures, literary as well as pictorial, of *El jardín de las delicias*. We transfer to them or they reveal to us our desires and affections (conscious or unconscious), inasmuch as Ayala, in a masterful way, is able to evoke primary experiences, be they real or fantasied. André Green, who follows Freud here, states the importance of these fantasies: "he [Freud] considered that any experience related to these primal fantasies would have an influence on psychic development which was not in proportion with the importance of the experience in reality. Primal fantasies acted, in his opinion, as if they had the power of categorizing, or classifying, all other experiences" ("Constituents of the Personal Myth" 68). However, these fantasies are articulated in the form of narrations or images, which make up the personal myth. Located in this double dimension of the mythic (or generic) and the personal is each individual's existence or truth: a truth only accessible when subjected to certain psychic structures, which in the process deform it. As Green says, "The truth we discover is, like myth, a distorted one. We have to accept the fact, as we have to accept the idea, that some truths can reach us only through a distortion that enables them to be told" (86). Of course, the same distortion follows when, as critics (analysts/analysands) we attempt to retell the stories we read and view or, if you wish, to interpret them, substituting narrative for factual truth.

# CHAPTER 7

## *Visions of a Painted Garden: José Donoso's Dialogue with Art*

The vision of the writer exiled in a garden of earthly pleasure and pain that informed the analysis of Francisco Ayala's work in the previous chapter may be extended equally well to the Chilean writer José Donoso, who spent long years in Spain away from his native country when it was under Pinochet's rule. "Exile," Donoso has remarked, "meaning both political and voluntary absence from one's own country . . . is one of those knots of live-wires, a shared, collective experience, from which I think the greater part of Latin American contemporary fiction derives its strength" ("Ithaca" 182). Mario Vargas Llosa and Guillermo Cabrera Infante, the subjects of the next two chapters, are certainly no exceptions to Donoso's observation. Although exile in itself constitutes a fundamental consideration in the works of Donoso and his literary colleagues from Spanish America, its presence may also be viewed as one component in the interartistic framework that we have been employing to perform our analyses. Paradise lost, which ties to political exile and psychic alienation, is transformed through writing into a metaphoric place where fantasies take shape as painting on the page.

It is this dialogue between painting and literature that José Donoso has cultivated in *El jardín de al lado* [The garden next door] (1981), which he declares is his "most realistic novel to date; it is a psychological study and there are few masks although I imagine scholars will find them" ("Conversation between Donoso and Gautier" 3). He also claims that it is "the portrait of a middle-aged literary couple whose love is starting to give way and the political defeat somehow breaks them but they stick together" ("Round Table" 33). Donoso's classification of this work as a portrait is far from arbitrary, and he is right in imagining that students of the novel will find masks where he consciously placed few. On close examination, the novel engages in a lively dialogue between literature and the visual arts in an attempt to answer the question, How can the eye/I see itself? The confessional mode, which normally entails intimate revelations, here becomes a device that instead produces a textual disguise of remarkable complexities. Julio Méndez, the primary narrator of *The Garden Next Door*, documents his failed efforts to produce a publishable version of his novel, whose subject is the military coup in his native Chile. But the whole of *The Garden Next Door* revolves around the hidden female narrator-author, Gloria Echeverría de Méndez, Julio's wife, who steps forward in the final chapter. In telling the story of exile, Donoso thus takes flight from his own *I*—always a potential empty shifter in literature, and always an other, as Rimbaud tells us—to take refuge in his writer-protagonist who himself is filtered through the eyes of an overriding narrator.

In this confessional work, then, the figure of the male author is twice masked or mediated in the text: through the narrative disguises of a male character with a fictional name and through a female author-character who purportedly writes the novel finally accepted for publication by literary agent Núria Monclús. Thus *The Garden Next Door* centers on a metaconfessional act: Gloria writing about Julio writing about his struggles to write an autobiographically inspired novel. This great unwritten novel of the Chilean experience, which is only spoken about in *The Garden Next Door,* constitutes the elusive core of the work in that it escapes Gloria, Julio, and perhaps even Donoso to remain trapped in layers of narrative and psychological cover.[1] When the novel first opens, Julio is seen avoiding his typewriter, the taskmaster that demands either a new version of his "novela-documento . . . ya rechazada una vez por la formidable Núria Monclús," "novel-testimonial . . . already rejected once by the formidable Núria Monclús," or the "tediosa traducción de *Middlemarch* de George Eliot, hecho en *tandem* con Gloria, labor que parecía eterna" (*Jardín* 13) "[tedious translation of George Eliot's *Middlemarch*, done in tandem with Gloria], a task that seemed endless" (*Garden* 5). In tandem—one behind the other—or a team. But for the team to operate, one partner must assume a leading position, and the apparent forerunner, Julio, wears blinders, since he remains unaware that throughout the entire work he is a textual object for his wife, the successful author. It is interesting that Julio and Gloria's translation is of a work by a female author who goes by a male pseudonym, which previews in ironic fashion the gender crossing that is unveiled in the final chapter of Donoso's novel. *Middlemarch* also echoes and redoubles the thematic structure of *The Garden Next Door*, focused as Eliot's novel is on the tension-filled marriages of two couples. Continuing along these lines, it is worth noting that the latest edition of Donoso's *Historia personal del "boom"* [Personal history of the "boom"] (1983) contains two appendixes. The first, "El 'boom' doméstico" [The domestic boom], was written by María Pilar Serrano, the writer's wife; the second is a postscript by Donoso, "Diez años después" [Ten years later]. Serrano, writing in tandem with her husband, exposes intimate gossip in her version, which is a triumph of the "minor tone" that appeals to Gloria.[2] And in 1987 she published a book of memoirs entitled *Los de entonces* [Those of yesteryear], which chronicles life before and after her marriage to José Donoso through a series of chapters based on social events such as "Té para cuatro" [Tea for four] or "*Beer party* en Iowa." The work ends with a change of tone. The final episode is a sober reflection on the Pinochet years in Chile, "Santiago tras las rejas" [Santiago behind bars]. Of particular relevance to our discussion of authority and authorship is Serrano's decision to publish the book under the name María Pilar Donoso. She remarks in the prologue: "Justifico mi firma . . . por considerar que al publicar un primer libro a mi edad, no puedo darme el lujo de perder las ventajas de la curiosidad que el apellido Donoso despierta en los círculos literarios. . . . Donoso es 'mejor apellido' que Serrano, al menos en las librerías." "I justify my signature . . . because I believe that in publishing a first book at my age, I cannot afford to give up the advantages of the curiosity that the name Donoso can generate in literary circles. . . . Donoso is a 'better name' than Serrano, at least in bookstores" (11). Donoso's wife, as we see, thus writes with him, and with his name.

In her insightful analysis of *The Garden Next Door*, Lucille Kerr concludes that "the contingent and mobile quality of the authority apparently held or wielded by the principal subjects undermines any notion of its absolute or permanent nature, even when the final inversion, the surprising reversal, would seem to put an end to its movements" ("Authority in Play" 60). Yet, we may add, it is precisely the unconscious fantasy of an integral and infallible narrative anchor that undergirds the novel. This figure corresponds psychologically to the preoedipal or phallic mother, whom Jane Gallop describes in Lacanian terms as "apparently omnipotent and omniscient until the 'discovery of her castration,' the discovery that she is not a 'whole'" (*Daughter's Seduction* 22). Omnipotent and omniscient—what better words to characterize the hidden Gloria, who has managed to pass off a convincing first-person narration in her husband's voice? She then becomes the all-seeing eye, the spy whose gaze penetrates into the most remote corners of Julio's being. It would be she who has Julio engage in ruthless self-examination, she who authors the devastatingly ironic remarks about herself: "la odio porque está fea o mal vestida o porque saló demasiado el tomate" (115) "I hate her because she's ugly or sloppily dressed or she salted [the tomato] too much" (100). In keeping with modern functions ascribed to the first person in a narrative, the *I* of Julio's text fails to be self-referential and instead stands for another. Thus, the masculine *I* harbors a latent *she*, who eventually dislocates the unstable *I* to subordinate it in the form of a third-person, *he*.[3] The narrative filter is thus a veil that cloaks the shocking, naked reality of the female author at the work's core. Here we have two veiled portraits, as the cover of *The Garden Next Door* graphically symbolizes with its version of René Magritte's *The Lovers* (Fig. 22). In this extratextual sign system, Magritte's painting is superimposed on portions of a draft of *El jardín de al lado*; the typewritten lines, containing crossed out words and handwritten corrections, extend from the front cover of the book to the back. The couple's shrouded faces partially block the traces of the text in progress, thus mirroring the process that occurs within the novel. Words, both in their semiotic and semantic powers, remain buried, literally under cover in this novel. As the book's cover illustrates, then, the association of text to art constitutes a key medium through which Donoso explores the couple's relationship to each other and to writing; an interartistic analysis may therefore gain us privileged access to the deep structure of desire in *The Garden Next Door*.[4]

The apartment in Madrid that is home to Julio and Gloria for the summer belongs to Chilean Pancho Salvatierra, a painter. Julio describes one wall of his friend's apartment: "En el salón, dos ventanas simétricas, desnudas, que descubren sólo cuadrados de verdure como si fueran tapices, y entre ellas, de exactamente las mismas dimensiones, un cuadro que reproduce los cortinajes blancos de toda la casa, cuadro en que reconozco la maestría para reproducir la engañosa realidad que es don de Pancho Salvatierra" (67)

# El jardín de al lado

## José Donoso

Figure 22
Front cover of José Donoso's *El jardín de al lado*.
Cover design by Josep Navas, based on Magritte's *The Lovers*.

"In the living room, two bare symmetrical windows that [reveal only squares of verdure as if they were tapestries], and between them, exactly the same size, a painting [that reproduces] the white curtains found throughout the apartment, [a painting in which] I recognize Pancho Salvatierra's gift for reproducing a false reality"

(54). Bijou, son of Chilean exiles living in Paris, bursts into laughter when he first spots Pancho's *trompe l'oeil* painting. Bijou's reaction gives Julio cause to reflect on Pancho's apparent success: "Poseer un punto de vista tan original que se acerque a lo cómico . . . , pienso en Dalí, en Chirico, en Magritte, que también son envolventes e instantáneos y divertidos. . . . Eso envidio" (142) "To [possess] a point of view so original that it verges on the comic . . . I'm thinking of Dalí, de Chirico, Magritte, who are also compelling, immediate, amusing. . . . I envy it" (126).

Pancho's *trompe l'oeil* consists of false curtains that cover only empty wall space, while the bare windows in the room create a painting-like impression as they open on the lush garden next door. Donoso's novel, itself a study in trickery with regard to characters and readers alike, also plays with the notion of naked revelations and veiled portraits. But to equate Pancho's work with Magritte's, as Julio does, is to err significantly, for while there are similarities in theme, an important difference stands out. Magritte creates not the *trompe l'oeil*, which hinges on deceiving one's perception of physical reality, but instead cultivates what Picasso has called the *trompe l'esprit* (Gablik 77), a type of metaphysical questioning. Pancho's work of art may best be understood in relation to some of Magritte's "cloud" paintings, such as *The Memoirs of a Saint* (Fig. 23). The circular red curtain in this painting refuses to fulfill the traditional function of shading out light, whereas the "sky lining" of the curtain defies even more dramatically the function of real draperies. A related painting, *The Gioconda,* shows two free-standing black curtains placed against a dark background; the superimposed panel in the shape of a curtain appears to be an isolated patch of sky with clouds. Similarly, *Wasted Effort* uses two bright sky and cloud curtain-shaped panels before a background of a sky with clouds in muted tones, and on the extreme right and left sides of the painting are smaller blue cloth curtains. All four curtains appear to be standing on a stage, as does the curtain in *The Memoirs of a Saint,* which underscores the notion that for Magritte physical objects may be transformed by the brush into players of roles or even wearers of masks. He endows objects (such as a chair, tuba, rock, or bell) with animate qualities by making them appear to fly, burn, or float, for example.

Magritte's well-known *The False Mirror* depicts a giant human eye: filling it is a reflection of blue sky and clouds. The "painting philosopher" thereby challenges the seeing function of

Figure 23
René Magritte, *The Memoirs of a Saint* (1960).
The Menil Collection, Houston. Photo F. W. Seiders. Copyright 1994
C. Herscovici, Brussels/Artists Rights Society, New York.

the eye and instead turns it into the object viewed.[5] Similarly, in *El jardín de al lado*, the fascinating woman in the garden next door, Countess Monika Pinell de Bray, has Magritte-like eyes, which serve as a false mirror to Julio:

> como en una cabeza clásica de mármol, sus ojos son vacíos. Pero con una diferencia: en vez de ser un vacío de piedra en blanco, son dos ventanas abiertas al cielo por el cual transitan nubes o donde juegan niños en sus triciclos o, cuando mi amor es más doloroso, los agujeros almendrados me dejan ver olas rompiendo sobre riscos, y más allá, el horizonte del mundo entero. (144–45)

> as in a classic marble head, her eyes are blank. But with a difference: instead of the [vacuum] of blank stone they are two windows opening to the sky [through which] clouds drift past or where children play on their tricycles or, when my love [is most painful], those [almond-shaped openings] let me see surf break-

ing on cliffsides and beyond them, the horizon of the whole world. (128)

Like Magritte, Donoso takes up the problematics of "seeing" in *The Garden Next Door*, where the subject sees himself reflected in the eyes of the (female) other, who in turn views herself through the male's desire.

To pursue the painting analogy, central to the confessional voice in Donoso's work, we now turn to the Odalisque paintings of Jean-Auguste-Dominique Ingres; it is here that we find the interplay of desire and vision carried out in full depth. Julio first associates Gloria with Ingres's Odalisque on their wedding night, and it is an image he continues to evoke throughout the decades of their marriage. He describes Gloria as she showers:

> el torneado de la otrora perfecta Odalisca de Ingres—deleitosa cadera plena, largo arco de la espalda para acariciar y pierna larga, largo cuello, y ojo alargado bajo el turbante envuelto en la cabeza volteada—se dibujaba más allá de esa puerta, pero, sobre todo, más allá del tiempo, por el reconocido roce de la ropa al caer por los contornos de aquel cuerpo. Hasta que, con-temporánea, doméstica, imperfecta otra vez, la oí dar la ducha y meterse debajo. (24–25)

> the once-perfect outlines of Ingres's Odalisque—[delightful full hip, long arch of her caressable back], long leg, long neck, and elongated eye beneath the turban around the half-turned head— were being sketched for me (beyond that door, but, above all, beyond time), by the familiar rustle of her clothes slipping down the contours of her body. And then I heard her, contemporary, [domestic], imperfect once again, turn on the shower and step under it. (15–16)

This description corresponds most exactly to the *Grande Odalisque* in the Louvre (Fig. 24), but may also be related to paintings such as the *Valpinçon Bather* or *Odalisque with the Slave*. For Julio, Gloria lives on as the imperfect, deformed Odal-isque whom he attempts to resuscitate through physical contact enhanced by mental fantasy. This comparison between Gloria and the Odalisque rests on a solid basis, as revealed by Julio's knowl-edge of the artist's techniques: "Ingres, pienso al mirarla ahora, sabía dibujar como nadie: le bastaba la más sutil modulación de una línea, variar su espesor, su densidad, hacerla más profunda o casi eliminarla, para hacer real la sugerencia de masa y de peso y

Figure 24
Jean-Auguste-Dominique Ingres, *The Grand Odalisque* (1814).
Louvre, Paris, France. Giraudon/Art Resource, New York.

el satinado y la sensualidad y el calor de la espléndida carne de su modelo" (155) "Looking at her now, I say to myself, Ingres knew how to draw like no one else: the subtlest modulation of a line, a variation of its thickness, its density, making it more pronounced or almost eliminating it, was enough for him to suggest realistically the mass and the weight, the satin texture, the sensuality and warmth of his model's marvelous flesh" (138). The equation Gloria-Odalisque serves to keep Julio's wife attractive to him—he clings to the fantasy of the female nude—but at the same time it shows painfully how she has aged and changed. The association also affects Gloria by keeping her in her marriage, as she discloses in the last chapter to Núria Monclús during their meeting to discuss Gloria's accepted manuscript: "¿Y por qué no abandonaste tú a Julio?" "And why didn't you leave Julio?" inquires Gloria's literary agent. She responds: "La Odalisca, que tan orgullosa me hace, no existe fuera del recuerdo y la fantasía de Julio. . . . ¿Qué otro ser puede restituirme mi cuerpo de entonces, hacer presente la realidad de esa Odalisca del pasado, sino Julio? Un beso, la toalla envuelta en la cabeza, basta" (257–58) "The Odalisque I'm so proud of doesn't exist except in Julio's memory and imagination. . . . Who else, except Julio, can restore [to me] the body I had then and make that Odalisque of the past real [in the present]? A kiss, a towel wrapped around my head, is enough"

(235–36). The subtle implications of this linkage become apparent when we examine Ingres's paintings, which reveal a remarkable similarity in artistic vision to Donoso's portrait of Gloria in *The Garden Next Door*. For example, Robert Rosenblum makes these comments on the *Grande Odalisque*: "the prodigious ductility of the line . . . suggests a flesh of voluptuous malleability, yet this pliant stuff is polished to a marmoreal firmness, so that it seems alternately warm-blooded and cold, slack and taut, a fusion of opposites" (107). Gloria is forged as a flesh-and-blood woman whom her husband believes to know completely, yet she is presented simultaneously as the unknowable, unreachable, *unreadable* controller of the text and consequently of its primary narrator. And while the *Grande Odalisque* has been compared to a titillating pin-up girl,[6] most critics instead agree that these paintings "generate erotic power precisely because they elude the imagination's hot embrace," as John Connolly puts it (17). More radical is Norman Bryson's opinion that sexuality in Ingres "is not a positive or *plenary* force, but a force of *vacuum*"; he claims that the *Grande Odalisque* "is not offering herself at all," but rather is presented in terms of highest unreality, and "constitutes a radical disruption of the standard and homogeneous image of woman" (*Tradition and Desire* 137). This self-dissolving and self-unraveling movement that Bryson sees in the implausible physical form of the *Grande Odalisque* causes her to be Ingres's most impossible creation.[7]

Paradoxically, it is this impossible creation that incarnates the structure of desire in both Ingres and Donoso. And, returning to our original thesis, what would represent the structure of desire better than the fantasy of the phallic-castrated woman who threatens the male protagonist or viewer with a terrifying *manque-à-être*? Any text, Sarah Kofman argues, "is always a tissue that, for fear of castration, disguises a terrible and most tempting nudity" (96). Like the spider, a phallic mother symbol, Gloria spins narrative threads to cover her nakedness and perhaps to entrap her victim. But she is also the odalisque, who, let us remember, is a female slave or concubine in a harem, to which all men except one are forbidden access. This is Gloria speaking in Tangiers, near the end of the text narrated in Julio's voice: "¡Qué pena que el idiota de Carlos Martel ganara en Poitiers! . . . Si no, andaríamos todos vestidos así, yo viviría cómodamente en un harem precioso. . . . En fin . . . por lo menos andaríamos con la cara velada" (235)

"What a pity that idiot Charles Martel had to win the battle of Poitiers! . . . If he hadn't, we'd all go around dressed like that, I'd live comfortably in a nice harem. . . . Anyway, at least we'd walk around with veils over our faces" (213). Julio wonders to himself if Gloria could mean "velada para disimular la vergüenza" "veiled to cover up their shame." The facial veil would of course constitute a displacement upward from the genital zone that supposedly provokes corporeal shame. And so it becomes clear that Donoso's evocation of the odalisque is far from casual: it symbolizes Gloria's conflictive double role as tempting slave and terrifying slave driver. Looking again at Ingres's paintings, we notice that the odalisque indeed remains partially veiled, yet her face is uncovered: rather, it is her genital nudity that remains out of sight, either because she has her back to us (*Grande Odalisque*) or because she is shrouded by the diaphanous cloth that extends provocatively from her thighs to other regions (*Odalisque with the Slave*). Ingres did indeed paint total nudes, but the odalisque guards her mysteries, like Gloria. Ingres and Donoso touch upon a common fantasy when they cast their odalisques in the mold of a veiled woman who defies man's attempts to possess her, and who remains alluringly attractive because of what she hides, or more accurately, because she hides it.[8]

This hidden schema of temptation and terror, of strength and impotence, of hostility and affection, goes beyond the immediate duo of Gloria and Julio. Let us consider the role of Núria Monclús, the literary agent who twice rejects Julio's novel. She is intimately associated with Gloria, first by Julio, who proclaims of his wife: "ella y Núria son, igualmente, mis verdugos" (225) "she and Núria are both my executioners" (204). A mythical devouring female, Núria represents all that is terrible: she preys on weaklings like Julio with her "carnívoro sadismo" (30) "bloodthirsty sadism" (21). While Julio finds some comfort in the *vox populi* that makes Núria out to be a frigid, avaricious and opportunistic woman, he cannot escape her tyranny:

> ¿Si recupero mi facultad de sentir placer en vez de aceptar pasivo mi ciudadanía en esa provincia tan extrañamente reglamentada que es la del fracaso personal . . . podré adquirir la libertad para escribir otra o la misma novela . . . ? No: aunque saque ahora mismo los papeles de la maleta, la figura de Núria Monclús con la telaraña velándole los ojos y la espada de fuego en su mano ensangrentada se interpondrá entre yo y el placer. (70–71)

> If I recover my ability to feel pleasure and renounce my passive
> citizenship in the [strangely regimented] province of personal
> failure . . . will I then be free to write another or even the same
> novel . . . ? No: I may take my papers out of the suitcase right
> now, but the vision of Núria Monclús with the spiderweb [veil
> covering] her eyes and the fiery sword in her bloodstained hand
> would come between me and the pleasure. (57)[9]

Julio feels himself imprisoned in his novel with Núria as his jailor.
Unlike his wife, this spiderwoman shows no positive reverse side
to Julio. Núria is *par excellence* the castrating, phallic mother who
impedes the son's absolute pleasure. Núria admonishes Julio to
"see" his novel: "verla," "see it," she says from beneath her own
veiled eyes. And yet sight belongs specifically to the phallic order,
since the discovery of "castration" revolves around a vision, a
prizing above all of that which is seen.[10] What Julio ultimately
sees is himself as failed writer: "Soy inerte, castrado, mal escritor"
(173) "I am [inert, castrated], a bad writer" (156); "el falso triun-
fador, el macho falsificado, el ladrón, el delincuente, el men-
tiroso" (230–31) "the false victor, the fake macho, the thief, the
delinquent, the liar" (209). And while Julio struggles to assume his
own failure, as he puts it, he nevertheless incriminates Núria,
agent of his literary nonexistence.

There is a curious aside to Donoso's textual story. It seems that
Isabel Allende, the Chilean novelist who fled her country following
her uncle's assassination, turned to Carmen Balcells, the literary
agent after whom Núria Monclús is modeled in *The Garden Next
Door*. Allende recounts that she got the idea of sending Balcells the
manuscript of the now-famous *La casa de los espíritus* [The house
of spirits] after reading Donoso's novel. Allende, who is currently
more popular in the United States than her compatriot Donoso (at
least in bookstores), has cultivated that melodramatic "minor
tone" that Núria appreciated in Gloria. It is ironic that this younger
Chilean author could be considered a modern-day Marcelo Chir-
iboga (Julio's nemesis) in a female version, someone who has
become a representative of *the* Latin-American author before an
international public. Needless to say, Donoso's literary reputation
is well-secured; he would have little reason to envy Allende's success
and has not, to our knowledge, shown any reaction to her triumphs
under Balcells's agency. Nevertheless, Donoso displays little gen-
erosity in claiming that the younger "generation in Latin America

has not given very interesting women writers" ("Conversation with Montenegro and Santí" 15).

Returning to the novel, we note that Julio's failure extends to Gloria, not only his spouse but also his collaborator and reader of his fiction: "El fracaso es de ambos, yo no la arrastré a él, yo tengo esperanza aún, y hasta ella suele tenerla, sólo que a veces todo se torna negro, como si todo ocurriera detrás del antifaz sin ojos" (102) "[The failure belongs to both of us], I didn't drag her into it, I still have hope and so has she, but sometimes everything looks black, as if everything went on behind the night mask [without eyes]" (87). Gloria's black night mask is one way of seeing, or rather, of blocking out a vision. For if Gloria "sees" Julio's novel when he reads it to her during her recovery from severe depression, she also is blinded because, as she states, "no puedo juzgarla porque es tan mía como tuya y te quiero" (217) "I can't judge it because it's mine as much as yours and because I love you" (196). Or we should say that the successful novel is hers alone. Julio is blinded to the fact that Gloria will write a triumphant version of their intimate story. He dons his wife's black mask to obliterate all visual sensations, a symbolic gesture that represents the overall irony of his textual predicament. In his naiveté he fears that Núria's rejection of his novel would be an equally terrible blow to his wife: "Núria tiene la culpa, puesto que ella me impide triunfar: ella tiene atrapada a Gloria en una telaraña, que es su cárcel" (178) "It's Núria's fault, because she keeps me from [triumphing]: she has Gloria trapped in a spiderweb, her prison" (161). But, instead, the two web-spinning women form an alliance in the book's final chapter. Gloria's opening line undoes the frightful picture Julio had painted of Núria: "Ninguna de las terribles leyendas que circulan sobre ella son verdad: es fina, encantadora, generosa, sensible" (247) "None of the terrible stories going around about her are true: she is charming, generous, sensitive" (225). Thus, the portrait of Gloria that Julio sketched throughout his part of the narration is shown to be distorted as well: no longer ensnared in anyone's net, she has instead become the trapper. Julio's derogatory comments about Gloria's creative abilities turn ironically against him when their source is revealed. Or do they? Must we disavow the authority who really engenders these transfigurations? Does not the figure of the male author—not the fictional Julio, but José Donoso—stand clearly behind the many masks assumed by the writer-characters in the text of *The Garden*

*Next Door*? After all, Gloria is his creation. Could we not apply to *The Garden Next Door* and to Gloria what Donoso himself has said of Manuela, the protagonist in his *El lugar sin límites* [translated as Hell hath no limits]: "a man who poses as a woman who poses as a man who poses as a woman" ("Round Table" 28). *The Garden Next Door* harbors a futile search that crosses gender boundaries; much like Ingres's odalisques, who exude desire and yet thwart it, the narrators and their masks seek through the other a knowledge impossible to attain. Every object of desire, according to Lacan, will show itself to be "necessarily ephemeral and destined to be supplanted because it is incapable of stopping up the lack inscribed in the subject from the start" (Lemaire 175). Donoso's characters cannot fathom the nature of lack in the other, because they fail to recognize it in themselves, and their incessant search for (phallic) plenitude edges them closer to the void.

If Gloria's apparition at the end of the work symbolizes the male narrator's blocked access to knowledge, vision, or truth, then so does the garden next door to the apartment building in Madrid where the couple is staying. Much like the self-representative figure of Hieronymus Bosch above the abyss in *The Garden of Earthly Delights* (Fig. 20) (discussed in chapter 7), Julio observes the spectacle of the neighbors as they dance, laugh, and splash about in the pool, a veritable "pond of lust" analogous to the one in Bosch's painting. Julio wishes to join them: "El anhelo es de pasar al otro lado del espejo, que ellos habitan" (106) "[The desire is] to pass through to the other side of the looking glass they live in" (91). This hallucinatory garden next door serves as a cruel mirror that forces Julio to "see" himself as incomplete or disassembled, the same image that Núria reflects back to him. Julio's fascination with this garden centers on the young countess, who changes before his ever-watchful eyes from ordinary hausfrau into passionate adulteress. In a reversal of the classic primal scene, Julio, the middle-aged adult, glimpses the youthful participants in their orgy: "me abro en una oquedad de melancolía al darme cuenta de la irreparable exclusión de mi cuerpo y mi mundo del desenfadado vigor de esos cuerpos que continúan nadando . . . abrazados en racimos" (109) "I feel a sad emptiness opening inside me when [I realize the irreparable exclusion] of my body and my world from the easy vigor of those bodies that go on swimming . . . with their arms around each other [like branches]" (94).

Julio describes the countess and her lover as follows: "el hombre desnudo toma en sus brazos a la mujer de la túnica que se entrega a su cuerpo en un abrazo tan sexual como el de la pareja de Klimt, en que sólo se ven las cabezas envueltas por la algarabía de colores de oro, pero que los ojos cerrados de la mujer describen como el placer de la entrega total" (146) "the naked man takes the woman in the tunic into his arms and she gives herself up to his body in an embrace as sexual as that of Klimt's couple, in which all you see is the heads wrapped in a riot of colors and of gold, but which the woman's closed eyes [describe as] the pleasure of total [submission]" (129). Klimt's *The Kiss* (Fig. 25) indeed transmits the total self-absorption of the embracing pair as they merge into one gold-laden sphere. But this bliss in Klimt is short-lived: the

Figure 25
Gustav Klimt, *The Kiss* (1907–1908). Oesterreichische Galerie, Vienna, Austria. Erich Lessing/Art Resource, New York.

erotic, the "doomed-to-transiency embrace," as Alessandra Comini calls it (19), leads to the specter of aging, destruction, and death. This stifling colorful ornamentation in works by Klimt such as *The Kiss* engulfs the couple in an over-lush garden that gives way to the stark, deathlike embrace of, for example, the clinging pair in the Beethoven frieze, done mostly in *grisaille*. According to one critic, Klimt's female is sexually destructive, "her eroticism cloaked, layered and ultimately kept untouchable by a glittering surface of elaborate gold painting" (Meisler 77), a vision close to Ingres's and Donoso's. It comes as little surprise at the end of *The Garden Next Door* when Gloria reveals that the countess has committed suicide. Gloria thinks: "tal vez no haya pasado de ser una fantasía cuya clave se encuentra en *El abrazo*, de Klimt" (252) "perhaps she was never more than a fantasy whose clue can be found in Klimt's *Embrace*"(230).[11] This fantasy, as we will see, interconnects with the other artistic themes so richly woven throughout Donoso's novel.

When at the end of chapter 2 Julio, from his darkened room, hears the sounds of splashing water in the pool, he mentally recites part of the third stanza of T. S. Eliot's "East Coker": "*The laughter in the garden, echoed ecstasy / Not lost, but requiring, pointing to the agony / Of death and birth*" (111–12). Donoso's interartistic dialogue once again strikes deep chords: T. S. Eliot's *Four Quartets*, which belongs to the confessional mode, treats precisely the writer's struggle to "see" his work and himself.[12] Further on in "East Coker" we read: "So here I am, in the middle way . . . Trying to learn to use words, and every attempt / Is a wholly new start, and a different kind of failure / Because one has only learnt to get the better of words" (30). Julio's lost garden, like Eliot's, is a paradise of words that could somehow magically take shape on the page to transmit feelings or to communicate experiences. But words, for both writers, remain insubstantial signs that call attention to themselves, that constantly threaten to unveil their status as "shabby equipment always deteriorating," as Eliot says (31).[13] Julio, like all humans, must mediate himself through words—doubly so, since he is a writer. When he becomes caught up in the other's look in his attempt to see himself, he only becomes further alienated from the truth he so desperately seeks. This predicament may explain Julio's desire to exchange himself, to become another, be it the adolescent Bijou, the Bacchic revelers next door, or the ailing beggar in Tangiers: "quiero ser ese hombre, meterme dentro de su piel enfermiza y de su hambre para así no tener esperanza de nada ni temer nada, eliminar sobre todo este temor al mandato de la historia de mi ser y mi cultura, que es el de confesar esta misma noche . . . la complejidad de mi derrota" (239) "I would like to be that man, to crawl into his sickly skin and into his hunger, to hope for nothing or fear nothing, and most of all to get rid of this fear that my background and my culture will make me confess tonight . . . the complex story of my defeat."[14]

Yet the deepest level of surrender to another, or of disappearance into another, occurs metafictionally when Gloria steps out as the "real" author of Julio's story. May we then say that she, too, wishes to be another, to trade in her identity for, perhaps, that of her husband, whose narrative voice she usurps? This undoubtedly is one reading that the novel allows. Let us not forget that Gloria presents herself as a potential author: "¡Si supieras cuántas novelas no escritas tengo encerradas dentro de mí, como gatos locos en un saco, que pelean y se destrozan . . . !" "If you only knew how many unwritten novels are sealed up inside me, like cats in a sack, gone wild, fighting and tearing one another apart!" This remark meets with Julio's scorn: "¡No digas leseras! ¿Me quieres convencer ahora de que eres una escritora frustrada?" "Cut out the nonsense! Are you trying to make me believe that you're a frustrated writer?" Gloria mockingly retorts: "En fin, ¿quién sabe? Puede ser sólo la clásica envidia del pene" (117–18) "Well, who knows? It may just be a classic case of penis envy" (102–3). That writing is a phallic activity has of course been questioned by feminists, and even silence has been called woman's true voice.[15] Silence serves as a way for Gloria to avenge herself; although it is not apparently "productive" in a social or cultural sense, it is in fact a weapon she uses effectively against Julio. But, as Kerr demonstrates, Gloria breaks silence and turns to a more recognizably powerful weapon to achieve her final revenge: writing her own and Julio's story (*Reclaiming the Author* 128–30). Through writing, Gloria shuns her exclusive role as Odalisque, object (and creation) of man's desire. By writing herself, Domna Stanton points out, women may reappropriate the female body, "which man has confiscated as his property" (76). These issues of gender and writing are firmly planted and debated on the multiple narrative planes of *The Garden Next Door*, not as detached, theoretical constructs but as an intimate portrait of two people's trials and triumphs.

This gender-writing conflict, however, leads not to the destruction of the couple's relationship, but to reconciliation and a "Glorious" triumph. Julio realizes that his wife has shared his vision of Tangiers and most likely would be able to write a superior chronicle of the experience; thus he encourages her to take up where he trails off. So the gender-crossing and transexual writing in *The Garden Next Door* may also be considered as a positive force, since it touches on an androgynous spirit, which, Carolyn Heilbrun says, may be identified in literary works "where the role of the male and female protagonists can be reversed without appearing ludicrous" (*Androgyny* 10). In his reversal of narrative voices Donoso perfects this structure of androgyny: Gloria is not only plausible, but also *invisible*, inasmuch as she actually passes unnoticed under Julio's cover.[16]

Despite Gloria's decision to stay with Julio, she nevertheless expresses dissatisfaction with her marital role and formulates this wish: "Ser yo, por fin, no parte incompleta de lo que Lawrence Durrell, falazmente, llama '*that wonderful two-headed animal that is a good marriage*,' ideal que durante tanto tiempo me sirvió para apoyar mi matrimonio" (257) "To be myself, at last, not just an incomplete part of what Lawrence Durrell wrongly calls 'that wonderful two-headed animal that is a good marriage,' an ideal that served me for such a long time to support my marriage" (235). Yet, ironically, the two-headed animal must be seen as the purported creator of this fragmented novel, since neither of the two main voices in *The Garden Next Door* would be possible without the other. When joined they form what may be called, in Melanie Klein's terminology, a "fantasy of combined parents," in which the mother retains her phallic powers through her link to the father. But if on the one hand the image of combined parents in *The Garden Next Door* stands for phallic power, on the other it disguises a lack-in-being. Much like the hydra, which replaces a slain head with two new ones, the fused narrative authorities of *The Garden Next Door* only manage a thin cover for their individual wounded selves. For, in order to generate new phallic heads, the hydra must first suffer decapitation, and that is precisely what Gloria undergoes by means of the portrait that Julio entitles *Retrato de la señora Gloria Echeverría de Méndez* [Portrait of Gloria Echeverría de Méndez].

After Julio learns from Núria that his novel has been rejected for a second time, he enters Pancho's study, where he spots a painting with an electric, phosphorescent blue background:

> un bello cuerpo de mujer desnuda, sentado, pero invadido por cientos de insectos meticulosamente pintados que cubren como joyas la carne fresca y bella de esa mujer, cochinillas, libélulas, moscardones, escarabajos, grillos, saltamontes, arañas. La figura sentada tiene un batracio sobre una rodilla, de modo que le cubre el sexo: los ojos del bicho son penetrantes, y la boca húmeda y lívida, abierta. El marco es un listón de plata que decapita la figura, cuya cabeza queda fuera del cuadro." (226–27)

> [the beautiful body of a nude woman], seated, but invaded by hundreds of meticulously painted insects, like jewels covering the cool lovely flesh [of the woman]: cochineal bugs, dragonflies, bluebottles, beetles, crickets, grasshoppers, spiders. The seated figure has a toad on one knee, arranged to cover her sex: the animal has penetrating eyes, and its moist, livid mouth is open. The frame is a silver strip that decapitates the figure, whose head is left out of the painting. (205–6)

On the back appears Pancho's title, *Retrato de la condesa Leonor de Teck* [Portrait of Countess Leonor de Teck], which Julio promptly blackens out and replaces with Gloria's name. He then wraps up the painting and proceeds to bootleg it.

This entire scene, in a dreamlike sequence, strings together familiar names, places, and events, but reassembles them in distorted fashion. Gloria, for example, has already been associated with the other Teck sister, Carlota. When Pancho calls to invite the couple to spend the summer in his apartment, he remarks to Julio:

> convence a Gloria que sea un ángel y consienta venir a Madrid a cuidar mis cositas. Dile que el primer polvo que le eché [sic] a la Carlota de Teck, que es totalmente frígida como se sabe en todo el mundo . . . se lo echaré murmurándole al oído que es idéntica a la Gloria, el primero de tantos amores no correspondidos de mi adolescencia, que es la pura verdad: tal vez así Carlota logre por fin un orgasmo. (20)

> see if you can talk Gloria into being an angel and agreeing to come [to Madrid to] look after the place. Tell her that the first time I lay Carlota de Teck, [who is totally frigid as everyone

knows] . . . I'll whisper in her ear that she [is identical to] Gloria, the first of so many unrequited loves of my teens, and that's the plain truth. Maybe Carlota will finally have an orgasm. (11–12)

Pancho's jocular comparison of Gloria to Carlota returns us to a familiar notion: one object of desire is substituted for another, but it is only the image of desire projected on the other that accounts for any fulfillment the couple may reach. And this is not the first time a painting of Pancho's disappears from the apartment: Bijou apparently stole one depicting a package wrapped in Manila paper, which Julio and Gloria desperately tried to recover (exactly like the couple in Donoso's "Atomo verde número cinco" [Green atom number five]). Nor is the countess's portrait the first object to be wrapped up and shipped off: Julio's novel manuscript received the same treatment. After hearing it read, Gloria exclaimed: "Mandémosla ahora mismo. En la despensa hay un rollo de papel de Manila y una madeja de cordel" (217) "Let's send it to her right now. There's brown paper and string in the pantry" (196). The manuscript, in its package form, is a material sign that reproduces the one contained in the painting Bijou stole: both packages disappear, their insubstantiality confirmed in loss.[17]

Julio's description of the portrait of Leonor-Gloria does not refer to a real work of art (at least not an easily identifiable one) but is instead the product of a character in a novel, and as such it is just a verbal construction, a painting on the page. It nevertheless may be related to works by artists such as Bosch, Magritte, and Dalí. Bosch of course captured on canvas the images of the nightmare of humanity in his *Garden of Earthly Delights*, including bestial torments not so different from the insect-covered body of Pancho's painting. Following Bosch's lead, the surrealists, particularly Salvador Dalí, cultivated horrifyingly beautiful dream imagery. In Dalí's *El torero alucinógeno* [The hallucinogenic toreador] (Fig. 26), with its shocking blue background (also present in a good number of his other works), we may appreciate affinities to the fictional *Portrait of Countess Leonor de Teck*. Like Magritte, Dalí often studies the duplication of a figure.[18] In *The Hallucinogenic Toreador* multiple versions of the Venus de Milo are depicted in floating positions throughout the center band of a coliseum-bullring, her lower torso draped in bright garb. Twice she is shown frontally; four figures of the statue in descending propor-

Figure 26
Salvador Dalí, *The Hallucinogenic Toreador* (1969–1970).
Collection of The Salvador Dalí Museum, St. Petersburg, Florida.
Copyright 1994 Salvador Dalí Museum, Inc.

tions appear with their backs to the viewer. Also visible are several heads and faces (one of whom represents Gala, the painter's wife) and tiny replicas of the Venus de Milo posed like classical statues around the upper ring of the coliseum and below the large female figures. What disturbs this serene beauty is the juxtaposition of life-sized flies at the base of the large statues; the motif is repeated in the sections of dots that sprout wings as they menacingly approach the Venuses. Most interesting is the misproportioned figure of the bullfighter seen from a lateral angle posed between two of the large Venuses. This male human form and his child-like double in the lower right-hand corner possess arms, in contrast to the dismembered female images. The bullfighter raises his arms, and his hands fuse with the hat that he offers up to Gala. Covering the upper torso of this figure are hundreds of the winged dots, creating the impression that the body of the bullfighter is victim of an insect attack. Typical of Dalí's work, in which erotic elements are often bound up with counterparts from the realm of the sadistic or the destructive, the *The Hallucinogenic Toreador* comes very close to the fantasies expressed in Pancho's portrait.

Carlos Rojas notes several elements in this complex painting that bear direct relation to our commentary here. The little boy dressed in a sailor's outfit, the same figure that appears in *The Specter of Sex Appeal*, is a self-portrait, "with a hoop and a big, petrified penis" (*Salvador Dalí* 178). The flabbergasted little boy would take in the spectacle of the endless Venus de Milo, whose classic beauty competes in the painting with the *trompe l'oeil* figures of the agonizing bull's head (lower left-hand corner) and the phantoms of Dalí's dead brother and slain poet Federico García Lorca (the two large Venus de Milo statues contain these images: her bust makes up the mouth and nose; her clothing forms shirts and ties). Rojas also studies the image of the peasant woman from Millet's *Angelus*, duplicated in *The Hallucinogenic Toreador* and *Portrait of My Dead Brother*, and relates this figure to the praying mantis. His conclusion: "Venus as the praying mantis is associated with a deadly mother who castrates and kills her sons. In other words, she emasculates them first with the terror she inspires, as shown by the petrified penis the little boy holds in his hand. Once their virility is eliminated, she eats them alive" (181).

In *The Hallucinogenic Toreador*, then, we find representations of extreme, complementary fantasies: the phallic, devouring mother in the presence of the sacrificial gorged bull or the stunned child, and, in the same pictorial or psychic space, numerous references to her "castration."[19] As we have noted, these themes also manifest themselves in the imaginary painting in Donoso's novel. The multiplicity of Dalí's versions of the Venus de Milo, with her truncated (castrated) arms, creates poliphallic cover for feared loss; Pancho's painting severs the woman's head, leaving it outside the frame. Dalí's abundance of winged insects serves as grotesque cover for the profiled figure of the bullfighter, much like Pancho's bugs and creatures provide a hideous cloak for his countess. The toad that obstructs view of the countess's sex organs itself creates a bulge where there is none; its eyes are described as "penetrating." This horrid phallic creature sees, but the woman who is the subject of Pancho's portrait is deprived of sight, similar to the woman's face in Magritte's *The Rape*, which is composed of breasts for eyes and sex organs for mouth.

Turning back to Magritte, we may discover a possible source for Pancho's painting style in *Les Liaisons dangereuses* [The dangerous relations] (Fig. 27), which depicts a nude woman holding a mirror that almost completely hides her. The frame of the mirror cuts off part of her head, which is downcast, with her eyes half shut. The woman shown in the mirror appears in profile, an impossible angle of reflection, given that the woman is holding the looking glass in a frontal position. The reflected image is completely headless, and, like the holder of the mirror, she attempts to shield her nude body from view. This deformation, according to Mary Ann Caws, may be read as central to the self, "for the woman divided is also watching herself—without seeing us see her from behind" ("Ladies Shot and Painted" 272). Caws proposes that Magritte's painting may be aptly titled *Woman Reading Woman* (274); in Donoso's novel, which could be titled *Woman Writing Man*, it is Julio (and the reader) who cannot perceive the female observer-author until she chooses to reveal herself.

Michel Foucault remarks of *The Dangerous Relations*: "Through all these scenes glide similitudes that no reference point can situate: translations with neither point of departure nor support" (*This Is Not a Pipe* 52). Pancho's painting also reveals a lack of departure point or support. Does not the woman whose head is cut off by the painting's frame represent the whole-hole of *The Garden Next Door*, where the female author rears her head only outside the main frame of the work, in the final chapter? And isn't woman's body covered over with layers of narration that shield her from view and turn her into a type of fetish?[20] Julio never sees Gloria in her role as triumphant writer, nor does he witness the unveiling of her nakedness at the work's end. He manifests affection and hostility (normally accompanying fetishism) toward that obscure, shifting,

Figure 27
René Magritte, *The Dangerous Relations* [Les Liaisons dangereuses]
(1936). Private Collection. Copyright 1994 C. Herscovici, Brussels/
Artists Rights Society, New York.

supportless construction that arouses insatiable desire in him but that he can never see or totally possess. The fetish is of course the Freudian metaphor for the maternal phallus,[21] a notion we have linked to several female figures in Donoso's work. We have also stressed Julio's ambivalence toward woman, and so if we interpret Gloria's writing as fetish, it comes as no surprise that "like all other compromises, the fetish can never be totally satisfying for either of the two positions, castration or its denial" (Kofman 89). Julio's text mutates before him into the female body, the other against whom man defines himself. The loss of mother, one key to Julio's crisis in *The Garden Next Door*, also signifies the loss of the garden of youth, the "beautiful land" of Melanie Klein's theory of artistic creation. The work of art, then, would stand for the mother's body, repeatedly destroyed in fantasy but restored or repaired through the act of creation (Klein 106).[22]

The double ending of *The Garden Next Door* deserves a few final remarks. Julio's ending to the chronicle of his failed career as an author also terminates his identity as such. He initiates his escape into the night world of Tangiers, purportedly to lose himself in the person of an ailing beggar: "Encontraré al mendigo que de ahora en adelante seré yo porque le meteré un cuchillo por donde se le escapará el alma, de la cual me apoderaré cargándolo con la mía llena de lacras y ansias y esperanzas y humillaciones. Y quedaré desposeído, a salvo de todas las depredaciones" (246) "I'll find the beggar I'm going to be from now on because I'll stick a knife into him to let his soul escape, [and I'll take possession of it; I'll carry it around with my own soul filled with wounds and longings and hopes and humiliations]. I'll be dispossessed, free from all depredations" (224). Julio expresses a desire: "borrar mis huellas para convertirme en otro" (240) "to erase my tracks in order to become another," a longing that is shared by the prototypical Donosian male character. To guide him in this inferno Julio turns imaginarily to Bijou, the bisexual adolescent who spurns the bourgeois moral code, much like Mauricio in "Gaspard de la nuit" of *Tres novelitas burguesas* [Sacred families]. Julio is willing to exchange his identity for a complete unknown in order to escape his stifling world, at the center of which lies Gloria. For what Julio despises in Gloria is also what he fears in her: her powerful and controlling sexuality, symbolized by the much-evoked figure depicted in Ingres's odalisque paintings. While Julio claims to have tired of his middle-aged wife and feels himself bound by conjugal duties, he nevertheless must acknowledge the deep desire she still arouses in him. His flight is motivated as much by his attraction to her and the power that she holds over him as by the repulsion he claims to experience.

Julio's apocalyptic end stands in opposition to the closure Gloria provides for her narration, which chronologically becomes the legitimate ending to the the text of *The Garden Next Door*.[23] If Julio manages to liberate himself from the chains of matrimony, it is only in his subordinated story: at the level of the discourse, Gloria, author of Julio's dramatized memoirs, seizes control of the textual authority and entraps her unsuspecting male victim. Her tale of the events following Julio's departure constitutes both the final chapter of *The Garden Next Door* and the missing chapter that literary agent Núria Monclús envisioned for the manuscript Gloria had sent her. We learn that Julio in reality returned to Gloria's arms at six o'clock in the morning: "Y como toda mujer a su marido que ha llegado a la cama después de una noche de juerga, le olí la boca, la cara, por si encontraba olor a alcohol, a kif, a perfume de alguien que no fuera yo: nada. ¿Además, qué sacaba con saberlo? Me levanté en puntillas de la cama, abrí la puerta de nuestro cuarto, y puse por fuera el aviso para la camarera: *Please do not disturb*" (263–64) "And like every woman whose husband comes to bed after a night on the town, I smelled his breath, his face, to see if there was any sign of alcohol, kif, or perfume that wasn't mine: nothing. Besides, what would be the good of knowing? I tiptoed out of bed, opened our bedroom door, and [put out the sign for the maid]: 'Please do not disturb'" (241). In Gloria's version, Julio merely takes leave for a few unaccounted hours that night, a void that fails to leave a discernible trace on his person, although this is a man who is shown to have a wounded soul. Unlike other Donosian characters whose night wanderings are revealed in chilling detail, Julio's activities, whatever their nature, remain an enigma. Upon hearing Gloria's version of the events, Monclús reacts by speaking what then become the novel's final lines: "Bueno, ¿no es éste el capítulo que falta, el que no has escrito?" (264) "Well, isn't this the missing chapter, the one you haven't written?" (242). Thus the bitter *The Garden Next Door* also ends with an ironic happy ending: a plea not to disturb the delicate reconciliation the couple has fashioned. As they drift into deep sleep in semi-fetal positions, Julio and Gloria recreate the bliss experienced in the symbiotic union of mother and child, a regressive pull that is echoed in all amorous findings, which are invariably *re*findings, according to Freud.

This act of sleep allows Julio to wake up from his nightmare; by renouncing the open door and its possibilities, Julio reaffirms his place in Gloria's garden of delights. For it is the image of the lost maternal garden that has thrown Julio into a state of crisis, and it is this image he sees reflected in the "garden next door." When he was observing his neighbors in their poolside orgy, Julio recalled T. S. Eliot's "East Coker." Eliot's poem starts as follows: "In my beginning is my end. In succession / Houses rise and fall, crumble, are extended, / Are removed, destroyed, restored, or in their place" (23). Julio too must choose between the crumbling house of the unknown world that he longs to inhabit and the comforts of the female (maternal) abode, where he is in his place, in order. His new beginning marks the end of his efforts to gain complete autonomy, yet this is an end that permits him to go on living: as Eliot's "East Coker" concludes, "In my end is my beginning" (32). For Donoso's character, this rebirth is not so much a matter of spiritual transcendence, but rather one of psychic survival.

If the text takes on the form of a palimpsest or, to use the artistic metaphor, a pentimento, then at most we have succeeded in uncovering a layer or two. Donoso charts the course for readers, following Julio and Gloria's lead, to "see" *The Garden Next Door* from a variety of angles, including some impossible ones similar to those of Magritte's paintings. Ingres said: "art never succeeds better than when it is concealed" (Pach 164). Magritte supplies a possible corollary: "What is invisible cannot be hidden from our eyes" (Matthews 220). Donoso tells us that we must go through the way of ignorance and dispossession to arrive at a vantage point from which we may contemplate the hallucinatory garden next door or within, a place that perhaps is devoid of ecstasy but never lacking in humanity.

# CHAPTER 8

## *In Ekphrastic Ecstasy: Mario Vargas Llosa as the Painter of Desire*

When authors such as Francisco Ayala or Mario Vargas Llosa place painting on the page alongside their writing, they invite readers to function also as viewers, and even to become cocreators in a joint interartistic venture. Thus when we process a text and an artwork coterminously, we get caught in a kind of slippage between the two media: the literary text refers explicitly to a visual representation, which, in turn, serves as the metaphoric mirror for the text. These reflections, which echo back and forth in the mirrored room of the interarts comparison, underscore in dramatic fashion that no viewing and no reading may be an isolated or decontextualized act. To interpret a literary interpretation of a painting forces us to make our rounds in the heavy traffic among sign systems: paintings can refer to other paintings, to myths, to biblical stories, and so on; a literary work can refer to other texts, to history, to human lives, and, ultimately, to everything, including language apparently denuded of its power to signify anything at all, as we will see in the next chapter. In the novel we are about to consider, Vargas Llosa has altered the tone of the dialogue between literature and the visual arts from the respectful gentility that may characterize Donoso, Ayala, or Salinas; We now arrive at a strident, flashy demonstration of how all art is artifice. This posture, which may be aligned to key aspects of postmodernism, seems fitting for an erotic novel of our times, times in which hardcore pornography has taken over where the subtle sensitivities of the literary and visual artist might once have reigned. Irony, humor, and self-mockery along with unabashed explicitness may be the best choice for a graceful storyteller like Vargas Llosa, who knows how to flaunt his talents, wink at the audience, and still manage to satisfy readers' desire for narrative pleasure while cutting short the absolute triumph of titillation.

Let us begin, then, with some words on literary erotica. Maurice Charney makes the following claim: "Despite the fact that sexual fiction is created primarily by males and with masculine values, the overwhelming interest in these books is in the representation of female sexuality. This is the central mystery. Is it the product of an oedipal striving to understand and master our earliest anxieties, especially in relation to our mothers?" (164). This rather bluntly formulated question may be precisely the one to which Vargas Llosa has responded in *Elogio de la madrastra* [In praise of the stepmother] (1988), which forms part of the popular erotica series *La sonrisa vertical* [The vertical smile], edited by Spanish film director Luis García Berlanga. It should not shock us in the least that Vargas Llosa, the lifelong admirer of Madame Bovary, has finally created his own fantasy of the adulterous woman.[1] Nor should it surprise us that one of the founding members of the "boom" in Latin American literature has now joined ranks with his contemporaries who have also explored the genre of sexual fiction, from the sexologist Guillermo Cabrera Infante in his confessional treatise of carnal knowledge, *La Habana para un infante difunto* [Infante's inferno] (1979) to José Donoso, in his marvelously decadent mock erotic novel, *La misteriosa desaparición de la Marquesita de Loria* [The mysterious disappearance of the marchioness of Loria] (1980), in which the protagonist is consumed by her fatal passions.

But Vargas Llosa's latest novel is far from an anomaly in his own literary production if we consider for a moment the implications of his autobiographical work, *La tía Julia y el escribidor* [Aunt Julia and the scriptwriter] (1977), an unbridled tribute to another mother-lover who eventually finds herself replaced as love object in the family constellation by her own niece. We have been anticipating this contribution for some time now, and it is with great excitement—intellectual, to be sure—that we finally witness the full play of this psychodrama that Vargas Llosa has been harboring in his earlier works. For the practice of feminist criticism, *In Praise of the Stepmother* constitutes a case study of unparalleled interest within the Peruvian writer's career. At long last we have overt fantasies that permit us to analyze the textual and sexual representations of women, a task that has been hindered by the rather stereotyped female characters who sparsely populate the "man's world" of his early novels. While the *machista* shadow that has loomed over Vargas Llosa will not be dispelled completely by the argument about to be made here, it may at least be understood for its unconscious meaning as revealed through the psychoanalytic framework that informs this reading.

Were it not enough that Vargas Llosa structured his novel around the basic conventions of literary erotica, including progression from light arousal to heavy violation of sexual taboos, his work would still be remarkable for its link to another mode of representation: the visual arts. Vargas Llosa has chosen to use paintings as illustrations for six of the fourteen chapters in the book, chapters which in reality contain ekphrastic fantasies, imaginary tales based on the content of the pictorial images reproduced on the pages of the novel. Vargas Llosa's dialogue with the language of images[2] becomes central to his representations of eroticism in the novel; yet even when the writer acts as the painter of desire, he naturally must use the artistic implements particular to the verbal sign system. It is through language that Vargas Llosa creates the female protagonist when he imagines a text to accompany a painting. Thus in this novel we not only come face to face—or face to behind, as it were—with the painted woman, but also with her linguistic counterpart in both the primary text and in the embedded stories, including the composition written by the character Alfonso ("Fonchito") entitled "Elogio de la madrastra" "In Praise of the Stepmother." Like Aunt Julia before her, the stepmother coexists on multiple narrative planes, yet she is further diffused among multiple artistic media as well.[3] Our interpretive act, then, must necessarily undergo a splitting along those same planes, since in essence, we are forced to offer an interpretation of Vargas Llosa's literary reinterpretation of pictorial images. So the painter of desire in reality holds no brush; rather, through words he tells stories that he imagines the paintings to be speaking. Yet even that statement puts things too simply, for in this thoroughly postmodern work, the fantasies are attributed not to some overseeing implied author but to the members of the oedipal triangle within the work, most particularly to the male protagonist, Don Rigoberto.

Thus we are up against some hybrid, even monstrous, creation, a text that subverts the very model of erotica to which it supposedly conforms, a novel that filters its fantasies through the visual arts. Worse yet, this book exhibits the marks of ironic self-consciousness, as if Vargas Llosa knowingly and laughingly took on the traditional psychoanalytic repertoire of perversions: pedophilia, incest, voyeurism, fetishism, fixations, and so on. The result, many would surely argue, is an erotic novel that lacks the essential ingredient of . . . eroticism, for in its delirious pursuit of the inner workings—understood as physiologically literal—of the protagonist in his amorous rituals, the text aims less to arouse us and more to disgust us, or at least to amuse us. So what use will it be to return to the psychoanalytic theory that allows us to speak of these concepts at all? Wouldn't that be playing into Vargas Llosa's hands? What could we attempt to show that he hasn't already flagrantly displayed with his mock erotic text? One of the challenges offered by an interartistic approach to literature is to reach new levels of meaning with respect to both the image and the word despite the self-conscious games that may be played out simultaneously. This means that we can still enjoy the pleasures of the text even though we take them seriously, but it also means that we will be forced to deconstruct the psychoanalytic play with those very instruments handed down to us from Freud. For if Freud proved anything, it is that jokes often reveal unconscious thoughts, that negation can be the vehicle to affirmation, and that unwillingness to take psychoanalysis seriously can in itself provide clues to the ways in which the unconscious speaks. Further, it is often the case that when we think we have arrived at a valid psychoanalytic interpretation, all that we have really done is edify another layer of defense, put up another screen of meaning that merely blocks deeper unconscious signification. As we approach Vargas Llosa's novel, then, we will be seeking to undo the tightly woven web of fantasy he has constructed, yet we will also have to reconcile our own critical tendencies of projection and disavowal—a rather frightening notion, since our readings would then harbor the potential to be knocked down or reversed with *our own evidence*. Perhaps meaning will be infinitely deferred, or perhaps it will never "arrive," to put it in Derridean terms. But by turning the text and its images back on themselves, and by turning back to the paintings stripped bare of Vargas Llosa's ekphrastic supplements, we can grasp not so much meaning as the process of sign production, which in this case takes us to a postmodern commentary on how representation functions—or fails. Although we inevitably end up assigning provisional interpretations, we must remain vigilant, even self-conscious, of the way we go about it: *In Praise of the Stepmother* demands at least this much of us.

It seems fairly obvious that in employing an approach derived from psychoanalysis, feminism, and theories of the visual arts, we are not at all claiming that Vargas Llosa has in some way posited a feminist reader or has consciously encoded the particular gaps and reversals upon which this analysis hinges. If there is a space for a feminist reading of *In Praise of the Stepmother*, it is one that we must open up forcefully by interrogating the female subject's identification in the narrative movement. Teresa de Lauretis asks: "What manner of seduction operates in cinema to solicit the complicity of women spectators in a desire whose terms are those of the Oedipus?" (137). We, too, will need to examine how a female spectator or reader negotiates the split between gaze and image, between sign and signified, as she positions herself in the complex structure of desire that undergirds the text and its illustrations.

How, then, does the structure of desire manifest itself in Vargas Llosa's novel? In the first chapter, the essential ingredients in the oedipal triangle are set out: on the day Doña Lucrecia turns forty, she receives a birthday note, a veritable billet-doux, from her stepson Fonchito, described as "un ángel de nacimiento, uno de esos pajes de los grabados galantes que su marido escondía bajo cuatro llaves" (*Elogio de la madrastra* 17) "a born angel, one of those court pages in the elegant erotic etchings that her husband kept under quadruple lock and key" (*In Praise of the Stepmother* 5). When Lucrecia reacts to Fonchito's presumably innocent caresses with womanly passion, she mentally declares herself depraved and wonders why she momentarily doubted the pure intentions of her adoring stepson. Initially worried that her husband would react suspiciously at her visibly aroused state, Lucrecia proceeds to subjugate her illicit pleasures into more conventional ones in the marital bed. But, in truth, her passion continues to be ignited by visions of the "little angel," and that excitement also applies to Don Rigoberto, who inquires: "¿Fonchito te ha visto en camisón? . . . Le habrás dado malas ideas al chiquito" (21) "Did Fonchito see you in your nightdress? . . . You may have given the [little] boy wicked thoughts" (9). The spouses' sexual encounter ends with the query that is repeated throughout the novel. Lucrecia asks: "¿Quién soy?" "Who am I?" which prompts Rigoberto to reveal the fantasy that has stimulated him on each occasion. In the first chapter, he responds, "La esposa del rey de Lidia, mi amor" (23) "The wife of the King of Lydia, my love" (11). Now the sexual fantasies as expounded in the first chapter are fairly easy to identify, for they are narrated rather explicitly, not only in their erotic detail, for that after all is one of the essential characteristics of this genre, but also in their classic psychoanalytic language. Thus Rigoberto is said to have *fantasized* ("fantaseó") that his wife appeared seminude before his son, and Lucrecia shows full awareness that her sexual enjoyment has been enhanced by the forbidden infantile kisses. What is not so readily apparent, it could be argued, is the relation between this story and the painting reproduced as illustration for the next chapter, a fantasy based on Jacob Jordaens's *Candaules, King of Lydia* (Fig. 28) in which the king displays his nude wife to his prime minister, Gyges. Further, as we will see upon examining this second chapter of the novel, the oedipal structure as outlined above allows for intricate permutations, beginning with the essential matter of the paths in which desire travels in search of its objects.

Jordaens's painting is predicated upon a showing of a woman's body, as indeed is much of Western art. But this painting does not merely offer the spectacle of a nude woman for the (supposedly masculine) gaze, one that may be construed alternately as now sadistic, now voyeuristic, now admiring, now indifferent. Rather, the queen is being shown by Candaules for the benefit of his underling, Gyges, who must then declare to the king whether this woman surpasses all others in her beauty. The Greek legend gives two versions of the story. According to Herodotus, Candaules, King of Lydia in the seventh century B.C., "fell in love with his own wife" (36) and coerced the doubting Gyges to look upon the queen as she undressed. When the queen discovered her husband's betrayal, she forced Gyges to choose between his own death or murdering the king. The wise Gyges elected to kill Candaules and become ruler of Lydia and husband of the queen.[4] In Vargas Llosa's version, the scene that Jordaens depicts gains some erotic enhancement. The presence of the third party in the bedroom incites Candaules's passion for his wife to such a degree that he is compelled to possess her in front of his prime minister, but the voyeuristic ménage-à-trois precipitates no death other than perhaps *la petite mort*.

In his painting, Jordaens supplements the threesome by introducing a requisite fourth party. Not only does the queen show her-

Figure 28
Jacob Jordaens, *Candaules, King of Lydia, showing his wife to Prime Minister Gyges.* National Museum, Stockholm, Sweden. Foto Marburg/ Art Resource, New York.

self unwittingly to her husband and his guard, but she knowingly meets the gaze of something outside the painting situated at the viewing place occupied by the spectator (and, by implication, at the real or imaginary vantage point of the artist who painted this scene). The terms *gaze* and *glance* require some precision here. As Norman Bryson defines them, the glance is a "furtive or sideways look whose attention is always elsewhere, which shifts to conceal its own existence, and which is capable of carrying unofficial, *sub rosa* messages of hostility, collusion, rebellion, and lust," whereas the gaze is "vision disembodied, vision decarnalised" (94–95). Our initial visual survey places us squarely before the queen's backside, the site upon which our vision is centered, but we gradually find our eyes lifting upward to meet her sidelong glance. The king, on the other hand, is depicted in a frontal position, with his eyes slightly turned toward Gyges, whose head is twisted laterally so he may take in the king's generous offering. Note, however, that Gyges looks intently toward the queen's face but can only see the back of her head: thus the guard does not yet make visual contact with the uncovered body nor the unveiled face that readily greet the external spectator. In fact, none of the figures within the painting meets the other's look; rather, the looks pass along in succession through a circuit of vision that goes from the king to the guard to the queen to the spectators (including the artist). Even the little dog becomes involved in the throwing of glances as it sets its sight on the two partially concealed men on the opposite side of the canvas.

There is only one possibility for a meeting of eyes, then, which would be the imaginary interlock of viewing subject's and female subject's mutual beholding. This potential space of visual interchange saves us from being cast in the role of Gyges, both from a formal perspective—we do not view from the place that he does— and from a psychological perspective—we are not simply voyeurs of the nude woman, but also onlookers of the voyeuristic duo, that is, of two forbidden scenes. Is that perhaps why the queen sports a mischievous look, if we can call it that? Does she express complicity with herself-as-spectacle, her "to-be-looked-at-ness," to use Laura Mulvey's term? And could not her right hand, which in its turned-out position sustains minimal contact with her robes, be a hand *signal* to the hidden duo, a sign that physically opens herself up to their glance as she consciously refuses their gaze? Or is she completely ignorant of the male eyes that seek her, and instead responds with her downward look to another woman, a female attendant who is spatially and socially beneath her? And what if she were contemplating herself in a mirror, a motif we have seen repeatedly in Dutch painting of this time? If this were the case, then the queen would be seeing herself being seen by the king and Gyges, but then the king would be facing the mirror and thus would be aware that he had been discovered, a revelation that would radically modify the legend in its classic version.

Ultimately, we are left to question the woman's position within the structure of desire in the painting, just as we are to question who sees and is seen, a matter that becomes increasingly relevant to our discussion of Vargas Llosa's novel when we learn where Lucrecia's erotic wanderings eventually will lead her. Yet no matter who the imbedded audience is in Jordaens's painting, the external spectator initially takes in the scene from the position of an embodied viewing subject who must look up toward the queen's nude behind, much like a reduplicated figure of the spying Gyges, much like a spying child—a Fonchito, whose father secretly delights in exhibiting his wife before the original oedipal rival, the real son. But in psychoanalytic theory it is the other way around. While the father may unconsciously experience feelings of rivalry toward the son, those feelings must be traced back to their origin in childhood when the young boy himself goes through the intense rivalry that results from the discovery that his mother belongs to another. Clearly, the voyeuristic satisfaction experienced by the king is derived from the feelings he ignites in Gyges, whom we may now regard as stand-in son in the oedipal triangle. The spectator's (disembodied) satisfaction, however, comes from catching all parties in the act, the act of seeing and not being seen. That is, the spectator in this case renounces the initial childlike pleasure of spying on the mother (and desiring to possess her) in order to experience the super-ego gratification of censuring and intercepting the illicit glances of others. The spectator thereby passes from purveyor of the glance to practitioner of the gaze, but in the process the viewer relinquishes the possible *jouissance* of that scene with the father absent. Thus, ironically, the satisfaction of imposing the law-of-the-father proportionally diminishes those joys that come about from escaping that law.[5]

The escape is doubly encoded in the painting in that the king himself refuses to heed the law, as does Gyges; therefore, the spectator could reproduce that violation and reinforce the king's impulse by acting out the scopophiliac role as well. The instinctual impulse that is symptomatically displayed in the voyeuristic position would signal the "return of the repressed," a mechanism that in psychoanalytic theory ushers in the representation of what had been expelled in the phase of repression proper.[6] But to follow that impulse, the spectator would have to occupy the place of the king or Gyges. Or, rather, their presence would first be recorded only to be subsequently obliterated in an attempt to satisfy unconscious desires. Thus the vision of the king (the father) apprehended by the subject would need to be suppressed: the king would have to be "murdered" by the spectator, just as the king will be murdered by Gyges. In that instance viewers could then claim the queen for their eyes only, yet this triumph would be fraught with the anxiety brought about by the unconscious act of patricide. In *Candaules, King of Lydia*, then, there is a denied potential for unpunished or infantile voyeurism: in its place is the installation of a chain of desire that offers no possibility for satisfactory linkage among the three subjects of the painting (taken together) and the viewers. The novelist Vargas Llosa accomplishes a similar feat in his text by casting the reader in the role of interceptor of the multiple sexual exchanges going on in Don Rigoberto's household. We see Fonchito spy on Lucrecia; we catch Rigoberto in his intimate preparations done for Lucrecia's benefit; we observe Lucrecia as she becomes aroused by her stepson; indeed, we are given privileged access to all the manifestations of desire among the trio, but we are denied (unless momentarily) the pleasures that exclusive identification with either the son, the mother, or the father might bring. As subjects we too are alienated from the objects of desire by the interposition of other figures, and we are therefore stripped of the vicarious enjoyment that the erotic novel normally seeks to provide.

The second chapter of Vargas Llosa's novel is an ekphrastic fantasy that may be attributed to Rigoberto, who identifies with King Candaules of Jordaens's painting: "Soy Candaules, rey de Lidia" (27) "I am Candaules, King of Lydia" (13). Based on this fantasy, the primary joy for the viewer of Jordaens's painting resides in beholding the queen's glorious rump, as the narrator Candaules, a projection of Rigoberto, proclaims: "Lo que más me enorgullece de mi reino . . . [es] la grupa de Lucrecia, mi mujer" "What I am most proud of in my kingdom . . . is the croup of Lucrecia, my wife" (27). If this seems like a highly degraded rendering of Jordaens's Queen of Lydia, a grasp at the obvious, then let us see what the character Candaules does with this image and how he uses it for his own erotic satisfactions.[7] When Rigoberto assumes the role of King Candaules, he describes his pleasures with the queen as follows: "cuando yo la cabalgo la sensación que me embarga es ésa: la de estar sobre una yegua musculosa y aterciopelada, puro nervio y docilidad" (27) "when I ride her the sensation that comes over me is precisely this: that of being astride a velvety, muscular mare, high-spirited and [docile]" (13). This conventional equestrian metaphor finds its match in another traditional equation, that is, woman as possession, "la más exquisita posesión de mi reino" (30) "the most exquisite possession in my kingdom" (16), as Rigoberto in his role as Candaules puts it. However, Rigoberto claims to have found true love in his Lucrecia, and, what is more important, continual sexual excitement, which makes the routine of marriage quite tolerable to him. But this image of the queen as object of possession and as source for marital satisfaction is deconstructed by the trafficking among men that makes her not so much object of exchange as catalyst for man's sexual anxieties.

If Vargas Llosa's Candaules boasts of his prowess with the "soft" and "delicate" (15) queen, he still needs to reaffirm his desire by putting it to the test before other men; or, rather, it is *only* through this test that his desire is fully aroused. Thus the narrator Candaules tells Gyges of the time he ordered his well-endowed Ethiopian slave, Atlas, to mount the queen ("le ordené que la montara," 29), which the slave failed to do after many valiant attempts, and as a consequence he was decapitated by his master in a gesture of respect for the humiliated Lucrecia. Candaules knows that his wife is a formidable object of desire: "Penetrarla no es fácil; doloroso más bien, al principio, y hasta heroico por la resistencia que esas carnes rosadas oponen al ataque viril" (28) "Penetrating her is not easy: painful, rather, at first, and even heroic, in view of the resistance [with which] those expanses of pink flesh oppose the virile attack" (14). So Lucrecia is "sweet and delicate," yet heroic in her resistance to the attacking male member. But the one who seems repelled in this amorous combat is the king; it is he who finds penetration painful. Surely we can read a homoerotic role play in the king's description of amorous combat with Lucrecia. Candaules seems to be casting himself in a female role, and his subsequent voyeuristic enjoyment before Gyges or Atlas may be derived from identification with his wife's position (the same may be said of the Candaules depicted by Jordaens or narrated by Herodotus).[8] It is no coincidence that Gyges, in response to the challenge to compare his wife's rump with Lucrecia's, says: "Su Majestad sabe que sus deseos son los míos" (32) "Your Majesty knows that his desires are mine" (18). Candaules recognizes that the malicious complicity that unites him with his prime minister is also the spark that reignites his passion toward that impenetrable filly, and thus he rushes to her avid arms with delight at knowing that Gyges is looking on. Candaules wonders if Lucrecia also senses the presence of a third party, and indeed he speculates that she might have found equal excitement in the game: "Acaso presentía que, aquella noche, quienes gozábamos en esa habitación enrojecida por la candela y el deseo no éramos dos sino tres" (36) "Perhaps she sensed that, that night, it was not two of us but three who took our pleasure in that bedchamber turned a glowing red by candlelight and desire set aflame" (21). Is this what Vargas Llosa reads into the eyes of Jordaens's queen? Does the faint outline of a smile, which might be read as complicit, give him licence to turn her into the consenting member of a triangle instigated for the king's pleasure? Or are her own pleasures legible in this story as well? In the first chapter of the novel Lucrecia does in fact mentally summon a third party to her bedroom, her stepson, Fonchito, and now Rigoberto brings his fantasy of the onlooker Gyges into the conjugal bed. The initial displacement that we have established in Jordaens's painting—Gyges-spectator-child—finds confirmation in the structure of desire revealed in the ekphrastic fantasy. If Lucrecia is guilty of becoming aroused by a child, Rigoberto is guilty of worse perversions. But as the end of the work shows, the punishment for oedipal guilt must be shifted directly onto the woman. In this manner, patriarchal order would be disrupted in the realm of the ekphrastic fantasies that are embedded in the novel, but this disruption would not necessarily carry over to the chapters of the main narrative, which do not declare themselves to be fictions, dreams, or imaginings in the way that the pictorial-based ones do.

This banishment of woman under a reified patriarchal order as Vargas Llosa presents it is not found in André Gide's play based on the theme of King Candaules, nor in the version of events given by Herodotus. In Gide's *Le Roi Candaules*, the queen orders Gyges to kill the king, rewards the murderer with the king's throne, and becomes his wife. Thus the classic oedipal tragedy is re-enacted in Gide's play when the subservient man murders his master and then assumes those social and marital roles that correspond to the once-powerful male. Gide's king receives death for his conduct, whereas in Vargas Llosa's story, the king and queen playfully diffuse the tensions generated by the situation in order to transport the residual sexual excitement into the routine of their marriage, even finding pleasure in the gossip spread about the kingdom by none other than the imputable Gyges. The potential for tragedy gives way to erotic farce, which, of course, relies heavily on wordplay to provoke scandalized laughter.

The play between tragedy and farce continues in chapter 4, where the maid, Justiniana, discovers Fonchito atop the skylight that overlooks Lucrecia in her bath. Imagining that Fonchito might fall to his death, Lucrecia thinks to herself: "Evita un escándalo. Evita, sobre todo, algo que podría terminar en tragedia" (63) "Don't create a scandal. Keep clear, above all, of something that might end in tragedy" (42). Instead of expressing alarm, then, Lucrecia steps out of the bath and knowingly exhibits her body to the voyeur on high. When she finally manages to get to sleep that night, she has a dream inspired in "uno de esos grabados de la secreta colección de don Rigoberto que él y ella solían contemplar y comentar juntos en las noches buscando inspiración para su amor" (65) "one of those etchings in Don Rigoberto's secret collection that he and she were in the habit of contemplating and commenting upon together at night, seeking inspiration for their love" (44). We presume that this is a reference to the painting by François Boucher that illustrates the next chapter, an ekphrastic fantasy called "Diana después de su baño" [Diana after her bath]. The painting in question, however, bears a slightly different title in the French original: *Diane sortant du bain* (Fig. 29). In chapter 5 Lucrecia incarnates the mythological figure of Diana as painted by Boucher, and she also functions as the female first-person narrative voice: "Esa, la de la izquierda, soy yo, Diana Lucrecia" (69) "That one, the one on the left, is me, Diana Lucrecia" (45). The "left" corresponds not to the vantage point of the spectator before the picture, but instead to the (subject) position of Diana within the painting. To her right (that is, to our left) is Justiniana, Lucrecia's servant, now transformed into Diana's favorite ("mi favorita"). Diana therefore addresses a reader/viewer outside the text/painting while simultaneously blocking the point of view of those possible receptors of the discourse. In other words, although she employs a demonstrative that invokes physical separation ("esa" "that"), the narrator does not take distance from herself in order to view herself as a spectator would see her (to the right of Justin-

Figure 29
François Boucher, *Diana Leaving the Bath* (1742). Louvre, Paris,
France. Alinari/Art Resource, New York.

iana). The notion of exterior space is thereby destroyed, and,
along with it, the presence of a viewing subject in that space.

We may also observe a strict literary-pictorial correlation in
that the Diana in Boucher's painting does not look out at the viewers of the work: she directs her sight toward the nymph, who in
turn observes the delicate foot of the goddess. A closed circuit is
thus formed, one that shuts out intrusions from third parties
(compare this painting to Jordaens's *Candaules, King of Lydia*
with its structural opening to viewers or voyeurs). The term
*absorption*, coined by Michael Fried, applies most appropriately
to the context of Boucher's work: "for French painters of the early
and mid–1750s the persuasive representation of absorption
entailed evoking the perfect obliviousness of a figure or group of
figures to everything but the objects of their absorption. Those
objects did not include the beholder standing before the painting"
(66).[9] At the same time, Fried recognizes that the mission of any
painting is to attract a spectator's attention. Paradoxically, then,

in the example of which we are speaking, "only by establishing the fiction of his [the beholder's] absence or nonexistence could his actual placement before and enthrallment by the painting be secured" (103). And, in psychic life, what better equivalent for this kind of painting than a primal scene, which also simultaneously attracts and distances or excludes the onlooker? Before these characters we all become spies or voyeurs, although we may also perform acts of identification with the *I* of the text (Diana Lucrecia), the principal subject of the painting, (Diana) and one or both of the participants in the primal scene.

In his story Vargas Llosa has responded to the impulse to introduce a third party, a representation of the reader in the text or the beholder before the painting. Thus after negating the existence of exterior space, Diana points to the presence of an invisible observer, on whom she additionally confers privileged status: "El personaje principal no está en el cuadro. Mejor dicho, no se le ve. Anda por allí detrás, oculto en la arboleda, espiándonos" (70) "The main character is not in the picture. Or rather, he is not in sight. He is there in the background, hidden in the shady grove, spying on us" (46). The two women not only display their uncovered beauty for the eyes of this voyeur, who displaces Diana as "main character," but they also enact erotic scenes for his benefit: "No hay ejercicio o función, desenfreno y ritual del cuerpo y del alma que no hayamos representado para él" (74) "There is no exercise or function, no wanton ritual of body or soul that we have not performed for him" (50). In this way, the author extends the moment represented in the painting. He starts by modifying the title: *Diane sortant du bain* [Diana leaving the bath] becomes "Diana después de su baño" [Diana after her bath]. Of course, Vargas Llosa's *after* allows a temporal sequence (a narrative) that the gerund *leaving*, which refers to a precise and limited moment, makes nearly impossible. Diana and her female companion therefore abandon the stasis of their enraptured look—the pictorial instant captured by Boucher—to instead perform in front of the hidden spectator, who is none other than Fonchito, here called Foncín, and turned into a delicate "niño pastor" "little goatherd." If we persist in seeking a plastic equivalent for the narrative, we should resort to a different kind of painting, one defined by Fried as a "shift from the primacy of absorption toward the primacy of action and expression—more accurately, from the representation of figures absorbed in quintessentially absorptive states and activities toward the representation of figures absorbed in action or passion (or both)" (107). In other words, we could say that in this imaginary theatre the border between the nude and the naked has clearly been crossed. As Lynda Nead says, "The live performance of theatre is perhaps the most risky situation for the display of the body, straining the 'sacred frontier' between high culture and vulgarity to its limit" (85).

In effect, we have been transported from the exquisite (perhaps even saccharine) art of the eighteenth-century French painter to the salaciousness of the Peruvian writer, who effaces—or at least interrogates—the distinction between "high art" and "dirty pictures." This novel, after all, is published in a series that accomplishes just that. In this regard, it is of interest that in one of the stories in the novel ("Las malas palabras" [Dirty words]) Rigoberto is reading (or eyeing) Sir Kenneth Clark's *The Nude* (165, 123), which he precipitously closes when Fonchito interrupts him. For the bourgeois patriarch, judging by his embarrassed reaction, the artistic nudes of the book trigger in him the same kind of arousal that he might experience looking at images in a magazine such as *Playboy*: "Con brusco sobresalto, retornaba a Lima, a su casa, a su escritorio, desde los vapores húmedos y femeninos del atestado *Baño turco* del pintor Ingres, en el que había estado inmerso" (165) "With a brusque start of surprise, he returned to Lima, to his house, to his study, from the damp female vapors of Ingres's crowded *Turkish Bath*, in which he had been immersed" (123).[10] In his own way, and with much less effort than an avant-garde critic, Rigoberto deconstructs the difference between the nude and the naked, and he knocks down the British "Sir" (a dignified representative of high culture or class) to the level of a pornographer. More in line with Rigoberto than with Sir Kenneth Clark, Vargas Llosa brings to life the two female nudes by Boucher, along with the unpainted observer, the "little goatherd": "Foncín, simplemente permaneciendo allí, entre el muro de piedra y la arboleda, actuará también para nosotras" (74) "Foncín, simply by remaining there where he is, between the stone wall and the grove, will also perform for the two of us" (50).

Narrative therefore allows Vargas Llosa to insert the presence of a voyeur into Boucher's painting, or, to put it another way, into the mind of Diana who appears in that artwork. The readers may align their look with that of the voyeur in a way that the viewers of *Diane sortant du bain* cannot: this route to textual pleasure is theoretically open to both masculine and feminine identificatory positions. In fact, male observers such as Foncín can *only* look (and of course act on their own). In order to identify with the participants in the scene, the male heterosexual viewer would have to cross gender identifications, which is quite possible at the level of fantasy; theoretically, a female-identified viewer would be able to summon a homoerotic nexus to this scene with more ease. Diana (or Justiniana) would invite female-identified viewers to take her place and enjoy the delights of lesbian eroticism by participating in the action triggered by the writer's imagination. The writer's fantasy is situated at the precise instant reflected in the painting, one that breaks the "eterna inmovilidad" (74) "eternal immobility" (50) of the work: "Ella se moverá, se inclinará y su boquita de labios bermejos besará mi pie y chupará cada uno de mis dedos como se chupa la lima y el limón en las calenturientas tardes del estío" (75) "She will move, will bend down, and her little vermilion-lipped mouth will kiss my foot and suck each one of my toes as one sucks lemons and limes on sultry summer afternoons" (50).

We have noted the added presence of the male voyeur in this classic painted scene that the novelist subverts into an erotic fantasy with two women as protagonists. The voyeur's function reminds us of pornographic films with their intended audience of male heterosexuals. Linda Williams has explored how the "lesbian" or "girl-girl number" in those films serves as titillation for the viewers, and as warm-up for the "real" (that is, heterosexual) scenes, which of course require the participation of on-screen males. The main narrative of *In Praise of the Stepmother* contains no enacted lesbian eroticism: these fantasies, attributed by the male novelist to the female protagonist, in fact serve as "warm-ups" for the lovemaking that takes place between Lucrecia and Fonchito or Rigoberto. These lesbian delights are thus co-opted back into the heterosexual structure of desire that informs the novel, and the women are never left to their own devices for long. Williams explains how some of this cross-identification works in a pornography film with a "lesbian" number (one that has defined active and passive roles, in this instance):

> Putting aside for the moment the question of how women might identify and take pleasure in such action, it certainly seems possible that male viewers can identify with the active woman, with her superior knowledge of how the more passive woman feels.

But perhaps we should not rule out less active forms of identification—that is, identification with the passive woman who is given pleasure and abandons herself to the control of the other. Spectatorial pleasure in such scenes may very well involve the ability to identify both ways. (140)

In Vargas Llosa's novel, this imagined relationship between two women encodes a dual tension: it (momentarily) excludes the male as protagonist in an erotic scene, but it also promises him access to female sexuality. The lesbian display is performed at least in part for his benefit, yet it also places him in a highly vulnerable position, since the contemplated female is none other than Diana. As we mentioned in chapter 4, the goddess Diana is both the moon-lover and the implacable huntress of men: she turns Actaeon, the most famous voyeur of her charms, into a stag, and she commands his own hounds to attack and kill him. Boucher's painting shows signs of this predatory act in that we see the dogs, the arrows, and the dead animals to either side, at a distance from the women's serene beauty. The association between Foncín and Actaeon is produced in Diana's mind: "Palidece y, cervatillo arisco, echa a correr hasta desdibujarse en el ramaje" (72) "He pales and, a shy little musk deer, breaks into a run, fading into the network of branches" (48). The goddess imaginarily relishes the thought of devouring her victim, as if he were one of those hares or pheasants that she hunted: "lo veo, lo huelo, lo acariño, lo aprieto y lo desaparezco dentro de mí, sin necesidad de tocarlo" (73) "I see him, I smell him, I caress him, I press him to my bosom and make him disappear within me, with no need to touch him" (49). And insofar as Diana is also Lucrecia, the maternal-filial nature of that relationship between the two sexes rears its angelic little head. The Virgin Goddess takes on the look of the Terrible Mother here.[11] How can the ill-fated Actaeon, or his stand-in, Foncín, escape this powerful force? The story concludes with a fantasy in Diana's voice. She envisions the three characters (Diana, Justiniana, and Foncín) as the theme of a future painting, which of course differs from the one by Boucher: "Allí estaremos los tres, quietos, pacientes, esperando al artista del futuro que, azuzado por el deseo, nos aprisione en sueños y, llevándonos a la tela con su pincel, crea que nos inventa" (76) "There the three of us will be, calm, patient, awaiting the artist of the future who, roused by desire, will imprison us in dreams and, pinning us to the canvas with his brush, will believe that he is inventing us" (51). For the reader, that artist has already arrived, although his instrument is the pen rather than the paintbrush: he is the author of the chapter in the novel entitled "Diana después de su baño." For Diana, however, that artist does not invent or fantasize any of it; or, more precisely, her fantasy declares itself with the uncontainable strength of an inner demon (as Vargas Llosa calls his creative impulses). He is her captive. To see or imagine Diana—the distinction between these acts is practically null—is the equivalent of falling into her trap (sexual symbolism intended), that is, the trap that imprisons all subjects of desire. If the artistic control of the painter or writer manages to immobilize Diana's figure within the limits of the painting or the text, then it may be said that the goddess plots her retaliation. Inaccessible, untouchable—as are all objects of desire, in the final analysis—she turns the voyeurs (or the visionaries) into stags whose destiny is to perish. And it isn't so much Diana herself who sets the hounds on their trail. Rather, it is desire that urges on the viewers of this far-off beauty and transforms them into metaphoric animals, propitiatory victims of a spec(tac)ular sacrifice.

Following a chapter in the primary narration called "Las abluciones de don Rigoberto," [Don Rigoberto's Ablutions], to which we will return shortly, Vargas Llosa appeals to another high artistic version of the female nude to illustrate chapter 7: Titian's well-known *Venus con el Amor y la Música* [Venus and Cupid with an Organist] (Fig. 30). Fonchito's voice, filtered through Cupid, now enters into play, in contrast to the previous ekphrastic fantasies that corresponded to the adults, Rigoberto-Candaules and Lucrecia-Diana. The trio in Titian's painting differs slightly from the threesome of Fonchito, Lucrecia, and Rigoberto, since the husband does not appear. Rather, the adult male is the young musician who plays the organ for Venus (Lucrecia) while she is caressed by Cupid (Fonchito). The mission of both males, according to the interpretation of the painting that the novel performs, is to excite the senses of this unclothed Venus to the maximum so that later, behind closed doors, Rigoberto may enjoy her splendors: "Así le gusta a don Rigoberto que se la entreguemos: ardiente y ávida, todas sus prevenciones morales y religiosas suspendidas y su mente y su cuerpo sobrecargados de apetitos" (98) "This is how Don Rigoberto likes to have us hand her over to him: ardent and avid, all her moral and religious scruples in abeyance and her mind and body filled to overflowing with appetites" (70).

Figure 30
Titian, *Venus and Cupid with an Organist*. Prado, Madrid.

The musician, then, carries out a function similar to that of the child-god's caresses: to submerge the woman in an ecstasy more of a carnal than a spiritual nature. The distinction between flesh and spirit is tenuous here, however. Music, like Love, merges the two realms and thus transports us from the "austeros retiros" (99) "austere retreats" (71) to the "procesiones callejeras que se transforman de pronto en pagano carnaval" (99–100) "street processions that are suddenly transformed into a pagan carnival" (71). Underneath beatific appearances there is always a Bacchanal ready to burst forth, for the eye that knows how to discern it. Vargas Llosa not only perceives this Bacchic note, but he evokes it with the kind of power that radiates from Cupid or the organist in Titian's painting. These words spoken by Cupid may be ascribed to Vargas Llosa as animator of the painting on the page: "Mi señora va viendo estas imágenes porque yo se las describo en el oído, con vocecilla aviesa, al compás de la música. . . . Eso es lo que ahora estoy haciendo . . . : susurrándole fábulas pecaminosas. Ficciones que la distraen y hacen sonreír, ficciones que la sobresaltan y enardecen" (100) "My lady sees this series of images because I describe them to her in her ear, in a soft, perverse voice, in time to the music. . . . That is what I am doing now . . . : whispering naughty stories to her. Fictions that distract her and make her smile, fictions that shock and excite her" (72). The creation of fictions is inseparable from erotic activities, something that Cupid displays (or sets in motion) better than anyone. Love (Eros or Cupid) remains faithful to his role as described by Plato in the *Symposium* (202d): "spirit" (*daimon*) that acts as an intermediary between gods and mortals. And accompanying Cupid's power—appropriated by the author of the text, we could say—is the talent of the painter, who is said to translate "en formas, colores, figuras y acciones incitantes las notas del órgano cómplice" (100) "the notes of that organ that is my accomplice into provocative shapes, colors, figures, actions" (72).

Nevertheless, the contemplated and narrated scene is presented as the product of Rigoberto's erotic imagination. He orders a series of actions at the same time that he sets limits on others: "El profesor no puede dejar un solo instante de tañer el órgano: le va en ello la cabeza. Don Rigoberto lo ha prevenido: 'Si aquellos fuelles dejan aunque sea un instante de soplar entenderé que cediste a la tentación de palpar'" (100) "The teacher cannot leave off playing the organ for a single moment: his life depends on it. Don Rigoberto has warned him: 'If those bellows stop working for one moment, I will know that you have yielded to the temptation to touch'" (72). Vargas Llosa has undoubtedly perceived the implications of Titian's painting. It should be noted that the Italian painter depicted this theme more than once, including two versions in the Prado. In the one that Vargas Llosa reproduces, Cupid is present, whereas in the other, *Venus recreándose en la música* [Venus and the organ-player], Venus rests her head on a pillow that takes the place of the child-god, while her left hand caresses a dog, which she looks at much in the way that her eyes meet Cupid's—serenely, but not wholly engaged. There is an earlier version in Berlin (Staatliche Museum) with notable differences. In the Berlin picture the organ player, with his back to the instrument, is absorbed in the act of contemplating Venus. He has thus ceased playing the organ in order to establish full visual contact with the goddess. In contrast, the two paintings in the Prado show the musician with one or both hands on the keyboard and his head partially turned toward the attractive—or distractive—female nude. In *Venus and Cupid with an Organist*, his body is almost perfectly aligned in reverse position to hers: they both recline, with an outstretched arm and turned head. Panofsky, in comparing the different versions, makes the following conclusion: "the supremacy of visible beauty (incarnated in the nude) over the audible charms of music is no longer uncontested [in the two Prado paintings]. Far from abandoning his instrument altogether, the player now attempts to enjoy the world of sight while not cutting himself off from the world of sound" (*Problems in Titian* 123). Vargas Llosa endows his musician with the balanced attitude of Titian's organist, suspended between two worlds (as in the Prado's versions), but denies him the audacity exhibited in the Berlin painting. Cupid as narrator nevertheless senses the aim of those sideward glances: "¿Qué encuentra o qué busca en ese venusino rincón el joven músico? ¿Qué tratan de perforar sus vírgenes pupilas?" (101) "What is the young musician finding, or what is he asking in that intimate Venusian retreat? What are his virgin pupils endeavoring to penetrate?" (73).[12]

The inevitable transition from the nude to the naked may also be related to the double temporal dimension of the story; that is, Lucrecia, a contemporary woman, is always present behind Venus (a classical goddess who herself is represented in another time— Titian's sixteenth century). Rigoberto says to her: "Hoy no serás Lucrecia . . . sino Venus y hoy pasarás de peruana a italiana y de terrestre a diosa y símbolo" (103) "You will not be Lucrecia today but Venus, and today you will change from a Peruvian woman into an Italian one and from a creature of this earth into a goddess and a symbol" (75). But despite the efforts of the lascivious Rigoberto, Lucrecia resists this passage and does not allow herself to be replaced by a goddess. Titian had already taken his Venus down from the Olympian heights and placed her in a Renaissance context, and Vargas Llosa prolongs this gesture by making Venus into a modern Peruvian woman. Margaret R. Miles's commentary is pertinent here: "In Clark's distinction between 'nakedness' and 'nudity' the nude body is a representation of a naked body from which subjectivity, along with moles and lumps, has been elided. . . . The nude achieves universality at the expense of particularity. The *subject* of a nude painting has been deleted, replaced by the role the nude plays in representing a 'far wider and more civilizing experience'" (14). Lucrecia seems to assert her right to be a subject and consequently to resist the attempt to idealize her, to turn her naked body into an unblemished nude. But, as we will see in the novel's last chapter, this very real Lucrecia succumbs to the man's world protagonized by Don Rigoberto and his offspring (or, at the least, she gets evicted from it—a crucial distinction).

In short, Rigoberto aspires to mold Lucrecia at will by merging her with Titian's Venus: "'Tú no eres tú sino mi fantasía', dice ella que le susurra cuando la ama" (103), "'You are not you but my fantasy,' she says he whispers to her when he makes love to her" (75). Insofar as Lucrecia is Vargas Llosa's fantasy, author and character coincide at this level; both take control of feminine beauty and possess the maternal figure. The male figure is split in two before this woman: he plays the role of the husband (Rigoberto) and that of the son-lover (Cupid-Fonchito). However, the woman also exerts her dominance over man, though the terms of this control are linked to her body. The "jugos secretos" "secret juices" of this Venus give off a "aroma a quesillo rancio" (105) "whiff of overripe cheese" (76) that drives Rigoberto wild. The fantasy literally overflows and cannot be contained. The domineering gaze of Titian's imitator gives way to the olfactory pleasure of one who is rendered vulnerable, who gets too close: "'Mientras huelas así, seré tu esclavo', dice ella que él le dice, con la lengua floja de los ebrios de amor" (105) "'As long as that is how you smell, I will be your slave,' she says that he says to her, with the loose tongue of those drunk on love" (77). Rigoberto now succumbs, overtaken by his desire; his artistic creation, so skillfully brought to life, possesses him. Or, in the words of Clark (but with a different meaning), the Venus restored by Vargas Llosa, her "delicate texture" removed, confronts and excites the Peruvian *macho* with her "almost brutal directness."

As the novel progresses, so too does the erotic relationship between Lucrecia and her stepson. Lucrecia is overcome by a passion that opposes all reason. The model presented in the text assumes that sexuality is a primitive force or drive traceable to the *id* and that it culminates in a death instinct: "Y, entonces fue como si dentro de ella un dique de contención súbitamente cediera y un torrente irrumpiera contra su prudencia y su razón, sumergiéndolas, pulverizando principios ancestrales que nunca había puesto en duda y hasta su instinto de conservación" (114) "And then it was as though a dam had suddenly burst within her and a flood descended upon her prudence and her reason, submerging them, pulverizing ancestral principles she had never doubted, and even her instinct for self-preservation" (83). Nevertheless, this desire

cannot be taken in isolation; it must be related to the novel's oedipal triangle, if only because the social fate of Lucrecia is linked to
it. *In Praise of the Stepmother* continually rearticulates this link
(or subordination): two lovers are never alone for long, either in
the ekphrastic tales or in the main narrative. Rigoberto thus
returns to the house to interrupt Lucrecia and Fonchito in their
amorous acts, and later, over dinner, the following scene takes
place: "Con risa saltarina celebró los chistes de su padre y le pidió
incluso que les contara otros, 'esos chistes negros papá, esos que
son algo cochinos'" (116) "He greeted his father's jokes with bubbling laughter and even asked him to tell some more, 'off-color
ones, Papa, the kind that are a tiny bit dirty'" (86). Freud has
remarked that the

> smutty joke was originally directed against the woman and may
> be comparable to an attempt at seduction. . . . The smutty joke
> is like a denudation of a person of the opposite sex toward whom
> the joke is directed. Through the utterance of obscene words the
> person attacked is forced to picture the parts of the body in ques-
> tion, or the sexual act, and is shown that the aggressor himself
> pictures the same thing. There is no doubt that the original motive
> of the smutty joke was the pleasure of seeing the sexual displayed.
> (*Wit and Its Relation to the Unconscious* 693–4)

Lucrecia therefore goes from her performance as a desiring, pas-
sion-driven woman to her silent denudation as the unspoken butt
of the jokes in question. Freud's terminology is fascinating with
respect to verbal-visual problems and sexuality: the smutty joke,
formed with words, evokes a picture and forces the (female)
hearer to *look* imaginarily. Telling becomes showing, and the
aggressor derives pleasure from sharing dirty (mental) pictures.
Isn't that what Vargas Llosa does at the metatextual level? He
shows us classic paintings and tells us dirty stories about them,
which forces us to picture the women in these paintings in sexualized or sexist ways. But do we have to assume one of two roles:
either that of the "feminized" hearer and viewer, who supposedly
would be scandalized and offended, or that of just another guy
sharing a dirty joke about women? Our contention is that the very
structure of the novel—with its pictorial intertexts, leveled narrations, range of gendered identificatory positions, and play
between high and popular culture—refuses the reader fixity and
provides several mirrored surfaces that echo among themselves,

producing countless reflections that implicate us in fragmented fashion.

It is precisely this image of the fragmented being that informs the next chapter of the novel, "Semblanza de humano" [Semblance of a human], which is illustrated by the first of Francis Bacon's *Head* paintings. The destructive potential of the love relationship may be read in this painting, which shows a severely distorted one-eyed head strung up from the ear, tilted back with its mouth agape. Although the narrator of this chapter has no name, it is clear that he is Rigoberto since in response to Lucrecia's query during lovemaking in the previous chapter, Rigoberto declared himself to be "un monstruo" "a monster." The reference to the nose is a further giveaway: "Tengo un olfato muy desarrollado y es por la nariz por donde más gozo y sufro" (122) "I have a very highly developed sense of smell and it is by way of my nose that I experience the greatest pleasure and the greatest pain" (90). The chapter immediately following this one (chapter 10) opens when Rigoberto, performing his nasal hygiene ritual, quotes the first line of Quevedo's famous sonnet, "Erase un hombre a una nariz pegado" (129) "Once . . . there was a man attached to a nose" (95). Although Bacon's painting shows a head that ends in a blob-like sea of white, the narrator of "Semblanza de humano" claims that his "sexo está intacto" (123) "My sex organ is intact" (91). The reduction of the speaker to little more than a sex organ should be seen as the cause rather than the consequence of the shattering that his person has undergone. And even though *Head I* by Bacon lacks explicit sexual connotations, other paintings by this artist show the physical union between two beings as a destructive phenomenon. Ernst van Alphen refers to this effect in the following commentary: "desire may bring the self and the other too close together. This seems to be the threat in many of Bacon's paintings. . . . [The bodies] have been transformed into one field of shattered fragments" (123, 126).

Ironically, it is excessive preoccupation with one's own body—brought to the surface in explicit detail in the earlier chapter, "Don Rigoberto's Ablutions"—coupled with minute control of the body of another (Lucrecia's in "Venus, with Love and Music") that leads to the complete loss of control, the absolute disintegration of the individual. For those who are possessed by desire, it is impossible to sustain any kind of affirmation of the limits of self. As a result, there is a regression to the fantasy or phantasm of the "fragmented body" that, for Lacan, antecedes the child's vision of his or her image in the mirror, from which a primordial form of the *I* is derived. Precisely, this specular image cannot be constituted either in Bacon's *Head* paintings or in Vargas Llosa's narration. As John Russell writes: "Perhaps the six *Heads* that formed part of Bacon's first show . . . are simply statements about what it feels like to be alone in a room. . . . What painting had never shown before is the disintegration of the social being which takes place when one is alone in a room which has no looking-glass" (38). Vargas Llosa places his character in a similar surrounding: "El cubo de vidrio donde estoy es mi casa. Veo a través de sus paredes pero nadie puede verme desde el exterior" (122) "The glass cube I live in is my home. I can see through the walls of it, but no one can see me from the outside" (90). Not only can he not been seen from the outside, but we could say that he, too, is unable to see, or identify, himself. Nevertheless, from the confines of his solitude, which cannot be eradicated through the mere contact of bodies, the narrator expresses his final plea: "Mírame bien, amor mío. Reconóceme, reconócete" (125) "Take a good look at me, my love. Recognize me, and recognize yourself" (93). In the final instance, then, the monster affirms his humanity; he functions as a mirror in which the (female, in this case) other can see herself and, through this act of seeing, can recognize him and return his image to him.

In the framework of our analysis, this painting by Bacon should be placed in relation to the female nude. That is, Lucrecia has been projected onto painted nude female figures, all of whom are involved with internal and external spectators in elaborate pictorial schemes of looking and "to-be-looked-at-ness," to use Mulvey's term again. Mulvey also notes that in the case of the female nude, the cosmetically finished surface of the body strives to conceal the abject matter of the interior; or, in psychoanalytic terms, the beautiful surface covers over the wound that the male psyche registers when it perceives sexual difference (in Nead, 66). In Vargas Llosa's novel, the male character, when finally represented pictorially, stands alone as a disintegrating head, its wounds, gapes, and abject matter of "inside" fully entangled with "outside." Van Alphen remarks that the male body in Bacon's work "shows no signs of stability, control, action, or production. Thus, the violent tension between body and representation . . . can be seen as an ongoing escape from the objectification of representation" (190). Lucrecia's figure has been subjected to this tension of objectification and also to idealization—a process that has been resisted, as we have shown—, but Rigoberto's portrait in the form of Bacon's *Head I* submits rather fully to the lack of control, to instability. In a sense, then, he resists fixity as did Lucrecia. To do so, however, he must surrender to the body gone wild. Rigoberto is depicted as a slave to his obsessive rituals of nose hair trimming, toenail clipping, anal cleansing, teeth picking, armpit washing, ear dewaxing, and so on (described in excruciating detail in "Don Rigoberto's Ablutions"); he calls these operations "un quehacer refinado que, aunque fuera por un tiempo fugaz, hacía de él un ser perfecto" (79–80) "an artful task that made of him, if only momentarily, a perfect being" (54). These rituals of perfection of course are pleasures in themselves: "lo hacía a conciencia y disfrutando, ni más ni menos que si se tratase de un placer prohibido" (92) "he did so conscientiously and at the same time thoroughly enjoying it, neither more nor less than if this were a forbidden pleasure" (65). But the pleasure of controlling the unruly body gives way to the logical antithesis, the pleasure of the body's unleashed excesses and abjections, now reclaimed by the "talking head" for erotic expression:

> Nunca lamentó alguno de mis amantes haberlo sido. Ellos y ellas me agradecen haberlos instruido en las refinadas combinaciones de lo horrible y el deseo para causar placer. Conmigo aprendieron que todo es y puede ser erógeno y que, asociada al amor, la función orgánica más vil, incluidas aquéllas del bajo vientre, se espiritualiza y ennoblece. (124)

> No one has ever regretted being my lover. Males and females alike thank me for having given them advanced instruction in the fine art of combining desire and the horrible so as to give pleasure. They learned from me that everything is and can be erogenous and that, associated with love, the basest organic functions, including those of the lower abdomen, become spiritualized and ennobled. (91–92)

This bisexual lover, then, asks to be recognized in relation to "lo horrible" "the horrible," and asks his interlocutor to "reconócete" "recognize yourself." Like Bacon's paintings in relation to the viewer, this textual monster-human allows the other to reconstitute him or herself as monstrous, and to resist secured positions. The journey into the abject by means of the shattered male self thus becomes a permutable pleasure trip, which constitutes a notable deviation from the preferred expression of visible/visual desire in this novel as symbolized by the painted female nude.

This painted symbol nevertheless undergoes a transformation in the last part of *In Praise of the Stepmother*. From the classic works of Jordaens, Boucher, or Titian, the female nude ultimately becomes associated with modern abstract painting. In chapter 11 the text breaks its pattern by introducing through narrative a pictorial theme by a specific artist in advance of the illustration, which instead accompanies chapter 12. The following declaration, spoken by Fonchito from the bed he is sharing with Lucrecia, introduces the painting in question: "Te voy a decir algo que no sabes, madrastra. . . . En el cuadro de la sala estás tú" (141) "I'm going to tell you something you don't know, stepmother. . . . You're in the painting in the living room" (105). Lucrecia responds: "Pero si en la sala hay un Szyszlo. . . . Un cuadro abstracto, chiquitín" (142) "But that's a Szyszlo in the living room. . . . An abstract painting, sweetie" (106). And, following a textual interval in which scenes of lovemaking between Lucrecia and Fonchito are focalized through the female protagonist, Fonchito continues: "Entonces, ahora ya sé lo que quiere decir un cuadro abstracto. . . . ¡Un cuadro cochino!" (143) "So I know now what's meant by an abstract painting. . . . A dirty picture!" (107). At this point in the novel, the reader has learned how to interpret visual products within the norms of the work; the relation between this verbal reference to a Szyszlo painting, and the reproduction of his *Camino a Mendieta 10* [Road to Mendieta 10] (Fig. 31) as epigraph for the next chapter, thus appears to be seamless. And yet this suturing device creates a monstrous text in which the demarcations between narrative levels and artistic media (verbal, visual) cannot be differentiated: they collapse "inside" and "outside," much like the paintings of Bacon and Szyszlo. *In Praise of the Stepmother* turns itself inside out and asks the reader/viewer to "see" (to picture, as Freud would say) the inner workings of desire and the inner workings of textual production.[13]

The female nude, dirty paintings, dirty words, dirty acts—how did this signifying chain end up on the *Road to Mendieta 10*? Lucrecia contemplates the Szyszlo painting in light of Fonchito's declaration: "Fue como si nunca lo hubiera visto antes, como si el cuadro, igual que una serpiente o una mariposa, hubiera mudado

Figure 31
Fernando de Szyszlo, *Road to Mendieta 10* (1977). Private Collection.

de apariencia y de ser" (151) "It was as if she had never seen it before, as if the painting, like a serpent or a butterfly, had changed appearance and nature" (115). Exactly. Vargas Llosa has uncovered the key role that interpretive context plays (something that is absolutely crucial to our analysis in the next chapter on Cabrera Infante and Duchamp). Further, it is the female body within the painting that mutates, serpent-like (how can we forget Eve here?) or in a way that resembles the butterfly, which after all starts out as a lowly worm. As this chapter closes, Lucrecia, in a reversal of their usual pattern, tells Rigoberto during lovemaking what her fantasy is: she claims to be "la del cuadro de la sala" "the woman in the painting in the living room" (116), which leads into the ekphrastic fantasy proper, "Laberinto de amor" [Labyrinth of love]. Following Fonchito's interpretive move, Lucrecia—and the receptors of the novel/painting—can in fact "read" the abstract *Road to Mendieta 10* for its narrative content, a process that transforms the elegant lines and muted colors of the Peruvian painter's work into an explicit tale of the erotic female body. Lucrecia, an Ariadne of sorts, guides us through this "labyrinth of love" that the painting represents. However, unlike Ariadne, she places herself at the center of the labyrinth, where, she says, one enters "como la novicia en el convento de clausura o el amante a la gruta de la amada" (157) "as the novice nun enters the cloister or the lover the cavern of his beloved" (117).[14] In Szyszlo's painting the figure on the right side may be seen as a reclining nude woman on a tripod table that functions as a kind of altar. The figure seems to have an arm bent behind her head. There are circular forms that look to be breasts, and it could be said that she has open legs; beneath the tangle of crisscrossing lines is a skinny phallic-like projection emerging from her sex organs. On the left side of the painting is what appears to be a monstrous creature with horns described as "medialunas sarracenas en la crisma" (158) "Saracen crescents on his head" (118), who watches the reclining figure. The texture of the paint seems thick, giving the impression of scales or feathers. This "Minotaur," let's call him, displays a rather visible erection. Or at least we can find a shape, in a lighter color than the rest of this figure, that may be read that way—by the eye that has been trained to discern it.

Lucrecia describes the female figure, with which she identifies as if it were a portrait of her:

> Sí, vida mía, aquello que yace sobre la piedra ceremonial (o, si prefieres, el decorado prehispánico), esa hechura viscosa de llagas malvas y tenues membranas . . . soy yo misma. Entiéndeme: yo, vista de adentro y de abajo, cuando tú me calcinas y me exprimes. Yo, erupcionando y derramándome bajo tu atenta mirada libertina de varón que ofició con eficiencia y, ahora, contempla y filosofa. (158)

> Yes, my treasure, what is lying on the ceremonial stone (or, if you prefer, the pre-Hispanic stage prop), that viscous creature with mauve wounds and delicate membranes . . . is myself. Understand me: myself, seen from the inside and from below, when you calcine me and express me. Myself, erupting and over-flowing beneath your attentive libertine gaze of a male who has

officiated with competence and is now contemplating and philosophizing. (118)

The painting hosts elements of pre-Columbian culture, [15] but it also may be seen as a new version of Picasso's theme of the Minotaur and the sleeping woman, which we discussed in relation to Francisco Ayala. Although the satyr is "contemplating and philosophizing," it is the woman's consciousness that is laid bare, if you will. She is not sleeping, but is instead very present as narrating subject and as one who experiences her ecstasy or *jouissance*. This *jouissance* derives from an erotic submission, as shown in the quotation above, as well as from an erotic performance in front of this male figure who has turned into a "mirón" (158) "voyeur." She in turn has become an "ofrenda" "offering": "Abierta en canal como una tórtola por el cuchillo del amor" (159) "Split open like a turtledove by love's knife" (119). Her own body functions as the labyrinth of love: "Dédalo y sensación, yo" (159) "labyrinth and sensation, I" (119); at the same time, she is Ariadne (or a nymph in her cavern) who embraces the monster-lover: "Aquí, nada nos frena ni inhibe, como al monstruo y al dios" (160) "Here, as is true as well of the monster and the god, nothing restrains or inhibits us" (120).

The fusion of bodies in an erotic embrace is not presented in the same destructive terms as it was in "Semblance of a Human": the sadomasochistic language here is the language of love, and as such appears to pose no threat. (For the moment, at least: when Lucrecia's full erotic passions are made known to Rigoberto, her *jouissance* turns into a real sacrifice since she is cut off from the father-and-son lovers.) The lovers abstracted from the Szyszlo painting strip each other of the marks of identity: "Hemos perdido el apellido y el nombre" (160) "We have lost name and surname" (120). They go from man and woman to "eyaculación, orgasmo y una idea fija. Nos hemos vuelto sagrados y obsesivos" (160) "ejaculation, orgasm, and a fixed idea. We have become sacred and obsessive" (120). In fact, they have incarnated the spirit of art as Fernando de Szyszlo himself defines it: "Just as the priest or sorcerer served a need for the primitive tribe, the artist today serves as a bridge and, as in the past, he expresses, conscientiously or not, the desires, the joys, the terrors of the age and its circumstances, and with it he fortifies the bases to accept them, to exorcise them and posses them" ("Reflections" 34). Further, Szyszlo claims that "art may not be the presence of the sacred but, in any case, it is the negation of the profane" ("Conversation" 26). Vargas Llosa, whose theories on artistic demons and their exorcisms are well known, aligns himself with his co-patriot artist friend in possessing and casting out the desires and terrors of the age in which they live. *In Praise of the Stepmother* ultimately upholds the sacred (high culture and art), while playfully subjecting it to the slashes and gashes of the profane. The artist, the "he" of Szyszlo's comments, remains. In this novel, the woman's fate, despite her erotic claiming, her coming-into-being, is another matter.

The female protagonist takes pleasure in the word as she describes the sacred rituals of sex: "yo te me entrego, me te masturbas, chupatemémonos" (161) "I give yourself to me, you masturbate myself for you, let's you and me suck our selves" (121). Strangely, the concretion with which these erotic acts are enumerated, once the identities of the lovers have been removed, takes us back to the abstract forms of Szyszlo's painting such as we first perceived them. They represent, then, the shape of things to come. Lucrecia's final words note that "aun antes de que nos conociéramos, nos amáramos y nos casáramos, alguien, pincel en mano, anticipó en qué horrenda gloria nos convertiría" (161) "even before we knew each other, loved each other, and married, someone, brush in hand, anticipated what horrendous glory we would be changed into" (121). One has to make an effort, or take an interpretive leap, to guess that the painting contains human beings, a "semblanza de humano" "semblance of a human," yet alone the traces of a love relationship. First Fonchito, then Lucrecia, then Rigoberto all perform this interpretive act, which the readers/spectators can prolong. But Lucrecia also carries out the reverse process. Once the two beings and the two sexes are demarcated, she fuses them anew; that is, she returns them to the mass of lines and colors where abstraction (sublimation) and concretion bordering on the pornographic coincide. In this fashion, the loss (of names, of limits) turns into a gain: "hemos ganado magia, misterio y fruición corporal"(160) "we have gained the power of magic, mystery, and bodily enjoyment" (120).

In the final pages of *In Praise of the Stepmother* the triangular crisis reaches its apparent resolution. Lucrecia and Fonchito have consummated their illicit passion, which has brought feelings of joy, rebirth, and renewed marital excitement into the stepmother's life. But Fonchito, enveloped in his aura of innocence and perversity, has obtained the object that he seemingly desired most from the relationship: a motorcycle. His "conquest" of the stepmother, then, has an apparent material motivation; once this need is satisfied, he turns away from Lucrecia and reaffirms his place beside his father. Or rather, he gives up the father's sexual role in order to resume his proper place as son. However, Fonchito's displacements finally set off the tensions that have been mounting throughout the novel. Don Rigoberto thus declares to Fonchito: "Si ustedes se quieren tanto que, a ratos, hasta celos tengo, pues me parece que tu madrastra te quiere más que a mí y que tú también la prefieres a ella que a tu padre" (168) "In fact, the two of you love each other so much that, every so often, I'm downright jealous, since it seems to me that your stepmother loves you more than she does me and that you, too, are fonder of her than you are of your father" (126). Father and son burst into peals of laughter at the ludicrous thought, whereby Fonchito inquires, "¿Qué quiere decir orgasmo, papá?" (168) "What does orgasm mean, Papa?" (126). The nervous encounter between father and son turns horrifying for Rigoberto when he hears that it is Lucrecia who has taught that word—and its meaning—to her stepson. Hoping to avoid further embarrassment, Rigoberto asks Fonchito to show him his homework, which turns out to be a composition entitled "Elogio de la madrastra" "In praise of the stepmother." Of course, Vargas Llosa has been saving the great incestual revelation for this metafictional moment when the imbedded story mirrors and mimics the erotic novel as a whole. Rigoberto reads in the words of his son's composition all the pleasures and the horrors that have been going on under his roof unbeknownst to him. At first he suspects it is one more fantasy in the chain of erotic stimula that have made up his own sexual life: "¿Qué significan estas . . . fantasías? . . . ¿Cómo has podido inventar unas suciedades tan indecentes?" (175–76) "What's the meaning of these . . . fantasies? . . . How could you have [invented such indecent filth]?" (133). Fonchito claims that his story is not a fabrication and that all the events have taken place. The composition is therefore not a work of fiction but an infantile confession that brings down Rigoberto's fragile "castillo de naipes" (170) "house of cards" (128), as he calls it.

Now it seems highly plausible that the final question—What do these fantasies mean?—is Vargas Llosa's own ironic, self-conscious query to the reader. What *are* we to make of this compendium of oedipal fantasies, and how can the text be resolved? In his ending to this erotic novel, Vargas Llosa deviates from the usual route. Most examples of the genre finish either with contrived amorous fulfillment—the protagonists renounce their libertine adventures when they find true love—or, on the other extreme, with a form of death, sexual exhaustion, or maddening repetition. When the oedipal crime in *Elogio de la madrastra* is finally revealed to Don Rigoberto, he contemplates Fonchito's "cara beatífica" "beatific face" and remarks: "Así debía ser Luzbel" (175) "This is what Lucifer must have looked like" (132). Rigoberto, on the other hand, manifests a wish to assume the (innocent) son's deserted place, that is, to cast off his devilish conduct and regress to an infantile or angelic state that would liberate him from sexuality entirely: "era un ser solitario, casto, desasido de apetitos, a salvo de todos los demonios de la carne y el sexo. Sí, sí, ése era él. El anacoreta, el santón, el monje, el ángel, el arcángel que sopla la celeste trompeta y baja al huerto a traer la buena noticia a las santas muchachas" (176–77) "he was a solitary being, chaste, freed of appetites, safe from all the demons of the flesh and sex. Yes, yes, that was how he was. The anchorite, the hermit, the monk, the angel, the archangel who blows the celestial trumpet and descends to the garden to bring the glad tidings to pure and pious maidens" (134). Thus Rigoberto goes from engaging in delightful polymorphous perversions to denouncing eroticism altogether; he descends from sexual ecstasy to the hell of his worst fantasies come true. Is that why he thinks, "Amar lo imposible tiene un precio que tarde o temprano se paga" (175) "Loving the impossible has a price that must be paid sooner or later" (132)? Who loved the impossible object here? How could it be Rigoberto, since his only sin was complete erotic devotion to his wife? The final ekphrastic chapter provides the clue. Here, Rigoberto once again assumes the role of the son and at the same time desexualizes all members of the oedipal triangle in a futile attempt to restore harmony.

The passage from apocalyptic revelation to blissful regression is signaled by the image that serves as illustration for the final chapter: Fra Angelico's large fresco, *The Annunciation*, from the Monastery of San Marco in Florence (Fig. 32). Of all the paintings that Vargas Llosa appropriates for his *Elogio de la madrastra*, we note immediately that *The Annunciation* is an anomaly, for not only is it chronologically the oldest of all the works reproduced in the book, but it is the only one that treats a Christian theme. Even

Figure 32
Fra Angelico, *The Annunciation* (large fresco). Museo di San Marco,
Florence, Italy. Scala/Art Resource, New York.

more significant is the fact that *The Annunciation* was painted by
an angelic monk, a veritable saint, if we heed what Vasari had to
say of him. The legend surrounding Fra Angelico depicts a man
who took up the paintbrush in a quasi mystical state, transformed
by abundant tears and intense prayer; his paintings supposedly
reflect the heavenly visions glimpsed in these fits of ecstasy, and
thus "his faces are divinely beautiful, his colors harmonious, his
forms infused with grace and gentleness" (Argan, *Fra Angelico*
10). Even if this is a mythic elevation of Fra Angelico's art, it nevertheless causes us to wonder what role *The Annunciation* should
play here among the ecstatic verbal renderings of physical rapture
or the clinical descriptions of lowly corporeal hygenic practices. Is
this a parodic intent on Vargas Llosa's part?

Clearly, we can say that there is some self-conscious irony in
Vargas Llosa's gesture. After having elevated carnal pleasures to
celestial heights and having plunged eroticism to grotesque
depths—often an undifferentiated process—it seems fitting that
the novelist should ultimately come face to face with an image of
the Virgin Mary and Gabriel. Our appropriate initial reaction,

then, may be to admire the way in which the novelist seeks to amuse by setting up an erotic farce based on long-standing tradition: a "mystery play," in this instance a profane play on Christ's genesis. But simply because there is an ironic subversion of the image's power to retain its original significance by placing it in a dislocated context, we should not presume that *The Annunciation* serves no other function in the novel. To begin, the description of the "joven rosado" "rosy youth" whom Rigoberto wishes to be would correspond more exactly to the figure of the once-angelic Fonchito. The Angel Gabriel is said to be "un ser tan armonioso y suave, de formas tan perfectas y voz tan sutil" "such a harmonious and gentle being, so seemly, with such a subtle voice," and upon contemplating him, Vargas Llosa's Mary feels a strange warmth overtaking her, like the burning passion aroused in Lucrecia by her stepson: "¿Eso será, magnificado a todo el cuerpo, lo que sienten las muchachas cuando se enamoran?" (182) "Can this be, magnified throughout the body, what young girls feel when they fall in love?" (136). Mary—the supposedly chaste antithesis of the naked female and even the painted female nude—is nevertheless infused with a passion equated to the effects of carnal love; but so in fact is Gabriel, at least earlier in the novel. In the ekphrastic chapter based on Bacon's *Head I*, the Rigoberto character declares: "tengo orgasmos prolongados y repetidos que me dan la sensación de ser aéreo y radiante como el arcángel Gabriel" (123) "I have prolonged and repeated orgasms that give me the sensation of being as ethereal and radiant as the Archangel Gabriel" (91).

After the angel makes his announcement and takes leave, the young girl is left to wonder: "¿Por qué me trató de señora si aún soy soltera? ¿Por qué me llamó reina? ¿Por qué descubrí un brillo de lágrimas en sus ojos cuando me vaticinó que sufriría? ¿Por qué me llamó madre si soy virgen? ¿Qué está sucediendo? ¿Qué va a ser de mí a partir de esta visita?" (186) "Why did he address me as señora if I am still an unmarried girl? Why did he call me queen? Why did I discover a gleam of tears in his eyes when he prophesied that I would suffer? Why did he call me mother if I am a virgin? What is happening? What is going to become of me after this visit?" (140). Here we observe the final fusion of father and son, for it was Fonchito who shed tears over Lucrecia, and it was he who was depicted as an angelic child capable of awakening her passions. But it was Rigoberto who once made her a queen: the

Queen of Lydia, the woman who has her husband killed by his impertinent subordinate. Indeed, what happens to Lucrecia after this chapter concludes is not a glorious ascent as the Queen of Heaven, but a banishment, or rather, a punishment for having become the sexualized mother. In this novel, the figure of Mary does not serve as the handmaiden of the Lord, but as the emissary of the devil. Yet it is Fonchito, the angelic Lucifer, who most explicitly incarnates that role. He, however, escapes with impunity, whereas Lucrecia is expelled from her home by the reigning patriarch.

The Latin inscription beneath Fra Angelico's fresco acquires particular significance here. It admonishes viewers to take great care when passing before the figure of the intact virgin that their *ave* not be silenced (VIRGINIS INTACTE CVM VENERIS ANTE FIGVRAM PRETEREVNDO CAVE NE SILEATVR AVE). In the solemn atmosphere of the rebuilt Monastery of San Marco in the mid-fifteenth century, the Dominican monks who passed before Fra Angelico's magnificent frescoes in the corridors or who contemplated them in their cells would most likely have felt inspired to meditate, to engage in self-communion. But according to the inscription, the figure of Mary in the north corridor should cause them to raise their voices in salutation in the manner of Gabriel as he greeted the fearful Virgin. Thus the inscription serves to caution the pious viewers not be dumbstruck by the glorious image painted by Fra Angelico; rather, the monks are instructed to direct their sights and their voices toward the Virgin herself. Giulo Carlo Argan claims that Fra Angelico devoted himself to "suggesting themes of meditation and enunciating the mysteries of the faith" and that he "demonstrated his power of laying symbols bare and creating forms that immaterially conveyed the symbol's ideational force" (*Fra Angelico* 84). If this were completely so, however, Fra Angelico need not have feared that the monks might silence their *ave* in the presence of his Virgin, whom Argan describes as "refined, transparent, intent, the exemplary reflection of beauty no longer earthbound, but wholly spiritual and free" (91). In the visual arts, the symbol "laid bare" can only be transmuted into another symbol system: Fra Angelico (or whoever may have added the inscription beneath the fresco) understood that *The Annunciation* might seduce the viewer into glorifying the stunning signifier rather than praising the signified.

The image of Mary commands the viewer's salutation and deserves praise, but in ironic contrast, the stepmother in this novel merits an erotic confessional story, the "In Praise of the Stepmother" written by Fonchito. This is the praise that rightfully should have been silenced. Fonchito betrays his father and his stepmother by transmitting the incestuous passion into words, and once these words are written, read, or spoken, they set into motion the final act of silencing when Rigoberto casts out the woman who knew too much. Both father and son, then, take vengeance on the woman who seemingly brought about the moral downfall of the family. In the epilogue, Justiniana, the maid, accuses Fonchito of having played a cruel game with the intention of forcing his father to react as he did. But Fonchito protests: "Yo no tengo la culpa de que él la botara. A lo mejor lo que él dijo era cierto. A lo mejor ella me estaba corrompiendo. Si mi papá lo dijo, así será" (194) "It's not my fault he threw her out. Maybe what he said was true. [Maybe she was] corrupting me. If my papa said that, it must be so" (146). In allying himself with patriarchal norms, Fonchito protects his own tenuous position. In fact he fortifies it when he then turns to his maid as a new romantic object, a typical move in bourgeois patriarchal households. Justiniana asks the boy: "¿Hiciste todo eso por doña Eloísa? ¿Porque no querías que nadie reemplazara a tu mamá?" "Did you do all that on account of Doña Eloísa? Because you didn't want anyone to replace your mama?" to which he responds, "Lo hice por ti, Justita . . . no por mi mamá. Para que se fuera de esta casa y nos quedáramos solitos mi papá, yo y tú" (197) "I did it for you, Justita . . . not for my mama. So she'd leave this house and leave the three of us alone together: my papa, you, and I" (148). On an unconscious level, Fonchito's love for the stepmother would of course be a displacement of his love for his deceased mother, a love which must find a new outlet. But Fonchito's actions would also result from the great feelings of loss, hatred, and resentment unconsciously experienced toward the woman who loved his father and abandoned the child through her early death. In seeking to re-enact that scenario, Fonchito masochistically banishes the object of his love before she can desert him and sadistically uses the father, the legitimate possessor of the mother under the marriage contract, to exact his double vengeance.

The pawn here is the patriarch himself, the displaced father who desperately attempts to re-establish order or to retain his own rights

over his wife. How can we not think of Vargas Llosa's other paternal characters, such as Don Fermín in *Conversación en La Catedral*
[Conversation in the cathedral] (1969), or the outraged father in
*La tía Julia y el escribidor*? In *La tía Julia*, during what can only
be a jealous fit of rage, Varguitas's father threatens to banish the
divorcée who "corrupted" his boy and to kill Varguitas "de cinco
balazos como a un perro, en plena calle" ( 414) "[with five bullets]
like a dog, right in the middle of the street" (345). Varguitas' father
re-establishes his power over the son and forbids him to marry
"Aunt Julia," but Varguitas gets his way and elopes with this
mother figure. In *Conversación*, Santiago Zavala's powerful father
is debased completely when he is shown to be a passive homosexual,
the worst insult in the *machista* repertoire that can be hurled against
a man. So what should we say with respect to the stepmother? She
also receives the worst insult in the patriarchal language; she stands
as Mary Magdalene or Eve in contrast to the Virgin figure that for
the masculine unconscious would save her from dangerous sexuality. Now she is the one who is thrown out "como un perro" (191)
"like a dog" (143). Powerless, defenseless, the previously adored
stepmother ultimately receives no praise at all: the *AVE* has been
reversed to uncover the archaic *EVA*.[16] The solitary Rigoberto,
equally defenseless in light of the circumstances, is forced to surrender his patriarchal privileges to the son, but Fonchito too stands
alone, unable to experience love without engaging in devastating
territorial disputes. Vargas Llosa's erotic farce thus harbors a complex oedipal relationship that returns us to some familiar
"demons," as the author calls his creative obsessions. In the final
analysis, the novel supports Maurice Charney's contention that
"our sexual fiction needs no apology. If it is not always attractive,
it is at least always true" (169). On the unconscious level it is particularly true, we might add. If Vargas Llosa as the "painter of
desire" sometimes reveals the darker side of eroticism in *Elogio de
la madrastra*, we can at least be sure that he has faced those angelic
demons with a frankness hereto unequalled in his literary career.

# CHAPTER 9

## *Dada at the Tropicana: Guillermo Cabrera Infante and Readymade Art*

This final chapter might be considered a stylistic exercise, performed in a duet, perhaps even a duel, with Guillermo Cabrera Infante's *Exorcismos de esti(l)o* [Exorcizing a sty(le)] (1976). The comparative arts approaches that we have employed in the previous studies have sought to explicate meaning and sign production in a context that privileges the unconscious through a feminist psychoanalytic account. Here, however, we shift ground a bit and direct even more attention to the surface and to play than we did with regard to Vargas Llosa's erotic novel. Cabrera Infante likes to claim that his writing is nothing more than words, words, words, written to amuse himself; the search for "deep meaning" would thus go against the spirit in which Cabrera purports to work. Naturally, that claim has not prevented critics from offering interpretations that go beyond the superficial, and word play indeed may be analyzed successfully in terms of "deep play." This study gives an artistic context for Cabrera's stylistic exercises, and in so doing attempts to rescue his work from the junkyard of literature; or rather, we should say that what some call the "junkyard" is itself worth studying, because it provides unique passage to determining what art and literature can be all about. The abject, as we have seen in our psychoanalytically based chapters, counterbalances and illuminates the sublime. We began this book with "decadent" literature, and we end with the decay of "literature." So let us now proceed to a setting similar to the Tropicana nightclub from Cabrera's *Tres tristes tigres* [Three trapped tigers] (1971), where it is once again "Showtime!" at the (Dada) cabaret.

At first glance, Cabrera Infante's *Exorcismos de esti(l)o* appears to be a collection of untranscendental fragments composed of puns, parodies, word games, and other airy prosaic or poetic forms that mesh well with the Cuban author's literary style as manifested in his highly acclaimed novel *Tres tristes tigres*, one of the cornerstones of the "boom."[1] It is not surprising that this minor work has attracted sparse critical attention because it gives the impression of being totally devoid of content.[2] The pieces in the collection flaunt their status as linguistic games, and even the author himself stresses their inconsequentiality when he remarks that the title may be taken literally; that is, the stylistic exercises/exorcisms may have been performed as a diversionary tactic to beat the summer heat (Acosta-Belén 106–7). In a reflective moment, however, Cabrera Infante declares that *Exorcismos* is a more ambitious work:

> El libro tiene pretensiones . . . de jugar con la literatura y al mismo tiempo establecer una relación entre la escritura y la metafísica, como otro juego posible. . . . Yo quería hacer ese juego . . . al nivel de la separación del lenguaje en sus componentes, jugando con los signos, con las representaciones de los signos, como son los diagramas de composición, por ejemplo. Esto lo habían hecho mucho antes los dadaístas.

> The book has pretensions . . . of playing with literature and at the same time establishing a relation between writing and metaphysics, as another possible game. . . . I wanted to play that game . . . at the level of the separation of language into its components, playing with signs, with the representations of signs, such as composition diagrams, for example. This is something that the Dadaists had done much earlier. ("Habla Cabrera Infante" 120)

This chapter explores the relation between Cabrera Infante's *Exorcismos* and what has been called the "Duchamp effect"[3] in an attempt to demonstrate the intellectual and artistic affinities that link the Cuban master of wordplay to the French inventor of the "readymade." The "effect" of which we are speaking may be best defined as an attitude of indifference or hostility toward "high" art and literature predicated on the notion of game and amusement, which in turn produces a playful celebration of the commonplace and of language itself. Cabrera Infante recognizes that the games he plays as neo-Dadaist (struck by the Duchamp effect, we might add) start from a refusal to signify and end up in the realm of metaphysics, beyond the material. Johan Huizinga would call this the "significant" function of play: "the very fact that play has a meaning implies a non-materialistic quality in the nature of the thing itself" (1). The formal characteristics of play as Huizinga defines them are most appropriate to our discussion. He notes that play is "a free activity standing quite consciously outside 'ordinary' life"; it is "an activity connected with no material interest, and no profit can be gained by it"; it "proceeds within its own proper boundaries of time and space according to fixed rules and in an orderly manner" (13). As will become clear in the course of this discussion, both Guillermo Cabrera Infante and Marcel Duchamp have deliberately situated themselves in their individual playgrounds of art, and we in turn now stand as players at the crossroads that rise up from the "small infinity" of technical possibilities specific to those games. If their games are objects in space, our critical play becomes an action in time, a re-presentation or a replay. In performing an analysis along these lines, the goals are to illustrate the parallels between the creative acts performed by both men in their respective times and artistic circumstances and to uncover the operative rules of their games. It should be emphasized that the primary aim of this study is not to furnish proof of direct artistic influence understood in the traditional sense, although a good case could be stated for this, beginning with the fact that Cabrera Infante has made explicit reference to Duchamp on at least one occasion.[4] Moreover, to speak of the connection between the visual and the verbal arts in the case of Cabrera Infante seems to be a logical extension of Dada, since the link was firmly established during the incipient stages of the avant-garde movements when there was an overt mingling of artistic and literary production along with a true association of writers and painters who worked side by side in formal or informal artistic societies.[5] Duchamp himself has reclaimed a vast pictorial tradition anchored as much in the verbal as in the visual: "I was interested in ideas—not merely in visual products. I wanted to put painting once again at the service of the mind. . . . In fact until the last hundred years all painting had been literary or religious: it had all been at the service of the mind" ("Painting" 394).

In approaching Cabrera Infante's work, as well as the texts that are the focus of the other chapters of our book, we have made use of what may be called "interartisticality" (although the term is somewhat awkward), a method that is theoretically akin to intertextuality. If we endeavor to situate a text within the framework of an infinite discursive chain, we soon come up against a mosaic of citations, or a grid of other texts that in turn establishes a context, a set of expectations. Interartisticality would further expand the grid to include the relation between the visual and the verbal. To speak of Cabrera Infante's work in the Dada tradition, then, is to construct a theoretical framework that may be used to explore kinship, but should not be taken as a license to establish paternity. At this juncture it is necessary to steer away from the question of whether the pieces comprising Cabrera Infante's *Exorcismos* and the ready-mades by Duchamp should be viewed as "mere real things" or whether they represent a "transfiguration of the commonplace,"[6] that is, a conversion into sanctioned works of art (indeed, the whole Dada movement turns on this problem). Although this topic will be indirectly addressed, we have chosen instead to concentrate for the most part on the structural significance of these artists' respective gestures, whether these gestures ultimately respond more faithfully to a conservative or to a radical impulse.

As a point of departure let us examine a section of *Exorcismos* that by all rights should be considered readymade art proper. The text in question (179) reads exactly as follows:

LAS MUY INQUISITIVAS AVENTURAS
DE DON ARCHIBALDO LYALL
POR LOS DUROS DOMINIOS DE CASTILLA
LA FONETICA

*(fragmentos)*

DISPENSAYMAY, kay ora ess? Moochass grahtheeahss.
Ah kay ora saleh el bookeh pahra _____ oy? Ah kay ora
lyayga el trayn a _____ manyahna?
- - - - - - - - - - - - - - - - - - - - - - - - - - - - - - - - - - - - - - - -
　Estah dessockoopahdo esteh asee-ento? Keereh
dahrrmeh lah leesta day lahss komeedahs, senyoreeta?
- - - - - - - - - - - - - - - - - - - - - - - - - - - - - - - - - - - - - - - -
　Lah kwentah, kahmarairo, prawnto, por fahvor. Estah
inklooeedo el sairveethyo?
- - - - - - - - - - - - - - - - - - - - - - - - - - - - - - - - - - - - - - - -
　Bwaynohss deeahss, kwahnto vahleh esto? Ess
daymahsseeahdo. Lo see-ento moocho. Ahdeeohss!
- - - - - - - - - - - - - - - - - - - - - - - - - - - - - - - - - - - - - - - -
　Bwaynohss deeahss, por dondeh say vah ah lah Plahtha
day lah Kahtaydrahl? Estah therrahda esta manyahna
lah eeglayseea vee-ahya? Ah kay ora say ahbreh esta
tharrdeh?
- - - - - - - - - - - - - - - - - - - - - - - - - - - - - - - - - - - - - - - -

The equivalent in translation would be fragments from a travel book intended for Spanish speakers who need "tourist English." The pronunciation would thus have to correspond to the Spanish sound system, but the translator of the piece would need to communicate a tone of mockery as well. Cabrera Infante's text, "The Very Inquisitive Adventures of Sir Archibald Lyall in the Difficult Dominions of Phonetic Castile," offers "translations" of the following English phrases: "Excuse me, what time is it? Thank you very much. What time does the ship leave for _____ today? What time does the train arrive at _____ tomorrow? Is this seat occupied? May I please see a menu, miss? Waiter, the check, quickly, please. Is the tip included? Good morning, how much does this cost? That is too much. I am very sorry. Good-by! Good morning, how do I get to the Cathedral Square? Is the old church closed this morning? What time does it open this afternoon?"

Upon reading "The Very Inquisitive Adventures of Sir Archibald Lyall," one might first suspect that Cabrera Infante has simply invented a literary vehicle through which he may mock the Anglophone's pronunciation of the Spanish language by "transcribing" stereotypical phrases of the type uttered by tourists. But in reality this linguistic farce has been extracted from a specific source and then reassembled by the author with some minor alterations: addition of a title, deletions of the English phrases and their translation into written standard Spanish, corruptions of the "respelling" (as they call the pronunciation system common to language guides for travelers). One such guidebook that we have in hand is *Grosset's Spanish Phrase Book and Dictionary for Travelers* by Charles A. Hughes, which very well could have been the original after which Cabrera Infante modeled his language lesson. In Grosset's phrase book, one finds many of the exact questions posed by the fictional Anglophone traveler of *Exorcismos*. The English is given in bold-faced type, followed by the standard Spanish, and, finally, in italics, the "respelling" for English speakers:

**What time is it?**
¿Qué hora es?
*Keh oh´-rah ehs?* (25)

Thus, if we so desired, we could reconstruct the whole of Don Archibaldo's adventures by going to the appropriate section of Grosset's phrase book. But after having read Cabrera Infante's (per)version, a return to the traveler's guide brings to light its ludicrous side. If we subject the manual to the process of interpretation, such as we do with a literary text, we come square up against a readymade of grotesque proportions that rivals or even surpasses Cabrera Infante's experiment. In the spirit of Dada, let us arbitrarily reproduce a portion of the real-world object-text, the handy Grosset's guidebook that could be purchased in an airport store or popular bookshop:

**This butter is not fresh.**
Esta mantequilla no está fresca.
*Eh´-stah mahn-teh-kee´-lyah noh eh-stah´ frehs´-kah.*

**This milk is warm.**
Esta leche está caliente.
*Eh´-stah leh´-cheh eh-stah´*
*kah-lyehn´-teh.*

**This milk is sour.**
Esta leche está agria.
*Eh´-stah leh´-cheh eh-stah´*
*ah´-gree-yah.*

**I would like a glass of cold milk.**
Quisiera un vaso de leche fría.
*Kee-syeh´-rah oon vah´-soh deh leh´-cheh free´-yah.*

**Another cup of coffee?**
¿Otra taza de café?
*Oh´-trah tah´-sah deh kahfeh´?*

**Another cup of tea?**
¿Otra taza de té?
*Oh´-trah tah´-sah deh teh?*

**Do you want some more tea?**
¿Quiere usted más té?
*Kyeh´-reh oos-tehd´ mahs teh?* (55)

If we read this page as dialogue, it naturally borders on the absurd. There is no indication who should speak the lines, although it is obvious that the tourist would voice the requests, whereas the waiter would offer the beverages. Let us imagine for a moment a hypothetical situation in which the Anglophone traveler, following the pronunciation guide, painstakingly utters some of the suggested phrases, her confidence boosted by the reassurance that "a slight mispronunciation is no embarrassment," as *Grosset's Spanish Phrase Book* confidently proclaims. First of all, she would obviously make a selection among the many possibilities listed here, unless of course she feels compelled to object to both the milk's temperature and its state of freshness. And the server, in turn, would probably not offer more coffee *and* tea to the same person. But there are more absurd factors at work in this "text," and these are the culturally based ones that Cabrera

Infante uses for his satiric parody.[7] Anglophone tourists, accustomed to the ways of their native lands, would find it logical that the waiter bring around second servings of coffee, whereas in Spanish-speaking countries, coffee puts an end to a meal and is not normally served repeatedly. It is also comic to note that most of the utterances on this page attributed to the Anglophone are complaints, which implies that when one is traveling in a Spanish-speaking country, one should expect to encounter spoiled butter, sour milk, or a dirty tablecloth and silverware, as noted in another part of the "Eating and Drinking" section. Thus the "implied Anglophone," if we may use this term, seems remarkably like the "ugly American" tourist who defines and evaluates a cultural-linguistic universe he or she does not understand very well and cannot manipulate from within; further, the tourist's depiction in this little phrase book (as well as in Cabrera Infante's text) makes him or her comparable to, say, an Ionesco character who sputters one non sequitur after another. And those who know Cabrera's *Tres tristes tigres* may have already noted the similarities between don Archibaldo and another famous pair of stereotypical American characters, a subject to which we will return shortly.

Our reading of Grosset's phrase book is possible because of Cabrera Infante's initial appropriation of its format; however, as we noted earlier, there are some key transformations in the "literary" version. The addition of a title makes the reconstituted found object into a narrative of sorts. Yet the "inquisitive" adventures merely refer back to an interrogative punctuation sign system. All Archibaldo's experiences in the land of "Castilla la Fonética" are linguistic in nature, and the "country" he visits exists exclusively as "black symbols on a white page," to cite one of Cabrera Infante's definitions of literature.[8] It appears that Archibaldo Lyall (Y'all? Lie-all?) is simply reciting random sections of his phrase book with no visible interlocutor, and he is predictably unable to formulate logical questions ("Ah kay ora lyayga el trayn a _____ manyahna?" "What time does the train arrive at _____ tomorrow?"). If Archibaldo is a buffoon, it is in part attributable to the ridiculous phrase book that would have him learning vital travel phrases such as "This is not my handkerchief," found in Grosset's guide (41). Cabrera Infante carries his parody further when he corrupts the "respelling" to reflect how uninitiated Anglophones really pronounce the Spanish language: instead of "prohn´-to" Archibaldo says "prawnto," and he asks "kay ora

ess? rather than "keh oh´-rah ehs?" And finally, Cabrera Infante
subjects his character to the hard lessons of Castillian pronunciation, with its characteristic "th" sound as in Archibaldo's
"grahtheeahss." Naturally, Archibaldo overgeneralizes the phonetic rules, so that he mispronounces *tarde* as "tharrdeh."

When we call this piece from *Exorcismos* a "readymade," or,
more precisely, a "readymade aided" we are using Marcel Duchamp's terms to describe his own creative work.[9] He makes the
following remarks about his famous readymades, such as the bicy-
cle wheel on a kitchen stool, the snow shovel renamed *In Advance
of the Broken Arm*, or *Fountain*, the urinal signed "R. Mutt":
"One important characteristic was the short sentence which I
occasionally inscribed on the 'Readymade.' That sentence instead
of describing the object like a title was meant to carry the mind of
the spectator toward other regions more verbal. Sometimes I
would add a graphic detail of presentation which in order to satisfy my craving for alliterations, would be called 'Readymade
Aided'" (*Writings* 141–42). Duchamp's readymades indeed carry
the spectator to regions more verbal because, in their resemblance
to their ordinary counterparts in the real world, they force the
spectator into an act of interpretation. In the words of Inez
Hedges, the readymade and the surrealist object "interrogate the
relationship between the work and the world" (54), to which we
must add, in Duchamp's and Cabrera Infante's cases, among the
*word*, the work, and the world.

One of the ways in which the readymade accomplishes this
interrogation is by alienating the object from its habitual context
or its original purpose, an effect André Breton has called "mutation de rôle."[10] This "change of role" has also been named *dépaysement*, which literally suggests that the object has been removed
or displaced from its homeland (Rubin 48). The term *dépaysement* applies particularly well to Cabrera Infante's readymade,
given that many of its playful possibilities hinge on Archibaldo's
displacement from his own linguistic ambience into the realm of
"Castilla la Fonética." The dissociation of Archibaldo's adventures from the phrase book that served as their model suspends the
text-object into a vacuum and divorces it from the utilitarian role
that publishers intend for works like it.[11] How can we not think
of Duchamp's *Hat Rack*, suspended from the ceiling, where it is
physically elevated above its real-world counterparts, isolated
from "mere real things" both on the material and on the spiritual

planes? And yet, all these artistic activities are executed with what Duchamp calls "meta-irony." As one critic puts it, the French artist's "works or 'jokes' flutter on the frontier between meaninglessness and deep metaphysical significance" (Shattuck 46). In passing critical judgment on his *Exorcismos*, Cabrera Infante also alternates between the poles of vacuousness and hypersignification, something that we, too, are inclined to do in our analysis of the work. The simple "exercises," purportedly a homage to Raymond Queneau, easily lend themselves to the type of overdetermination that probably characterizes our way of reading; however, this interpretative excess is precisely what is demanded by the artistic context we are defining in relation to the readymade.

The notion of *dépaysement* takes on further significance with respect to Cabrera Infante when we take into account that much of his *oeuvre* plays with the interlinguistic possibilities of English and Spanish; in fact, it has often been said that Cabrera Infante's reader must be bilingual—or at least conversant in bits and pieces of popular American English—in order to participate in the word games that lie at the core of his writings. The adventures of Archibaldo, as we have indicated, take place in the realm of language exercises, a predicament that recalls the trials and tribulations of the memorable Anglophones in *Tres tristes tigres*, the Campbells. In "Los visitantes" [The visitors], the fifth section of Cabrera Infante's masterpiece, the adventures of Mr. and Mrs. Campbell during their weekend in Havana are told and retold (supposedly by the Campbells themselves) in a hilarious *exercise de style* that achieves its humor through mistranslations from English into Spanish and vice-versa. Thus Mrs. Campbell is reported to have said upon landing in steamy Havana: "*Miel*, éste es *el* Trópico!" (186) "Little dear, this is *the* Tropic" (186). When Mrs. Campbell writes her version of the events, she claims: "Mi español no es, por amor de Dios, un idioma perfectamente hablado. . . . También lo cepillé un poco antes de venir. Nunca exhibiré afuera un idioma que no conozco bien" (203) "My Spanish is not, I swear to God, a perfectly spoken idiom. . . . I also gave it a good scrubbing before coming to Cuba. I will never exhibit outside a language I do not well know" (203). If the Spanish text is to emerge from its condition as complete nonsense, or the chaos of literalness, one must look to English for the source of these erroneous translations ("Also I brushed it [my Spanish] up shortly before coming"; "I will never show off a language I don't know well").[12] Of course, the English version of *Tres tristes tigres* retains the literalness that gives the Spanish its zest and humor, for otherwise, the game of translation and mistranslation would have no impact in English at all. Cabrera Infante constructs the visitors' adventures from the stuff of language, and shows how the failure to transmit a meaningful message or to comprehend the intended signified places the Campbells in a risible predicament, first as tourists on the island and subsequently as writers of their tale.

There are other indications that in *Tres tristes tigres* Cabrera Infante has explored the realm of readymade art and what we are identifying as its inherent *dépaysement*. In the section called "Bachata," three friends, Cué, Eribó, and Silvestre, spend their days cruising in cars, pursuing women, and, above all, engaging in the prodigious verbal jousts that give this novel much of its originality. At one point the "tigers" spot a sign as they go down the street, which initiates a lengthy discussion of the implications of the (road) sign as signifier:

> Una vez más vimos el letrero que decía *No tiren piedras ay mujeres y niños* y Cué habló del Lorca impensado que lo pintó, como de aquel otro de la Vía Blanca, el aviso de *Solamente para Gancedo,* que quería decir que no se podía doblar sino para coger la calle Gancedo y Cué decía que era una exclusiva más del industrial del mismo nombre o . . . ante el anuncio en la carretera de Cantarranas, *Deliciosos moros sabrosos negros, Entre* queriendo anunciar frijoles negros y el arroz con frijoles apodado en La Habana moros y cristianos, que dijo que era una invitación expresa a André Gide. . . . Fue él mismo quien recordó esa última ratio leída por alguien en México, que advertía a los cargadores de materiales que no podían parquear sus camiones, de esta manera: SE PROHIBE A LOS MATERIALISTAS ESTACIONARSE EN LO ABSOLUTO. (316–17)

> Once more we saw the handwritten sign saying *Think twise— would you thro bricks to woman with baby?* and Cué said,— Nobody but W.C.! Fields could have done it, like that other sign on the Via Blanca which read OPEN ONLY TO GANCEDO meaning you couldn't turn except into Gancedo Street, and Cué said that it was one more exclusive property of the industrialist of the same name or . . . when he passed the sign on the Cantarranas highway which said DELICIOUS BLACKS AND DELECTABLE MOORS. DRIVE IN, an ad for black beans and rice, called "Moors and Christians" in Havana, he said it was a standing invitation

for André Gide. . . . It was he who also found this last beautiful piece of Sign Buddhism in Mexico, which notified truck drivers carrying building materials: MATERIALISTS ARE FORBIDDEN TO STOP IN THE ABSOLUTE. (331–32)

If we follow the pattern of the game as devised by the "tigers," we see that they have excised the signs from their habitual context, and have conferred on them a meaning that is derived either from what appears to be the literal sense, or from metaphoric connotations. When exiled from their natural element and blatantly subjected to the hermeneutic process, the signs yield a chain of signifieds that are in turn themselves bound to the newly created normalizing context in which they occur.

Stanley Fish cites a most felicitous example of the sign and its interpretation in his essay "Normal Circumstances, Literal Language, Direct Speech Acts, the Ordinary, the Everyday, the Obvious, What Goes without Saying, and Other Special Cases." It is a notice affixed to the door of a university club that reads PRIVATE MEMBERS ONLY. When asked to tell what the sign means, Fish's students offer a variety of interpretations, ranging from the predictably obvious to the humorously erotic. Unlike Duchamp's famous sign-saying, *Ovaire toute la nuit*,[13] Fish's example ostensibly lacks a built-in play on words or ambiguity of meaning. But as Fish convincingly demonstrates, the sign is *always* situated within a context, which in turn defines the parameters of the interpretative assumptions at work in the minds of readers who form a community. Thus the context of the PRIVATE MEMBERS ONLY sign when attached to a club door would create certain expectations as to what it means, just as the DELICIOUS BLACKS AND DELECTABLE MOORS. DRIVE IN sign outside a restaurant would have culinary connotations for native Cubans, rather than extend a homoerotic invitation to Gide, a meaning which the "tigers" adduce in their linguistic inebriation. Similarly, when we encounter a snow shovel in its place as a utilitarian object, we bring to bear a set of assumptions (it is used to remove snow; it may be purchased in a store, etc.), whereas when we view the same object as a readymade in the institutional setting of a museum or gallery, we locate it within the context of art.[14] And, in parallel fashion, when we come across the fragments of a Spanish phrase book in a text published as literature, we recognize the legitimacy—even the necessity—of reading it as such. Fish concludes that "irony and ambiguity are not properties of language but are functions of the expectations with which we approach it. If we expect a text to be ambiguous, we will in the act of reading it imagine situations in which it means first one thing and then another . . . and those plural meanings will, in the context of that situation, be the text's literal readings" (276–77). In other words, we should not speak dichotomously of a "literal" sense and a "figurative" sense, for this would reduce the signifying process to an easily accessible avenue of meaning which in turn would cut off the free play of the linguistic sign system. The signified is contextually commutable, as Fish, among others, has demonstrated, and it is this notion that allows us to locate Duchamp's and Cabrera Infante's art at a crucial point in the development of modern acts of creativity.

It has frequently been said that Duchamp's greatest works are words, and in this regard the French master shares a great deal with the author of *Exorcismos de esti(l)o.* Many sections of Cabrera Infante's book contain puns whose essence is erotic, scatological, and notably infantile, such as the following:

EROTESIS

¿Es que méamas porque me amás?   (90)

REGLAS DE HIGIENE

mano

ano

no                    (275)

The first pun, "Erotesis," plays with the verbs *mear,* "to pee", and *amar,* "to love." However, the incorrect placement of the written accents makes the phrase simultaneously nonsensical and polysemous ("Does she pee more because you love me," "Does she pee more because she pees more," etc.). The second example, "Rules of Hygiene," reduces the word *mano,* "hand," to *ano,* "anus," and *no,* "no." An equivalent in English might go something like this:

Passion

ass

sin

Of course, this version turns the rules of hygiene into a prohibition against anal eroticism.

Returning to Duchamp, we find among his writings a series of puns that play with the same basic notions as those employed by Cabrera Infante: "Ruiner, uriner" "Ruined, urined" (115); "Question d'hygiène intime: Faut-it mettre la moelle de l'épee dans le poil de l'aimée?" "Question of intimate hygiene: should you put the hilt of the foil in the quilt of the goil?" (106). Even the title Duchamp gave to some of his writings, *Texticules*, forces the written word to be subjected to the eroticized body, a process that has completely dominated the literary production of Cabrera Infante. After all, the Cuban's "Pornografía" from the "Vocalbur-lario" section of *Exorcismos* reads simply "V de vagina" (273).[15] For both creators, the erotic potential of language—especially its plastic representation as typographical symbols—furnishes an interminable source of inspiration for their work, absorbed as they are in the pleasure of the text(icle).[16]

Marcel Duchamp extended the eroticized pun to his ready-mades, such as the painting of the Mona Lisa, to which he added a mustache, a goatee, and a title: L.H.O.O.Q. ("elle a chaud au cul" "she has a hot ass"). Artist Gianfranco Baruchello's remarks on Duchamp's wit are most appropriate and equally applicable to Cabrera Infante:

> Some of his plays on words and arrangements of alphabets are almost embarrassing. They're almost a kind of whorehouse wit, or the sorts of things that get passed around a classroom by the kids who've been made to sit in the last row of desks. What do you say about somebody who could keep a box under his bed full of pages and pages of phonetic puns like LMAP, or LHIEOPI, or MOAGBZDDSOSLARNU. LHOOQ was really the most innocent of the lot. Things like that can make you wake up in the middle of the night and wonder if your attempts to look for a philoso-phy in this man aren't after all a little delirious. (71)

Baruchello has defined the spirit of Dada as it is incarnated by Duchamp and, by extension, as it resurfaces in Cabrera Infante decades later. The attempt to find philosophy here seems contrain-dicated, but then Cabrera would have been the first to tell us so. And still we persist, because there is something compelling in the kind of delirium that is at least as old as *Tristram Shandy*, and probably as old as the acquisition of language itself. Speech, after all, is word play, or word work, and Cabrera and Duchamp make a good argument that these facets are one and the same.[17]

This spirit that the two artists share derives much of its force from their stance *against* "art" or "literature," from their irreverence and their ability to shock. Both artists seek a variety of means by which they can interrogate the notion of art, and both take as a departure point the concept of the game. In *Tres tristes tigres*, the jocular banter of the three friends harbors an attitude that reflects this "anti-art" stance:

> —¿Y eso qué? Estamos hablando de literatura, ¿no? . . .
> —*Jugando* con la literatura.
> —¿Y qué tiene de malo eso?
> —La literatura, por supuesto.
> —Menos mal. Por un momento temí que pudieras decir, el juego. ¿Seguimos? (416).

> —So? Weren't we talking about literature? . . .
> —Not talking about, p*laying with* literature.
> —And what's so bad about that?
> —Literature, of course.
> —That's better. For a moment I was afraid you were going to say the game. Shall we go on? (439)

In a compelling way, this dialogue typifies most of Cabrera Infante's creative acts. He consistently places the intrinsic value of the game above the concept of literature. Rather, for Cabrera Infante, literature *is* a game, and it loses all interest for him when divorced from its power to amuse. Or to baffle. In this endeavor, Marcel Duchamp has also distinguished himself. His *To Be Looked at (from the Other Side of the Glass) with One Eye, Close to, for Almost an Hour* is a composition that is, among other things, an exercise in perspective. Contents of the work aside, what are we to make of the title instructions? Does the piece *only* take on significance when looked at in the prescribed manner? That is, does the spectator's pose *vis-à-vis* the composition create its meaning?[18] Cabrera Infante formulates equally enigmatic questions in *Exorcismos de esti(l)o*, where we find an exercise that consists of these directions: "Mirar con un ojo un retrato de Marx, con el otro el de Engels, mientras se piensa en Eng y Chang" "Look with one eye at a picture of Marx, with the other eye at a picture of Engels, while thinking about Eng and Chang" (222). Where is the creative act here? It is either in the writing of those instructions or in the rendezvous of Marx, Engels, Eng, and Chang that comes about when the reader executes the act both optically and mentally. But, as Cabrera Infante would certainly protest, this exercise is a game; we are only playing with literature, and we already know what is wrong with that: the attempt to see "literature" there at all, no matter how long we stare with both eyes open.

From the foregoing discussion, it is apparent that both Cabrera Infante and Duchamp have embraced what we may view as a variant of the "pleasure principle," the most expeditious route to joyful self-gratification produced through their infantile puns and scatological humor.[19] It is worthy to note that the two men execute self-portraits and create alter egos for themselves that also bear affinities. Granted, Duchamp's invented other, "Rrose Sélavy," is a transvestite version of self, whereas Cabrera Infante's "Cain," as the name suggests, is a fratricidal brother to his creator.[20] But the fact remains that both artists devised an elaborate game with their alter egos at the center and engaged in many creative activities, and anxieties, under their pseudonyms. If artistic creativity may be envisioned as amusement, it is quite understandable that the participants should wish to don costumes and masks from time to time, and even to change gender. The consummate example of the mask, however, is Duchamp's 1959 self-portrait, *With My Tongue in My Cheek* (Fig. 33), composed of plaster, pencil, and paper. Rosalind Krauss describes it as follows:

> On a sheet of paper Duchamp sketches his profile, depicting himself in the representational terms of the graphic icon. On the top of this drawing, coincident with part of its contour, is added the area of chin and cheek, cast from his own face in plaster. Index is juxtaposed to icon and both are then captioned. "With my tongue in my cheek," is obviously a reference to the ironic mode, a verbal doubling to redirect meaning. But it can also be taken literally. To actually place one's tongue in one's cheek is to lose the capacity for speech altogether. And it is this rupture between image and speech, or more specifically, language, that Duchamp's art both contemplates and instances. (*Originality of the Avant-Garde* 206)

Krauss has hit upon an essential feature of Duchamp's creative act, one that we also recognize on the pages of Cabrera Infante's *Exorcismos de esti(l)o*: that literalness is itself a relative term sub-

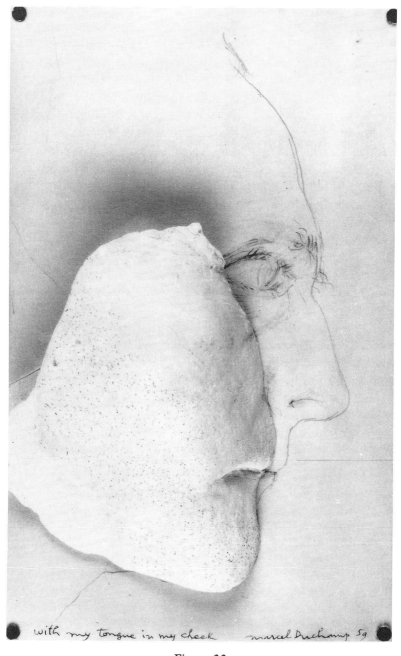

with my tongue in my cheek     marcel Duchamp 59

Figure 33
Marcel Duchamp, *With My Tongue in My Cheek* (1959). Musée
National d'Art Moderne, Centre Georges Pompidou, Paris, France.
Photo Philippe Migeat.

ject to interpretation (and subversion), as Fish has demonstrated
in his discourse on the sign PRIVATE MEMBERS ONLY. It is Duchamp's attempt at the literal depiction of himself in the jocular
mode that leads to aphasia, the breaking down—or, in this
instance, the cracking up—of language. When Duchamp's tongue
is physically placed in his cheek, the joking ceases on the verbal
level, but commences on the pictorial or iconographic level.

Cabrera Infante displays similar aims in his mock self-portrait
printed on the last page of *Exorcismos*, a text that the author hails
as a parodic quotation (with appropriate substitutions) of the last
paragraph of the epilogue from Jorge Luis Borges's *El hacedor*
[The maker].[21] The "Epilogolipo" harmonizes well with the
whole of *Exorcismos de esti(l)o* in that it conforms to the structural pattern of readymade that we have outlined here. Cabrera
Infante's text concludes:

> *Un hombre se propone el empeño de escribir el mundo. En el
> discurrir del tiempo construye un volumen con trozos de pueb-
> los, de reinos, de montes, de puertos, de buques, de islotes, de
> peces, de cubiles, de instrumentos, de soles, de equinos y de gen-
> tes. Poco tiempo previo de morir, descubre que ese minucioso
> enredo de surcos en dos dimensiones compone el dibujo de su
> rostro.* (293)

> *One person gives himself the job of writing the world. In the
> flow of time he constructs his volume with pieces of towns, of
> kingdoms, of hills, of ports, of ships, of isles, of fish, of rooms,
> of instruments, of suns, of horses, of people. Shortly before
> dying, he discovers how the minute mesh of furrows in two
> dimensions composes the sketch of his profile.*

By placing himself in mocking opposition to the Argentine master,
Cabrera Infante alienates his own reflection from the Borgesian
model that is reproduced on the pages of *Exorcismos*. But despite
his protests to the contrary, Cabrera Infante has indeed penned a
parodic self-portrait. By virtue of having chosen Borges's epilogue
for inclusion in his own book, he authorizes us to resituate the
autobiographical quotation in its new context and thus to ascribe
it to the executor of the parody. Further, Cabrera Infante's face
would be marked not so much by *"pieces of towns, of kingdoms,
of hills"* as by *pieces of texts*, and thus his readymade self-portrait,
like Duchamp's, would be drawn *with* and *by* the instruments of
his creative craft. The black-and-white symbols on the page,

reconstructed and reassembled in infinite verbal puns, would signify the essence of the punster; however, the traces that comprise the self-portrait would themselves only be signs or signifiers that refer the spectator to another level of signification, one that escapes "literalness." These artists construct themselves out of language in literal fashion, but, like all humans, they can *only* represent themselves through language. Thus, their play on words, their play with words, signals in graphic fashion the impossibility of escaping the labyrinth of signification. In sketching their self-portraits, they find themselves caught up in the failure of representation. Clearly, they know very well how to savor the pleasures of that paradox.

By way of conclusion, let us consider the following declaration, which is printed in such a manner that it spreads out over pages sixteen and seventeen of *Exorcismos de esti(l)o* like so:

| | |
|---|---|
| Literatura es todo lo que se lea | como tal |
| Literature is all that may be read | as such |

If we respect the typographical spacing of the statement, we arrive at two possible stances: everything that we happen to read *is* literature, and anything that we read *as* literature consequently *is* literature. This Dada-inspired maxim may also be applied to Duchamp, who in essence could have declared:

| | |
|---|---|
| Art is anything that may be seen | as such |

In the final analysis, Duchamp's most memorable Dada gesture was to utter the magic words that arbitrarily turned a urinal into *Fountain*, or a snow shovel into *In Advance of the Broken Arm*, and through his alchemy of the verb he forever changed our ways of seeing. Duchamp's work furnishes a most appropriate context in which to situate Cabrera Infante's *Exorcismos de esti(l)o*, for without it, the Cuban author's verbal games may appear totally weightless. In reality, they carry the heavy baggage of Dadaism, even if they take the form of an airy *trompe-l'oeil* much like Duchamp's *Why Not Sneeze Rose Sélavy* (Fig. 34), the birdcage filled with deceptive sugar cubes made of marble, which Octavio Paz has aptly called "the plastic equivalent of a pun" (22).[22] The context sketched here becomes especially crucial to this type of art if we follow Claude Lévi-Strauss's view that readymades "in themselves have very uncertain meanings, they are almost devoid of significance and only acquire a sense from their context. . . . it is the

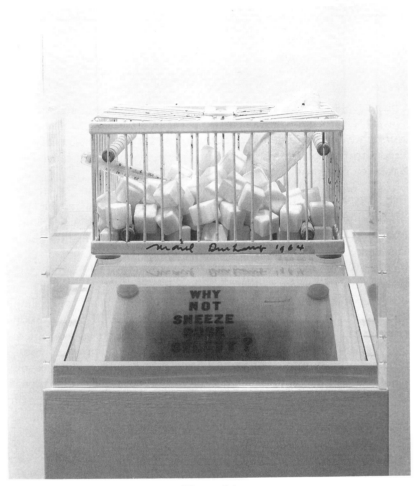

Figure 34
Duchamp, *Why Not Sneeze Rose Sélavy?* (1921).
Albright-Knox Art Gallery, Buffalo, New York.
George B. and Jenny R. Mathews Fund, 1972.

'sentences' made with objects which have a meaning and not the single object in itself" (80–81). If we extend this statement to the status of literary language and representation in their broader sense, then we arrive at a posture similar to the one formulated by Michel Foucault when he speaks of a given text as forming a node within a network, which thereby causes the book's unity to be variable and relative since it is constructed on the basis of a complex field of discourse (*Archaeology of Knowledge* 23). Through our own experiment in approximating the creative genius of Guillermo Cabrera Infante to that of Marcel Duchamp we have squeezed the Cuban's work into one of those Duchamp-like contraptions such as the birdcage, or the boxes filled with word plays that the Frenchman kept stashed under his bed, in our effort to liberate the text from its habitual place. We have sought to forge a link in the interpretive chain that will strengthen our view of those style-summer exercises performed by the author of *Tres tristes tigres,* which are in fact *exorcisms.* If we are right, we have uncovered another spirit lurking behind the ghost of Queneau, one who assumes the profile of the man "with his tongue in his cheek."

# Epi(dia)logue

CF: To tie up some loose ends I'd like to return here to the *Mirrored Room* of our first chapter, the cube that reflects on its surfaces the multiple image of whoever enters into it, and that serves as a metaphor for our commentaries. The specular reflection connects most easily to the *stade du miroir* as enunciated by Lacan, at least for the psychoanalytically informed reader. Yet according to the theoretical model developed by Winnicott, the face of the mother functions as precursor to the mirror in the development of each human being. What children contemplate in that mirror may thus differ essentially; as a consequence, psychic variations emerge that shape the particular individual. In the best possible scenario the mother returns the child's own image to him or her; that is, children see themselves—find themselves—in and through the mother. The encounter of oneself in the maternal mirror/face—or what Heinz Lichtenstein calls the emergence of a primary identity through the act of (maternal) mirroring (214)—can nevertheless be disturbed by the spectacle of a mother who, in Winnicott's words, "reflects her own mood or, worse still, the rigidity of her own defences" (112). The alienation of the subject would already begin here, before reaching the Lacanian mirror stage. On the other hand, when children contemplate themselves in a real mirror, they search there for the image of the mother capable of returning their own image back to them, of establishing a dialogue with them. The degree of alienation felt when one looks at oneself in a mirror would depend on the extent to which the imaginary presence of the responsive maternal face fails or succeeds to introduce itself in the mirroring experience. In this sense I am in disagreement with critics cited in the first part of chapter 1, such as James W. Fernandez, who turns the mirror into an instrument of confirmation of a strictly masculine identity. The "sensation of relief" that, according to Fernandez, comes over the subject would perhaps obey to the supposition of having avoided an intruding female image, as you indicate in your comments. It is better to exclude the mother (and, by extension, any feminine presence) than to have to observe a mother who shows herself as absent, unable to respond, or as an intrusive being: a voracious abyss rather than an empathic mirror.

It is understandable that the *Mirrored Room* constitutes a singular attraction for children. As a maternal, labyrinthic environment it beckons a child to lose himself or herself within its walls in order to emerge triumphantly, following the adventure, like a miniature Theseus. Of course, the maternal does not reside only in the labyrinthic sensation caused by infinite projections; it owes equally to the specular material of that attractive yet abysmal cloister cube. True, in that room we lose ourselves, we disperse psychotically in multiple fragments, but we also recreate ourselves following that process of dissociation. Even if we are no longer children, we can imaginarily regress when we enter the "children's section." The presence of the mother by the child's side naturally aids him or her in combatting archaic fears, that is, fears of the archaic mother. Thus the mother restrains the attraction and dissipates the terror that she herself originates. It is Ariadne, a woman and a maternal figure, who paradoxically aids Theseus (and us, his followers) in escaping from the maternal (or infantile) prison. And, although the father can carry out the same function, his presence does not seem to be absolutely necessary, provided of course that the mother is indeed good enough.

Painting also has the potential to evoke in us reactions analogous to those produced by the *Mirrored Room*; Samaras's work may thus be viewed as emblematic of all the paintings in the museum (or any museum), and not only of the ones that are reflected on its mirrored exterior walls. I think of Goya's *El Aquelarre*, which constitutes an obsessive presence in several of the texts that we analyze in this book. Doesn't this painting confront us, and doesn't it confront the literary characters who contemplate it (or who observe a similar vision) with archaic fantasies of the kind mentioned earlier? It is like a dream—a nightmare—populated by the most infantile fantasies of abandonment or destruction at the hands of those who gave us life. For the male spectator either in the museum or in the book where the vision is produced, the he-goat can hold appeal as a model (a negative one, to be sure) able to counterbalance maternal power. Or, to the contrary, the *macho cabrío* can be transformed into a fitting representation of the terrible father. The vision of *El Aquelarre* thus takes us into a mirrored room of sorts; not only do we see, but we are also seen—reflected—in this space, which contemplates us, which uncannily returns to us our own conscious and unconscious fantasies. In the process, we, like the artist (according to Anton Ehrenzweig), experience a kind of disintegration or psychosis, followed by an integration that art makes possible.

In *Spring Sonata* the Marquis of Bradomín exemplifies the attitude of identification with the artist. The world for him is reduced to a museum, a gallery of images that threaten him, but that may be kept at bay through the power of an aggressive and distancing look. The young marquis acts in this fashion like a Renaissance nobleman or painter and also effectuates a change in the surroundings onto which he projects himself. He fends off the danger of absorption or annihilation posed by the maternal palace of Liguria (another mirrored room) by transforming it into a surface that must only reflect the apparitions of his grandiose self (Kohut's term)—Narcissus, even more than Moses, saved from the devouring waters.

Michael Fried differentiates two modes of painting, which he calls "absorption" and "theatricality." In the former, the figures in the painting are drawn inward, absorbed in a world beyond the reach of any intrusion from the outside. In the theatrical mode, however, a relationship is established among these figures that invites the beholder to insert himself or herself in the group. Although Fried is referring to French painting of the Enlightenment, his concepts may be extended to other periods. In *Spring Sonata* the figures that are the principal object of Bradomín's contemplation—Princess Gaetani's five daughters—may be linked to pictorial groups such as the one in Botticelli's *Spring* or to those found in Pre-Raphaelite paintings. These groups do not appear to ask the male observer, the aloof marquis, to join in. To the contrary, the five sisters form a unitary, exclusively female world. And although they relate among themselves, they seem absorbed in the community of their actions; in this way, the five sisters merely duplicate the figure of a solitary woman, inaccessible and remote. Bradomín in turn counteracts the dangerous attraction to that world with his distancing look. The remoteness of the observed figures thereby answers largely to Bradomín's efforts to separate himself from those women. It is the marquis as narrator who configures the female universe to his liking: simultaneously attractive and distant.

The maximum distancing effect is of course attained with the death of the female character. Elisabeth Bronfen refers to this event: "if the alterity is perceived as potentially dangerous to the self it is successfully eliminated by virtue of death" (191). The death of the other—that threatening other who cannot be assimilated into one's own world—spares the subject from dreaded extinction or self-disintegration. This motif appears in *The House of Ulloa, Spring Sonata,* and *Time of Silence*, represented in the deaths of Nucha, María Nieves, Florita, and Dorita—far too many deaths to be coincidence alone. Literary works as diverse as these therefore achieve unity by means of a trajectory that leads to an analogous outcome: the death of the disturbing object (or an object in close proximity).

In the works of Pedro Salinas and Francisco Ayala pictorial referents tend to point in another direction. I am particularly interested in the presence of the museum in stories by these two authors. In both "Delirium of Poplar and Cypress" and "True Aurora" the couple meets in a museum, be it the Prado or an unnamed art gallery. But here paintings no longer function as in Valle-Inclán's *Sonata*, as simple Echoes to a Narcissus, that is, reflections of the grandiose self. In Salinas, the act of contemplation sets in motion an intimate dialogue between the spectator and the poplar which, in human form, coincides with a portrait by El Greco. In this context the museum is an image of the world (the reverse of Valle-Inclán's vision), one that gestures or "makes signs" (*hace señas*). In "Delirium," the absorption of the character portrayed does not alienate his beholders. In "True Aurora" the museum may be taken as a whole to represent, through paintings from different periods, a continuous progression comparable to the one love accomplishes. Or, in other words, the museum functions as a maternal medium—what Winnicott calls a "holding" or "facilitating environment"—that makes possible the harmonious development of a subject.

Here I am obviously recalling another idea of Winnicott's: the location of cultural experience in a "potential space." That is, art (and the museum as the meeting place with art) transports us to that borderland between me as motherly extension and the not-me. I remember my frequent visits to the Prado Museum during my years as a student in Madrid. The images of those paintings remain engraved in my memory; they populate it like internal objects, which are added to the ones resulting from infantile experiences or visions. They therefore function as good objects that support my sense of trust in an environment modeled after the maternal one.

Ayala, exiled from his country for many long years, also remembers paintings in the Prado: Rubens, Goya, and Alonso Cano meet in his imagination. They animate the fictions—the exile—of a modern writer, who via these representations may connect with a lost past (or paradise), with the "happy days." Of course, the made-up story is not always a happy one. Observing his companion's face, the narrator of "Magic, I" does not find the desired response. Under another woman's guise, the absorbed (and absorbing) mother—not the one who supports one's sense of self—intrudes on this scene catastrophically. Other narrations by Ayala restore the lost equilibrium. It is significant that in several of them the sustaining presence of a woman is related to a visit to an artistic site, be it the Hospital de la Caridad in Seville or the Sistine Chapel. The figure of a mother-painter and the existence of an art collection in the writer's childhood home doubtless contribute to accentuate the maternal nature of those artistic surroundings. Yet, I hasten to add, these biographic data are nevertheless quite expendable if we wish to affirm a general connection between an art space and the figure of a trustworthy mother. For me a museum, such as the Albright-Knox Art Gallery, whether I visit it alone or in agreeable female company, is always an eminently pleasurable place. There, in silent contemplation, I recover my true self; there, exempt from alien pressures, I am happy.

RGF: I'm afraid I will be seen as disagreeable feminist company if I fail to join you in celebrating the pleasurable, calming effects that the good enough maternal museum is said to offer. Or if I resist the conflation or interchangeability of "woman" and "mother." Why is it that Winnicott envisions the male subject in such a way that, when the mother "reflects her own moods," she ceases to be good enough and cannot provide mirroring (that is, allow the child to "find himself")? While it makes sense to me that a fundamental recognition of the child on the part of primary adult caregivers (or "mother") is absolutely crucial to the formation of the child's identity, why does it have to be posited at the expense of the mother's subjectivity? As Claire Kahane remarks, Winnicott's formulations are problematic "in their exclusion of the cultural context of meaning in which the mother and infant move, a symbolic network structured along the axis of the masculine subject which holds them both" (287). And yet, the museum stands precisely as a monument of and to culture, in all senses. It is, among other things, a gallery of symbols, often structured along the axis of the masculine. (I think of Mañara's staging of the artistic experience in the Hospital de la Caridad.)

At this point, Lacan's mirror from the *stade du miroir*, which we have called on to explicate key aspects of the formation of an identity with respect to text and art, might best be contrasted with that other famous Lacanian looking glass: the sardine can from "Of the Gaze as *Objet Petit a*." "You see that can? Do you see it?" fisherman Petit-Jean goads the young intellectual Jacques, "well, it doesn't see you!" (*Four Fundamental Concepts* 95). Lacan expends great effort to postulate a theory around this shame-inducing event, a theory that both claims that the tin (mirror) does in fact "see" the beholder by grasping or seeking him or her, and also refutes that the beholder can "be" in the picture except as "screen," "stain," or "spot." In a context beyond Lacanian fragmentation, the human desire to see ourselves in the picture may be paralleled to the viewing-mirroring process as it relates to identity and a concept of self, something that is evident in what you say in the first part of this epi(dia)logue. Let's shift focus for a minute and consider the female spectator as she looks at paintings. Maybe she wonders about female subjectivity in works such as Picasso's *La Toilette* in the Albright-Knox, which shows an unclothed woman contemplating herself in a mirror held up to her by a female other. The contrast between the two women—naked vs. clothed, warm pink flesh tones vs. cool blues, served vs. server—signals the kinds of differences that are not easily attributed to sex or gender alone. For me, this particular painting exemplifies the staging of the drama of female subjectivity, a key concern that we both have foregrounded in our interartistic commentaries.

I am struck, in rereading our analyses, that the inquiry into female subjectivity has in many instances uncovered identical psychic scenarios produced through a multiplicity of visual representations. While I certainly do not believe in some kind of timeless constancy to symbols or to myths, it nevertheless seems plausible, following Freud, to adduce a psychoanalytic repertoire, with its well-known scenes, tensions, conflicts, and their corresponding expressions in sign and symptom. It therefore makes sense to me, for example, that the image of the spiderwoman, with its phallic connotations, should emerge from within two very different contexts: the fin de siècle culture in which Emilia Pardo Bazán writes, with its exaggerated fear of the *femme fatale*, and the twentieth-century odyssey of exile and identity, protagonized textually by José Donoso's character-author-persona, Chilean Julio Méndez. Our interpretations of these two verbal and visual scenes elucidate the differences between them. In the first instance, the male protagonist, Julián, raised in a repressive and misogynist culture, struggles with an ambivalence linked to degradation and idealization of women; in the second instance, the male protagonist, Julio, struggles for authorship and authority in an international setting where women are increasingly "on top" with their power, pleasure, and bids for dominance. Or at least that is how Julio sees it. Gloria, particularly during her time of mute depression, expresses her own anxieties around identity and mastery of self and surrounding.

One particular issue that has intrigued us both is the nature of these authors' dialogues with the visual arts. How do writers appeal to painting or sculpture, and what interpretations do they encode in their texts? Do the textual and artistic visions overlap, and in what ways? Often we have remarked on the deep affinities or the analogous visions that the writers and visual artists share. We have called this process "interartisticality" when it refers more narrowly to the kind of sign and citation traffic that bustles about between text and art. More broadly, however, we must admit to forging (in a double sense) a relationship where none is apparently plotted out, and this, I think, is the kind of look that theory facilitates. In fact, I want to argue that in Vargas Llosa's novel, this relationship between text, art, and theory culminates in a veritable collapse of all categories (a postmodern strategy for sure). What happens when text makes art theory? That is, when the text produces theories of art, and when the text turns art into little more—nothing less—than theory?

In Vargas Llosa's case, the "art theory" that the text produces aligns itself nicely, and ironically, with feminist revisions of the great traditions of Western painting, such as views on the female nude expounded by Lynda Nead. But Vargas Llosa's art theory also looks quite similar to what Linda Hutcheon discerns with respect to postmodern parody, which can "use and abuse the conventions of both popular and élite" culture to challenge the commodification process of the invasive culture industry from within (*Poetics* 20). If the paintings recirculated as narration in *In Praise of the Stepmother* open up a space to interrogate female desire and subjectivity, they do so while debasing in parodic fashion the high artistic culture that originally produced them and set out their interpretive parameters. Vargas Llosa's novel theorizes these paintings as expressions of the pornographic or obscene. The look in this text may therefore be considered productive or perverse in the sense that Kaja Silverman gives to these terms when she claims that, since the Lacanian gaze marks things as given to be seen, the "productive look" must swerve away from what is most valorized, and instead attach itself to that which is marginal ("Productive Look").

Vargas Llosa's novel thus offers perverse readings of these well-known paintings and, in so doing, presents a way of "looking awry" at art. In popular culture this "perverse looking" is a long-standing tradition that takes many guises, like the parodic and salacious alteration of paintings such as Titian's *Venus with an Organist* that the Bécquer brothers performed in nineteenth-century Spain in their *Los Borbones en pelota* [The Bourbons in the buff]. A more contemporary example is the hilarious spoof from *Saturday Night Live* in the late 1970s in which characters E. Buzz Miller (Dan Aykroyd) and strip artist Christie Christea (Laraine Newman) host a public access cable television show called "Art Classics." Buzz displays a series of female nudes, beginning with Titian's *Venus of Urbino*: "This is a really nice painting of a broad on a couch," he says, noting that "it was painted in 1538 by a guy in Venice, and this is for real, his name is . . . TIT-ian, honest to God." Christie breaks into a high-pitched giggle. I have thought of this sketch many times as I read Vargas Llosa's mock-modernist text (which he himself calls "precious, affected"). There is a raunchy streak in him that either reinscribes misogyny or else radically loosens it up (or does both things simultaneously) by slashing the moorings that keep high art anchored to seriousness, that prevent the nude from frolicking with the naked, that bind Eve to Mary in strict dichotomy. When we compare Vargas Llosa's disrespectful reading of Titian's paintings to the reverence of, say, Francisco Ayala before *Sacred and Profane Love*, we can be sure that, if nothing else, *theory* indeed is in the making, and that the works of art, the paintings on the page, have been assimilated into the textual sign system as an integral part of this process. As the Lucrecia character mentally says to Rigoberto when she fantasizes herself to be represented in the Szyszlo painting, "you would like to dissolve me in a theory" (*In Praise* 119). The paintings in the text might very well be speaking the same line to the receptors, including the creator, Vargas Llosa.

In a sense, *In Praise of the Stepmother* serves up postmodern commentary on the kinds of literary and artistic traditions that were the focus of the previous chapters. But the theory making found in this chapter may also be perceived throughout our entire critical endeavor. As anthropologist Jacques Maquet remarks on the polysemy of the visual sign: "When [by means of conceptualism] a painting visually represents what is thought rather than what is seen, it certainly suggests different meanings to different beholders; it also suggests different meanings to the same beholder in other circumstances" (221). So while there are some constants and overlapping interpretations in this book, there are also multiple readings of the same visual representations or textual engagements, depending on which of us is speaking or looking, and in what context.

I'd like to say a few words here about words: Cabrera Infante's, to be precise. Although many of our commentaries have explored psychoanalytic questions related to desire, sexuality, fantasies, terrors, and all the other "vocabulary of psychoanalysis," the last chapter restricts itself to Cabrera's and Duchamp's verbal and visual play, which certainly contains a great deal of erotic humor and tensions. This particular analysis did not open up the space for a psychoanalytic exploration of fantasy and desire in quite the same terms that inform the rest of our book. But those familiar with Duchamp's artistic production have already put their eyes to the peepholes of the *Etant donnés*, and those who have read Cabrera Infante's *La Habana para un infante difunto* have already traveled, along with the narrator, through the swallowing vagina that draws him back to the womb in the final pages of the novel. In Duchamp's installation, which he worked on in secret during the last decades of his life, viewers peep through two holes in a wooden door at a splayed, nude female figure made of "leather stretched over an armature of metal and other materials," as the Philadelphia Museum of Art's description of the work reads. Amelia Jones's recent commentary on *Etant donnés* shows how Duchamp engages in a highly complex discourse on desire, masculinity, phallic assertion and erasure, sexual difference, and so forth, themes, of course, that we have looked at repeatedly with respect to the six male and one female authors whom we studied in chapters 2 through 8. Duchamp's private pornography made public reminds me that eroticism might manifest as puns and witty word play ("Words are plastic and may be moulded into almost any shape," Freud declares in *Wit and Its Relation to the Unconscious*, 649), or it might appear as a staged scene of voyeurism replete with notes of violation, mutilation, and death. Full circle back to Pardo Bazán and Valle-Inclán, by means of that postmodern Vargas Llosa, who knows that "fantasy [corrodes] life," and adds, "Thank God" (104).

Full circle back to the *Mirrored Room*, too. Samaras explains that the idea for a completely mirror-covered cube room occurred to him around 1963 when he incorporated the idea into a short story. It turns out, then, that his creation has an interartistic origin. It began as a (fictitious) artwork on the page of a literary text. He put a table and a chair in the *Mirrored Room* "for someone to sit down and imagine or think or discover" (in Moore 235). Of course, you can't really sit on that chair, but we assuredly can take him up on his invitation to think and discover. After all, Samaras has called his creation a "theoretical room" (235), which provides me with just the right setting to take a good look at your reflections and mine. And it is here, among all the contradictions and tensions of a theoretical room, that I am quite content.

CF:  I am aware of the feminist critiques addressed to Winnicott, critiques that basically amount to a defense of the rights or needs of the mother or, in your own words, of her subjectivity. Yet subjectivity is formed through interpersonal relations. The bad (or not so good enough) mother, in Winnicott's terms, would be the one who retreats (not just temporarily but chronically) into a private, narcissistic universe, thus hampering both the creation of the child's identity and the development of her own subjectivity. She would also be the possessive mother who understands the child as an extension of herself, no matter how intensely she may care for the physical needs of that child. The good enough mother, then, together with good mirroring or with infusing a sense of trust, promotes separation. And this implies that she must affirm her own subjectivity and attend to her own interests, something she does by provoking what Winnicott has called "optimal frustration."

If we turn to the artists that we have studied in this book, we are entitled to say that in many instances we witness a dramatization of the lack of good mirroring or good parent-infant relationships (not necessarily as psychobiographic event, of course). Take, for example, Francis Bacon. After referring to him as that "challenging artist of our time who goes on and on painting the human face distorted significantly," Winnicott makes the following comment: "in looking at faces he [Bacon] seems to me to be painfully striving towards being seen" (114). Vargas Llosa, in "Semblance of a Human," would arrive at the same conclusion when he has the character identified with one of Bacon's heads, Rigoberto, exclaim: "Take a good look at me, my love. Recognize me, and recognize yourself" (*In Praise* 93). Other visions found in paintings, such as Goya's *El Aquelarre*, also reveal a universe in which any worthy communication among humans has failed: children sacrificed by their mothers, who in turn become the victims of a terrible domineering male. Psychoanalytic interpretation, as exemplified by Winnicott, traces these obsessive images to childhood. Adult experiences must nevertheless confirm these atrocious representations in some way. As Jay Greenberg writes, "any memories of failed mirroring are themselves re-representations that must be understood on the basis of subsequent dynamic developments" (202). We might add that these developments can be both of a personal and of a collective nature. Thus, in Goya as well as in Martín-Santos, the figure of the "bad mother" is buttressed by the vision of Spain, the motherland, as a cruel stepmother. Or we could say that the image of the domineering male corresponds more to a social phenomenon (Hispanic *machismo*, if not simply universal *machismo*) than to a specific father. In like fashion, the cultural and religious context in *The House of Ulloa* informs Julián's particular vision. For the priest, women appear exclusively in one of two guises, the virgin or the witch-prostitute, but this spectacle is occasionally counterbalanced by the female narrative voice or viewpoint. Similarly, in Donoso's *The Garden Next Door*, Gloria refutes Julio's fantasy of Núria as a spider-woman.

When these visions emerging from infantile and/or cultural experiences are transferred to the realm of art, however, they undergo a fundamental change. Not only do they appear to the artist (as an obsession, a demon, an inspiration, an idea), but the artist in turn uses them in an exercise of his or her own creative power. And I am inclined to think, along with Winnicott once again, that creativity has its origins in childhood play: "Cultural experience begins with creative living first manifested in play"

(100). A similar notion was expressed by Huizinga, whom you cite in regard to Dada and Cabrera Infante, and also by Ortega y Gasset in *La deshumanización del arte* [The dehumanization of art] (1925), although Ortega restricts his observations to what he calls new (avant-garde) art. To consider the cultural world as masculine territory (that is, to ignore its roots in the "potential space" between child and mother) seems to me to be a very partial understanding of culture. I want to mention an anecdotal detail here. In my native city of La Coruña, situated in a prominent place in the main park, there is a statue of the only female author we have studied in this book, Emilia Pardo Bazán, also born in that city. Seated majestically, Doña Emilia flourishes a pen in her right hand, a symbol of the cultural power she succeeded in conquering. Children play all around her statue. To put Winnicott's theory into practice, we may note the subtle transition from the universe of play to the realm of art, represented here by a woman. And what about the other "great mother" of my native land, the highly acclaimed poet Rosalía de Castro, whose museum-house in Padrón (province of La Coruña) is visited by more men and women than all the other museums in the Galician region put together? Is this a world structured along the axis of the masculine subject?

True, artistic creations have often been viewed as the transformation of matter (supposedly feminine) into form or spirit (supposedly masculine). In this sense, men may resort to the "works of the spirit" in self-interested fashion to confirm their always precarious masculine identity once they dispose of the abject maternal body (Kristeva, *Powers of Horror*). But unless I am very mistaken, our analyses give a coincident critique of traditional values. If Vargas Llosa, as you say, can be aligned with feminist revisions of the great Western artistic traditions or with postmodern parodies, I think something comparable may be said about the Spanish authors studied here. Thus in *Time of Silence* the association made between the he-goat and the cultured lecturer, "with eighty years of European idealism behind him" (134), effectively deconstructs the difference between "high" (masculine-encoded) and "low" culture. The novel situates Ortega in his condition as subject of desire, one more he-goat, whose brilliant ideas may be related to the fetishes or false idols of those who remain on the margin of Western civilization, the supposed embodiment of truth and reason. Similar remarks could be made with respect to Pedro, the young researcher who aspires to the world represented by Ortega and who unwittingly falls ever deeper into the domains where the he-goat rules. In other instances, culture is manifested through Julián (the priest) or Bradomín (the nobleman), victims nonetheless of their uncontainable desire, which at the end of *The House of Ulloa* propels Julián, a "man used to repress[ing] every outburst of passion," toward kissing "the grave [of Nucha] ardently, crying like a child or a woman" (259), or which ultimately forces Bradomín to incarnate the character of an evil "murderer," always engaged in a struggle with the irresistible power (and attraction) of the maternal *imago*.

In Salinas, there is also a challenge to masculine values such as the emphasis on rationality or artistic idealization (de-eroticizing) of the feminine body. In "Rendezvous for Three," the narrator immerses himself in a "naked" (pre-symbolic) time, a time behaving like a body that "loosens corset and suspenders, garters and clasps, . . . and reveals itself free and easy, rosy, leaving no doubt of its complete surrender" (*Prelude* 34). In addition to evoking the idealist tradition of Renaissance painting (Titian's *Bacchanal*), this image subverts all notions of high culture through the spectacle of the time/woman undressing in the context of "a Bacchic festival." This nude/naked, then, is and is not similar to the distant, sleeping Ariadne immortalized by Titian in his famous painting in the Prado. Thus, by escaping the symbolic order, Salinas reaches *jouissance,* a surplus of enjoyment that becomes "the unconfessable crime . . . pursued by the law of the father" (Benvenuto and Kennedy 191) and which, according to Lacan, man (but not woman) has had to renounce.

Finally, Ayala, though he remains basically faithful to the principles of high culture—at least in the stories from his *Garden of Earthly Delights* analyzed in our book (there are more "earthy" ones in the other section, "Diablo mundo")—never quite adopts a reverential attitude toward painters like Titian, in opposition to the "disrespectful" pose of Vargas Llosa. In "Sacred and Profane Love" we may note how difficult it is to achieve the ideal of "tense equilibrium" or "miraculous suspension" between the spirit and the senses. The sensual order is not so easily ruled, and the image of the "splendid woman" in the magazine who holds up her glass in a toast, inviting the narrator to join her, plunges the couple in an imaginary orgy (reminiscent of the orgiastic images in several of the etchings from Picasso's Vollard Suite). As in Picasso, or earlier, in Salinas, the cloister of art opens up here to Bacchic impulses, destroyer of all norms, of all Renaissance-Platonic idealism. Titian's sublime painting, a background for the narration of a mature man at the end of a series of loves, is framed (and deconstructed) between two paragraphs in which the "splendid woman" of the advertisement is evoked, with the added feature of a cup in her hand. Another "sota de copas" "maid of cups," like the one in *The House of Ulloa*, who attracts the narrator into her world of commercial art, "low culture," and carnal senses, thereby forcing him—helping him—to forget for a while the Uranian Venus, the great myths and works of Western art.

RGF: Your comments about the "tense equilibrium" or "miraculous suspension" in relation to the object of the gaze and to the gendered (and engendering) look permit me to recast what I said earlier about the productive look. It is problematic to claim that there is a perverse or productive look operating along a line (or misalignment) of vision in texts by Vargas Llosa, or by Ayala in the example you give, unless we also consider that the pornographic readings of high cultural art objects are perfectly in line with what is given to be seen. As you insinuate, artists like Picasso or Titian, and writers like the ones we study, are never far from a complete Bacchic breakout, understood as the eruption of that which (elite) culture rejects or represses: the exaltation of the naked, the insistence on excess. Pleasure and terror to the extreme—it would be perverse *not* to notice. Looking through the peepholes at the *Etant donnés* is not productive in this sense either. It is "given," as the French title suggests, and we therefore entrench ourselves in a culturally coded space of voyeurism that Duchamp meticulously mapped out. "But nothing," says Rosiland Krauss, "breaks the circuit of the gaze's connection to its object or interrupts the satisfaction of its desire. Having sought the peephole of *Etant donnés*, Duchamp's viewer has in fact entered a kind of optical machine through which it is impossible *not* to see" (*Optical Unconscious* 112). The perverse look must direct itself elsewhere.

These final reflections have allowed me to focus on an aspect of visual studies that I have known instinctively but that I have never quite articulated. Museums simultaneously attract me and repel me like no other environment. Our discussion of the *Mirrored Room* with its inherent properties of facilitating environment or fun house or theoretical space still strikes me as authentic; nevertheless, I must conclude that it is the terror rather than the repose of Samaras's other work, the *Mirrored Cell*, that predominates for me. Perhaps my ambivalence grows out of the very tension that we have been weaving throughout this epi(dia)logue, which may be crystalized in a passive-voiced question: what is seen? At each stage of our critical journey we have asked, am *I* on view, and in what way? Further, we have wondered, how does the *I*-eye construct what it sees, what is given to be seen? And we have asked what it means to see interdiscursively, to read, to view, and to perform analytical operations with our verbal sutures on the written or painted scenes.

What is seen when I stand in the museum setting, surrounded not only by an empathic accompanist (I think here of the *órgano cómplice* of Titian's painting as read by Vargas Llosa), but also by strangers—tourists, guards, art historians, school children? A scene. I become part of this scene/seen of others, and I confess to often feeling very much not-at-home, *unheimlich*. So this Winnicottian scenario, which you and I have been debating, of good mirroring emanating from the art objects, seems at times inaccessible to me in the museum space. I simply cannot immerse myself for long enough in those paintings as they are displayed in public settings; call it self-consciousness or distraction, or even resistance. Maybe I do not want to be inscribed in that scene in that way. You see, the *Mirrored Room* offers a refuge within the museum from the rest of the museum.

So do books. Here is the strange part: I am often more at ease with a reproduction of an artwork than I am with the real thing. I can examine the representation *as* representation, and I can read it as text, much as I do with the literature that forms the basis of our study. Further, by turning to books that reproduce images, you can line up an artist's entire production for a personal "viewing," if you like, or you could compare one set of works with another grouping from other places and times that you select and arrange. This process of constructing a context and staging an ordered show is of course one that a scholar of the visual arts undertakes in the analysis of any given image, as does a textual analyst in her choice of quotations, references, and so forth. And so I confess to being a devotee of the painting on the page, and to enjoying, in the solitary confinement of my study, an interartistic monodialogue with the works that I may or may not have seen (and been seen with). Would it be so farfetched to suggest that Rigoberto's use of Kenneth Clark's *The Nude* in *In Praise of the Stepmother* should be reconsidered as a possible model for visual analysis? Sometimes for me the textual experience actually surpasses the live viewing, I must add. When I visited the Magritte show at the Metropolitan Museum of Art in New York in 1992 and saw paintings that had been the focus of my personal and professional interest, I was struck by the awkwardness of the technique, the almost crude rendering of the (mutilated) female body, and the loss of the uncanniness that makes Magritte so compelling.

I now wish to return to José Donoso's *The Garden Next Door*, which takes up many of the issues that you and I have tried to work out here. How can I not think autobiographically when I read those fictitious and real-life triumphs and struggles between a husband-and-wife team of writers? At many points during the writing process you and I have made imaginary footnotes to the other's analysis when we have taken issue with what each of us wanted to say. Most of these disputes are resolved, or glossed over, because we have come to see—and be seen—in terms that are either compatible or acceptable. Donoso says, in reference to his novel: "I didn't know whether I was telling my story or I was telling hers. There was a confusion of identity at that point and I think it is this confusion, this interchangeability of identities, which I have lived through so many times with her" ("Conversation with Montenegro and Santí" 9–10). Frankly, there are moments in this study when we might say the same thing, but there are other times when, like Donoso, we must alert the other if he or she "salted the tomato too much" (*Garden* 100). In this epi(dia)logue we opened up a discursive mode that would not have worked for the entire project: it could only happen as frame or postscript. We need solitude with the texts and artworks that we bring together, and I imagine that we each create our own mental museums and libraries to explore independently first. For me, it has been, and has to be, that way.

Fernando de Szyszlo says that art is terrible: "It's supportable only because the terror is not total" ("Conversation" 25). The same could naturally be said of literature and of the endeavor to place text and art in dialogue. But another formulation is equally valid: art is pleasurable, and it is only bearable because the pleasure is not total. As Gilbert Rose remarks, art "provides a normative mode or opportunity for stimulating and assimilating potentially dangerous degrees of affect—in short, extending the limits of the bearable. . . . At its greatest, it extends the limits of the imaginable" (227–28). One final image, then, to mirror your memory of the statue of Emilia Pardo Bazán in your native Galicia. I am thinking of an outdoor sculpture by another Galician artist, who goes by the name of Buciños, entitled *Homenaje al libro* [Homage to the book]. Buciños often uses Celtic mythology in his semi-abstract metal sculptures, but this particular work shows a rather realistic "sacred family" threesome (terror) gathered around a book, in the act of reading (pleasure). This sculpture, then, literally infuses a representation of text into an artistic production and celebrates, albeit with more sucrose than I might like, the intermingling of book (and the reading process), art (and the act of viewing), and human relatedness. *Homage to the Book* is not in La Coruña, however. It stands on Recoletos, the elegant avenue a short distance from the Prado Museum, in front of the Biblioteca Nacional. You and I found it once, after we exited from the museum and looked for it among the trees, asking what may be seen there. I'll tell you now. I saw that art is all too brief and that life, from a vantage point where the pleasure and the terror are not total, is long indeed.

# NOTES

## 1. REFLECTIONS ON THE *MIRRORED ROOM*: FROM WORK TO WORD

1. Fernandez does make a valid point here, however: he contrasts two "lessons" to be learned from the mirror, the first consisting of "self-objectification," and the second, "object-subjectification." The reciprocal function of the mirror resides in its ability to allow one to be "a subject seeing itself in the object, the object living itself in the subject" (36).

2. An earlier study by Heinrich Schwartz surveys the use of the mirror in painting with emphasis on premodern periods but does not go into the wide symbolic detail found in Schneider's work. See also Wolfgang Zucker's "Reflections on Reflections," which examines the philosophical implications of the use of the mirror by such painters as Jan van Eyck, Petrus Christus, and Velázquez, and relates these findings to the literary works of Cocteau and to Sir David Brewster's invention of the "Teleidoscope."

3. Michael Fried's *Absorption and Theatricality* looks deeply at these concepts. For a fine discussion and application of Fried's concepts, see Bal's *Reading "Rembrandt"* 45–53; Bal also takes up the problem of mirrors and self-representation in chapter 7 of her book. Another fine analysis of the mirror and its relation to interpretation is found in David Carrier's "Art and Its Spectators."

4. Or, as W. J. T. Mitchell says, "we have this compulsion to conceive of the relation between words and images in political terms, as a struggle for territory, a contest of rival ideologies." He suggests that, in part, this competition stems from our conception of the image as "the sign that pretends not to be a sign, masquerading as (or, for the believer, actually achieving) natural immediacy and presence. The word is its 'other,' the artificial, arbitrary production of human will that disrupts natural presence by introducing unnatural elements into the world" (*Iconology* 43).

5. Ronald Foust connects Frank with structuralism to the extent that both point to a collective psychic dimension beyond the individual: "both Frank and the Structuralists emphasize the partially unconscious function of the creative ego and its subordination to a collective mind—

that is, its function as a mediation between an individual personality and a broader social category" (200).

6. Michael Ann Holly summarizes Panofsky's thinking on this point: "we must become familiar not only with the work of art in both its stylistic form and its storied content but also with all of the possible ineffable and ultimately unverifiable forces (psychological, societal, cultural, political, spiritual, philosophical, and so forth) that have jointly shaped its singular existence" (160). It is within the context of this true interdisciplinarity that we wish to situate out own analyses.

7. Tickner expresses her indebtedness to the earlier work of Thalia Gouma-Peterson and Patricia Mathews, whose "The Feminist Critique of Art History" traces the emergence and evolution of feminism and art history in terms of art production, reception, criticism, and theory. This article not only provides a summary of the trends in the field, but also includes an indispensable wealth of bibliographic material.

8. Foster briefly discusses these concepts in his preface to *Vision and Visuality* (ix–xiv). Bryson defines them more extensively in his "The Gaze in the Expanded Field," included in Foster's collection: "Between the subject and the world is inserted the entire sum of discourses which make up visuality, that cultural construct, and make visuality different from vision, the notion of unmediated visual experience. Between retina and world is inserted a *screen* of signs, a screen consisting of all the multiple discourses on vision built into the social arena" (91–92). Bryson would most likely consent to our adding the discourse of the unconscious to the sign system interposed between the world and the eye—or the I, the *ego*.

9. Bryson's and Mitchell's critiques of the theories of Ernst Gombrich are the departure point for reformulating the notion of vision and visuality. See "The Essential Copy," chapter 2 of Bryson's *Vision and Painting: The Logic of the Gaze*, and "Nature and Convention: Gombrich's Illusions," chapter 3 of Mitchell's *Iconology: Image, Text, Ideology*. Murray Krieger has also critiqued Gombrich, but not for his *Art and Illusion*: "in his later work it [the natural-sign myth] has been reemerging explicitly—and embarrassingly for those of us who thought of ourselves as following him" (257). Gombrich rejects the charge that there is discontinuity in his ideas; he therefore denies having subverted "the old idea of mimesis" and does not believe "that all that remained were different systems of conventional signs which were made to stand for an unknowable reality" (in Krieger 257).

10. Peter Brooks remarks: "A transferential model . . . allows us to take as the object of analysis, not author or reader, but reading, including of course the transferential-interpretive operations that belong to reading" ("Idea" 13–14). For Brooks, good criticism "involves a willingness, a desire, to enter into the delusional system of texts, to espouse their hal-

lucinated vision, in an attempt to master and be mastered by their power of conviction" (16).

11. Jeffrey Berman takes a different route to the same conclusion: "literary critics need to recognize countertransference problems awakened by fictional characters" (254). Using the concept of countertransference, Berman places the critic in the traditional role of analyst; he clearly recognizes, however, that the dialogic model is a viable one.

12. For Lis Møller these two types of analytic truth—narrative (construction) and historical (reconstruction)—were already differentiated by Freud, whom one must not, therefore, consider a simple archaeologist of the mind (as Spence does): "In rereading Freud in light of *Narrative Truth and Historical Truth*, one discovers . . . rather the fundamental heterogeneity of Freud's arguments" (5).

## 2. THE TEMPTATION OF SAINT JULIAN IN EMILIA PARDO BAZÁN'S *THE HOUSE OF ULLOA*: BOSCH, GOYA, AND SPAIN'S FIN DE SIÈCLE

1. For example, the paintings by Bosch in the Museu Nacional de Arte Antiga, Lisbon; the Walter P. Chrysler Collection, New York; Rijksmuseum, Amsterdam; and the Museo del Prado, Madrid. Flaubert's influential *La Tentation de saint Antoine* (1874) caused the theme to flourish anew at the end of the nineteenth century: Dijkstra (254–56) reproduces a series of paintings by artists such as Ferdinand Götz, Louis Corinth, John Charles Dollman, and Paul Cézanne in which Saint Anthony tries to escape from the women who pursue him. Flaubert in turn was influenced by a painting by Brueghel, which he describes as follows: "Saint Anthony among three women, turning his head away in order to avoid their caresses" (14).

2. "Of these [the animal appearances of the Devil] the most frequent were serpent (dragon), goat, and dog" (J. B. Russell 67). "The witches of Zugarramurdi took the form of goats and other animals during the witches' sabbath" (Mariño Ferro 131).

3. Several recent articles establish this basic point: "a sensitivity to the role of gender as a factor shaping fiction allows the reader to discern a certain tension between a dominant patriarchal or paternal discourse and an often submerged matrilineal or maternal subtext" (Ordóñez 122). "In adopting the realist-naturalist mode, she [Pardo Bazán] also positions herself within a male genre tradition without entirely disengaging her fiction from the influences of either male-voiced *costumbrismo* or the female-voiced sentimental novel" (Bieder 131). Along these lines see also Carlos Feal's "La voz femenina."

4. The relationship between *The Witches' Sabbath* and the passage quoted from the novel has been pointed out by Edward Stanton when he says that "the whole scene displays a spiritual kinship with *The Witches' Sabbath*" (282). Stanton, however, does not delve into the possible significance of this parallel and restricts his comments to the following: "Whatever the intentions of the author were, the mute allusion to Goya marvelously enriches and deepens the scene in the novel" (283).

5. In her article entitled "Goya," Pardo Bazán presents a vision of the Spanish painter that lends itself well to the atmosphere of *The House of Ulloa*: "La *Maja*, más inquietante aún bajo la ropa, entre la nube de la mantilla blonda, es la que vemos en *Los caprichos*, con todo su carácter de bruja moza, acompañada de la bruja vieja, halduda y barbuda" "The *Maja*, even more disquieting beneath her clothes, covered in a cloud of blond mantilla lace, is the one we see in the *Caprichos*, in her total girl witch nature, accompanied by the old witch, skirted and bearded" (1288). To express herself in these terms, however, Pardo Bazán must adopt the viewpoint of a man, the object of the seduction presented as bewitchment: "una bruja joven, que fascina y hace sortilegios; una tentación de asceta" "a young witch, who enchants and casts spells; a temptation to ascetics" (1288). In *The House of Ulloa*, Julián functions as that "ascetic" (or as a new Saint Anthony).

6. Teresa Lorenzo de Márquez, commenting on other works by Goya such as *Caprichos 44* ("Hilan delgado" "They spin finely") and 73 ("Mejor es holgar" "It is better to be lazy"), says the following: "A subgroup within this topic of Lust is based on the double meaning of *hilar* (to spin) as *futuere* (to copulate), frequent in [Spanish] Golden Age erotic poetry and familiar to Carnival language" (lxxxvi). And she also remarks with respect to Goya's works: "The obvious idea of Gluttony insinuates the metaphorical one of Lust" (lxxxvi).

7. Steiner writes: "I think that one of the 'claims' of a Boschian or Brueghelesque vision painting is that 'this painting is what the figure in it imagines, and not what anyone else would actually see'" (*Colors of Rhetoric* 65).

8. The Spanish card deck contains the following suits: *copas* (goblets), *bastos* (clubs), *oros* (coins), and *espadas* (spades). The high cards are *rey* (king), *reina* (queen), *caballo* (horse), and *sota* (maid). We have modified the English version by employing the literal translations, which are necessary for our interpretation.

9. It is interesting that Lacan in another place mentions "the visionary Hieronymus Bosch" as someone who gave pictorial form to the "fragmented body" (*corps morcelé*), that is, to the experience, usually manifested in dreams, of "a certain level of aggressive disintegration in the individual" ("Mirror Stage" 4).

10. Lacan says: "A gaze surprises him in the function of voyeur, disturbs him, overwhelms him and reduces him to a feeling of shame" (*Four Fundamental Concepts* 84). By identifying with Julián, the reader of the novel would also function as a voyeur who engages in spying rooted in infantile experiences. André Green points to this specular relation between the reader and the text: "He [the reader] has switched, in his voyeurism, from an active position to a passive one. One may blush at the reading of a text as if someone were looking at you, guessing at your feelings" ("Unbinding Process" 344).

11. Ralph B. Little remarks that "in the unconscious the spider symbolizes the female" (175). We should keep in mind that the word *spider* derives from the name Arachne (the Latin *aranea*), the woman whom the goddess Athena turned into a spider.

12. The appearance of Saint George in the dream is related to Nucha's cry of fear, heard by Julián, when she sees the spider: "¡San Jorge . . . , para la araña" (187) "Saint George, stop the spider!" (167). According to Montes-Huidobro, "Nucha is desperately calling to Julián to save her from the grip of her husband, who at that moment is the Dragon" (49).

13. Munich says: "In the sense that the Andromeda myth took the fancy not of women but of men artists during the years between 1830 and 1895, it can be thought of as a male myth. . . . The myth counters feminist aspirations by telling the maiden that she needs the hero, she needs marriage" (13, 33). Since in *The House of Ulloa* no man is granted the possibility of liberating the woman (liberating her, that is, from a disastrous marriage), it is suggested that emancipation could only come from the woman herself. Pardo Bazán would thus be introducing an original variation on the treatment of this myth.

14. For an eloquent pictorial example, see the two paintings by Edward Burne-Jones that Munich analyzes (118–21). There is further evidence of the link between Nucha and the spider figure in the description of her hysterical fit: "Sus manos crispadas arrancaban los corchetes de su traje, o comprimían sus sienes, o se clavaban en los almohadones del sofá, *arañándolos* con furor" (197–98, our emphasis) "Her hands twitched, tugged at the hooks of her dress, or pressed her temples, or dug into the cushions of the sofa and scratched them [*arañándolos*] furiously" (176). The Spanish verb *arañar* (to scratch) is obviously related to *araña* (spider). See Carlos Feal's "La voz femenina" (217–18) for a detailed analysis of this passage.

15. Munich states: "The close association between Rossetti, Morris, and Burne-Jones . . . clearly emerges in their similar typological iconography, connecting Andromeda, Virgin Mary, and Eve. . . . The meeting of eyes between Andromeda and Perseus is a charm against the other, the

Medusan meeting, in which passion may be the woman's as well as the man's—or, worse, may be hers alone" (108, 116).

16. Peter Gay's commentary is relevant here: "the general preoccupation with nervousness impinged on the burgeoning mid-nineteenth-century woman's movement. . . . The feminists read nervousness not as a cause but as an effect. The passage of time would prove them right" (335).

17. Ordóñez says: "I suggest that we have here an intertextual motif in women's literature which speaks of the solitude of the female condition once woman has left her paternal home to become a possession of her husband" (130).

18. Cirlot makes the link between both saints: "In hagiography, the patron saints of knights, Saint George and the Archangel Saint Michael, appear in the very act of fighting it [the dragon] in an abundance of prodigious works of art" (175–76).

19. Kronik cites this eloquent testimony offered by the author of *The House of Ulloa*: "The decadent phase of literature interests me most deeply, and in its best documents I always find something that moves my spirit" (175–76).

## 3. ALL THE WORLD'S A MUSEUM: THE MARQUIS OF BRADOMÍN'S TEXTUAL EXHIBITION

1. Concerning the absence of the father in the *Sonatas*, see Carlos Feal, "Realidad psicológica" 45 and "Rivales amorosos" 47–48. Guillermo Díaz-Plaja also notes this absence: "Significantly, there is no allusion to the father, which explains Bradomín's infancy, 'blond like a treasure,' among the women who were present at the family palace" (201).

2. Serge Leclaire, following Lacan, defines the phallus in these terms: "It is a copula, a hyphen . . . *the signifier par excellence of the impossible identity*" (in Lemaire 86).

3. "'Imaginary' is the term used by Lacan to designate that order of the subject's experience which is dominated by identification and duality. Within the Lacanian scheme it not only precedes the symbolic order, which introduces the subject to language and Oedipal triangulation, but continues to coexist with it afterward" (Silverman 157).

4. The Christ-child's smile, as Leo Steinberg observes (*Sexuality of Christ* 21–22), appears in Roger van der Weyden's *Madonna and Child* and Antonio Rossellino's *Virgin with Laughing Child*. Steinberg notes in these works "the motif of the infant Christ, in childlike innocence, earnestly or in play, pulling his dress to expose his sex" (21). Valle-Inclán also reconciles sexuality and innocence: "juego cándido y celeste" "innocent and celestial play."

5. The *Summer Sonata* (1903) provides one instance in which the sexuality of Christ is visibly manifested. Niña Chole wishes to drink from a convent fountain; two lay sisters stop her:

— ... Es agua bendita, y solamente la Comunidad tiene bula para beberla. ...
Y las dos legas, hablando a coro, señalaban al angelote desnudo, que enredador y tronera vertía el agua en el tazón de alabastro por su menuda y cándida virilidad.
Nos dijeron que era el Niño Jesús. (*Sonatas* 197)

" ... it is holy water; only the Community has dispensation to drink it. ..."
And both speaking at once, the lay-sisters pointed out the [naked angel who mischievously spouted] the waters into an alabaster basin [with his small and innocent virility]. They told [us] it was the Infant Jesus. (*Pleasant Memoirs* 99–100)

Fortunately, Bradomín comes to the aid of the woman who passes for his wife: "Yo aseguré a las legas que la Marquesa de Bradomín también tenía bula para beber las aguas del Niño Jesús. Ellas la miraron mostrando gran respeto, y disputáronse ofrecerle sus ánforas, pero yo les aseguré que la Niña Marquesa prefería saciar la sed aplicando los labios al santo surtidor de donde el agua manaba" (197) "I assured the sisters that [the Marquise of Bradomín] also had a dispensation to drink the waters of the Infant Jesus. They showed [her] great deference at this and each one desired to offer [the marquise] her jar, but [I assured them that the marquise] preferred to satisfy [her] thirst by applying [her] lips at the holy spout from which the water was flowing" (100).

6. The wedding ceremony took place by proxy in Florence. As a reflection of this circumstance, King Enrique IV does not appear in the painting, but in his stead we see the Grand Duke Ferdinando de' Medici, Maria's uncle. (Thuillier 77).

7. It is worth noting that Augusta in *Epitalamio* [Wedding song] (1897), one of Valle-Inclán's first works, was called "Dalila tentadora" (190) "Dalila the temptress." A later echo of this theme of the decapitating or castrating woman appears in *La cabeza del Bautista* [The Baptist's head] (1924).

8. The influence of the Pre-Raphaelites on Valle-Inclán has been noted by critics such as Zamora Vicente (94–95), Rodolphe Stembert (475–76), Hans Hinterhäuser (107), and Dianella Gambini (600–3). Hinterhäuser points out the frequency in Valle-Inclán's descriptions of "Pre-Raphaelite props: the rose, the lily and the dove, symbols of purity, virginity and holiness (and also of the Virgen Mary herself)" (107).

9. Juan Ramón Jiménez testifies to the admiration Valle-Inclán felt for *Spring*: "We go to a café. ... Valle ... sits at the last table, he takes out an issue of *Alrededor del mundo* [Around the world], a magazine

that publishes classic artworks on the cover, he props it up against a bottle of water and he looks fascinated, smiling ineffably *[inefablemente sonreído]* before Botticelli's *Spring"* (47).

10. Robert Abirached provides information about this woman in his edition of the *Mémoires* of Casanova: "Marianna Corticelli, born in Bologna in 1747, made her début in Florence before going to dance in Prague, Berne, and finally Paris . . . : she is known to have had several liaisons in Paris" (1194). In the *Mémoires*, Marianna Corticelli is at first a girl to whom the seducer becomes attached (like Bradomín to the innocent María Rosario): "Marianna Corticelli was barely thirteen years old, and she was so dainty that she only looked about ten . . . she was . . . spiritual, and her skin was a pale white that is rare in Italy" (716). Later, however, she is presented as destructive, "always making sure to cause me all possible sorrow" (905), "she had done everything in her power to hurt me" (908). And, in fact, she ends up deceiving Sir Seingalt with a canon (2, chap. 39) and with Sir Ville-Fallet (2, chap. 40).

11. Walter Pater—connected so closely with European modernism—transmits this supposition: "He [Botticelli] paints the story of the goddess of pleasure. . . . The same figure—tradition connects it with Simonetta, the mistress of Giuliano de' Medici—appears again as Judith, returning home across the hill country, when the great deed is over" (47). In his edition of Pater's work, Donald L. Hill has this to say about *The Return of Judith*: "Judith carries in her right hand the sword with which she has cut off the head of Holofernes; in her left is an olive branch. Her maid follows her with the severed head in a basket" (339). Another painting by Botticelli in the Uffizi deserves mention here: *Judith with the Head of Holofernes*, which is the exact title of the work that Bradomín contemplates in the Gaetani palace.

12. Another display of interest in Pre-Raphaelite painting may be found in one of Emilia Pardo Bazán's late novels, *La Quimera* [The chimera] (1905), contemporaneous with the *Sonatas*. The Swede Limsoe tells the protagonist, the painter Silvio Lago, in one of their conversations: "Eternos son ya los nombres de Holman Hunt, Millais y Dante Gabriel Rossetti. Fueron iniciadores, y fueron, sobre todo, poetas; sintieron, se elevaron" "The names of Holman Hunt, Millais, and Dante Gabriel Rossetti are now eternal. They were initiators, and they were, above all, poets: they had feelings, they lifted themselves higher" (860). Silvio does not give in easily: "He oído que los prerrafaelistas son unos histéricos, unos degenerados" "I have heard that the Pre-Raphaelites were a bunch of hysterics, degenerates" (861). As for Valle-Inclán, he would find Pre-Raphaelite art attractive for its mysticism as well as for its degeneracy.

13. We should mention here that Botticelli's Venus in *Spring* has also been frequently associated with Mary. Gombrich corroborates this

opinion: "The many critics who sensed the affinity of Botticelli's Venus with his Madonnas were certainly right. . . . What we witness is . . . the opening up, to secular art, of emotional spheres which had hitherto been the preserve of religious worship" (*Symbolic Images* 63, 64).

14. Paglia notes this change in artistic sensibility: "The Renaissance liberated the western eye, repressed by the Christian Middle Ages. In that eye, sex and aggression are amorally fused" (140). In analogous fashion, Paglia defines the decadent style as "freezing word to image to propitiate the pagan eye" (421).

15. Eugene Goodheart writes: "The modernist imagination ambiguously affirms and resists the claim of desire, and it does so by dividing writing from living" (9).

16. "Almost alone of all the princes of that time, he [Cesare Borgia] has left behind no portrait of himself that one can cite with absolute certainty. The one in the Borghese Gallery, formerly attributed to Raphael, truly resembles him: that is all that one can say" (Sizeranne 89).

17. Gonzalo Sobejano (*Nietzsche* 215) points to Nietzsche's influence, through D'Annunzio, on the Valle-Inclán who exalts Borgia, the barbarous impulse, and the will to power: "The prototype of the healthy man, instinctual, prehensile, and 'tropical,' is, for Nietzsche, Cesare Borgia, whose pontificate would have constituted a life triumph on the very throne of Christendom. D'Annunzio's heroes strive for this life triumph. Several of Valle-Inclán's characters also covet that triumph: Augusta del Fede and Attilio Bonaparte, the Marquis of Bradomín, Don Juan Manuel Montenegro." For a positive view of barbarism in Valle-Inclán, see Leda Schiavo.

18. Joseph Frank cites Wylie Sypher, who sees the loss of the self as one of the prevailing tendencies of both modernism and postmodernism. Frank adds: "The self no longer feels itself to be an active, individual form operating in the real world of history and time; it exists, if at all, only through its assimilation into a mythical world of eternal prototypes" ("Spatial Form: Thirty Years After" 228–29).

19. There is already a comparable division in the Renaissance between the transcendent self and the historical self: "the Renaissance system reinforced the distinction between the isolated or transcendent self and the self modified by circumstance" (Steiner, *Pictures* 3).

20. This idea is commonplace in psychoanalytic criticism about *Hamlet*: "Polonius is yet another father figure who comes between Hamlet and his love, even as Hamlet's father stood and Claudius now stands between Hamlet and his first love, his mother" (Lidz 93).

21. "Polonius has been exhibited as something of a fool in his own right, a dotard version of the father figure" (Barber and Wheeler 259).

22. Julio Casares (65–72) indicated the literary source of this episode: a passage from the *Mémoires* of Casanova. Valle-Inclán replied to

Casares's criticism: "Cuando escribía yo la *Sonata de primavera*, cuya acción pasa en Italia, incrusté un episodio romano de Casanova para convencerme de que mi obra estaba bien ambientada e iba por buen camino" "When I was writing the *Spring Sonata*, the action of which takes place in Italy, I incrusted a Roman episode of Casanova to convince myself that my work was well oriented and headed in the right direction" (Dougherty 196).

23. The corresponding passage in Casanova possesses less intensity: "Certainly I would not have let you die, she [the old woman] told me, but I would have made you fall in love and be unhappy" (in Casares 69). Valle-Inclán does not follow Casanova as literally as Casares claims.

24. Charles Bernheimer remarks: "Castration . . . is the seminal fantasy of the decadent imagination" ("Fetishism" 62). For Bernheimer, the importance that Freud accords to castration fantasy is rooted in the same cultural context: "the misogynist fears of his fin de siècle" (62).

25. Peter A. Bly sees the girl's death as the highest representation of a desire for calm, which compels the narrator to describe actions as if they were paintings: "artistic stasis is only a representation of that great stasis of death when the truth of all life is fully revealed" (262).

26. Concerning *King Lear*, Adelman wonders if the last scene (where Cordelia lies dead in her father's arms) should be interpreted as a union or as an irrevocable separation between the two: "is death their new home, the final version of prison as kind nursery? Or does the reversed pietà of his gesture—the mortal father/son now carrying the holy virgin mother, dead as earth—signal the permanent loss of this possibility, the final separation?" (126).

27. The fragility of the female, cut down in the prime of life by physical or nervous illness, is inscribed in the Pre-Raphaelite aesthetics: "Passivity is the dominant trope; beauty renders those so designated an object of another's desiring gaze; illness—suggested in terms such as 'fragile', 'tragic life'—implies dependency, incapacity, inactivity, suffering" (Pollock 96). Another female protagonist in Valle-Inclán's work, Eulalia, shows certain commonalities with the drowned Ophelia as she appears in Millais, for example: "Arrastrada por la corriente . . . iba el cuerpo de Eulalia. La luna marcaba un camino sobre las aguas, y la cabellera de Eulalia, deshecha ya, apareció dos veces flotando" "Dragged by the current . . . went the body of Eulalia. The moon traced a path on the waters, and Eulalia's hair, already loose, floated to the surface two times" (*Corte de amor* 81–82). Before drowning, Eulalia also manifests symptoms of delirium.

28. Insofar as Hamlet and Bradomín coincide in their lack of a father, Adelman's comments are most applicable: "This father [Hamlet's] cannot protect his son; and his disappearance in effect throws Ham-

let into the domain of the engulfing mother, awakening all the fears incident to the primary mother-child bond" (30).

29. According to Joseph Frank, myth forms "the common content of modern literature, that finds its appropriate aesthetic expression in spatial form" ("Spatial Form in Modern Literature" 60).

30. Alan Wilde underscores an aspect of modernism that is relevant to our discussion: "we need to recognize in the unresolved quality of modernist irony . . . a refusal to easy answers and, at the same time, to acknowledge in its absolute poise not confidence and rest but crisis and arrest—to concede, that is, the *humanity* of the modernist enterprise" (47).

## 4. THE INFINITE PROGRESSION:
## LOVE AND ART IN *PRELUDE TO PLEASURE*
## BY PEDRO SALINAS

1. There has been a tendency to isolate Spanish literature of the first decades of the twentieth century from other countries' literature of that time. Ricardo Gullón, who criticized the term *Generation of '98*, reacted against this stance: "The error in particularizing the general, in considering that which happened in so many places to be a native phenomenon, has hindered us from observing deep affinities, and instead has led us to extol superficial differences" (13). According to Gullón, the Generation of '98 is inseparable from modernism, which of course is not limited to the Hispanic world. J. J. Macklin, who calls an author such as Ramón Pérez de Ayala a modernist, proposes a similar chronology for Spanish and European letters: "we can state with certainty that modernism is a historic term that should be employed, for example, like realism, and that refers to a movement in European art lasting approximately between the years 1900 and 1930" (35).

2. Salinas coincides with W. J. T. Mitchell, for whom spatial and temporal notions are mutually implicated: "We cannot experience a spatial form except in time; we cannot talk about our temporal experience without invoking spatial measures" ("Spatial Form" 276).

3. This hypothesis is more likely in view of the fact that Ortega y Gasset, in his essay "Tres cuadros del vino" [Three paintings on wine] included in *El Espectador, I* [The spectator, I] (1916), devotes a commentary to Titian's *Bacchanal*, which he sees as an expression of a moment of perfect pleasure exempt from routine time: "there are sublime moments in which we feel ourselves in union with the entire universe. . . . Titian has painted one of these moments. . . . Like an object of unlimited elasticity the moment has been stretched out and it reaches those vague

confines of time from one end to the other" (51–52). Ortega, of course, was the intellectual luminary of Salinas's generation.

4. T. J. Clark defines the nude as follows: "[It] is a picture for men to look at, in which Woman is constructed as an object of somebody else's desire" (131).

5. Lynda Nead writes: "even at the most basic levels the body is always produced through representation" (16). But Peter Brooks offers the contrary viewpoint: "The body, I think, often presents us with a fall from language, a return to an infantile presymbolic space in which primal drives reassert their force" (*Body Work* 7).

6. As we discussed in chapter 2, the figure of Saint George was linked in Victorian times to Perseus as liberator of Andromeda: "In Victorian England the legend of St. George and the dragon is an analogue of the mythological rescue scene, the hero transformed to a knight of chivalric romance. . . . [M]any English Victorian representations favor the version of the myth where the Saint kills the dragon then marries Princess Sabra" (Munich 13).

7. Jacqueline Rose remarks: "femininity is assigned to a point of origin prior to the mark of symbolic difference and law. The privileged relationship of women to that origin gives them access to an archaic form of expressivity outside the circuit of linguistic exchange" (Introduction 54).

8. In "Números" [Numbers] from *Seguro Azar* [Steadfast chance] (1924–28), Salinas compares a metaphoric constellation made up of numbers with "Ariadna, desnuda allí / en islas del horizonte" "Ariadne, naked there / on islands at the horizon" (*Poesías* 66). That naked Ariadne is precisely the figure painted by Titian in his *Bacchanal*, the setting for which is none other than an island. It should also be noted that this figure departs from tradition: "Unlike Titian's 'Ariadne,' the Roman and Hellenistic sculptures of this type are virtually always clothed, but with one breast exposed" (Wethey 40). Obviously Salinas had Titian's painting in mind.

9. The young nobleman of Sigüenza, who died in the war of Granada, is once again associated with Alfonso de Padilla; his real name, however, was Martín Vázquez de Arce; see Gaya Nuño 184.

10. Gaya Nuño places the cathedral of Sigüenza within the context of the battles between Moors and Christians: "Preoccupations concerning religious wars, which were prevailing in that meridional Castile, determined the strong military appearance of the exterior, turreted with the same solidity as a castle" (131).

11. Lacan claims: "A signifier is that which represents a subject. For whom? not for another subject, but for another signifier" (*Four Fundamental Concepts* 198).

12. Compare these lines: "¡Gloria a las diferencias / entre tú y yo que llaman / nuestro amor a la alerta, / cara a cara, a probarse! / ¡Qué fácil unidad / de los que son iguales!" "Glory to the differences / between you and me that place / our love on alert, / face to face, to be proven!/ What easy unity / of those who are the same!" (*Razón de amor, Poesías* 240).

13. C. B. Morris points out the similarities between Salinas and Proust: "And the Aurora who finally ends Jorge's wait observes the principle Proust laid down in *A l'ombre des jeunes filles en fleur* that 'Chaque être est détruit quand nous cessons de le voir; puis son apparition suivante est une création nouvelle, différente de celle qui l'a immédiatement précédée, sinon de toutes' ['Each being is destroyed when we no longer see it; its later appearance is thus a new creation, different from the one that immediately preceded it, if not from all of them'] (*Recherche*, Paris, 1955–56, 1, 917)" (200).

14. "Curiously enough, *even the beloved woman is negated* by Salinas; I don't know of any love poetry in which the pair of lovers is reduced so narrowly to the *I* of the poet, in which the woman only lives in function of the spirit of the man and is nothing more than a 'phenomenon of consciousness' for him" (Spitzer 194). "Salinas believes that things perceived by the senses are simple accidents of essence, that 'other reality,' an essential reality in the Platonic sense" (Zardoya 106). "If the spirit is felt to be concrete, substantial, then its dreams and visions become also concrete and the material world, on the other hand, becomes insubstantial in comparison" (Stixrude 21). "For Salinas there is no reality. It becomes reality when it is created inside ourselves through intuition of its essence" (Cirre 29). For a critique of Spitzer and other opinions that adhere to his views, see Carlos Feal, *La poesía de Pedro Salinas* 157–58 and "Lo visible y lo invisible en los primeros libros poéticos de Salinas." Also in reference to Spitzer's judgment, Jorge Guillén remarks: "A monstrous conclusion. This time, for once, the great Spitzer was in error" (11).

15. In his book review of 1926, Fernando Vela remarks: "In *Víspera del gozo*, the simple, but full presence produces 'the perfect abolition of intermediate times,' of the interpolated imaginings between two meetings. It is not felt as the lamentable rupture of illusion" (129). This contemporaneous critical evaluation stands in marked contrast with later opinions: "When Aurora finally arrives, the real Aurora, Jorge suffers a true deception because she does not correspond at all to the ideal created in his imagination" (Spires 250). "'Aurora de verdad' . . . ends with a disillusion, with an emotional fall downward from the heights of hope" (Newman 424).

16. Of course, this kind of vision, far from natural, would be the result of a learning process: "The 'innocent eye' is a metaphor for a

highly experienced and cultivated sort of vision" (Mitchell, *Iconology* 118).

17. Sanford Schwartz writes: "Many philosophers at the turn of the century regarded conceptual abstractions as instrumental forms that we impose upon the flux of sensations" (20). For Schwartz, those philosophers (Bergson, William James, Nietzsche, among others) had a decisive influence on the poetics of European modernism. The following words by Bergson, from his *Essai sur les données immédiates de la conscience* (1889), are most applicable to the ideas under analysis here: "Every day I perceive the same houses, and as I know that they are the same objects, I always call them by the same name to me. But if I recur, at the end of a sufficiently long period, to the impression which I experienced during the first years, I am surprised at the remarkable, inexplicable change which has taken place" (in Schwartz 22).

18. Although the theme of dawn occurs frequently in Turner, there is no particular painting with that exact title. The closest would be *Morning amongst the Coniston Fells* (Tate Gallery, London), which Salinas could very well have seen since he was a lecturer in Spanish at Cambridge University from 1922 to 1923.

19. Gombrich describes Turner's paintings in these terms: "[He] had visions of a fantastic world bathed in light and resplendent with beauty, but it was a world not of calm but of movement, not of simple harmonies but of dazzling pageantries" (*Story* 302). John Ruskin's remarks on Turner from *Modern Painters* (1856) are also of interest here. Norman Bryson summarizes them as follows: "Turner's paintings are said by Ruskin to record how Turner perceives what is there: some paintings by Turner may look 'visionary'—deviating from what is there—but, Ruskin argues, they are actually grounded in a perceiving consciousness" ("Semiology" 61). Salinas's affinity to Ruskin may be gleaned from these words written by the English critic: "the whole technical power of painting depends upon our recovery of what may be called the *innocence of the eye*" (in Danto, "Description" 207).

20. Lacan, in *Four Fundamental Concepts* (53), also proclaims an analogous orientation toward the real, although he is less optimistic than Merleau-Ponty: "For what we have in the discovery of psycho-analysis is an encounter, an essential encounter—an appointment to which we are always called with a real that eludes us." In their study of Lacan, Bice Benvenuto and Roger Kennedy mention Merleau-Ponty, "whose work affected his [Lacan's] greatly" (69). Frequent references to Merleau-Ponty may in fact be found throughout the section "Of the Gaze as *Objet Petit a*" in *Four Fundamental Concepts*.

21. For Angel del Río, *Víspera del gozo* (along with *Seguro azar* and *Fábula y signo*) constitutes an anomaly in Salinas's work: "It could be said that during a long phase of his slow poetic evolution Salinas tries to

go beyond himself in order to become immersed in life around him, thereby promising a happiness that in the end fades away. This is what takes place in the beautiful pages of *Víspera del gozo*" (13). This opinion, which seeks to establish differences between those three works by Salinas and his later ones, does not hold up. Salinas's poetic trajectory does not display essential deviations; his postwar work (with which Angel del Río had no familiarity when he wrote his article) corroborates his early attitudes. Take, for example, that ode to vision *El Contemplado* [The Contemplated One] (1946), the title of which announces its theme, or these lines from his posthumous work *Confianza* [Confidence] (1954): "Quisiera más que nada, más que sueño, / ver lo que veo" "I would like more than anything, more than dreams, / to see what I see" ("Ver lo que veo," *Poesías* 461).

## 5. MALE (DE) SIGNS: ART AND SOCIETY IN LUIS MARTÍN-SANTOS

1. "Goya's mockery lies in his insinuation that these witches are more engaged in passions of the flesh than with magic" (Pérez Sánchez and Sayre 62).

2. The description of this lecture is based on a real experience, according to Jo Labanyi: "[Martín-Santos] heard him [Ortega] speak in person—at the lecture parodied in the novel, which Martín-Santos attended in 1949 with Juan Benet" (*Myth and History* 56).

3. At the end of the nineteenth century autopsies were frequently performed on women (especially prostitutes). Perhaps Martín-Santos was familiar with that information, which populated the medical literature and art of the time. Elaine Showalter, who notes this practice, also remarks: "They [men] gain control over an elusive and threatening femininity by turning the woman into a 'case' to be opened or shut" (*Sexual Anarchy* 134).

4. Juan Carlos Curutchet sees Goya's painting as a "critique of *machismo*" (46). He does not relate this point with the totality of the novel, however, which makes his interpretation restricted: "Ortega has turned into the he-goat, and the humble country women have turned into conceited high Spanish society ladies offering their feeble sexuality" (46). In addition, Curutchet (45) confuses *El Aquelarre* from the Lázaro Galdiano Museum with another painting by Goya of the same title in the Prado.

5. Labanyi noticed this point: "In *Tiempo de silencio* the lower classes (the shanty town), the middle classes (the *pensión*) and the upper classes (the reception for Ortega) coincide in their adulation of a patriarch, whether present (Muecas, Ortega) or absent (as in the *pensión*

which tries to make Pedro fit the role of the founding father)" (*Myth and History* 71).

6. Richard Lee and Richard Daly write: "Male domination is one part of a complex of power relations fundamental to the maintenance of a class society; the other two parts are social inequality and militarism. . . . Patriarchy can best be understood as the reproduction of state hierarchy within the family" (30, 41).

7. We are aware that, in *Time of Silence*, multiple narrators or narrative voices coexist. References to the narrator, in general, indicate a voice that is not identified with any one of the characters in the novel, although on some occasions the narrator cannot be distinguished from Pedro. Normally, however, there is distance between the narrator and the protagonist: "The preferred target for the narrator's critiques is Pedro" (Rey 103).

8. In Juan Goytisolo's *Reivindicación del Conde don Julián* (1970), a novel obviously indebted to *Time of Silence*, the *capra hispánica* functions as a symbol of the Spanish man. Note that Ortega is not left out of this presentation either:

> a la hora del aperitivo, cuando el tráfico urbano suele ser más intenso, un paradigmático ejemplar de capra hispánica hace su aparición en el cruce de Callao y Granvía, frente a la boca del metro: sucesivamente lo vemos en el stand de bonetería de Galerías Preciados, de visita en diferentes museos e iglesias, dar una charla sobre "Ortega y la Caza" en los salones del Ateneo, brindar con una copa de vino español en Chicote, departir de oligarquía clasista en el Pelayo y de verso plurimembre en el Gijón (254)

> at the cocktail hour, when city traffic is usually heavier, a perfect specimen of the *capra hispanica* makes [his] appearance at the corner of Callao and Granvía, in front of the subway entrance: we then see [him] successively standing at the [hat] counter at the Galerías Preciados, visiting different museums and churches, giving a talk on "Ortega and [Hunting]" at the Ateneo, having a drink of Spanish wine with friends [at Chicote's], holding forth on economic oligarchy at the Pelayo and on polymembrous verse at the Gijón. (*Count Julian* 157–58)

Martín-Santos also depicts the café Gijón—a meeting place for artists—in a sarcastic way (*Tiempo* 78–86; *Time* 64–70).

9. Jean Laplanche and J.-B. Pontalis explain this unconscious fantasy: "some psychoanalysts have uncovered . . . an anxiety-generating phantasy in which the mother has kept the phallus received in coitus inside her body" (312).

10. "Overcoming cosmic terror is concomitant with destroying the magical universe of the primitive or of the child. . . . This universe gradually disappears, in proportion to the establishment of rational and causal connections in reality" (Martín-Santos, *Libertad, temporalidad y transferencia* [Liberty, temporality and transference] 242).

11. Alfonso Rey posits a basic coincidence between author and narrator in the novel: the narrator "influences our reading" so that we adhere to "the ideology that the author attempts to communicate" (112). While what Rey says is true, it must be noted that Martín-Santos is conscious of the mythical aspects in any ideology. He states, in response to Janet W. Díaz (237) on the social function of the novelist: "His function is what I call desacrilizing-sacrogenetic [*desacrilizadora-sacrogenética*]: Desacrilizing—destroying by means of a sharp criticism of injustice. Sacrogenetic—collaborating simultaneously in the edification of the new myths that go on to form the Sacred Scriptures of tomorrow."

12. The idea that *Time of Silence* constitutes a psychoanalysis of Spain was formulated by critics such as Curutchet (39) and José Schraibman. Also see Carlos Feal, "En torno al casticismo de Pedro." Martín-Santos himself favors this type of interpretation: "Psychiatry does not deal only in individual subjects. There is also a psychology of peoples and nations. Each people has its complexes" (*Apólogos* 104).

13. Fernando Morán calls Martín-Santos's novel a "semi-esperpento" (388). Curutchet places it in "the tradition of Quevedo and Goya (or even Valle-Inclán at his best)" (67). Max Estrella's pronouncement from Valle-Inclán's *Luces de Bohemia* [Bohemian lights] comes to mind: "El esperpentismo lo ha inventado Goya" "Esperpentism was invented by Goya" (132).

14. Gemma Roberts (166) connects this citation with the following words by Sartre, which she takes as an indication of the influence of the French writer on Martín-Santos: "l'acte amoureux est castration de l'homme" "the act of love is man's castration." Here is Sartre's more complete statement: "Sans aucun doute le sexe est bouche, et bouche vorace qui avale le pénis—ce qui peut bien amener l'idée de castration" "Without any doubt the sexual organ is a mouth, a voracious mouth that swallows the penis—which could well lead to the idea of castration" (*L'être et le néant* 706).

15. Another way to read the triad Dorita/mother/grandmother is through the mythic three aspects of woman: maiden/mother/crone. Since these aspects are contained in one figure, it is impossible to separate them; thus Dorita could not be wrenched from the other two. We thank Amy Katz Kaminsky for this insight.

16. In this respect, it is interesting to compare *El Aquelarre* with another painting by Goya, *Escena de brujas* [Scene of witches], also in the Lázaro Galdiano Museum. José Gudiol offers this description: "A group of witches surrounds a frightened woman. . . . Of the black witches, one holds a basket of infants, one torments an infant, one gestures hideously, and one reads the incantation by the light of a sputtering candle" (98). Note that the he-goat does not appear as an object of adoration in this painting.

17.  Madelon Sprengnether refers to the precariousness of the patriarchal mentality in these terms: "patriarchy itself is founded on a continual repression that takes its toll in terms of an anxiety about mastery,
which Freud refers to, appropriately, as the death instinct. At the heart
of phallogocentrism lies the terror as well as the certainty of its own
undoing" (244).

18.  José Luis Aranguren characterizes the tone of the novel as "ironically liturgical or ritual" (260).

19.  Carlos Fuentes makes the following point with respect to Goya:
"But perhaps reason, when it forgets its own limits and believes too
uncritically in itself and its brainchild, progress, deserves this nightmare.
Perhaps it is only the sleep of monsters that begets reason" (226–28).

20.  Gonzalo Sobejano has pointed out this character's importance
and function in the novel: "Muecas's wife is . . . the character through
whom we perceive the corrective spirit of the author and his capacity to
commiserate, within a context of what could seem only to be implacable
satire" (*Novela* 556).

21.  Carlos Rojas's comments on Goya's well-known painting *Los
fusilamientos en la montaña del Príncipe Pío* [The executions at the
Príncipe Pío mountain] are of relevance: "Perhaps as he goes to his death,
arms spread open before his executioners, the shirtless man whom you
painted will shout out the same sinister roar, *Long live the chains!*" (*Yo,
Goya* 182). It is interesting that the Príncipe Pío mountain is also invoked
in Pedro's final reflections by means of the name of the north train sta-
tion in Madrid, through which the beleaguered protagonist travels when
he abandons the city: "Llegué por Príncipe Pío, me voy por Príncipe Pío"
(287) "I arrived at Príncipe Pío, and I'm leaving from Príncipe Pío"
(239). Pedro's vicissitudes are therefore framed between two allusions to
Goya's *Los fusilamientos*, that is, the attempt by an invading power to
exterminate the people of Madrid.

22.  Eugenio d'Ors's words on Goya are appropriate here: "Popularity has unshakably granted him the highest rank. Goya is Spanish painting; he is the Prado Museum. . . . For the 'good people' of Madrid . . .
there is no possible rival" (87).

23.  It does not seem gratuitous that the author has assigned the
name Dora (rather uncommon in Spanish) to the mother and daughter
pair in the novel. Dora is of course the name of one of Freud's first
patients, immortalized in his "Fragment of an Analysis of a Case of Hysteria" and the object of much attention in recent years among feminist
scholars. Lisa Appignanesi and John Forrester remark: "The story of
Dora provides a paradigm case for catching patriarchy with its pants
down, of tracing how 'sexual union is understood accurately as a power
relation' and is irrevocably cast in terms of dominance and submission"
(146). The phrase in quotations is from Maria Ramas (51). Concerning

Martín-Santos's familiarity with Freud's works, Carlos Castilla del Pino says: "Martín-Santos began to have direct contact with Freud's writing in 1956. It is a late contact: this is not surprising, however, if one remembers that for sociopolitical reasons most or all of Freud's works were excluded from the official psychiatric *status* in Spain" (22). Castilla refers, of course, to the years of the Franco regime.

24. Such an extreme critique of the country places the novel in a venerable tradition, acutely noted by Paul Ilie: "Spanish literature—despite its diversity—is obsessed with Spain as *la madre-madrastra* [the mother-stepmother]" (31). The obsession registered by Ilie is also present among Spanish painters. These are the words of the great artist Jusepe de Ribera, lo Spagnoletto, who spent most of his life in Italy: "I judge that Spain is a pious mother to foreigners and a very cruel stepmother to her own native sons" (in Brown, *Golden Age* 179).

25. Elisabeth Bronfen's remarks make sense in this context: "Annihilation can be an indication of the presence of the death drive as well as a defence against an experience of desire by annihilating the desired object and that part of the self desiring the object" (192).

26. In his exaltation of Cervantes, Martín-Santos is heir to the legacy of Ortega and the Generation of '98 who, in Rockwell Gray's words, "marked the beginning of Spain's decline from her golden age about the time *Don Quijote* was published. A rereading of that classic seemed a way both to recover the national patrimony and to celebrate Spain's cultural awakening from a long slumber" (93). With respect to Martín-Santos's attitude of simultaneous attraction and repulsion toward Ortega, see Rey 201–38 and 238–49.

## 6. EXILED IN *THE GARDEN OF EARTHLY DELIGHTS*: FROM HIERONYMUS BOSCH TO FRANCISCO AYALA

1. In commenting on his story "Nuestro jardín" [Our garden] included in *El jardín de las delicias* Ayala writes in his *Recuerdos y olvidos* [Remembrances and omissions]: "That wasn't the first story of mine that originated in one of the paintings hanging on the walls of my childhood home. Many years before writing it I had published a short novel, *San Juan de Dios*, in which the figure of the saint rises up from a painting from our collection of ancient artworks to take on an imaginary life" (57). In another essay, Ayala says this about his story "El Hechizado": "When . . . I conceived and wrote the story 'El Hechizado' from my exile, . . . the figure that I trace there of the unfortunate Carlos II of Spain . . . is a verbal transposition, along with other elements, of the portraits painted by his Court painter, Juan Carreño de Miranda, and in particular the one that I had stopped to look at so many times during my

visits to our Art Gallery [the Prado Museum]" (*El tiempo y yo* [Time and I] 21).

2. All quotes from *El jardín de las delicias* refer to the first edition: Seix Barral, 1971. The book was republished twice in expanded editions by Espasa-Calpe (1978) and Mondadori (1990). There is no published English translation to date.

3. Rudolf Arnheim remarks: "A round shape is so complete and stable in itself that it adapts itself badly to the context of a composition unless it can hold the center and have all other shapes conform to it" (87).

4. "' . . . [T]he circle expresses Heaven or eternal existence,' says George Ferguson in his book on Christian symbols" (Arnheim 79–80).

5. Ayala is aware of the symbolic meaning of his story: "Our garden. It is my grandfather's garden, which I never got to see; but it is also at the same time the garden for which the human species yearns. The we, subject of the possessive our, are all children of Eve, and our garden is Paradise lost. It is located in a mythic time, anterior to our birth" (*El tiempo y yo* 62).

6. "The pig is a symbol of the Archetypal Feminine and occurs everywhere as the sacrificial beast of the Earth Goddess" (Neumann, *Great Mother* 139).

7. Walter Burkert makes these comments about the fact that Aphrodite, enamored of Adonis, sends him to Persephone (who then tries to keep him for herself): "what an idea to hide the beloved one in a *lárnax*, a coffin, and send him to the nether world, of all places!" (110). The anomaly may be resolved if we view the two goddesses as "one goddess in dual form," in Joseph Campbell's words (48). It is also worth mentioning that in the garden of Flora (one of the characters in Botticelli's painting and, like Venus, goddess of spring), flowers grew that were "born of the blood of handsome young men who have been mortally wounded, like Hyacinthus or Adonis" (Detienne 99).

8. It is of interest to note Dante's influence on Botticelli: the artist illustrated the first Florentine edition of the *Divina Commedia* (1481) with twelve etchings. See Giulio Carlo Argan, *Botticelli* 7, 94–95.

9. John Freccero remarks with respect to the cited lines from Dante: "Dante is himself in a sense searching for a prelapsarian Persephone, an erotic innocence which he recaptures, at one remove, in his encounter with Matelda at the top of the Mountain of Purgatory" (125). Let us also remember the association between the Venus of Botticelli's *Spring* and the Madonna (see chapter 3, note 13).

10. Ricardo Arias (422) and Carolyn Richmond (222) observe that the two lateral panels of Bosch's painting are reproduced in Ayala's book in reversed position; they therefore equate the first part of Ayala's *El jardín* (*Diablo mundo*) with hell, and the second part (*Días felices*) with heaven.

While this is an astute observation, we may add that the contrast between hell and paradise is not only established between the two parts, but also within several of the stories of the second part, such as "*Au cochon de lait.*" Andrés Amorós thinks along the same lines when he asks whether one cannot find "such atrocious things" (10) in *Días felices* as in *Diablo mundo*. Ayala answers this question in the affirmative, although he points out a difference in tone; he also stresses the "eternal nostalgia for paradise" (Amorós 4) in several of the stories in *Días felices*.

11. In his conversation with Amorós, Ayala recognizes "the myth of original sin" as a basic truth, but he also admits the need for "redemption" (10). From a purely psychological point of view, André Green sets forth the dual nature of this universal idea: "The world before the fall is always a reconstruction. Nevertheless paradise lost is not only a memory trace or a fantasied retrospection, it includes also a hope, or an illusion, of refinding such a condition, in earthly life or after death" (74).

12. Francesco La Cava, a physician, was the first to mention this fact in a work published in 1925, *Il Volto di Michelangelo scoperto nel Giudizio Finale* (Steinberg, "Line of Fate" 102). Tolnay, among others, shares this opinion: "On the skin held by St. Bartholomew, there is a tragic mask with a grimace of pain: the portrait of Michelangelo himself" (*Michelangelo* 44).

13. Tolnay highlights this motif: "The fresco of Michelangelo marks a turning-point in the iconography of the Last Judgment by introducing a revolving dynamism which unites the earthly and heavenly spheres—a sort of cosmic whirlpool" (*Michelangelo* 23).

14. "The relative paucity of mythological works by Spanish artists has usually been attributed to the influence of church doctrine, which regarded antique subjects as a pretext for representing the naked body and thus arousing the baser instincts of the viewer" (Brown, *Golden Age* 211).

15. "A Picasso watercolor of the Blue Period presents the artist at twenty-three. He is doing none of the things self-portrayed artists usually do. He is . . . watching a girl asleep" (Steinberg, "Picasso's Sleepwatchers" 93). According to Mary Mathews Gedo (144), the woman in the painting is Fernande Olivier, one of Picasso's first lovers.

16. Steinberg writes: "like the sculptor with whom he consorts, he [the Minotaur] stands for the artist himself" ("Picasso's Sleepwatchers" 101). Steinberg is referring to the Vollard Suite, in which the Minotaur appears in the sculptor's studio. In this series of one hundred etchings, the Minotaur theme is present in fifteen (Bolliger, numbers 83–97), dated from May 17 to June 18, 1933. The work that Ayala reproduces is posterior (June 12, 1936); Bolliger lists it under the title *Satyr and Sleeping Woman* (number 27).

17. John Golding highlights a similar attitude in Picasso's Minotaurs, who differ from the surrealists' versions of them as representatives of the Freudian *id*: "For Picasso he [the Minotaur] was a more human and more complex creature" (119).

18. Wendy Steiner's remarks on Picasso have bearing here: "The sleepwatcher in such works represents the pause before violation less often than the arrest at the inviolability of the dreamer and the incommunicability of thought and desire" (*Pictures* 131–32).

19. However, the comma after the title disappears in the 1978 and 1990 editions of *El jardín*.

20. In Titian's *Bacchanal* (which we mentioned in chapter 4 with respect to Salinas), the sleeping figure of Ariadne also rests her head on her bent arm.

21. Carlos Rojas, in his comments on etching 88, *Dying Minotaur* (May 26, 1933) from the Vollard Suite, points out a connection between the Minotaur and Ariadne: "he slips toward death in the same position as Ariadne—his step-sister, after all—lies sleeping in the Vatican's statue: her head in the the hollow of her crooked arm, like the model Fernande Olivier was resting or dreaming nearly thirty years earlier" (*Mundo mítico* 172).

22. In Spanish painting, the theme of Saint Geronimo was treated several times by Ribera, who in turn found imitators in other painters besides Cano, like Francisco Collantes, Antonio de Pereda, and Diego Polo (Brown, *Golden Age* 196). In fact, in the 1978 and 1990 editions of *El jardín*, Cano's *Saint Geronimo* is substituted respectively by another painting from the Ribera School (Lázaro Galdiano Museum) and a work by Ribera himself (Prado Museum). The angel is not present in any of them, however; rather, there is a prominent image of a skull near the saint. In the Lázaro Galdiano painting, the saint is shown writing, which highlights his intellectual standing.

23. The temptations of Saint Geronimo have been represented pictorially by artists such as Zurbarán (Monasterio de Guadalupe) and Valdés Leal (Museo de Bellas Artes, Seville) (Brown, *Golden Age* 174, 270). With respect to the link between the dove and human desire, we may cite this line by Dante as he contemplates Paolo and Francesca in hell, where they were sent for their sin of lust: "Quali colombe dal disio chiamate" (*Divina Commedia, Inferno 5*, 82), "As doves called by desire" (*Divine Comedy* 40).

24. Ayala comments elsewhere on this central theme in *El jardín*: "this book cries out for Paradise lost from many of its pages, and in some places one may glimpse the illusion of having recuperated it for fleeting moments" (*El tiempo y yo* 63).

25. Plato formulates the distinction between the heavenly (Uranian) Aphrodite, goddess of pure love, and the common (Pandemian) Aphro-

dite, goddess of carnal love, in the *Symposium* (180d–e). Plato's ideas recirculate in the Renaissance through authors such as Ficino. Thus Panofsky has related Titian's *Sacred and Profane Love* precisely to Neoplatonic doctrines of the Italian Renaissance (*Studies in Iconology* 150–51).

26. Ayala's attraction to Renaissance art may be better understood if we consider the intimate connection between arts and letters during this period. As Wendy Steiner writes, "Both these possibilities [literary texts based upon paintings and vice versa] characterized significant portions of Renaissance art. It was the combination of visual detail and abstract concept in the symbol that facilitated interartistic sharing" (*Colors of Rhetoric* 9).

27. Clark has the following to say of the nude woman in *Sacred and Profane Love*, even after he recognizes that she represents the heavenly Venus: "Beyond almost any figure in art, she has what Blake called 'the lineaments of gratified desire'" (124). Clark thereby prolongs the narrative that we have sketched out by insinuating an amorous union between two beings. We are left to wonder just what desire has been gratified here, the woman's or the man's. Nevertheless, the distinction between the naked and the nude is harder to sustain in the modern world. Stephen Kern remarks: "The striking shift in the depiction of the body in art across this period is from the classical nude to the naked woman" (79). Kern also says concerning the naked woman (Victorine Meurent) surrounded by two dressed men in Manet's famous picture *Le Déjeuner sur l'herbe*: "she had undressed in the presence of men and was therefore not acceptably nude but rather unacceptably naked" (79).

28. Martin Jay makes this point: "In addition to its de-eroticing of the visual order, it [Cartesian perspectivalism] had also fostered what might be called de-narrativization or de-textualization" (8). By "Cartesian perspectivalism" Jay understands a mixture of "Renaissance notions of perspective in the visual arts and Cartesian ideas of subjective rationality in philosophy" (4).

29. "Ariadne . . . lies asleep with wine here," writes Wethey (151).

30. See chapter 2, note 5. For his part, Eugenio d'Ors calls the two *Majas* "true monuments of obscenity; especially, of course, the clothed one" (94).

31. Some critics deny that the two women in Titian's painting represent the twin Venuses: "The possibility arises that the clothed lady is Chastity, who resists the blandishments of Venus, a solution which was first advanced by Charles de Tolnay" (Wethey 21). According to this conjecture, the two Venuses are reduced to one—the earthly Venus—who attempts to conquer all resistance to carnal love.

32. Picasso's *Faun Unveiling a Sleeping Woman* draws from Rembrandt's etching *Jupiter and Antiope*, especially the larger plate (1659)

of two on the same subject. Rembrandt, in turn, must have been familiar with similar works by Annibale Carracci and Correggio (Hind 1, 119). Another undeniable precedent is Titian's *Jupiter and Antiope* (the so-called Pardo Venus, now in the Louvre, and formerly in the palace of El Pardo, near Madrid). Wethey writes in this regard: "In Renaissance versions of Jupiter's seduction of Antiope, he appears as a satyr, and the source, a favorite of Titian . . . , is Ovid's *Metamorphoses*. . . . Ovid does not specify that Antiope was asleep, and there are examples in Renaissance art where she is awake. However, the pictorial tradition of the subject, in which the satyr-Jupiter approaches the sleeping Antiope with seduction unmistakably his intention, does exist in a print by the monogramist LD after Primaticcio" (54–55).

33. It is interesting to note that, on the front of the fountain where the two Venuses are posed in *Sacred and Profane Love*, there is a simulated relief that represents a scene described as follows by Panofsky: "the principal motif is a huge, unbridled horse which a rather indistinct figure seeks to control by getting hold of its mane. On the left, a man grabs the hair of a woman as if to capture her by force" (*Problems in Titian* 117). According to Panofsky, this is an example of what Renaissance Platonists like Ficino and Pico della Mirandola call by the names *amor ferinus* or *amore bestiale* in contradistinction to both *amor divinus* and *amor humanus*. Panofsky interprets Titian's painting as an expression of a force that, in Ficino's words, "induces all lower things to turn toward the better and higher ones" (119). We should not ignore the possibility of the inverse process either.

## 7. VISIONS OF A PAINTED GARDEN: JOSÉ DONOSO'S DIALOGUE WITH ART

1. Donoso has remarked that *La desesperanza* [Curfew] (1986) is the novel that Julio Méndez never succeeded in writing. This statement, however, does not give us license to view Julio as an unmediated autobiographical stand-in for Donoso, which would be incompatible with the critical aims of this analysis.

2. For a convincing interpretation of *El jardín* as a novel inspired in Donoso's *Historia personal*, see Oscar Montero.

3. Of course, from a grammatical point of view any text is always narrated by a first person. As Mieke Bal points out, it is the concept of focalization that may establish a relation between "the vision and that which is 'seen,' perceived" (*Narratology* 100). In *El jardín*, it is essential to distinguish between (s)he who speaks and (s)he who sees, precisely because of the unconventional shift in narrative function.

4. Donoso has acknowledged: "In me there is an extreme preoccupation with painting which has always been a big thing in my life. I am a passionate student of painting and it's extremely central in all my work" ("Round Table" 23). The author's novella entitled "Naturaleza muerta con cachimba" [Still life with a pipe], written in 1988, is based on the title of a painting, and it treats familiar Donosian themes of loss, recuperation, and formation or destruction of one's identity through artistic creation. As for María Pilar Serrano, Donoso notes: "My wife was, before I met her, a painter who had had several reasonably successful shows. . . . I told her, first of all, that I thought her painting stank, it was very bad. . . . I also said that I thought that perhaps she could write" ("Conversation with Montenegro and Santí" 9)

5. As Hammacher remarks: "Magritte avoids here the eye's active function—looking—by showing only its reflective function—the reflection in the cornea of sky and clouds. The reflection in the mirror is passive, dead, but the reflection in the eye penetrates the interior and it is there, instead of the eye, that the image comes into being" (86).

6. This view is set forth energetically (and simplistically) by John Berger, who juxtaposes the *Grande Odalisque* with an image from a "girlie magazine" (55). He remarks: "Women are there to feed an appetite, not to have any of their own. . . . She is offering up her femininity as the surveyed" (55).

7. Bryson speaks of the *Valpinçon Bather* in these terms:

> Certain aspects of the bather are obviously intended for the spectator alone: the soft, yielding underside of the foot, the nape of the neck, and the gently modelled back are zones the bather cannot herself see; but while these details increase sensual enjoyment of the figure, they also isolate the viewer in voyeurism and erotic deflection, pushing viewing out still further from the image. Instead of satisfaction, the viewer experiences the interval between the viewer's and the figure's existence, the lack, not the presence, in desire. (*Tradition and Desire* 130).

In her analysis of female/male spectator response to Ingres, Wendy Leeks discusses how the figures in these paintings "attend to the sights and sounds of their own world; they are intent on their own pleasures" (31). She also holds that the "turbanned figure is both the sexual mistress/ Odalisque and the asexual Madonna/mother" (34).

8. Sandra Gilbert and Susan Gubar's comments on George Eliot's "The Lifted Veil" are most relevant. Eliot transforms the veil into "a multitude of webs, nets, snares, bandages, shawls, masks, and curtains" (469); the veil is an ambiguous symbol that cloaks an obscure visage, one that reflects male dread of woman (472). Gilbert and Gubar conclude that "the recording of what exists behind the veil is distinctively female because it is the woman who exists behind the veil in patriarchal society, inhabiting a private sphere invisible to public view" (474).

9. If there were any doubt that Núria is patterned after literary agent Carmen Balcells, who represented the major figures of the "boom," we have only to cite from Donoso's testimony in *Historia personal*: "Carmen Balcells parecía tener en sus manos las cuerdas que nos hacían bailar a todos como a marionetas, y nos contemplaba, quizá con admiración, quizá con hambre, quizá con una mezcla de ambas cosas" "Carmen Balcells seemed to hold the strings in her hands that made us all dance like marionettes, and she contemplated us, perhaps with admiration, perhaps with hunger, perhaps with a mixture of both things" (87–88), and in "Diez años después" where he tells us of her "lujoso velito que ahora caracteriza su cabeza" "luxurious little veil that now characterizes her head" (147).

10. Jane Gallop remarks: "Freud articulates the 'discovery of castration' around a sight: sight of a phallic presence in the boy, sight of a phallic absence in the girl, ultimately sight of a phallic absence in the mother. Sex difference takes its actual divisive significance upon a sighting. The privilege of the phallus as presence, the concomitant 'disappearance' of any female genitalia marks the phallic order, is based on the privilege of sight over other senses" (*Daughter's Seduction* 27).

11. It is unclear by the title whether "*El abrazo* de Klimt" refers here to the final section of the Beethoven frieze, in which a man with his nude back to the spectator engulfs a woman in a desperate embrace, or if the painting called *El abrazo* instead refers to Klimt's better known work, *The Kiss*, an ornate vision of a blissfully submissive woman with her lover. However, these two interpretations of the kiss motif are not so distant: lurking beneath the mask of passivity in Klimt's females is the face of death and destruction. For a study of the theme of the embracing lovers in Klimt, see Patricia McDonnell.

12. See chapter 5 of James Olney, in which he analyzes the *Four Quartets* as a paradigm for poetic autobiography.

13. The situation could not be any other way, if we accept Lacanian thought: "The subject's accession to the verb does, however, cause him to experience a sort of lack of being: speech is no more than a mediator; it relates to appearance alone and fails to reach the essence. . . . Caught up in the symbolic, where he is simply represented, obliged to translate himself through the intermediary of discourse, the subject will become lost, lured away from himself, and will shape himself in accordance with the other's look" (Lemaire 179).

14. The themes of disappearance and identity change form the basis for much of Donoso's work, especially *Tres novelitas burguesas* [Sacred families] (1973), "Paseo" [The walk] (1960), *El lugar sin límites* [Hell hath no limits] (1966), *La misteriosa desaparición de la marquesita de Loria* [The mysterious disappearance of the marchioness of Loria] (1980), and of course *El obsceno pájaro de la noche* [The obscene bird

of night] (1970). For an excellent study of these themes, see Sharon Magnarelli's "The Dilemma of Disappearance and Literary Duplicity in José Donoso's *Tres novelitas burguesas*" and her recent book on Donoso.

15. On gender and writing, see especially Showalter and the discussion of her work by Heilbrun and Gallop in *Writing and Sexual Difference*. The view of silence as true voice is backed by many of the so-called French feminists (although we would hardly wish to view manifestations of feminist theory and practice in France as monolithic). For example, Xavière Gauthier comments: "And then, blank pages, gaps, borders, spaces and silence, holes in discourse. . . . If the reader feels a bit disoriented in this new space, one which is obscure and silent, it proves, perhaps, that it is a woman's space." (164).

16. Flora González observes an association between the androgynous narrator and the elongated, sexless Brancusi figure that in the novel is used to represent the countess in the garden next door. One of the problems with the androgynous ideal, however, is the insidious smoothing over of the tensions inherent in sexual difference. Our link of the female narrator to the pictorial works of Magritte, Dalí, Klimt, and Ingres in part seeks to reproject the unconscious tensions onto the polished surface that Donoso, like Brancusi, presents to the audience.

17. For an analysis of the bonds between Julio-Gloria and the interrelated couples of Roberto-Marta from "Atomo verde," and Blanca-Francisco from "Los habitantes de una ruina inconclusa" [Inhabitants of an inconclusive ruin], see Rosemary Geisdorfer Feal, "'In my end is my beginning.'"

18. Gablik compares the two painters in this regard and concludes that Dalí "hopes to induce a paranoid state in the spectator. . . . Dalí's world, in contrast to Magritte's, is one in which nothing is what it seems to be because everything is something else" (94).

19. Kristeva discusses the fantasy of the phallic mother in her study of Bellini's paintings: "if the mother were not, that is, if she were not phallic, then every speaker would be led to conceive of its Being in relation to some void, a nothingness asymmetrically opposed to this Being, a permanent threat against, first, its mastery, and ultimately, its stability" (238).

20. Klimt's unfinished painting *The Bride* deserves special mention with regard to the deep content of the artistic visions under analysis here. On the right side of the canvas lies the sole figure of a nude young girl; her open legs expose a detailed pubic region covered over with ornamentation, and directly over her genitals is a phallic-like green projection. Comini points out that the bride appears decapitated and mutilated owing to the mufflerlike wrap at the throat, a motif found in several of Klimt's paintings of women (5). Klimt's "devouring woman" and inno-

cent, submissive bride become fused, and thus man feels compelled to symbolically castrate (decapitate) the bride while simultaneously endowing her with the phallic cover of the fetish.

21. Freud remarks: "the fetish is a substitute for the woman's (mother's) phallus which the little boy once believed in and does not wish to forgo. . . . It [the fetish] remains a token of triumph over the threat of castration and a safeguard against it" ("Fetishism" 215–16).

22. Along these lines, it is interesting to note, as does Gablik, that Magritte's *The Lovers* may be inspired by "the unconscious memory of his mother, who drowned with her nightgown wrapped round her face" (49). Magritte's veiled portrait, too, would be an act that brings to the surface the hidden need to restore the mother's mutilated body.

23. Donoso's comments on the genesis of the "real" ending to his novel are relevant: "It was only in the page proofs that I deleted all the end that I had in the other novel, and in about two or three days I wrote, in quite a frenzy, the end as you know it" ("Conversation with Montenegro and Santí" 10).

# 8. IN EKPHRASTIC ECSTASY:
## MARIO VARGAS LLOSA AS THE PAINTER OF DESIRE

1. See Vargas Llosa's *La orgía perpetua: Flaubert y "Madame Bovary"* (1975), published in English as *The Perpetual Orgy* (1986).

2. This usage is borrowed from W. J. T. Mitchell's book of the same name.

3. This technique of weaving the main narrative strand with another level of fiction has served Vargas Llosa well in recent years: Aunt Julia's story must compete with the mock radio soaps attributed to the hack Pedro Camacho; the storyteller of *El hablador* [The speaker] (1987) supposedly is the source of the tales told in the chapters that alternate with those that communicate the primary plot; in the play *La señorita de Tacna* [The girl from Tacna] (1981), the on-stage division graphically recreates the two spaces in which the double-stranded action takes place; and his other plays, *Kathie y el hipopótamo* [Kathie and the hippopotamus] (1983) and *La Chunga* [Chunga] (1986), also use the theatrical convention of staged fantasy whereby the characters mentally recreate stories from the past and act them out as if they were happening. See Rosemary Geisdorfer Feal's "La ficción como tema: la trilogía dramática de Mario Vargas Llosa" for a discussion of this meta-dramatic mode and chapter 3 of her *Novel Lives* for a detailed analysis of the narrative structure of *La tía Julia y el escribidor*.

4. The way in which Herodotus wrote his *History* is of particular interest for our purposes. David Grene remarks: "Herodotus makes no

effective discrimination in his *History* between the skeletal act—for instance, the murder of Candaules by Gyges, which is "historical"—and the imaginative reality toward which the story reaches. His *History* is that of a storyteller who is never quite out of the frame of narrative and never quite in it. . . . But it is never an acknowledged artistic fiction; it is never an artistic fiction, completely, at all" (in Herodotus 12). Herodotus reconstructs verifiable fact through the interaction between experience and dreams, like the master storyteller Vargas Llosa, who himself continually transgresses the boundaries that separate fiction from reality, history from myth, and truth from falsehood.

5. This is a Kristevian view of the role of the father and of preoedipal *jouissance*, which is derived especially from her "Giotto's Joy." It is through identification with the law-of-the-father (and acceptance of castration, of course) that Giotto would save himself from a plunge into a psychotic abyss, according to her interpretation.

6. This is Freud's account from his essay "Repression" (1915).

7. Vargas Llosa is not the only one to arrive at this view. Anne Hollander, in her *Seeing through Clothes*, also assumes the position of a (degraded) voyeur when she remarks:

> In *Gyges and Candaules* Jordaens chose a nude rear view of the lady, otherwise clad in a lace cap and a partially removed smock. Her face turns back toward the spectator with express consciousness, and she caresses her right buttock for us with the back of her own hand. We are certainly supposed to look at her rump, even if she does not know of the presence of the hidden peeking men. The near presence of the shiny chamber pot adds even more modern smut to the allegedly mythological image. (231)

8. Otto Fenichel speaks of certain types of altruism in which a man offers a woman to another man. He concludes that the person who desires to witness the sexual activities of another couple really wishes to share their experience by a process of empathy, generally in a homosexual sense, that is, empathy with the experience of the partner of the opposite sex. See *The Psychoanalytic Theory of Neurosis* 328–37.

9. *Diane sortant du bain* is dated to 1742, the age of rococo. Fried (35) sees the primacy of absorption in French painting and criticism of the early and mid-1750s as a reaction against the rococo. With specific reference to Boucher, he nevertheless states: "All of this is not to say that Boucher himself was unaffected by the new emphasis on absorptive values and effects or at any rate that none of his paintings could be seen as satisfying the new demands" (192). Undoubtedly, subjects involving absorptive states and activities are present in numerous paintings that antedate 1750, and did not wholly disappear from French painting with the rise of rococo, as Fried himself remarks (43–44).

10. In the previous chapter we discussed paintings by Ingres in terms of eroticism by noting their association to pin-up girls on the one hand (Berger), and, on the other, to distant self-enclosed figures (Bryson). With regard to Vargas Llosa's novel, there is a movement toward creating narrative or visual pleasure that parallels Mel Ramos's impulse. His parodic works such as *Ode to Ang* (based on *The Source*) or *Plenty Grand Odalisque* approximate Ingres's classical paintings to the pin-up genre, something that Rigoberto accomplishes mentally (and Vargas Llosa, textually).

11. Ruth El Saffar, in reference to another case (the character of Marcela in *Don Quijote*), establishes this parallel: "The huge statue of Artemis in the Temple of Diana at Ephesus shows her with many breasts, as the mother who feeds all, suggesting an early affiliation of Artemis with the Great Mother. . . . In the time of Homer, however, the more archaic aspects of Artemis' Great Mother characterization gave way to her more sisterly, virginal aspects" (162).

12. Sir Kenneth Clark, however, manages to remain dispassionate before this splendid nude. His sober words concerning these paintings by Titian might be judged as a corrective to the frenzied imagination of the Peruvian (or "Latin") writer: "in spite of this pleasure in the flesh, the Venuses of this series are not provocative. Now that their delicate texture has been removed by restoration, the almost brutal directness with which their bodies are presented to us makes them singularly unaphrodisiac" (128–29).

13. The impetus for this novel is of interest here. Vargas Llosa recounts how he and Szyszlo had originally planned to do a book together: "the idea was not that he would illustrate a story of mine nor that I would write a text for some of his drawings, but instead that the entire gestation of the book would be reciprocally influenced" ("Entrevista" 373). Although the project never materialized as such, *Elogio de la madrastra* was born of it; the novel uses as its central focus what Vargas Llosa calls "the plastic imagination" (373).

14. In her book on erotic fantasies, *Fantasías eróticas*, Cristina Peri Rossi discusses the ritual transformation of base instinctual activity into the aesthetics of eroticism, where the participants are high priests and priestesses whose artful artifice win admirers and imitators. Her ideas on eroticism are obviously in keeping with this novel.

15. Fernando de Szyszlo: "I still have a very beautiful collection of pre-Columbian art. . . . For me it has been a great source of inspiration" ("Conversation" 25).

16. On the idea of the Virgin as the second Eve through whom the sin of the first was ransomed, see chapter 4 of Marina Warner's *Alone of All Her Sex*, which also appropriates Fra Angelico's *The Annunciation* (in this case, for the cover illustration).

## 9. DADA AT THE TROPICANA:
## GUILLERMO CABRERA INFANTE AND READYMADE ART

1. Although translations from *Exorcismos de esti(l)o* are ours, the English version of the title, *Exorcizing a Sty(le)*, is by Suzanne Jill Levine, who has translated one selection from *Exorcismos* entitled "The Ides of March."

2. Stephanie Merrim asserts that in *Exorcismos*, "the style devours the content" (278); Isabel Alvarez-Borland claims that "the narrator expresses the desire to dominate and control the style of the different narrative modalities, without paying much attention to content" (130); Edna Acosta-Belén shows less charity when she observes that Cabrera Infante's constant use and abuse of wit "can turn into a monotonous and often senseless exercise that leaves the reader with greater expectations for a more profound or artistically complex work of the caliber of *Tres tristes tigres*" (109).

3. This is the term employed by artist Gianfranco Baruchello to describe the aesthetic impact of Duchamp on the succeeding generation: "Or what about defining the Duchamp Effect? The effect we're defining by drifting this way through everything he thought and wrote, the effect we're defining by the way he confuses us. And this confusion is important" (73).

4. With respect to *La Habana para un infante difunto* [Infante's inferno] (1979), the author acknowledges: "I have called her [his character Violeta del Valle] Margarita del Campo in order to make, many pages further on, that joke on Marguerite Duchamp by Marcel Duchamp, at the moment when Margarita ascends the staircase clothed—that is, the reverse of Duchamp's famous painting, *Nude Descending a Staircase*" ("Cain by Himself" 11).

5. Wendy Steiner proposes a model to approximate literary and artistic Cubism in her pioneering study, *The Colors of Rhetoric*, which, as we stated in chapter 1, addresses broad questions concerning the interrelations of visual and verbal arts.

6. These are Arthur Danto's terms. For a thorough discussion of this polemical question, see the excellent article by Steven Goldsmith, in which he argues that the readymade may be legitimately reinserted into its original radical context even though Danto, among others, has made it assume a conservative function by admitting it into the "artworld."

7. The term *parody* is not to be taken automatically in a pejorative sense, but rather denotes the "quotation" or borrowing system prevalent in twentieth-century art forms. Linda Hutcheon devotes an entire study to the theory of parody, a term that she likens to "trans-contextualizing" (*Theory of Parody* 101).

8. Cabrera Infante also says: "Writing itself is a continuous present

that unfolds itself as the type prints while the ribbon runs and the paper goes from white to black, from blank space into crowded time. Writing is an island in itself, and no word is ever alone. . . . That island is my eternal island, the only kingdom I really owe allegiance to, the only country I inhabit, the house I live in, the house of words, the country of writing, the kingdom of language" ("Cain by Himself" 11).

9. It would be instructive to review some definitions of the readymade and its genesis that have been formulated by critics. Readymade is "the conscious decision to take an object and, by an act of will, wrest it into another context of meaning, so that its use, its worth, its symbolic value are bleached of their associations and must be reassessed, fundamentally reinterpreted" (Bailly 42); "an industrial object raised to the status of art by the artist's act of perception" (Hedges xiii). Richard Wollheim views readymades as a kind of minimal art, "in that they are to an extreme degree undifferentiated in themselves and therefore possess very low content of any kind, or else the differentiation that they do exhibit, which may in some cases be very considerable, comes not from the artist but from a nonartistic source, like nature or the factory" (101).

10. This is Haim Finkelstein's synthesis of the views put forth by Breton and others on the object in surrealism (39).

11. Werner Hofmann speaks of Duchamp's readymades in terms of their divorce from the utilitarian realm (62–63).

12. Another possible "readymade" source for Cabrera's humorous language-learning lessons might be popular advertisements, such as the kind found in reviews of books, that ask: "Want to brush up on a foreign language?" The particular advertisement series from which this line was taken has as its illustration a cast of odd cartoon-like characters, such as the figure with his hand across his chest, Napoleon-style, or the one of a woman garbed in layers of "medieval" dress. We guess these enigmatic characters are meant to signal "foreign people" for North Americans.

13. The pun here is on *ouvert* ("open") and *ovaire* ("ovary").

14. Rosalind E. Krauss remarks: "Given its function as the physical vehicle of exhibition, the gallery wall became the signifier of inclusion and, thus, can be seen as constituting in itself a representation of what could be called *exhibitionality*" (*Originality of the Avant-Garde* 133).

15. The title "Vocalburlario" announces its intentions to play with words in that it is derived from *vocal, vocabulary,* and *to mock.* Cabrera's "Pornography" works the same in English and Spanish: "V as in vagina." (Although it fails to correspond anatomically. Perhaps he should have selected the V as in mons *veneris?*).

16. Duchamp's work, especially *The Large Glass,* is frequently analyzed in terms of onanism, and Cabrera Infante's writings may be seen as a form of what he has called "masturhablarse," a play on the verbs *to masturbate* and *to talk to oneself.* See "*La Habana para un infante*

*difunto:* Fiction, Film, Pornography" in *Novel Lives* by Rosemary Geis-dorfer Feal for a discussion of word play and sex play in Cabrera Infante.

17. We should note at this point another resurfacing of Dada in Cabrera Infante, which is the link between Dadaist concrete poetry and the section entitled "Carmen Figuranta" in *Exorcismos*. These verbal/visual compositions surely bear the mark of Dada phonetic poems, such as those created by Christian Morgenstern and Man Ray, among others. Steiner analyzes the dynamics of concrete poetry in the section called "Res Poetica" in *The Colors of Rhetoric*.

18. Albert Cook deals with issues of this sort in his remarks on the "meta-irony" of Duchamp, and he offers a lucid model through which we may uncover the operational mode of readymade art. See also Mary Ann Caws's notes on the "Ready Maid."

19. Freud extensively studied what he called "word-pleasure" (*Wit and Its Relation to the Unconscious* 717). He notes that "wit serves to acquire pleasure" (761) and that one of its impulses is "to substitute for the adult an infantile state of mind" (720).

20. For a discussion of Cabrera Infante and his "Cain" with respect to literary creation and self-portraiture, see chapter 1 of Rosemary Geis-dorfer Feal's *Novel Lives*. Amelia Jones analyzes "Rrose Sélavy" in terms of gender and authorship, and concludes: "Through his assumption of the persona Rrose Sélavy, Duchamp unmasks the insecurity of identity" (160).

21. Para parodiarlo no había más que reducirlo no al absurdo sino a su mínima expresión. Así tomé su "Epílogo" de *El hacedor* y lo reproduje íntegro—pero con una salvedad. Lo salvé de la letra *a*, tan común en español, y al escribir su "Epílogo" Borges no podía ser más pretencioso (mientras pretendía no serlo), más trascendental y más lastimoso. En mi "Epilogolipo" todos esos defectos se convierten en efectos y el texto resulta una parodia perfecta: ahí está todo Borges pero de alguna manera ése no es Borges.

To parody [Borges] all I had to do was reduce him not to the absurd but to his minimal expression. Thus I took his "Epilogue" from *The Maker* and I reproduced it in its integrity—save one thing. I saved it from the letter *a*, so common in Spanish, and in writing his "Epilogue" Borges couldn't be any more pretentious (while claiming not to be), more transcendental and pitiful. In my "Epilogolipo" all those defects are turned into effects, and the text becomes a perfect parody: Borges is there but in some way that isn't Borges. ("21 en el 21" 26–27)

Cabrera Infante's complete omission of the letter *a* entailed a creative search for synonyms to replace Borges's original lexical choices (*montes* for *montañas, islotes* for *islas*, and so forth). In our translation we have respected this omission of the letter *a*, but in so doing have had to resort to some slight rewording in order to translate Cabrera's slight rewording of Borges!

22.  Paz claims that readymades "are not creations but signs, questioning or negating the act of creation" (22). Duchamp liked to trick his visitors by asking them to lift the birdcage. The unexpected weight made the visual pun perceivable through a sense other than vision.

# WORKS CITED

Abel, Elizabeth, ed. *Writing and Sexual Difference*. Chicago: University of Chicago Press, 1982.

Acosta-Belén, Edna. "The Literary Exorcisms of Guillermo Cabrera Infante." *Crítica Hispánica* 3 (1981): 99–110.

Adelman, Janet. *Suffocating Mothers: Fantasies of Maternal Origin in Shakespeare's Plays, Hamlet to The Tempest*. New York: Routledge, 1992.

Aldrich, Virgil. "Mirrors, Pictures, Words, Perceptions." *Philosophy* 55 (1980): 39–56.

Alpers, Svetlana, and Paul. "Ut Pictura Noesis? Criticism in Literary Studies and Art History." *New Literary History* 3.3 (Spring 1972): 437–58.

Alphen, Ernst van. *Francis Bacon and the Loss of Self*. Cambridge, MA: Harvard University Press, 1993.

Alvarez-Borland, Isabel. *Discontinuidad y ruptura en Guillermo Cabrera Infante*. Gaithersburg, MD: Hispamérica, 1983.

Amorós, Andrés. "Conversación con Francisco Ayala sobre *El jardín de las delicias.*" *Insula* 302 (1972): 4–11.

Appignanesi, Lisa, and John Forrester. *Freud's Women*. New York: Basic, 1992.

Aranguren, José Luis L. "El curso de la novela española contemporánea." In *Estudios literarios*, 212–310. Madrid: Gredos, 1976.

Argan, Giulio Carlo. *Botticelli*. Lausanne: Skira, 1957.

———. *Fra Angelico and His Times*. Trans. James Emmons. Lausanne: Skira, 1955.

Arias, Ricardo. "Relación entre *El jardín de las delicias*, del Bosco, y el de Ayala en el contexto de sus obras." *Cuadernos Hispanoamericanos* 329–30 (1977): 414–28.

Arnheim, Rudolf. *The Power of the Center: A Study of Composition in the Visual Arts*. Berkeley and Los Angeles: University of California Press, 1988.

Ayala, Francisco. *El jardín de las delicias*. Barcelona: Seix Barral, 1971.

———. *El jardín de las delicias*. Prologue by Carolyn Richmond. Selecciones Austral. Madrid: Espasa-Calpe, 1978.

———. *El jardín de las delicias*. Madrid: Mondadori, 1990.

———. *Recuerdos y olvidos*. Madrid: Alianza, 1988.

———. *El tiempo y yo, o El mundo a la espalda.* Madrid: Alianza, 1992.

———. *Los usurpadores.* Ed. Carolyn Richmond. Madrid: Cátedra, 1992.

Bailly, Jean-Christophe. *Duchamp.* Trans. Jane Brenton. London: Art Data, 1986.

Bal, Mieke. *Narratology: Introduction to the Theory of Narrative.* Trans. Christine von Boheemen. Toronto: University of Toronto Press, 1985.

———. *Reading "Rembrandt": Beyond the Word-Image Opposition.* Cambridge, MA: Cambridge University Press, 1991.

Barber, C. L., and Richard P. Wheeler. *The Whole Journey: Shakespeare's Power of Development.* Berkeley and Los Angeles: University of California Press, 1986.

Baruchello, Gianfranco, and Henry Martin. *Why Duchamp: An Essay on Aesthetic Impact.* Documentext. New Paltz, NY: McPherson, 1985.

Benvenuto, Bice, and Roger Kennedy. *The Works of Jacques Lacan: An Introduction.* New York: St. Martin's, 1986.

Berenson, Bernard. *The Italian Painters of the Renaissance.* 1952. Ithaca: Cornell University Press, 1980.

Berger, John. *Ways of Seeing.* London: British Broadcasting Corporation/Penguin, 1972.

Berman, Jeffrey. *Narcissism and the Novel.* New York: New York University Press, 1990.

Bernheimer, Charles. "Fetishism and Decadence: Salome's Severed Heads." In *Fetishism as Cultural Discourse,* ed. Emily Apter and William Pietz, 62–83. Ithaca: Cornell University Press, 1993.

———. "The Uncanny Lure of Manet's *Olympia.*" In *Seduction and Theory: Readings of Gender, Representation, and Rhetoric,* ed. Dianne Hunter, 13–2. Urbana: University of Illinois Press, 1989.

Bettelheim, Bruno. *The Uses of Enchantment: The Meaning and Importance of Fairy Tales.* New York: Knopf, 1976.

Bieder, Maryellen. "Between Genre and Gender: Emilia Pardo Bazán and *Los Pazos de Ulloa.*" In *In the Feminine Mode: Essays on Hispanic Women Writers,* ed. Noël Valis and Carol Maier, 131–45. Lewisburg: Bucknell University Press, 1990.

Bly, Peter A. "Pictorial Stasis in the *Sonatas* of Valle-Inclán." *Romance Quarterly* 36 (1989): 261–69.

Bolliger, Hans. *Picasso for Vollard.* New York: Abrams, 1956.

Borges, Jorge Luis. *El Aleph. Prosa completa.* Vol. 2. Barcelona: Bruguera, 1985. 4 vols.

Bronfen, Elisabeth. *Over Her Dead Body: Death, Femininity and the Aesthetic.* New York: Routledge, 1992.

Brooks, Peter. *Body Work: Objects of Desire in Modern Narrative.* Cambridge, MA: Harvard University Press, 1993.

——. "The Idea of a Psychoanalytic Literary Criticism." In *Psychoanalysis and Literature,* ed. Shlomith Rimmon-Kenan, 1–18. London: Methuen, 1987.

Brown, Jonathan. *The Golden Age of Painting in Spain.* New Haven: Yale University Press, 1991.

——. "Hieroglyphs of Death and Salvation: The Decoration of the Church of the Hermandad de la Caridad, Seville." In *Images and Ideas in Seventeenth-Century Spanish Painting,* 128–46. Princeton: Princeton University Press, 1978.

Bryson, Norman. "The Gaze in the Expanded Field." In Foster, 87–108.

——. "Semiology and Visual Interpretation." In Bryson, Holly, and Moxey, 61–73.

——. *Tradition and Desire: From David to Delacroix.* Cambridge: Cambridge University Press, 1984.

——. *Vision and Painting: The Logic of the Gaze.* New Haven: Yale University Press, 1983.

Bryson, Norman, Michael Ann Holly, and Keith Moxey, eds. *Visual Theory: Painting and Interpretation.* Cambridge: Polity, 1991.

Bulfinch, Thomas. *Bulfinch's Mythology: The Greek and Roman Fables Illustrated.* New York: Viking, 1979.

Burkert, Walter. *Structure and History in Greek Mythology and Ritual.* Berkeley and Los Angeles: University of California Press, 1982.

Cabrera Infante, Guillermo. "Cain by Himself: Guillermo Cabrera Infante, Man of Three Islands." Comp. William L. Siemens. *Review* 28 (1981): 8–11.

——. *Exorcismos de esti(l)o.* Barcelona: Seix Barral, 1976.

——. "Habla Cabrera Infante: Una larga entrevista que es una poética." With Rosa María Pereda in her *Guillermo Cabrera Infante,* 99–141. Escritores de todos los tiempos 3. Madrid: EDAF, 1978.

——. *Three Trapped Tigers.* Trans. Donald Gardner and Suzanne Jill Levine in collaboration with the author. 1971. New York: Avon/Bard, 1985.

——. *Tres tristes tigres.* Barcelona: Seix Barral, 1970.

——. "21 en el 21: Una entrevista de larga distancia con Guillermo Cabrera Infante." With Sharon Magnarelli. *Prismal/Cabral* 5 (1979): 23–42.

Campbell, Joseph. *The Masks of God: Occidental Mythology.* New York: Viking, 1970.

Carpenter, Thomas H. *Art and Myth in Ancient Greece.* London: Thames and Hudson, 1991.

Carrier, David. "Art and Its Spectators." *Journal of Aesthetics and Art Criticism* 45 (1986): 5–17.

Casanova, Giacomo. *Mémoires*. Ed. Robert Abirached. Vol. 2. Paris: Gallimard, 1958–60. 3 vols.

Casares, Julio. *Crítica profana: Valle-Inclán, "Azorín," Ricardo León*. Buenos Aires: Espasa-Calpe, 1944.

Castilla del Pino, Carlos. "La obra psiquiátrica de Luis Martín-Santos." Prologue to Martín-Santos, *Libertad*, 11–24.

Castillo-Feliú, Guillermo, ed. *The Creative Process in the Works of José Donoso*. Winthrop, SC: Winthrop Studies on Major Modern Writers, 1982.

Caws, Mary Ann. "Ladies Shot and Painted: Female Embodiment in Surrealist Art." In *The Female Body in Western Culture*, ed. Susan Rubin Suleiman, 262–287.Cambridge, MA: Harvard University Press, 1986.

———. "Partiality and the Ready Maid, or Representation by Reduction." *Journal of Aesthetics and Art Criticism* 42 (1984): 255–60.

Charney, Maurice. *Sexual Fiction*. New York: Methuen, 1981.

Cirlot, Juan-Eduardo. *Diccionario de símbolos*. 6th ed. Barcelona: Labor, 1985.

Cirre, José Francisco. *El mundo lírico de Pedro Salinas*. Granada: Don Quijote, 1982.

Clark, Kenneth. *The Nude: A Study in Ideal Form*. New York: Pantheon, 1956.

Clark, T. J. *The Painting of Modern Life: Paris in the Art of Manet and His Followers*. New York: Knopf, 1985.

Comini, Alessandra. *Gustav Klimt*. New York: George Braziller, 1975.

Connolly, John L. "Ingres and the Erotic Intellect." In *Woman as Sex Object: Studies in Erotic Art, 1730–1970*, ed. Thoman B. Hess and Linda Nochlin, 17–31. New York: Newsweek, 1972.

Cook, Albert. "The 'Meta-Irony' of Marcel Duchamp." *Journal of Aesthetics and Art Criticism* 44 (1986): 263–70.

Curutchet, Juan Carlos. "Luis Martín-Santos: el fundador." In *Cuatro ensayos sobre la nueva novela española*, 29–69. Montevideo: Alfa, 1973.

Dante Alighieri. *La Divina Commedia*. Ed. C. H. Grandgent. Revised by Charles S. Singleton. Cambridge, MA: Harvard University Press, 1972.

———. *The Divine Comedy*. Carlyle-Wicksteed Trans. New York: Modern Library, 1932.

Danto, Arthur C. "Description and the Phenomenology of Perception." In Bryson, Holly, and Moxey, 201–15.

———. *The Transfiguration of the Commonplace*. Cambridge, MA: Harvard University Press, 1981.

De Lauretis, Teresa. *Alice Doesn't: Feminism, Semiotics, Cinema*. Bloomington: Indiana University Press, 1984.

Detienne, Marcel. "The Powers of Marriage in Greece." In *Greek and Egyptian Mythologies*. Comp. by Yves Bonnefoy and trans. under the direction of Wendy Doniger, 95–100. Chicago: University of Chicago Press, 1992.

Díaz, Janet Winecoff. "Luis Martín-Santos and the Contemporary Spanish Novel." *Hispania* 51 (1968): 232–38.

Díaz-Plaja, Guillermo. *Las estéticas de Valle Inclán*. Madrid: Gredos, 1972.

*Diccionario de Autoridades*. 3 vols. Madrid: Gredos, 1964.

Dijkstra, Bram. *Idols of Perversity: Fantasies of Feminine Evil in Fin-de-Siècle Culture*. New York: Oxford University Press, 1986.

Doane, Mary Ann. *Femmes Fatales: Feminism, Film Theory, Psychoanalysis*. New York: Routledge, 1991.

Doménech, Ricardo, ed. *Ramón del Valle-Inclán*. Madrid: Taurus, 1988.

Donoso, José. "A Conversation between José Donoso and Marie-Lise Gazarian Gautier." In Castillo-Feliú, 1–13.

———. "A Conversation with José Donoso." With Nivia Montenegro and Enrico Mario Santí. *New Novel Review* 1.2 (1994): 7–15.

———. *The Garden Next Door*. Trans. Hardie St. Martin. New York: Grove, 1992.

———. *Historia personal del "boom."* Appendix 1, "El 'boom' doméstico," by María Pilar Serrano. Appendix 2, "Diez años después," by José Donoso. Barcelona: Seix Barral, 1983.

———. "Ithaca: The Impossible Return." In *Lives on the Line: The Testimony of Contemporary Latin American Authors,* ed. Doris Meyer, 181–195. Berkeley and Los Angeles: University of California Press, 1988.

———. *El jardín de al lado*. Barcelona: Seix Barral, 1981.

———. "A Round Table Discussion with José Donoso." In Castillo-Feliú, 14–34.

Donoso, María Pilar. *Los de entonces*. Barcelona: Seix Barral, 1987.

Dougherty, Dru. *Un Valle Inclán olvidado: entrevistas y conferencias*. Madrid: Fundamentos, 1983.

Duchamp, Marcel. "Painting . . . at the Service of the Mind." 1946. In *Theories of Modern Art: A Source Book by Artists and Critics,* ed. Herschel B. Chipp, 392–95. Berkeley and Los Angeles: University of California Press, 1968.

———. *The Writings of Marcel Duchamp*. 1973. Ed. Michel Sanouillet and Elmer Peterson. New York: Da Capo, 1989.

Ehrenzweig, Anton. *The Hidden Order of Art: A Study in the Psychology of Artistic Imagination*. Berkeley and Los Angeles: University of California Press, 1971.

Eliot, T. S. *Four Quartets*. 1943. New York: Harvest-Hartcourt, 1971.

El Saffar, Ruth Anthony. "In Marcela's Case." In *Quixotic Desire: Psychoanalytic Perspectives on Cervantes,* ed. El Saffar and Diana de Armas Wilson, 157–78. Ithaca: Cornell University Press, 1993.

Feal, Carlos. "En torno al casticismo de Pedro: El principio y el fin de *Tiempo de silencio.*" *Revista Iberoamericana* 116–17 (1981): 203–11.

———. *La poesía de Pedro Salinas.* Madrid: Gredos, 1965.

———. "La realidad psicológica en la *Sonata de otoño.*" *España Contemporánea* 2.4 (1989): 41–60.

———. "Rivales amorosos y modelos masculinos en las *Sonatas* de Valle-Inclán." *España Contemporánea* 4.1 (1991): 47–64.

———. "Lo visible y lo invisible en los primeros libros poéticos de Salinas." *Bulletin Hispanique* 93 (1991): 183–206.

———. "La voz femenina en *Los pazos de Ulloa.*" *Hispania* 70 (1987): 214–21.

Feal, Rosemary Geisdorfer. "La ficción como tema: la trilogía dramática de Mario Vargas Llosa." *Texto Crítico* 36–37 (1987): 137–45.

———. "'In my end is my beginning': José Donoso's Sense of an Ending." *Chasqui: Revista de Literatura Latinoamericana* 17. 2 (1988): 46–55.

———. *Novel Lives: The Fictional Autobiographies of Guillermo Cabrera Infante and Mario Vargas Llosa.* University of North Carolina Studies in the Romance Languages and Literatures 226. Chapel Hill: University of North Carolina Department of Romance Languages, 1986.

Fenichel, Otto. *The Psychoanalytic Theory of Neurosis.* New York: Norton, 1945.

Fernandez, James W. "Reflection on Looking into Mirrors." *Semiotica* 30. 1–2 (1980): 27–39.

Finkelstein, Haim N. *Surrealism and the Crisis of the Object.* Ann Arbor: University of Michigan Research Press, 1979.

Fish, Stanley. *Is There a Text in This Class? The Authority of Interpretive Communities.* Cambridge, MA: Harvard University Press, 1980.

Fisher, Alden L., ed. *The Essential Writings of Merleau-Ponty.* New York: Harcourt, 1969.

Flaubert, Gustave. *Oeuvres complètes*, vol. 4. Paris: Club de l'Honnête Homme, 1972. 16 vols. 1971–75.

Foster, Hal, ed. *Vision and Visuality.* Seattle: Bay, 1988.

Foucault, Michel. *The Archaeology of Knowledge and the Discourse on Language.* Trans. A. M. Sheridan Smith. New York: Pantheon, 1972.

———. *This Is Not a Pipe.* Trans. and ed. James Harkness. Berkeley and Los Angeles: University of California Press, 1983.

Foust, Ronald. "The Aporia of Recent Criticism and the Contemporary Significance of Spatial Form." In Smitten and Daghistany, 179–201.

Frank, Joseph. "Spatial Form in Modern Literature." In *The Widening Gyre: Crisis and Mastery in Modern Literature,* 3–62. New Brunswick: Rutgers University Press, 1963.

———. "Spatial Form: Thirty Years After." In Smitten and Daghistany, 202–43.

Freccero, John. *Dante: The Poetics of Conversion.* Cambridge, MA: Harvard University Press, 1986.

Freud, Sigmund. *The Collected Papers.* Ed. Philip Rieff. New York: Collier, 1963.

———. *Dora: An Analysis of a Case of Hysteria.* 1905. In *Collected Papers.*

———. "Fetishism." 1927. Trans. Joan Riviere. *Sexuality and the Psychology of Love.* In *Collected Papers,* 214–19.

———. "Repression." 1915. In *A General Selection from the Works of Sigmund Freud.* 1937. Ed. John Rickman, 87–97. Garden City, NY: Doubleday, 1957.

———. *Wit and its Relation to the Unconscious.* 1905. In *The Basic Writings of Sigmund Freud,* ed. A. A. Brill, 631–803. New York: Modern Library, 1966.

Fried, Michael. *Absorption and Theatricality: Painting and Beholder in the Age of Diderot.* Berkeley and Los Angeles: University California Press, 1980.

Fuentes, Carlos. *The Buried Mirror: Reflections on Spain and the New World.* Boston: Houghton Mifflin, 1992.

Gablik, Suzi. *Magritte.* New York: Thames and Hudson, 1970.

Gallop, Jane. *The Daughter's Seduction: Feminism and Psychoanalysis.* Ithaca: Cornell University Press, 1982.

———. "The Difference Within." In Abel, 283–90.

Gambini, Dianella. "Tipología femenina *fin-de-siècle* en las *Sonatas* de Valle-Inclán." In *Suma valleinclaniana,* ed. John P. Gabriele, 599–609. Barcelona: Anthropos, 1992.

Gauthier, Xavière. "Is There Such a Thing as Women's Writing?" Trans. Marilyn A. August. In *New French Feminisms,* ed. Elaine Marks and Isabelle de Courtivron, 161–164. New York: Schocken, 1981.

Gay, Peter. *The Tender Passion.* New York: Oxford University Press, 1986. Vol. 2 of *The Bourgeois Experience: Victoria to Freud.* 3 vols. to date. 1984–.

Gaya Nuño, J. A. *Historia del arte español.* 2nd ed. Madrid: Plus Ultra, 1957.

Gedo, John E. "Interdisciplinary Dialogue as a *Lutte d'amour.*" *Psychoanalytic Perspectives on Art* 2 (1987): 223–35.

———. "Paul Cézanne: Symbiosis, Masochism, and the Struggle for Perception." *Psychoanalytic Perspectives on Art* 2 (1987): 187–201.

Gedo, Mary Mathews. *Picasso: Art as Autobiography*. Chicago: University of Chicago Press, 1980.

Gilbert, Sandra, and Susan Gubar. *The Madwoman in the Attic: The Woman Writer and the Nineteenth Century Imagination*. New Haven: Yale University Press, 1979.

Glendinning, Nigel. "Art and Enlightenment in Goya's Circle." In Pérez Sánchez and Sayre, lxiv-lxxvi.

Golding, John. "Picasso and Surrealism." In Penrose and Golding, 77–121.

Goldsmith, Steven. "The Readymades of Marcel Duchamp: The Ambiguities of an Aesthetic Revolution." *Journal of Aesthetics and Art Criticism* 42 (1983): 197–208.

Gombrich, E. H. *The Story of Art*. 13th ed. New York: Dutton, 1978.

———. *Symbolic Images: Studies in the Art of the Renaissance*. London: Phaidon, 1972.

González, Flora. "The Androgynous Narrator in José Donoso's *El jardín de al lado*." *Revista de Estudios Hispánicos* 23 (1989): 99–114.

Goodheart, Eugene. *Desire and Its Discontents*. New York: Columbia University Press, 1991.

Goodman, Nelson. *Languages of Art: An Approach to a Theory of Symbols*. Indianapolis: Hackett, 1976.

Gouma-Peterson, Thalia, and Patricia Mathews. "The Feminist Critique of Art History." *Art Bulletin* 69.3 (1987): 326–57.

Goya y Lucientes, Francisco. *Los Caprichos*. New York: Dover, 1969.

Goytisolo, Juan. *Count Julian*. Trans. Helen R. Lane. New York: Viking, 1974.

———. *Reivindicación del Conde don Julián*. Ed. Linda Gould Levine. Madrid: Cátedra, 1985.

Gray, Rockwell. *The Imperative of Modernity: An Intellectual Biography of José Ortega y Gasset*. Berkeley and Los Angeles: University of California Press, 1989.

Green, André. "On the Constituents of the Personal Myth." In *The Personal Myth in Psychoanalytic Theory,* ed. Peter Hartocollis and Ian Davidson Graham, 63–87. Madison, CT: International Universities Press, 1991.

———. "The Unbinding Process." In *On Private Madness,* 331–59. Madison, CT: International Universities Press, 1986.

Greenberg, Jay. *Oedipus and Beyond: A Clinical Theory*. Cambridge, MA: Harvard University Press, 1991.

Grimal, Pierre. *Dictionnaire de la mythologie grecque et romaine*. Paris: Presses Universitaires de France, 1958.

Grosz, Elizabeth. *Jacques Lacan: A Feminist Introduction*. London: Routledge, 1990.

Gudiol, José. *Goya*. Trans. Priscilla Muller. New York: Abrams, 1965.

Guillén, Jorge. Prólogo. *Poesías completas,* by Pedro Salinas, ed. Soledad Salinas de Marichal. 2nd ed. Barcelona: Barral, 1975.

Gullón, Ricardo. *La invención del 98 y otros ensayos.* Madrid: Gredos, 1969.

Hall, James. *A History of Ideas and Images in Italian Art.* New York: Harper, 1983.

Hammacher, A. M. *Magritte.* New York: Abrams, 1974.

Hedges, Inez. *Languages of Revolt: Dada and Surrealist Literature and Film.* Durham, NC: Duke University Press, 1983.

Heilbrun, Carolyn G. "A Response to *Writing and Sexual Difference.*" In Abel, 291–97.

———. *Toward a Recognition of Androgyny.* 1964. New York: Norton, 1982.

Helman, Edith. *Trasmundo de Goya.* Madrid: Revista de Occidente, 1963.

Herodotus. *The History.* Trans. David Grene. Chicago: University of Chicago Press, 1987.

Hilton, Timothy. *The Pre-Raphaelites.* London: Thames and Hudson, 1989.

Hind, Arthur M. *A Catalogue of Rembrandt's Etchings.* 2nd ed. London: Methuen, 1924. 2 vols.

Hinterhäuser, Hans. *Fin de siglo: Figuras y mitos.* Trans. María Teresa Martínez. Madrid: Taurus, 1980.

Hofmann, Werner. "Marcel Duchamp and Emblematic Realism." In Masheck, 53–66.

Hollander, Anne. *Seeing Through Clothes.* New York: Avon, 1980.

Holly, Michael Ann. *Panofsky and the Foundations of Art History.* Ithaca: Cornell University Press, 1984.

*Holy Bible.* King James Version. New York: American Bible Society, 1967.

Hughes, Charles A. *Grosset's Spanish Phrase Book and Dictionary for Travelers.* New York: Grosset and Dunlap, 1971.

Huizinga, Johan. *Homo Ludens: A Study of the Play-Element in Culture.* 1950. Boston: Beacon, 1960.

Hutcheon, Linda. *A Poetics of Postmodernism: History, Theory, Fiction.* New York: Routledge, 1988.

———. *A Theory of Parody: The Teachings of Twentieth-Century Art Forms.* New York: Methuen, 1985.

Ilie, Paul. "Autophagous Spain and the European Other." *Hispania* 67 (1984): 28–35.

Irizarry, Estelle. "La cultura como experiencia viva en *El jardín de las delicias* de Francisco Ayala." *Papeles de Son Armadans* 68 (1973): 249–61.

James, Carol P. "Duchamp's Early Readymades: The Erasure of Boundaries between Literature and the Other Arts." *Perspectives on Contemporary Literature* 13 (1987): 24–32.

———. "'No, Says the Signified': The 'Logical Status' of Words in Painting." *Visible Language* 19.4 (1985): 439–61.

Jay, Martin. "Scopic Regimes of Modernity." In Foster, 3–23.

Jiménez, Juan Ramón. "Ramón del Valle-Inclán [Castillo de quema], 1899–1925." In Doménech, 46–57.

Jones, Amelia. *Postmodernism and the En-Gendering of Marcel Duchamp*. Cambridge: Cambridge University Press, 1994.

Kahane, Claire. "Object-relations Theory." In *Feminism and Psychoanalysis: A Critical Dictionary*, ed. Elizabeth Wright, 284–90. Oxford: Blackwell, 1992.

Kern, Stephen. *The Culture of Love: Victorians to Moderns*. Cambridge, MA: Harvard University Press, 1992.

Kerr, Lucille. "Authority in Play: José Donoso's *El jardín de al lado*." *Criticism* 25 (1983): 41–65.

———. *Reclaiming the Author: Figures and Fictions from Spanish America*. Durham: Duke University Press, 1992.

Klein, Melanie. "Love, Guilt and Reparation." 1937. In *Love, Hate and Reparation*, by Klein and Joan Riviere, 57–119. New York: Norton, 1964.

Kofman, Sarah. *The Enigma of Woman: Woman in Freud's Writings*. Trans. Catherine Porter. Ithaca: Cornell University Press, 1985.

Krauss, Rosalind E. *The Optical Unconscious*. Cambridge, MA: MIT Press, 1993.

———. *The Originality of the Avant-Garde and Other Modernist Myths*. Cambridge, MA: MIT Press, 1987.

Krieger, Murray. *Ekphrasis: The Illusion of the Natural Sign*. Baltimore: Johns Hopkins University Press, 1992.

Kristeva, Julia. "Giotto's Joy." In *Desire in Language: A Semiotic Approach to Literature and Art*, ed. Leon S. Roudiez, and trans. Thomas Gora, Alice Jardine, and Roudiez, 210–36. New York: Columbia University Press, 1980.

———. "Motherhood According to Giovanni Bellini." In *Desire in Language*, 237–70.

Kronik, John W. "Entre la ética y la estética: Pardo Bazán y el decadentismo francés." In Mayoral, 163–74.

Labanyi, Jo. *Ironía e historia en "Tiempo de silencio."* Madrid: Taurus, 1985.

———. *Myth and History in the Contemporary Spanish Novel*. Cambridge: Cambridge University Press, 1989.

La Belle, Jenijoy. *Herself Beheld: The Literature of the Looking Glass*. Ithaca: Cornell University Press, 1988.

Lacan, Jacques. *The Four Fundamental Concepts of Psycho-Analysis.* Trans. Alan Sheridan. New York: Norton, 1981.

———. "The Mirror Stage as Formative of the Function of the I as Revealed in Psychoanalytic Experience." 1949. In *Ecrits: A Selection,* trans. Alan Sheridan, 1–7. New York: Norton, 1977.

Lafuente Ferrari, Enrique. "Goya grabador o la búsqueda de un lenguaje universal." In *Goya: Toros y toreros,* 23–26. Madrid: Ministerio de Cultura, 1990.

Laplanche, Jean, and J.-B. Pontalis. *The Language of Psycho-Analysis.* Trans. Donald Nicholson-Smith. New York: Norton, 1973.

Lassaigne, Jacques, and Robert L. Delevoy. *Flemish Painting: From Bosch to Rubens.* Trans. Stuart Gilbert. Lausanne: Skira, 1958.

Lavin, Marilyn Aronberg. "The Joy of the Bridegroom's Friend: Smiling Faces in Fra Filippo, Raphael, and Leonardo." In *Art the Ape of Nature,* ed. Moshe Barasch and Lucy Freeman Sandler, 193–210. New York: Abrams, 1981.

Lee, Richard, and Richard Daly. "Man's Domination and Woman's Oppression: The Question of Origins." In *Beyond Patriarchy,* ed. Michael Kaufman, 30–44. Toronto: Oxford University Pres, 1987.

Leeks, Wendy. "Ingres Other-Wise." *The Oxford Art Journal* 9.1 (1986): 29–37.

Lemaire, Anika. *Jacques Lacan.* Trans. David Macey. London: Routledge and Kegan Paul, 1977.

Lévi-Strauss, Claude. "Natural Art and Cultural Art: A Conversation with Claude Lévi-Strauss." With Georges Charbonnier. In Masheck, 77–83.

Licht, Fred. *Goya: The Origins of the Modern Temper in Art.* New York: Universe, 1979.

Lichtenstein, Heinz. *The Dilemma of Human Identity.* New York: Jason Aronson, 1983.

Lidz, Theodore. *Hamlet's Enemy: Madness and Myth in* Hamlet. New York: Basic, 1975.

Liebert, Robert S. *Michelangelo: A Psychoanalytic Study of His Life and Images.* New Haven: Yale University Press, 1983.

Little, Ralph B. "Oral Aggression in Spider Legends." *American Imago* 23 (1966): 169- 79.

Lloréns, Eva. *Valle-Inclán y la plástica.* Madrid: Insula, 1975.

Lorente, Manuel. *The Prado, Madrid.* 2 vols. New York: Appleton-Century, 1965.

Lorenzo de Márquez, Teresa. "Carnival Traditions in Goya's Iconic Language." In Pérez Sánchez and Sayre, lxxxv-xciv.

McDonnell, Patricia. "*The Kiss:* A Barometer for the Symbolism of Gustav Klimt." *Arts Magazine* 60.8 (1986): 65–73.

Macklin, J. J. "Pérez de Ayala y la novela modernista europea." *La novela lírica*, ed. Darío Villanueva, 34–50. vol. 2 Madrid: Taurus, 1983. 2 vols.

Magnarelli, Sharon. "The Dilemma of Disappearance and Literary Duplicity in José Donoso's *Tres novelitas burguesas*." *Prismal/Cabral* 3–4 (1979): 29–46.

———. *Understanding José Donoso*. Understanding Modern European and Latin American Literature. Columbia: University of South Carolina Press, 1993.

Maquet, Jacques. *The Aesthetic Experience: An Anthropologist Looks at the Visual Arts*. New Haven: Yale University Press, 1986.

Mariño Ferro, Xosé Ramón. *Satán, sus siervas las brujas y la religión del mal*. Vigo: Edicións Xerais de Galicia, 1984.

Martín-Santos, Luis. *Apólogos y otras prosas inéditas*. Barcelona: Seix Barral, 1970.

———. *Libertad, temporalidad y transferencia en el psicoanálisis existencial*. Barcelona: Seix Barral, 1975.

———. *Tiempo de silencio*. 24th ed. Barcelona: Seix Barral, 1985.

———. *Time of Silence*. Trans. George Leeson. New York: Columbia University Press, 1989.

Masheck, Joseph, ed. *Marcel Duchamp in Perspective*. Englewood Cliffs, NJ: Prentice-Hall, 1975.

Matthews, J. H. *The Imagery of Surrealism*. Syracuse, NY: Syracuse University Press, 1977.

Mayoral, Marina, coord. *Estudios sobre "Los Pazos de Ulloa"*. Madrid: Cátedra/Ministerio de Cultura, 1989.

Meisler, Stanley. "Vienna's Anguished Artists." *Smithsonian* (Aug. 1986): 70–81.

Merleau-Ponty, Maurice. "Cézanne's Doubt." In Fisher, 233–51.

———. "Eye and Mind." In Fisher, 252–86.

———. *The Visible and the Invisible*. Trans. Alphonso Lingis. Evanston: Northwestern University Press, 1968.

Merrim, Stephanie. Rev. of *Exorcismos de esti(l)o*, by Guillermo Cabrera Infante. *Revista Iberoamericana* 44 (1978): 276–79.

Miles, Margaret R. *Carnal Knowing: Female Nakedness and Religious Meaning in the Christian West*. Boston: Beacon, 1989.

Mitchell, W. J. T. *Iconology: Image, Text, Ideology*. Chicago: University of Chicago Press, 1986.

———, ed. *The Language of Images*. Chicago: University of Chicago Press, 1980.

———. "Spatial Form in Literature: Toward a General Theory." In Mitchell, *The Language of Images*, 271–99.

Moliner, María, *Diccionario de uso del español*. 2 vols. Madrid: Gredos, 1973.

Møller, Lis. *The Freudian Reading: Analytical and Fictional Constructions.* Philadelphia: University of Pennsylvania Press, 1991.

Montero, Oscar. "*El jardín de al lado*: La escritura y el fracaso del éxito." *Revista Iberoamericana* 49 (1983): 449–67.

Montes-Huidobro, Matías. "Corrientes ocultas en *Los pazos de Ulloa*." *España Contemporánea* 4.2 (1991): 33–50.

Moore, Ethel. "Lucas Samaras." *125 Masterpieces from the Collection of the Albright-Knox Art Gallery,* 235. New York: Rizzoli, 1987.

Morán, Fernando. *Novela y semidesarrollo (Una interpretación de la novela hispanoamericana y española).* Madrid: Taurus, 1971.

Morris, C. B. "Pedro Salinas and Marcel Proust." *Revue de littérature comparée* 44 (1970): 195–214.

Mulvey, Laura. "Visual Pleasure and Narrative Cinema." *Screen* 16.3 (1975): 6–18.

Munich, Adrienne Auslander. *Andromeda's Chains: Gender and Interpretation in Victorian Literature and Art.* New York: Columbia University Press, 1989.

Nead, Lynda. *The Female Nude: Art, Obscenity and Sexuality.* London: Routledge, 1992.

Neumann, Erich. *The Great Mother: An Analysis of the Archetype.* 1955. Trans. Ralph Manheim. New York: Pantheon, 1963.

———. *The Origins and History of Consciousness.* 1949. Trans. R. F. C. Hull. Princeton: Princeton University Press, 1970.

Newman, Jean Cross. "Víspera del gozo, tema saliniano." In *Actas del Sexto Congreso Internacional de Hispanistas,* ed. Alan M. Gordon and Evelyn Rugg, 523–26. Toronto: Dept. of Spanish and Portuguese, University of Toronto, 1980.

Olney, James. *Metaphors of Self: The Meaning of Autobiography.* Princeton: Princeton University Press, 1972.

Ordóñez, Elizabeth J. "¿Y mi niña?: Another Voice in *Los pazos de Ulloa*." *Discurso Literario* 3 (1985): 121–31.

Ors, Eugenio d'. *Tres horas en el Museo del Prado.* 1923. 2nd ed. Madrid: Caro Raggio, n.d.

Ortega y Gasset, José. "Tres cuadros del vino." In *El Espectador,* vol. 2 of *Obras completas,* 48–56. Madrid: Revista de Occidente, 1946. 12 vols. 1946–83.

Pach, Walter. *Ingres.* New York: Harper, 1939.

Paglia, Camille. *Sexual Personae: Art and Decadence from Nefertiti to Emily Dickinson.* New Haven: Yale University Press, 1990.

Pallucchini, Anna, Carlo Ludovicio Ragghianti and Licia Ragghianti Collobi. *Prado. Madrid.* New York: Newsweek/Mondadori, 1968.

Panofsky, Erwin. *Problems in Titian: Mostly Iconographic.* New York: New York University Press, 1969.

———. *Studies in Iconology: Humanistic Themes in the Art of the Renaissance.* 1939. New York: Icon, 1972.

Pardo Bazán, Emilia. "Goya." 1906. In *Obras completas*, vol. 3, 1281–95.

———. *The House of Ulloa.* Trans. Roser Caminals-Heath. Athens: University of Georgia Press, 1992.

———. *La Madre Naturaleza.* In *Obras completas,* vol. 1.

———. *Obras completas.* 3 vols. Madrid: Aguilar, 1964–73.

———. *Los Pazos de Ulloa.* 12th ed. Madrid: Alianza, 1985.

———. *La Quimera.* In *Obras completas,* vol. 1.

Pater, Walter. *The Renaissance: Studies in Art and Poetry. The 1893 Text.* Ed. Donald L. Hill. Berkeley and Los Angeles: University of California Press, 1980.

Paz, Octavio. *Marcel Duchamp: Appearance Stripped Bare.* Trans. Rachel Phillips and Donald Gardner. New York: Seaver, 1981.

Penrose, Roland. "Beauty and the Monster." In Penrose and Golding, 157–95.

Penrose, Roland, and John Golding. *Pablo Picasso, 1881–1973.* New York: Portland, 1988.

Peri Rossi, Cristina. *Fantasías eróticas.* Colección Biblioteca Erótica. Madrid: Ediciones Temas de Hoy, 1991.

Pérez Sánchez, Alfonso E. Introduction. In Pérez Sánchez and Sayre, xvii–xxv.

Pérez Sánchez, Alfonso E., and Eleanor A. Sayre, eds. *Goya and the Spirit of Enlightenment.* Boston: Bulfinch, 1989.

Plato. *Symposium.* Trans. Tom Griffith. Berkeley and Los Angeles: University of California Press, 1985.

Pollock, Griselda. *Vision and Difference: Femininity, Feminism and the Histories of Art.* London: Routledge, 1988.

Ragland-Sullivan, Ellie. *Jacques Lacan and the Philosophy of Psychoanalysis.* Urbana: University of Illinois Press, 1986.

Ramas, Maria. "Freud's Dora, Dora's Hysteria." In *In Dora's Case: Freud-Hysteria-Feminism,* ed. Charles Bernheimer and Claire Kahane, 149–80. New York: Columbia University Press, 1985.

Real Academia Española. *Diccionario de la lengua española.* 19th ed. Madrid: Espasa Calpe, 1970.

Reff, Theodore. "The Author, the Authority, the Authoritarian." *Psychoanalytic Perspectives on Art* 2 (1987): 237–43.

———. "John Gedo and the Struggle for Perception." *Psychoanalytic Perspectives on Art* 2 (1987): 203–21.

Rey, Alfonso. *Construcción y sentido de "Tiempo de silencio".* Madrid: Porrúa Turanzas, 1977.

Richmond, Carolyn. "La complejidad estructural de *El jardín de las delicias* vista a través de dos de sus piezas." In *El jardín de las delicias,* by Francisco Ayala, 211–22. Madrid: Mondadori, 1990.

Ries, Martin. "Picasso and the Myth of the Minotaur." *Art Journal* 32 (1972–73): 142–45.

Roberts, Gemma. *Temas existenciales en la novela española de postguerra*. Madrid: Gredos, 1973.

Rojas, Carlos. *El mundo mítico y mágico de Picasso*. Barcelona: Planeta, 1984.

———. *Salvador Dalí, Or the Art of Spitting on Your Mother's Portrait*. Trans. Alma Amell. University Park: Pennsylvania State University Press, 1993.

———. *Yo, Goya*. Barcelona: Planeta, 1990.

Rose, Gilbert J. *The Power of Form: A Psychoanalytic Approach to Aesthetic Form*. Expanded ed. Madison, CT: International Universities Press, 1992.

Rose, Jacqueline. Introduction. In *Feminine Sexuality: Jacques Lacan and the "école freudienne,"* ed. Juliet Mitchell and Rose, 27–57. New York: Norton, 1982.

———. *Sexuality in the Field of Vision*. London: Verso, 1986.

Rosenblum, Robert. *Jean-Auguste-Dominique Ingres*. New York: Abrams, 1967.

Rubin, William. "Reflexions on Marcel Duchamp." In Masheck, 41–52.

Russell, Jeffrey Burton. *Lucifer: The Devil in the Middle Ages*. Ithaca: Cornell University Press, 1984.

Russell, John. *Francis Bacon*. Revised and updated ed. New York: Thames and Hudson, 1993.

Salinas, Pedro. *To Live in Pronouns: Selected Love Poems*. Trans. Edith Helman and Norma Farber. New York: Norton, 1974.

———. *Poesías completas*. Ed. Juan Marichal. Madrid: Aguilar, 1955.

———. *Prelude to Pleasure: A Bilingual Edition of Víspera del gozo*. Trans. Noël Valis. Lewisburg: Bucknell University Press, 1993.

———. *Víspera del gozo*. Madrid: Alianza, 1974.

Sartre, Jean-Paul. *L'Etre et le néant*. Paris: Gallimard, 1943.

Schiavo, Leda. "La 'barbarie' de las *Comedias bárbaras*." In *Estelas, laberintos, nuevas sendas: Unamuno. Valle-Inclán. García Lorca. La Guerra Civil,* ed. Angel G. Loureiro, 191–203. Barcelona: Anthropos, 1988.

Schneider, Carl. *Shame, Exposure and Privacy*. Boston: Beacon, 1977.

Schneider, Laurie. "Mirrors in Art." *Psychoanalytic Inquiry* 5 (1985): 283–324.

Schor, Naomi. "Female Paranoia: The Case for Psychoanalytic Feminist Criticism." *Yale French Studies* 62 (1981): 204–219.

Schraibman, José. "*Tiempo de silencio* y la cura psiquiátrica de un pueblo: España." *Insula* 365 (1977): 3.

Schwarz, Heinrich. "The Mirror in Art." *Art Quarterly* 15 (1952): 96–118.

Schwartz, Sanford. *The Matrix of Modernism: Pound, Eliot, and Early Twentieth Century Thought*. Princeton: Princeton University Press, 1985.

Shattuck, Roger. *The Innocent Eye: On Modern Literature and the Arts*. New York: Washington Square, 1986.

Showalter, Elaine. "Feminist Criticism in the Wilderness." *Critical Inquiry* 8 (1981): 179–205. Rpt. in *Abel, 9–35*.

———. *Sexual Anarchy: Gender and Culture at the Fin de Siècle*. New York: Viking, 1990.

Silverman, Kaja. "The Productive Look." Buffalo Symposium in Literature and Psychoanalysis: Impulses of the Perverse. Buffalo, NY, 30 April 1994.

———. *The Subject of Semiotics*. New York: Oxford University Press, 1983.

Sizeranne, Robert de la. *César Borgia et le duc d'Urbino*. Paris: Hachette, 1924.

Skira-Venturi, Rosabianca. *Italian Painting: The Renaissance*. Critical studies by Lionello Venturi, historical surveys by Skira-Venturi, and trans. Stuart Gilbert. Geneva: Skira, 1951.

Smitten, Jeffrey R., and Ann Daghistany, eds. *Spatial Form in Narrative*. Ithaca: Cornell University Press, 1981.

Sobejano, Gonzalo. *Nietzsche en España*. Madrid: Gredos, 1967.

———. *Novela española de nuestro tiempo*. 2nd ed. Madrid: Prensa Española, 1975.

Spector, Jack J. "The State of Psychoanalytic Research in Art History." *The Art Bulletin* 70 (March 1988): 49–76.

Spence, Donald P. *Narrative Truth and Historical Truth: Meaning and Interpretation in Psychoanalysis*. New York: Norton, 1982.

Spires, Robert C. "Realidad prosaica e imaginación transcendente en dos cuentos de Pedro Salinas." In *Pedro Salinas*, ed. Andrew P. Debicki, 249–57. Madrid: Taurus, 1976.

Spitz, Ellen Handler. *Art and Psyche: A Study in Psychoanalysis and Aesthetics*. New Haven: Yale University Press, 1985.

Spitzer, Leo. "El conceptismo interior de Pedro Salinas." In *Lingüística e historia literaria*, 188–246. Madrid: Gredos, 1955.

Sprengnether, Madelon. *The Spectral Mother: Freud, Feminism, and Psychoanalysis*. Ithaca: Cornell University Press, 1990.

Stanton, Domna C. "Language and Revolution: The Franco-American Dis-Connection." In *The Future of Difference*, ed. Hester Eisenstein and Alice Jardine, 73–87. New Brunswick: Rutgers University Press, 1985.

Stanton, Edward. "*Los Pazos de Ulloa* y la Pintura." *Papeles de Son Armadans* 58 (1970): 279–87.

Steinberg, Leo. "The Line of Fate in Michelangelo's Painting." In Mitchell, *The Language of Images*, 85–128.

———. "Picasso's Sleepwatchers." In *Other Criteria: Confrontations with Twentieth-Century Art*, 93–114. New York: Oxford University Press, 1978.

———. *The Sexuality of Christ in Renaissance Art and in Modern Oblivion*. New York: Pantheon, 1983.

Steiner, Wendy. *The Colors of Rhetoric: Problems in the Relation between Modern Literature and Painting*. Chicago: University of Chicago Press, 1982.

———. "Intertextuality in Painting." *American Journal of Semiotics* 3.4 (1985): 57–67.

———. *Pictures of Romance: Form against Context in Painting and Literature*. Chicago: University of Chicago Press, 1991.

Stembert, Rodolfo. "Don Ramón del Valle-Inclán y la pintura." *Cuadernos Hispanoamericanos* 311 (1976): 461–76.

Stixrude, David L. *The Early Poetry of Pedro Salinas*. Madrid/Princeton: Castalia, 1975.

Szyszlo, Fernando de. "Conversation with a Peruvian Master: Fernando de Szyszlo." With Alice Thorson. *Latin American Art* 2.1 (1990): 23–27.

———. "Reflections of Artistic Creation in Latin America." *Review: Latin American Literature and Arts* 39 (1988): 31–34.

Taminiaux, Jacques. "The Thinker and the Painter." In *Merleau-Ponty Vivant*, ed. M. C. Dillon, 195–212. Albany: State University of New York Press, 1991.

Taylor, Mark C. *Altarity*. Chicago: University of Chicago Press, 1987.

Thomas, Ronald R. *Dreams of Authority: Freud and the Fictions of the Unconscious*. Ithaca: Cornell University Press, 1990.

Thuillier, Jacques. *Rubens' Life of Marie de' Medici*. New York: Abrams, 1967.

Tickner, Lisa. "The Body Politic: Female Sexuality and Women Artists Since 1970." *Art History* 1 (1978): 241–42.

Tolnay, Charles de. *Hieronymus Bosch*. New York: Reynal, 1966.

———. *Michelangelo: The Final Period*. Princeton: Princeton University Press, 1960.

Torgovnick, Marianna. *The Visual Arts, Pictorialism, and the Novel*. Princeton: Princeton University Press, 1985.

Unamuno, Miguel de. "El habla de Valle-Inclán." In Doménech, 42–45.

Uspensky, Boris. *A Poetics of Composition: The Structure of the Artistic Text and Typology of a Compositional Form*. Berkeley and Los Angeles: University of California Press, 1983.

Valle-Inclán, Ramón del. *La cabeza del Bautista. Retablo de la avaricia, la lujuria y la muerte*. 2nd ed. Madrid: Espasa-Calpe, 1968.

————. *Corte de amor.* 5th ed. Madrid: Espasa-Calpe, 1970.

————. *Epitalamio.* Selecciones Austral. Madrid: Espasa-Calpe, 1978.

————. *Luces de bohemia.* Ed. Alonso Zamora Vicente. Madrid: Espasa-Calpe, 1973.

————. *The Pleasant Memoirs of the Marquis de Bradomín: Four Sonatas.* Trans. May Heywood Broun and Thomas Walsh. New York: Howard Fertig, 1984.

————. *Sonatas. Memorias del Marqués de Bradomín.* 2nd ed. Madrid: Espasa-Calpe, 1979.

Vallentin, Antonina. *El Greco.* Paris: Albin Michel, 1954.

Vargas Llosa, Mario. *Aunt Julia and the Scriptwriter.* Trans. Helen Lane. New York: Avon, 1983.

————. *Elogio de la madrastra.* Barcelona: Tusquets, 1988.

————. "Entrevista a Mario Vargas Llosa." With Leopoldo Bernucci. *Hispania* 74 (1991): 370–74.

————. *In Praise of the Stepmother.* Trans. Helen Lane. New York: Penguin, 1991.

————. *La tía Julia y el escribidor.* Barcelona: Seix Barral, 1977.

Vela, Fernando. "Pedro Salinas: *Víspera del gozo.*" *Revista de Occidente* 13 (1926): 124–29.

Villanueva, Darío. "*Los Pazos de Ulloa,* el naturalismo y Henry James." *Hispanic Review* 52 (1984): 121–39.

————. "*Los Pazos,* novela en la encrucijada." In *Mayoral,* 17–36.

Wallis, Brian, ed. *Art after Modernism: Rethinking Representation.* New York: New Museum of Contemporary Art, 1984.

Warner, Marina. *Alone of All Her Sex: The Myth and the Cult of the Virgin Mary.* New York: Vintage, 1983.

Wehle, Harry B. *Great Paintings from the Prado Museum.* New York: Abrams, [1963].

Wethey, Harold E. *The Paintings of Titian,* vol. 3. London: Phaidon, 1975. 3 vols.

Wilde, Alan. *Horizons of Assent: Modernism, Postmodernism, and the Ironic Imagination.* Philadelphia: University of Pennsylvania Press, 1987.

Williams, Linda. *Hard Core: Power, Pleasure, and the "Frenzy of the Visible."* Berkeley and Los Angeles: University of California Press, 1989.

Winnicott, D. W. *Playing and Reality.* New York: Basic, 1971.

Wollheim, Richard. "Minimal Art." In *On Art and the Mind,* 101–111. Cambridge, MA: Harvard University Press, 1974.

Zamora Vicente, Alonso. *Las sonatas de Valle-Inclán.* 2nd ed. Madrid: Gredos, 1983.

Zardoya, Concha. "La 'otra' realidad de Pedro Salinas." In *Poesía española del siglo XX,* 106–48. Vol. 2 Madrid: Gredos, 1974. 4 vols.

Ziolkowski, Theodore. *Disenchanted Images: A Literary Iconology.* Princeton: Princeton University Press, 1977.

Zucker, Wolfgang. "Reflections on Reflections." *Journal of Aesthetics and Art Criticism* 20 (1962): 239–50.

# INDEX